More Praise for *Dreamland*

"Journalist Quinones weaves an extraordinary story, including the personal journeys of the addicted, the drug traffickers, law enforcement, and scores of families affected by the scourge, as he details the social, economic, and political forces that eventually destroyed communities in the American heartland and continues to have a resounding impact." —*Booklist* (starred review)

"Quinones deftly recounts how a flood of prescription pain meds, along with black tar heroin from Nayarit, Mexico, transformed the once-vital blue-collar city of Portsmouth, Ohio, and other American communities into heartlands of addiction. With prose direct yet empathic, he interweaves the stories of Mexican entrepreneurs, narcotics agents, and small-town folks whose lives were upended by the deluge of drugs, leaving them shaking their heads, wondering how they could possibly have resisted." —*Mother Jones*

"Smack is back in the news as heroin use spikes and busts pile up at the border, making *Dreamland* a timely book. Veteran journalist and storyteller Sam Quinones provides investigative reporting to explain the latest surge. But he also goes way deeper; he tells the social and human stories at the heart of the opiate trade and how it tortures the souls of America and Mexico." —Ioan Grillo, author of *El Narco*

"*Dreamland* spreads out like a transnational episode of *The Wire*, alternately maddening, thrilling, depressing, and with writing as sharp and insightful as a razor blade. You cannot understand our drug war and Mexican immigration to the United States without reading this book." —Gustavo Arellano, syndicated columnist, *¡Ask a Mexican!*

"Quinones recounts individual tales—from junkies in Portland, Ore., to pill mills in Appalachia to entrepreneurial heroin traffickers from small-town Mexico—to describe a 'catastrophic synergy' in which over-prescription of opioid painkillers begets addicts, many of whom then turn to heroin, which is cheaper and just as ubiquitous." —Best Books of 2015, *Boston Globe*

"Unflinching . . . Compellingly investigated." —*Kirkus Reviews*

"The path of heroin from America's urban slums to its trim suburban subdivisions is traced by a *Los Angeles Times* reporter. Quinones' deeply researched and readable book says well-heeled addicts got hooked first on pain-killing medications like OxyContin—but then switched to much cheaper Mexican heroin, feeding a problem across the nation." —Best Books of 2015, *St. Louis Dispatch*

"Fascinating . . . A harrowing, eye-opening look at two sides of the same coin, the legal and illegal faces of addictive painkillers and their insidious power." —*Publishers Weekly*

"Fascinating." —*Salon*

"You won't find this story told better anywhere else, from the economic hollowing-out of the middle class to the greedy and reckless marketing of pharmaceutical opiates to the remarkable entrepreneurial industry of the residents of the obscure Mexican state of Nayarit . . . *Dreamland*—true crime, sociology, and exposé—illuminates a catastrophe unfolding all around us, right now." —Laura Miller's 10 Favorite Books of 2015, *Slate*

"This book is as much of a page-turner as a good mystery, as well as being thoroughly and disturbingly illuminating about a national crisis." —*Christian Science Monitor*

"A gripping read and hard-hitting account of a ubiquitous plague that has flown under the radar." —*Portland Business Journal*

"Quinones's absorbing narrative is deep in research, on-site reporting, personal interviews and insight. Spanning the central U.S. and crossing the Mexican border, *Dreamland* adroitly unsnarls the tangled business that feeds a growing lust for chemical euphoria and relief." —*Shelf Awareness*

"Everybody should read this book. Everybody." —Rod Dreher, *The American Conservative*

"An important frame of reference for understanding America's opiate epidemic." —*Portland Press Herald*

"[A] powerful investigation into the explosion of heroin abuse in suburban America that combines skilful reporting and strong research with a superb narrative." —*The Spectator*

"A page-turning tale of America's opiate epidemic and a heartbreaking and thought-provoking journey into the lives of those whose dignity has been stolen by addiction." —Matt Bevin, Governor of the Commonwealth of Kentucky

"An eye-opening, enlightening and mesmerizing account of one of the most important stories of the last few decades . . . Quinones is a master storyteller, with a knack of bringing hundreds of characters to life . . . *Dreamland* stands as a model of meticulous investigative reporting providing important insights not only the current opiate epidemic but also into the sometimes negative symbiosis between our country and our neighbors to the south." —*New York Journal of Books*

"Quinones' research ensures that there is something legitimately interesting (and frequently horrifying) on every page." —*Entertainment Weekly*

DREAMLAND

The True Tale of
America's Opiate Epidemic

SAM QUINONES

BLOOMSBURY PRESS
NEW YORK · LONDON · OXFORD · NEW DELHI · SYDNEY

To my girls

Bloomsbury Press
An imprint of Bloomsbury Publishing Plc

1385 Broadway	50 Bedford Square
New York	London
NY 10018	WC1B 3DP
USA	UK

www.bloomsbury.com

BLOOMSBURY and the Diana logo are trademarks of Bloomsbury Publishing Plc

First published 2015
This paperback edition published 2016

ISBN: HB: 978-1-62040-250-4
PB: 978-1-62040-252-8
ePub: 978-1-62040-251-1

LIBRARY OF CONGRESS CATALOGING-IN-PUBLICATION DATA

Quinones, Sam, 1958–
Dreamland: the true tale of America's opiate epidemic / by Sam Quinones.
pages cm
Includes bibliographical references and index.
ISBN 978-1-62040-250-4 (hardcover)
978-1-62040-252-8 (paperback) 978-1-62040-251-1 (ebook)
1. Drug traffic—Mexico. 2. Drug addiction—United States.
3. Heroin abuse—United States. 4. Oxycodone—United States.
5. Narcotics—United States. 6. American Dream. I. Title.
HV5840.M4Q56 2014
362.29'30973—dc23
2014025398

20 19 18 17 16

Typeset by Hewer Text UK Ltd, Edinburgh
Printed and bound in the U.S.A. by Berryville Graphics Inc., Berryville, Virginia

To find out more about our authors and books visit www.bloomsbury.com
Here you will find extracts, author interviews, details of forthcoming
events and the option to sign up for our newsletters.

Bloomsbury books may be purchased for business or promotional use. For
information on bulk purchases please contact Macmillan Corporate and
Premium Sales Department at specialmarkets@macmillan.com.

CONTENTS

Preface: Portsmouth, Ohio 1
Introduction 5

Part I 11
Part II 185
Part III 271
Part IV 301
Part V 331

Afterword 346
Acknowledgments 354
Source Notes 359
Index 363

The Xalisco Boys Heroin Cells
in the United States

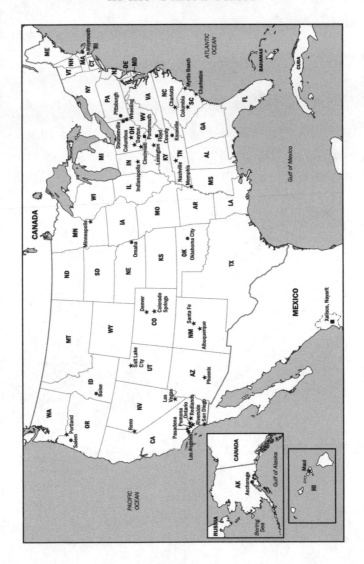

U.S. cities where the traffickers from Xalisco, Nayarit, have heroin cells (stars) or have at one time had cells working (dots). In most cases, the market for their black tar heroin stretches far beyond each city, sometimes for hundreds of miles.

Xalisco county in Nayarit, Mexico

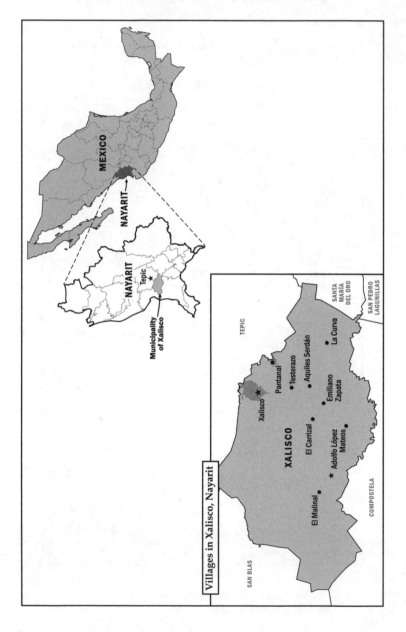

A word on terminology: I have used the term "opiate" throughout this book to describe drugs like morphine and heroin, which derive directly from the opium poppy, and others that derive indirectly, or are synthesized from drugs derived, from the poppy and resemble morphine in their effects. These derivative drugs are often described as opioids. But I felt that going back and forth between the two terms throughout the book would confuse the lay reader.

TIME LINE

1804: Morphine is distilled from opium for the first time.

1839: First Opium War breaks out as Britain forces China to sell its India-grown opium, and the British take Hong Kong. A second war erupts in 1957.

1853: The hypodermic syringe is invented. Inventor's wife is first to die of injected drug overdose.

1898: Bayer chemist invents diacetylmorphine, names it heroin.

1914: U.S. Congress passes Harrison Narcotics Tax Act.

1928: What eventually becomes known as the Committee on the Problems of Drug Dependence forms to organize research in pursuit of the Holy Grail: a nonaddictive painkiller.

1935: The Narcotic Farm in Lexington, Kentucky, opens as federal prison/drug rehabilitation and research center.

1951: Arthur Sackler revolutionizes drug advertising with campaign for antibiotic Terramycin.

1952: Arthur, Raymond, and Mortimer Sackler buy Purdue Frederick.

1960: Arthur Sackler's campaign for Valium makes it the industry's first $100 million drug.

1974: The Narcotic Farm closes and is transformed into a medical center and prison.

1980: Jan Stjernsward made chief of the cancer program for the World Health Organization. Devises WHO Ladder of pain treatment.

1980: The *New England Journal of Medicine* publishes letter to editor that becomes known as Porter and Jick.

Early 1980s: First Xalisco migrants set up heroin trafficking businesses in the San Fernando Valley of Los Angeles.

1984: Purdue releases MS Contin, a timed-release morphine painkiller marketed to cancer patients.

1986: Drs. Kathleen Foley and Russell Portenoy publish paper in the journal *Pain*, opening a debate about use of opiate painkillers for wider variety of pain.

1987: Arthur Sackler dies, having revolutionized pharmaceutical advertising.

Early 1990s: Xalisco Boys heroin cells begin expanding beyond San Fernando Valley to cities across western United States. Their pizza-delivery-style system evolves.

1996: Purdue releases OxyContin, timed-released oxycodone, marketed largely for chronic-pain patients.

1996: Dr. David Procter's clinic in South Shore, Kentucky, is presumed the nation's first pill mill.

1996: President of American Pain Society urges doctors to treat pain as a vital sign.

1998: "The Man" takes Xalisco black tar heroin east across the Mississippi River for the first time, lands in Columbus, Ohio.

1998: In Portsmouth, Ohio, Dr. David Procter has an auto accident that leaves him unable to practice medicine but still capable of running a pain clinic. He hires doctors who go on to open clinics.

Late 1990s: Xalisco Boys heroin cells begin to spread to numerous cities and suburbs east of the Mississippi River.

1998–99: Veterans Administration and JCAHO adopt idea of pain as fifth vital sign.

2000: Operation Tar Pit targets Xalisco heroin networks—the largest joint DEA/FBI operation and first drug conspiracy case to stretch from coast to coast.

2001: Injured workers covered under Washington State's workers' comp system start dying of opiate overdoses.

2002: Dr. David Procter pleads guilty to drug trafficking and conspiracy and serves eleven years in federal prison.

2004: Washington State Department of Labor & Industries Drs. Gary Franklin and Jaymie Mai publish findings on deaths of injured workers due to overdoses on opiate painkillers.

Mid-2000s: Xalisco black tar heroin cells are now in at least seventeen states. Portsmouth, Ohio, has more pill mills per capita than any U.S. town. Florida's lax regulations make it another center of illicit pill supply.

2006: Operation Black Gold Rush, a second DEA operation targeting Xalisco heroin cells across the country.

2007: Purdue and three executives plead guilty to misdemeanor charges of false branding of OxyContin; fined $634 million.

2008: Drug overdoses, mostly from opiates, surpass auto fatalities as leading cause of accidental death in the United States.

2010: Drug violence between Los Zetas and Sinaloa cartels spreads to Xalisco, Nayarit.

2011: Ohio passes House Bill 93, regulating pain clinics.

2013: The College on the Problems of Drug Dependence turns seventy-five without finding the Holy Grail of a nonaddictive painkiller.

2014: Actor Philip Seymour Hoffman dies, focusing widespread attention for the first time on the United States' opiate-abuse epidemic and the transition from pills to heroin in particular.

2014: The FDA approves Zohydro, a timed-release hydrocodone painkiller with no abuse deterrent. It also approves Purdue's Targiniq ER, combining timed-release oxycodone with naloxone, the opiate-overdose antidote.

PREFACE: Portsmouth, Ohio

In 1929, three decades into what were the great years for the blue-collar town of Portsmouth, on the Ohio River, a private swimming pool opened and they called it Dreamland.

The pool was the size of a football field. Over the decades, generations of the town grew up at the edge of its crystal-blue water.

Dreamland was the summer babysitter. Parents left their children at the pool every day. Townsfolk found respite from the thick humidity at Dreamland and then went across the street to the A&W stand for hot dogs and root beer. The pool's french fries were the best around. Kids took the bus to the pool in the morning, and back home in the afternoon. They came from schools all over Scioto County and met each other and learned to swim. Some of them competed on the Dreamland Dolphins swim team, which practiced every morning and evening. WIOI, the local radio station, knowing so many of its listeners were sunbathing next to their transistor radios at Dreamland, would broadcast a jingle—"Time to turn so you won't burn"—every half hour.

The vast pool had room in the middle for two concrete platforms, from which kids sunned themselves, then dove back in. Poles topped with floodlights rose from the platforms for swimming at night. On one side of the pool was an immense lawn where families set their towels. On the opposite side were locker rooms and a restaurant.

Dreamland could fit hundreds of people, and yet, magically, the space around it kept growing and there was always room for more. Jaime Williams, the city treasurer, owned the pool for years. Williams was part owner of one of the shoe factories that were at the core of Portsmouth's industrial might. He bought more and more land, and for years Dreamland seemed to just get better. A large picnic area was added, and playgrounds for young children. Then fields for softball and football, and courts for basketball and shuffleboard, and a video arcade.

For a while, to remain white only, the pool became a private club and the name changed to the Terrace Club. But Portsmouth was a largely integrated town. Its chief of police was black. Black and white kids went to the same schools. Only the pool remained segregated. Then, in the summer of 1961, a black boy named Eugene McKinley drowned in the Scioto River, where he was swimming because he was kept out of the pool. The Portsmouth NAACP pushed back, held a wade-in, and quietly they integrated the pool. With integration, the pool was rechristened Dreamland, though blacks were never made to feel particularly comfortable there.

Dreamland did wash away class distinctions, though. In a swimming suit, a factory worker looked no different from the factory manager or clothing-shop owner. Wealthy families on Portsmouth's hilltop donated money to a fund that would go to pay for summer passes for families from the town's East End, down between the tracks and the Ohio River. East End river rats and upscale hilltoppers all met at Dreamland.

California had its beaches. Heartland America spent its summers at swimming pools, and, down at a far end of Ohio, Dreamland took on an outsized importance to the town of Portsmouth. A family's season pass was only twenty-five dollars, and this was a prized possession often given as a Christmas present. Kids whose families couldn't afford that could cut a neighbor's grass for the fifteen cents that a daily pool pass cost.

Friday swim dances began at midnight. They hauled out a jukebox and kids spent the night twisting by the pool. Couples announced new romances by walking hand in hand around Dreamland. Girls walked home from those dances and families left their doors unlocked. "The heat of the evening combined with the cool water was wonderful," one woman remembered. "It was my entire world. I did nothing else. As I grew up and had my own children, I took them, too."

In fact, the cycle of life in Portsmouth was repeated over and over at Dreamland. A toddler spent her first years at the shallow end watched by her parents, particularly her mother, who sat on a towel on the concrete near the water with other young moms. When the child left elementary school, she migrated out to the middle section of Dreamland as her parents retreated to the grass. By high school, she was hanging out on the grass around the pool's ten-foot deep end, near the high dive and the head lifeguard's chair, and her parents were far away. When she married and had children, she returned to the shallow end of Dreamland to watch over her own children, and the whole thing began again.

"My father, a Navy Vet from WWII, insisted that his 4 children learn not only how to swim but how not to be afraid of water," one man wrote. "My younger sister jumped off the 15-foot high diving board at age 3. Yes, my father, myself & brother were in the water just in case. Sister pops up out of the water and screams . . . 'Again!'"

For many years, Dreamland's manager, Chuck Lorentz, a Portsmouth High School coach and strict disciplinarian, walked the grounds with a yardstick, making sure teenagers minded his "three-foot rule" and stayed that far apart. He wasn't that successful. It seems half the town got their first kiss at the pool, and plenty lost their virginity in Dreamland's endless grass.

Lorentz's son, meanwhile, learned to swim before he could walk and became a Dreamland lifeguard in high school. "To be the lifeguard in that chair, you were right in the center of all the action, all the strutting, all the flirting," said John Lorentz, now a retired history professor. "You were like a king on a throne."

Through these years, Portsmouth also supported two bowling alleys, a JCPenney, a Sears, and a Montgomery Ward with an escalator, and locally owned Marting's Department Store, with a photo studio where graduating seniors had their portraits taken. Chillicothe Street bustled. Big U.S.-made sedans and station wagons lined the street. People cashed their checks at the Kresge's on Saturdays, and the owners of Morgan Brothers Jewelry, Herrmann's Meats, Counts' Bakery, and Atlas Fashion earned a middle-class living. Kids took the bus downtown to the movie theater or for cherry Cokes at Smith's Drugstore and stayed out late trick-or-treating on Halloween. On Friday and Saturday nights, teenagers cruised Chillicothe Street, from Staker's Drugs down to Smith's, then turned around and did it again.

Throughout the year, the shoe factories would deduct Christmas Club money from each worker's paycheck. Before Christmas, they issued each worker a check and he would cash it at the bank. Chillicothe Street was festive then. Bells rang as shoppers went shoulder to shoulder, watching the mechanical puppets in displays in store windows painted with candy canes, Christmas trees, and snowmen. Marting's had a Santa on its second floor.

So, in 1979 and 1980, Portsmouth felt worthy to be selected an All-American City. The town had more than forty-two thousand people then. Very few were wealthy, and the U.S. Labor Department would have gauged many Portsmouthians poor. "But we weren't aware of it, nor did we care," one woman recalled. Its industry supported a community for all. No one had pools in their backyards. Rather, there were parks, tennis and basketball courts, and window-shopping and levees to slide down. Families ice-skated at Millbrook Park in winter and picnicked at Roosevelt Lake in summer, or sat late into the evening as their kids played Kick the Can in the street.

"My family used to picnic down by the Ohio River in a little park, where my dad would push me so high on the swings I thought I'd land in Kentucky," another woman said.

All of this recreation let a working-class family feel well-off. But the center of it all was that gleaming, glorious swimming pool. Memories of Dreamland, drenched in the smell of chlorine, Coppertone, and french fries, were what almost everyone who grew up in Portsmouth took with them as the town declined.

Two Portsmouths exist today. One is a town of abandoned buildings at the edge of the Ohio River. The other resides in the memories of thousands in the town's diaspora who grew up during its better years and return to the actual Portsmouth rarely, if at all.

When you ask them what the town was back then, it was Dreamland.

INTRODUCTION

In the middle-class neighborhood on the east side of Columbus, Ohio, where Myles Schoonover grew up, the kids smoked weed and drank. But while Myles was growing up he knew no one who did heroin. He and his younger brother, Matt, went to a private Christian high school in a Columbus suburb. Their father, Paul Schoonover, co-owns an insurance agency. Ellen Schoonover, their mother, is a stay-at-home mom and part-time consultant.

Myles partied, but found it easy to bear down and focus. He went off to a Christian university in Tennessee in 2005 and was away from home for most of Matt's adolescence. Matt had attention deficit hyperactivity disorder and schoolwork came harder to him. He started partying—smoking pot and drinking—about his junior year in high school.

The two brothers got to know each other again when Matt joined Myles at college for his freshman year in 2009. His parents were never sure when exactly Matt began using pills that by then were all over central Ohio and Tennessee. But that year Myles saw that pills were already a big part of Matt's life.

Matt hoped school would be a new beginning. It wasn't. Instead, he accumulated a crew of friends who lacked basic skills and motivation. They slept on Myles's sofa. Myles ended up cooking for them. For a while he did his brother's laundry, because Matt could wear the same clothes for weeks on end. Matt, at six feet six and burly, was a caring fellow with a soft side. His cards could be heartfelt and sweet. "I love you, mommy," he wrote the last time to his mother, after his grandmother had been hospitalized for some time. "All this stuff with grandma has made me realize you really don't know how long you have on this earth. You're the best mom I could ask for." Yet the pills seemed to keep him in a fog. Myles once had to take him to a post office so he could mail their mother a birthday card, as Matt seemed otherwise incapable of finding the place.

Myles was a graduate teaching assistant and saw kids his brother's age all the time. It seemed to him that a large chunk of Matt's generation could not navigate life's demands and consequences. Myles had taught English in Beijing to Chinese kids who strove ferociously to differentiate themselves from millions of other young people. American kids a world away had enormous quantities of the world's resources lavished on them to little result; they coasted along, doing the bare minimum and depending on their parents to resolve problems, big and small.

At year's end, Matt returned home to live with his parents. Myles spent the next years at Yale getting a master's degree in Judaic and biblical studies and never knew all that happened later. At home, Matt seemed to have lost the aimlessness he displayed in college. He dressed neatly and worked full-time at catering companies. But by the time he moved home, his parents later realized, he had become a functional addict, using opiate prescription painkillers, and Percocet above all. From there, he moved eventually to OxyContin, a powerful pill made by a company in the small state of Connecticut—Purdue Pharma.

In early 2012, his parents found out. They were worried, but the pills Matt had been abusing were pharmaceuticals prescribed by a doctor. They weren't some street drug that you could die from, or so they believed. They took him to a doctor, who prescribed a weeklong home detoxification, using blood pressure and sleep medicine to calm the symptoms of opiate withdrawal.

He relapsed a short time later. Unable to afford street OxyContin, Matt at some point switched to the black tar heroin that had saturated the Columbus market, brought in by young Mexican men from a small state on Mexico's Pacific coast called Nayarit. Looking back later, his parents believe this had happened months before they knew of his addiction. But in April 2012, Matt tearfully admitted his heroin problem to his parents. Stunned, they got him into a treatment center.

Myles hadn't spoken to his brother for some time when he called his parents.

"He's in drug rehab," said his mother.

"What? For what?"

Ellen paused, not knowing how to say it.

"Matt is addicted to heroin."

Myles burst into tears.

Matt Schoonover came home from three weeks of rehab on May 10, 2012, and with that, his parents felt the nightmare was over. The next day, they bought him a new battery for his car, and a new cell phone.

He set off to a Narcotics Anonymous meeting, then a golf date with friends. He was supposed to call his father after the NA meeting.

His parents waited all day for a call that never came. That night, a policeman knocked on their door.

More than eight hundred people attended Matt's funeral. He was twenty-one when he overdosed on black tar heroin.

In the months after Matt died, Paul and Ellen Schoonover were struck by all they didn't know. First, the pills: Doctors prescribed them, so how could they lead to heroin and death? And *what* was black tar heroin? People who lived in tents under overpasses used heroin. Matt grew up in the best neighborhoods, attended a Christian private school and a prominent church. He'd admitted his addiction, sought help, and received the best residential drug treatment in Columbus. Why wasn't that enough?

But across America, thousands of people like Matt Schoonover were dying. Drug overdoses were killing more people every year than car accidents. Auto fatalities had been the leading cause of accidental death for decades until this. Now most of the fatal overdoses were from opiates: prescription painkillers or heroin. If deaths were the measurement, this wave of opiate abuse was the worst drug scourge to ever hit the country.

This epidemic involved more users and far more death than the crack plague of the 1990s, or the heroin plague in the 1970s; but it was happening quietly. Kids were dying in the Rust Belt of Ohio and the Bible Belt of Tennessee. Some of the worst of it was in Charlotte's best country club enclaves. It was in Mission Viejo and Simi Valley in suburban Southern California, and in Indianapolis, Salt Lake, and Albuquerque, in Oregon and Minnesota and Oklahoma and Alabama. For each of the thousands who died every year, many hundreds more were addicted.

Via pills, heroin had entered the mainstream. The new addicts were football players and cheerleaders; football was almost a gateway to opiate addiction. Wounded soldiers returned from Afghanistan hooked on pain pills and died in America. Kids got hooked in college and died there. Some of these addicts were from rough corners of rural Appalachia. But many more were from the U.S. middle class. They lived in communities where the driveways were clean, the cars were new, and the shopping centers attracted congregations of Starbucks, Home Depot, CVS, and Applebee's. They were the daughters of preachers, the sons of cops and doctors, the children of contractors and teachers and business owners and bankers.

And almost every one was white.

Children of the most privileged group in the wealthiest country in the history of the world were getting hooked and dying in almost epidemic numbers from substances meant to, of all things, numb pain. "What pain?" a South Carolina cop asked rhetorically one afternoon as we toured the fine neighborhoods south of Charlotte where he arrested kids for pills and heroin.

Crime was at historic lows, drug overdose deaths at record highs. A happy façade covered a disturbing reality.

I grew consumed by this story. It was about America and Mexico, about addiction and marketing, about wealth and poverty, about happiness and how to achieve it. I saw it as an epic woven by threads from all over. It took me through the history of pain and a revolution in U.S. medicine. I followed the tale through a small town of sugarcane farmers in Nayarit, Mexico, and a town of equal size in the Rust Belt of southern Ohio. The story transported me through Appalachian Kentucky and the gleaming suburbs of the cities that most benefited from our age of excess that began in the late 1990s. I met cops and addicts, professors and doctors, public health nurses and pharmacists, as I tried to follow the threads.

And I met parents.

On New Year's Day 2013, I was in Covington, Kentucky, and beginning full-time research on this book. The only place open for lunch was Herb & Thelma's Tavern—a cozy, darkened place for chili. Inside were a dozen members of a family celebrating a girl's birthday. I sat in a corner, eating and writing for an hour in the glow of the college football games on TV and the neon BAVARIAN BEER sign on the wall.

I rose to leave when, seeing the Berkeley sweatshirt I wore, the grandmother in the group asked, "You're not from around here, are you?"

I told her I was from California. She asked why I was so far from home. I told her I was just beginning to research a book about heroin and prescription pill abuse.

The party stopped. The tavern hushed.

"Well, pull up a chair," she said, after a pause. "I have a story for you."

Her name was Carol Wagner. Carol went on to tell me of her handsome, college-educated son, Chad, who was prescribed OxyContin for his carpal tunnel syndrome, grew addicted, and never got unstuck after that. He lost home and family and five years later lay dead of a heroin overdose in a Cincinnati halfway house. Carol's daughter-in-law had a nephew who'd also died from heroin.

"I no longer judge drug addicts," Carol said. "I no longer judge prostitutes."

I left Herb & Thelma's and drove the streets, stunned that so random an encounter in America's heartland could yield such personal connections to heroin.

Later, I met other parents whose children were still alive, but who had shape-shifted into lying, thieving slaves to an unseen molecule. These parents feared each night the call that their child was dead in a McDonald's bathroom. They went broke paying for rehab, and collect calls from jail. They moved to where no one knew their shame. They prayed that the child they'd known would reemerge. Some considered suicide. They were shell-shocked and unprepared for the sudden nightmare opiate abuse had wreaked and how deeply it mangled their lives.

Among the parents I met were Paul and Ellen Schoonover. I found them anguished and bewildered a year after Matt's death.

"I kept trying to figure out what just happened. Why did our lives become devastated?" Paul Schoonover said to me the day we first got together at his insurance agency in Columbus. "How could this have happened?"

Here's how.

PART I

Enrique

Yuma, Arizona

One hot day in the summer of 1999, a young Mexican man with tight-cropped hair, new shoes, a clean cream-colored button-down shirt, and pressed beige pants used a phony U.S. driver's license to cross the border into Arizona.

He took a cab to the Yuma International Airport, intending to fly to Phoenix.

Also in the airport, waiting for a plane, stood a dozen Mexican men. Short and brown, they wore dusty baseball caps, jeans, and faded T-shirts. They looked weather-beaten and callused—just like their hands, he imagined. He figured them for illegals, maybe construction workers, proud of their capacity for hard work, but without much else on their side.

He sometimes went by the name Enrique. He was tall, light-skinned, and handsome. The calluses on his hands, there since childhood, had softened. He had grown up in a hovel on the outskirts of a village in the Mexican state of Nayarit, fifteen hours by car south of Arizona. His father was a sugarcane farmer. His village depended on sugarcane, and thus it was poor, and life there was violent and mean. His relatives were split by a feud that began before he was born. He didn't know its cause, only that the two sides didn't get along.

But he had moved on; he had a business now, with employees and expenses. It allowed him to buy his first Levi's 501s and pay for his fade at the barbershop. His false U.S. ID allowed him to cross the border posing as another man, Alejandro Something.

Still, it wasn't hard for Enrique to see himself in those men at the airport in Yuma that day.

As he waited for his plane, he watched an immigration officer in the airport spot the men and make the same calculation he had. The officer asked them for identification. There was a discussion Enrique couldn't hear. But in the end, the men could produce none. As the other passengers watched, the officer led them off single file to be, Enrique assumed, deported.

Growing up in a poor Mexican village had attuned Enrique to the world's unfairness. Those who worked hard and honestly got left behind. Only those with power and money could insist on decent treatment. These facts, which he believed had been proven to him throughout his life, allowed him to rationalize what he did. Yet moral qualms still came like uninvited guests. He told others that he hadn't been raised to be a heroin trafficker and believed it when he said it, though he was one. Scenes like this convinced him that he was doing what he had to do to survive. He didn't make the rules.

Still, as the officer paraded the men by, he thought to himself, "I'm the dirtiest of them all and they don't ask me anything. If I'd have come to work *derecho*—honestly—they'd have treated me badly, too."

A while later he boarded a plane that took him to Phoenix and from there to Santa Fe, New Mexico.

Dr. Jick's Letter

Boston, Massachusetts

One day twenty years earlier, in 1979, a doctor at Boston University School of Medicine named Hershel Jick sat in his office pondering the question of how often patients in a hospital, given narcotic painkillers, grew addicted to these drugs.

He would not remember, years later, exactly why this question had occurred to him. "I think it was maybe a newspaper story," he said.

Hershel Jick was in a better position than most to gather findings on the topic. At Boston University, he had built a database of records of hospitalized patients. The database charted the effects of drugs of all kinds on these patients while they were in the hospital. The database grew from the thalidomide scandal of 1960, when babies were born with defects after their mothers were prescribed the drug. Only anecdotally did doctors discover the risk of thalidomide. In the early 1960s, Dr. Jick was asked to begin building a database of drugs used in hospitals and their effects.

The database grew as computers became more accessible. Today the Boston Collaborative Drug Surveillance Program, as it's known, includes millions of patients' hospital records in four databases. Yet even by the late 1970s, the database was a substantial thing, holding the records of three hundred thousand patients and the drugs they were given while hospitalized. Dr. Jick grew used to entertaining his curiosity with forays into the data. The doctor years later would say, "I don't even know how to turn on a computer." But he did have the sense to hire a bright computer technician, who had built the database and to whom Dr. Jick turned often with these requests.

This time, Dr. Jick asked for the numbers of patients in the database who had developed addictions after being given narcotic painkillers. Soon he had the data in hand. Figuring others might find it interesting, he wrote a paragraph in longhand describing the findings. Then he gave it to his secretary to type. The paragraph she typed said this: Of almost twelve thousand patients treated with opiates while in a hospital before 1979, and whose records were in the Boston database, only four had grown addicted. There was no data about how often, how long, or at what dose these patients were given opiates, nor the ailments the drugs treated. The paragraph simply cited the numbers and made no claim beyond that.

"That's all it pretended to be," Dr. Jick said later.

A graduate student named Jane Porter helped with his calculations in some way that Dr. Jick could not remember years later. As is the practice in medical research papers, she received top byline, though Dr. Jick said he wrote the thing. The secretary put the letter in an envelope and sent it off to the prestigious *New England Journal of Medicine*, which, in due course, in its edition of January 10, 1980, published Dr. Jick's paragraph on page 123 alongside myriad letters from researchers and physicians from around the country. It bore the title "Addiction Rare in Patients Treated with Narcotics."

With that, Hershel Jick filed the paragraph away and gave the letter scant thought for years thereafter. He published dozens of articles— including more than twenty in the *NEJM* alone. Jane Porter left the hospital and Dr. Jick lost track of her.

All from the Same Town

Huntington, West Virginia

One Monday in September 2007, Teddy Johnson, a well-to-do plumber in Huntington, West Virginia, visited the apartment of his son, Adam.

Adam Johnson was a chubby, redheaded kid. As a fan of alt-rockers like the New York Dolls, Brian Eno, and Captain Beefheart, he was a bit of a misfit in socially conservative West Virginia. He played the drums and guitar and grew up in a wealthy neighborhood. He was twenty-three and just starting college at Marshall University in Huntington. He already had a radio show, the *Oscillating Zoo*, which featured his eclectic taste in music on the school's station. Adam's mother was an alcoholic and he had used drugs off and on for several years. He started with cough syrup, but quickly moved on to other substances, including prescription painkillers, his friends said.

Adam had dropped out of high school, gotten his GED. He cast about for something to do with his life. He worked for Teddy. It seemed to Teddy that Adam was turning things around. He was playing music with friends and seemed sober. Teddy was heartened when his son enrolled in Marshall, planning to major in history.

Then, that Monday morning, Teddy came to Adam's apartment and found his son dead in bed.

Adam's autopsy showed a heroin overdose; police said Adam was using a sticky, dark substance known as "black tar," a semiprocessed heroin that comes from Mexico's Pacific coast, where opium poppies grow. That stunned Teddy almost as much as Adam's death. Heroin? That was for New York City. Huntington was in the middle of Appalachia.

"I had no clue," he said later. "We're a small town. We weren't prepared."

Two other men also died of black tar heroin overdoses in Huntington that weekend: Patrick Byars, forty-two, a Papa John's Pizza employee, and George Shore, fifty-four, former owner of an antique store. One black tar heroin overdose after another racked Huntington over the next five months. The town had seen only four heroin deaths since 2001. But twelve people died in five months; another two had died the previous spring. Dozens more would have died had paramedics not responded quickly.

"We had scores of overdoses occurring—medics finding [people] unresponsive," said Huntington police chief Skip Holbrook. Police in Huntington had never seen black tar before 2007.

Two years later, I stood on the southern banks of the Ohio River on what is uncharacteristically flat land for West Virginia. To the north is Ohio and to the west, Kentucky. Huntington lies in a long, narrow grid next to the flat, quiet river. The town was founded as a western terminus for the Chesapeake and Ohio Railway. Railcars carried the coal the region mined to Huntington, where river barges shipped it to the rest of the country.

The city is at the nexus of America's North and South—much like West Virginia itself. Democrats ran the state like a Tammany Hall. They created a legal and political system supportive of coal and railroad interests. The name of the state's best-known senator, Robert C. Byrd, is on a dozen public buildings in Huntington alone—including a bridge over the Ohio River. Yet West Virginia sent its raw materials elsewhere to be transformed into profitable, higher-value products. Parts of the South threw off this third world model of economic development. West Virginia did not. Resource extraction mechanized and jobs left. Railroads declined and economic turbulence set in. But the state's political system prevented a robust response or new direction. Poverty intensified. Marijuana became the state's number one crop. In 2005, the state produced more coal than ever, but with the fewest workers ever.

Immigrants avoided West Virginia. Only 1 percent of the state's population is foreign-born, ranking it last in that category in the United States. West Virginians with aspirations streamed north, thinking always of returning. The state does significant business in family reunions. Many of the families who remained lived on government assistance.

Huntington's population fell from eighty-three thousand in 1960 to forty-nine thousand today. The three R's became "reading, writing, and Route 23" as people headed north on the famous highway to Columbus, Cleveland, or Detroit. In 2008, the city was selected as the fattest in America; it had, the Associated Press reported, more pizza places than the entire state of West Virginia had gyms and health spas.

Through all this, what grew steadily in Huntington, besides the waistlines of its dwindling population, was drug use and fatalism. Dealers called the town Moneyington. Dealers from Detroit moved in and cops grew suspicious of any car with Michigan plates.

Yet Mexican drug traffickers avoided the town, police told me. This made Huntington rare. Mexican traffickers operated all over America— in Tennessee and Idaho and Alaska. But not in West Virginia. West Virginia was one of the seven states with no known Mexican drug-trafficking presence, according to a U.S. Department of Justice 2009 report I had seen. Police had a simple reason for this: There was no Mexican community in which to hide. Mexican immigrants followed the jobs, functioning as a sort of economic barometer: Mexicans in your community meant your area was growing. Huntington and West Virginia had no jobs, no Mexicans either.

So, I wondered, how is it black tar heroin from Mexico could have killed so many people here over so many months? And what's more, since when did West Virginia have heroin of any kind?

I began my journalism career as a crime reporter in Stockton, California. Up to then, I knew heroin only from the 1970s movies about New York City: *The French Connection*, *Serpico*, and *Prince of the City*, the drug was always white powder. New York City was our national heroin hub. But in Stockton I saw only this stuff called black tar. Narcotics officers told me black tar was made in Mexico. It was semi-processed opium base. Like other forms of heroin, it could be smoked or injected, and was just as potent as the more refined white powder I'd seen in *The French Connection*. The difference was that it had more impurities. Also, they said, black tar was a West Coast drug, sold in California, Oregon, and Washington. Denver had a lot, as did Arizona. But it was unknown east of the Mississippi River. For years, DEA reports showed that as well.

So what was black tar heroin now doing east of the Mississippi River?

Those questions brought me to Huntington and that Ohio River bank. I was a reporter for the *Los Angeles Times* on a team covering Mexico's drug wars. My job was to write about Mexican trafficking in the United States, a topic no one covered much at all. Searching for a story to do, I had come upon reports of Huntington's 2007 black tar outbreak and called a Huntington police narcotics sergeant.

All our black tar heroin comes from Columbus, Ohio, he told me.

I called the DEA in Columbus and spoke with an especially loquacious agent.

"We got dozens of Mexican heroin traffickers. They all drive around selling their dope in small balloons, delivering it to the addicts. They're like teams, or cells. We arrest the drivers all the time and they send new ones up from Mexico," he said. "They never go away."

He discoursed at some length on the frustration of arduous investigations ending with the arrest of young men who were replaced so quickly. They hide among Columbus's large Mexican population, he said. The drivers all know each other and never talk. They're never armed. They come, give false names, rent apartments, and are gone six months later. This was not the kind of heroin mafia Ohio and the eastern United States was used to.

"Crazy thing," he said. "They're all from the same town."

I sat up in my chair.

"Yeah, which one's that?"

He called over a colleague. They talked in muffled tones for a couple minutes.

I had lived in Mexico for ten years as a freelance writer after I left Stockton. I spent a lot of time in small towns and villages writing about people who migrated north. I wrote two books of nonfiction stories about Mexico. Many of the stories took place in the smallest villages, known as *ranchos*.

Ranchos were villages on the outskirts of civilization. Throughout history, rancheros had moved to the outback to escape the towns' stifling classism. They formed outposts and tried to carve a living from tough land that no one else wanted. Rancheros embodied Mexico's best pioneering impulse. They fled the government's suffocating embrace. They were dedicated to escaping poverty, usually by finding a way to be their own bosses.

Rancheros had little access to education. They learned a trade from relatives—farming or ranching, mostly. But I also knew villages where all the men were itinerant construction workers. Families from one village in the state of Zacatecas I knew started tortilla shops all over Mexico; in another, men hired out as cops around the state. I wrote about Tocumbo, Michoacan, where everyone learned to make popsicles, and run popsicle shops, known as Paleterias La Michoacana, that spread across Mexico, transforming the town and the lives of these rancheros. I had also been to Tenancingo, Tlaxcala, where the young men are all pimps, exporting country girls to Mexico City and to Queens, New York, and building garish mansions back home.

The DEA agent came back to the phone.

"Tepic," he said.

No, that's wrong, I thought. Tepic is the capital of one of Mexico's smallest states—Nayarit, on the Pacific coast. But it's still a big city, population 330,000. The agent wasn't lying. But my hunch was that the family and personal connections crucial to the system he was describing would only be forged in a small town or rancho. By the time I got off the phone, that prospect had me mesmerized. I imagined some rancho of heroin traffickers expert enough to supply a town the size of Columbus.

It helped that I loved ranchos. They were lawless, wild places, full of amazing tales of family feuds, stolen women, pistoleros, caciques (town bosses), and especially the tough guys—*valientes*—rebels who backed down from no one, and thus leapt like superheroes from the rancho into a place in Mexican movies, novels, and ballads.

Mine was a romantic infatuation. I didn't have to live in a rancho. They were brutish places and received outsiders uneasily. Rancho families wove together in vast clans, where everyone was related to almost everyone else. You did not penetrate that easily. To learn their secret stories, you had to spend a lot of time. But I could sit for hours listening to old men tell how their village had, say, split in half over a family feud. The stories melded fact and myth into accounts of doomed bravery or steel-cold vengeance. One tale I included in a book was about Antonio Carrillo, who went to the United States in the 1920s, worked in a steel mill, bought a pistol, then wrote to the man who killed his father, telling him his time had come. He went home and in the town plaza he shot the man to death with that pistol.

I learned, too, that *envidia*—envy, jealousy—was a destructive force in the rancho. That people were related didn't mean they got along. Families split over what one had and another did not. In the rancho, I saw that immigration was powered by what a poor man felt when he returned home with new boots, a new car, better clothes. That he could buy the beer in the plaza that night, pay for his daughter's *quinceañera* equal to that of the daughter of the local merchant, and act the magnanimous *don* if only for a week; that was a potent narcotic to any poor man. A have-not's success was sweeter if he could show it off to the backbiters back home. Thus few Mexicans started out aiming to melt into America. Returning home to the rancho was *the* point of going north. This homecoming had no power in anonymous big cities.

Migrants wanted to display their success to those who'd humiliated them years before. In the rancho.

I'd learned too that venturing into the unknown was in rancheros' DNA. The United States was the one place where the promise of the unknown had paid off. In turn, the Mexican rancho had become a huge influence in American life. It gave rise to millions of our new working class. Mexican immigrant customs and attitudes toward work, sex, politics, civic engagement, government, education, debt, leisure—they were forged in the rancho. They arrived intact in the United States, and changed slowly.

I ponder this all that day after the chat with the Columbus DEA agent. Only a small town or rancho could forge the connections that sustained the kind of heroin business the agent described. A village of master heroin retailers. Could it be?

I wrote to a dozen of the drivers arrested in Columbus who were doing time in federal prisons. I asked if they wanted to talk to a reporter. Weeks passed. I heard nothing from them. I was about to turn to other stories when one of them called collect. He'd worked, and was arrested, in Columbus. He was now doing many years in prison. He had lots of information. Most startling: Columbus was not the only town they worked, he told me.

"They're in many others. All over the country," he said. Salt Lake, Charlotte, Las Vegas, Cincinnati, Nashville, Minneapolis, Columbia, Indianapolis, Honolulu. They were working full-time in seventeen states. They'd been in another seven or eight states at one time or another. He went on. The cities he mentioned all had large white middle classes that benefited hugely from the economic booms of the previous dozen years, and now had large Mexican immigrant populations as well. I hardly associated these cities with heroin. Were there heroin markets in these towns? I wondered. Yes, he assured me, they were big and getting bigger. He hadn't even mentioned America's traditional heroin capital, I noticed.

"No, in New York are gangs, with guns," he said. "They're afraid of New York City. They don't go to New York."

Mexican traffickers afraid of gangs and gunplay? From one tiny town? Selling tar heroin in not just Columbus, but as much as half the United States, including now a bunch of cities east of the Mississippi River for the first time?

Right there, I was hooked.

Cops say they're from Tepic, I said finally.

"No, they're not from Tepic," he said. "That's what they say, but they're not."

Liberace in Appalachia

South Shore, Kentucky

In tiny South Shore, Kentucky, huddled next to the Ohio River, Biggs Lane amounts to a rural strip mall.

For its entire hundred yards, Biggs Lane hugs Route 23. Wright Pharmacy has been on Biggs a long time. Near Wright's is a dentist's office and a chiropractor, a gas station and a Subway sandwich shop. Farther down is a flooring shop. Next to that stands a good-sized beige metal-framed building.

To the south of Biggs is a street named Tootsie Drive and a neighborhood of small white wood houses that would be called quiet except that would be redundant. Everything in South Shore, Kentucky, population 2,100, is quiet, including the majestic Ohio River a hundred yards north. Across the river is Portsmouth, Ohio, wedged onto land where the Scioto River angles into the Ohio. In Portsmouth and South Shore is where another part of our story begins.

In 1979, the same year that Hershel Jick up in Boston wrote his letter to the *New England Journal of Medicine*, a doctor named David Procter moved into that beige metal-framed building on Biggs Lane in South Shore and called his new clinic Plaza Healthcare.

Procter had come to South Shore at the behest of Billy Riddle, the town's family doc. Billy Riddle had been in South Shore for years. He delivered many of the kids in town, and treated every ailment as best he could. He had trouble turning down patients and needed help. Somehow he found Procter, a Canadian, who'd just completed an internship in Nova Scotia, and enticed him to South Shore in 1977.

But within two years, Riddle had separated his practice from Procter's and changed the locks on his doors. Not long after that, in 1979, Billy Riddle died of a heart attack and then only David Procter remained.

Procter was a talkative and easygoing fellow. But he was flashy in a way foreign to the Ohio River valley. He wore diamond rings. He wore fur jackets. He drove a Porsche. "He dressed like Little Richard or Liberace," said one nurse.

PORTSMOUTH IS AN INDUSTRIAL town in the rural heartland, an outpost on the Ohio River far from other towns. In their glory days, river towns were places for rambunctious men to explode after days cooped up on barges. Portsmouth once felt it necessary to outlaw swimming naked in the river. Back then, seven shoe factories and the country's largest shoelace manufacturer were in downtown Portsmouth. A brickyard, a foundry, and the massive Detroit Steel Company attracted people from Ohio and Kentucky and employed thousands. Detroit Steel made bombs during World War II. Hundreds of people attended the inauguration of its new blast furnace in 1953, marveling at its size and happy with the jobs it would provide. Meanwhile, railroads took Portsmouth's steel and shoes to the rest of the country. For years, sons took jobs at the factories where their fathers worked, and, like a Bruce Springsteen song, that's how life went.

The town was a cradle of professional football. Jim Thorpe coached the Portsmouth Shoe-Steels. Later, the Portsmouth Spartans joined the National Football League. The Spartans moved to Detroit during the Great Depression and became the Detroit Lions.

Some say Portsmouth's long trip down began with the flood of 1937, when the Ohio River rose seventy-four feet after forty days of rain. What is true is that by the 1970s, Portsmouth was collapsing, along with the rest of what was becoming the American Rust Belt—a region unprepared for globalization, competition, and the cheaper labor in countries like Mexico. The shoe factories began closing. Selby Shoes was long gone. Williams Shoes hung on longer, trying to compete with Italy and Taiwan and Mexico. But soon Williams left, too, and the factories' empty shells remained as reminders of what had been.

Detroit Steel departed in 1980, the year Portsmouth was named an All-American City for the second time. Thousands of jobs went with it. The city didn't recover from that. The brickyard closed, too. So did the atomic energy plant up in Piketon. The coke plant that supplied Detroit Steel, meanwhile, closed in stages and finally gave up in 2000. A Walmart replaced them both. Near the retailer still stands the coke plant's smokestack.

Families fled to Columbus or Cincinnati or Nashville. A group of artists moved to Austin, Texas. Portsmouth's population deflated to twenty thousand. Unsellable houses were rented out or stood empty after landlords moved away. Stores on Chillicothe Street closed one by one until there wasn't much left there at all.

Remaining behind was a thin slice of educated people. They found work in the schools or the hospitals, in some way or other tending to those for whom factory closings were the beginning of an American nightmare.

About the only new folks who came to Portsmouth then were merchants of the poor economy. Portsmouth got its first check-cashing places and its first rent-to-owns. Pawnshops and scrap metal yards opened. And David Procter expanded his practice.

Many swore by Procter. Hard work was part of life in the area, and by then so was unemployment. The region slumped and the numbers of people applying for disability or workers' compensation shot up. Federal disability became long-term unemployment insurance for many in the Ohio River valley. Some were legitimately hurt or disabled; some weren't. But they all needed a doctor's diagnosis. Procter processed workers' comp paperwork fast. At Portsmouth's small Southern Hills Hospital, where Procter had privileges, nurses remembered him as the top admitter to the psych ward—mostly in an attempt to make patients eligible for disability.

Procter was married, with two sons living in Kentucky. He was also a flirt, and staff saw him out in the parking lot at times in a lovers' quarrel with a nurse.

At Southern Hills, Procter ran through his rounds—literally ran. He was at high speed, animated. A new attitude was taking hold in American medicine at the time. The patient, it held, was always right, particularly when it came to pain. The doctor was to believe a patient who said he was in pain. David Procter embodied this new attitude, and then some. He had a folksy style, with a little of the evangelist in him.

"His patients loved him because he had the ability to figure out what that person believed or needed or wanted," said Lisa Roberts, who was a hospital nurse at the time. "He was brilliant in that way, to forensically identify vulnerable people and figure out what they needed or believed. He would tell them they had all these things wrong with them."

Procter was paid in cash at his South Shore clinic. In the mid-1980s, the medical world wrestled with how to use the new opiates that pharmaceutical companies were developing to treat pain. David Procter was an early and aggressive adopter. He prescribed opiates for neck, leg, and lower back pain, arthritis, and lower lumbar spine pain. He combined them with benzodiazepines—anxiety relievers, of which Valium and

Xanax, Procter's favorite, are the best known. In Portsmouth, people had anxiety and they had pain. Appalachia had a long history of using benzodiazepines—dating to the release of Valium in the early 1960s. Little old ladies used it. In this part of the country, anything that relieved pain was welcome. But opiates and benzos together also led quickly to addiction.

By the mid-1990s, Procter was also known to prescribe a lot of diet pills and stimulants, even to those who weren't fat. A modest industry evolved in and around Portsmouth of scamming prescriptions for diet pills from willing docs like Procter, then selling the pills for a profit. His Plaza Healthcare clinic boomed.

In 1996, one who went to visit him was a man named Randy, a guard at the state prison in Lucasville ten miles north of Portsmouth. Randy suffered deep bruises to his back in a fight with an inmate. He was given a list of approved doctors to see. One was David Procter.

"Several guys from the prison went there because his office could take care of the [workers' compensation] paperwork," Randy remembered.

Procter took him off work for six months and, sure enough, handled all the paperwork, charging him two hundred dollars cash. He also prescribed a drug called OxyContin—40 mg, twice a day, for thirty days. The drug was a new painkiller, he said, and they were having good results with it.

"Looking back on it, [the injury] was nothing that warranted that harsh of a drug," Randy recalled. "But at the time, you're thinking this is great because I don't feel my back."

Thirty days later, Randy figured he was better and didn't return to Procter for a refill. Soon he was gripped by what he thought was the worst flu of his life. He ached, couldn't get out of bed, had diarrhea, and was throwing up. He talked to some friends. One suggested he might be going through withdrawal.

Then it hit him: You've got to go back.

Procter prescribed him more of the same. Randy returned every month, paying two hundred dollars cash for a three-minute visit with Procter and an Oxy prescription. Procter's waiting room overflowed. People fought over space in line. Only a handful of patients were there for injuries. The rest were feigning pain, scamming prescriptions, with the doctor's connivance. Randy saw six fellow prison guards in the waiting room. He kept his head down, got his Oxy prescription, and left.

"You're seeing people who you know are probably going to be locked up in one of your cellblocks," he said. "It really humbles you.

You think you're doing stuff the way it's supposed to be done. You're trusting the doctor. After a while you realize this isn't right but there really isn't anything you can do about it. You're stuck. You're addicted."

Before long, he found street dealers he could go to if he ran out during the month. He returned to his prison job. But by then fully addicted to an opiate, he began arriving late and making excuses. Desperate, he finally went to a deputy warden. He got into treatment and got clean. Three and a half years after going to David Procter the first time, the addiction was over for Randy.

For the Ohio River valley and America, it was just beginning.

The Adman

New York, New York

In 1951, an adman named Arthur Sackler from a little-known marketing firm met with the sales director of a small hundred-year-old chemical concern named Charles Pfizer and Company in New York City.

Arthur Mitchell Sackler was thirty-nine and already had a career of achievement as a psychiatrist behind him.

He and his brothers, Raymond and Mortimer, had grown up in New York, the sons of eastern European Jewish immigrants. They attended college during the Depression and all three passed briefly through the Communist Party, according to Alan Wald, author of *American Night: The Literary Left in the Era of the Cold War*. Arthur Sackler began his publishing career on his high school newspaper. During the Depression he printed single-handedly what Wald called a "crude strike bulletin" for the Communist Party. Sackler took art classes at night and paid for his schooling with odd jobs.

Finishing his medical studies, Sackler became a psychiatrist at Creedmoor, a New York mental hospital. There, he wrote more than 150 papers on psychiatry and experimental medicine, and identified some of the chemical causes in schizophrenia and manic depression. He was an antismoking crusader long before it was popular, and prohibited smoking at the companies he would later own. At Long Island University, he started Laboratories for Therapeutic Research, which he later directed and supported with large donations. Meanwhile, he established the first racially integrated blood bank in New York City.

Sackler watched medicine change radically during the postwar years. Scientific advances were allowing companies to produce life-altering drugs—antibiotics and vaccines in particular. It was an effervescent time, though less so for medical advertising, which remained plodding and gray even as the new drugs it promoted were changing the world. Sackler saw no reason this should be. He switched careers in the 1940s

28

and hired on at William Douglas McAdams, a small, rather staid medical advertising firm.

Before long one of his clients was Charles Pfizer and Company, then the world's largest manufacturer of vitamin C. The company's newly formed pharmaceutical research department had developed a synthetic antibiotic, first derived from soil bacteria, that it called Terramycin and that had proven effective on more than fifty diseases, including pneumonia. The company was moving from chemical manufacturing to pharmaceuticals. Instead of licensing it to a drug company, Pfizer wanted to sell the antibiotic itself.

In the office that day, Sackler told the company's sales director, Thomas Winn, that with a large enough advertising budget for Terramycin, he could turn Charles Pfizer and Company into a household name among doctors.

Winn gave him a budget larger than any company had ever spent to advertise a drug. Sackler "plastered the media with what would be called now a teaser campaign," said John Kallir, a copywriter at William Douglas McAdams at the time.

The Terramycin campaign aimed at frequent contact with individual doctors—a radical new concept. Sackler put large color ads in medical journals with plays on the word "terra" (Italian for earth): "Terra Bona" and some others. When the drug was finally released in America, he placed ads in the same font and color, saying "Terramycin."

Meanwhile, Sackler's ad writers in New York wrote thousands of postcards meant to appear as if they were from Egypt, Australia, Malta, and elsewhere. They mailed these cards, addressed individually to thousands of U.S. family doctors, pediatricians, and surgeons, describing how Terramycin was combating diseases in these exotic locales—"milk fever" in Malta, "Q fever" in Australia. The cards were signed "Sincerely, Pfizer." Doctors already known to prescribe a lot of drugs got extra direct mail.

Then Sackler sent salesmen on visits to doctors' offices. "They were intensive drives," Kallir said. "At the same time, we had a very heavy schedule of direct mailings, several mailings at a time to these doctors, along with journal ads."

Kallir remembered that Sackler paid to have a Pfizer *Spectrum*, an eight-page glossy house organ, inserted in the monthly *Journal of the American Medical Association* for a year.

All that combined with the drug's efficacy to make Terramycin a blockbuster—with forty-five million dollars in sales in 1952. Based on its Terramycin success, Charles Pfizer and Company expanded to thirteen countries, and eventually changed its name to Pfizer.

Sackler's campaign marked the emergence of modern pharmaceutical advertising, a field that up to then, in the words of one executive, "existed but it didn't." Seeing the future, Sackler bought the firm he worked for, William Douglas McAdams.

As an aside, he and his brothers also purchased an unknown drug company: Purdue Frederick, formed in the 1890s, during the days of patent medicines, by John Purdue Gray and George Frederick Bingham. The company had limped along since then, and until our story begins to unfold in the 1980s, it was still known mainly for selling antiseptics, a laxative, and an earwax remover.

Arthur Sackler, meanwhile, continued to transform drug marketing. In 1963, he licensed from Hoffman-La Roche the right to import and sell a new tranquilizer called Valium. Sackler again emphasized direct doctor contact to promote the drug. "Detail men"—salesmen—frequently visited doctors' offices bearing free samples of Valium. He put booths at medical conventions, and frequent multipage color ads in medical journals. He published another glossy monthly magazine with stories about what well-known doctors were up to, along with other news, and Valium ads.

Part of the campaign aimed to convince doctors to prescribe Valium, which the public saw as dangerous. Ads urged doctors to view a patient's physical pain as connected to stress—with Valium the destresser. If a child was sick, maybe her mother was tense. Valium was marketed above all to women, pitched as way of bearing the stress of lives as wives and mothers. Before the feminist movement, women were presumed to need that kind of help for the rest of their lives, thus there was no worry then about its addictiveness.

Among Arthur Sackler's many talents was that he thought like a family practitioner. Docs were barraged with patients who were tense, worried. "The patient would walk in, 'I'm nervous all day long, doctor.' Or 'My son's in the army,'" said Win Gerson, who worked for Sackler for years and later became president of William Douglas McAdams. "People were walking around nervous, worried, and this drug absolutely calmed them. It worked for certain types of back pains. It kind of made junkies out of some people, but that drug worked."

Yet if Terramycin was an unmitigated benefit to humankind, Valium was less so; or rather, any benefits were offset by significant risks. There was a little of nineteenth-century patent medicine in Valium's DNA. It didn't treat any root cause of stress. Instead, it treated vague symptoms and thus allowed doctors to avoid the complicated work of understanding the causes of that stress. Like patent medicines, Valium was a name-brand drug, promoted together with the idea that a pill could solve any ailment. Four decades later, and well after Arthur Sackler was gone, his company, Purdue, would produce and promote through his ad firm, William Douglas McAdams, a painkiller with similar characteristics.

Valium became the pharmaceutical industry's first hundred-million-dollar drug, and then its first billion-dollar drug. By the midseventies Valium was found indeed to be addictive and a street trade grew up around it. Hoffman-La Roche was accused of not warning of the drug's addictive potential.

Sackler, meanwhile, kept combining remarkable energy with great intellectual curiosity. He founded the *Medical Tribune*, a biweekly newspaper full of ads from the now-burgeoning pharmaceutical industry. In the newspaper, he wrote a column, One Man and Medicine. He became a world-class collector of Chinese art, and at parties at his house, guests hobnobbed with Luciano Pavarotti and Isaac Stern. As doctors raced to keep up with rapidly changing medicine, Sackler saw another marketing opportunity. He pushed his drug-company clients to fund CME—continuing medical education—seminars that were increasingly required for doctors to keep their licenses. By funding CME seminars, he saw, drug companies could grab the ears of physicians.

Arthur Sackler never retired. In 1987, at age seventy-three, he had a heart attack and died. He left behind a wife and two ex-wives, a spectacular fortune, and an industry so indebted that it referred to him by his first name. Today, his name is on galleries or wings of the Smithsonian Institution, the Metropolitan Museum of Art in New York City, the Royal Academy in London, as well as at Princeton, Harvard, and Beijing universities. Medical facilities bear his name at Tel Aviv, Tufts, and New York Universities. In 1996, he was one of the five first inductees into the Medical Advertising Hall of Fame.

But Arthur Sackler is important to this story because he founded modern pharmaceutical advertising and, in the words of John Kallir, showed the industry "that amazing things can be achieved with direct selling and intensive direct advertising."

Years later, Purdue would put those strategies to use marketing its new opiate painkiller OxyContin.

Enrique Begins

A Rancho in Nayarit, Mexico

Enrique's mother hated rain. It dripped through the corrugated-tin roof of their cardboard shack, keeping them damp for weeks. She placed pans and buckets around the shack to catch the new streams of water finding their way through the roof. As a toddler, Enrique ran about in the rain, splashed in puddles, and chased after the town's stray dogs. But to his mother, cold and relentless rain embodied their poverty and reminded her of her husband.

Enrique's parents lived at the bottom of a rancho with no paved streets or electricity, in the Mexican state of Nayarit. His parents had married young and without land. They eked a living from selling charcoal and wood. Enrique was their second child. The family was wedged into a four-room house with two other families. A few years later, they found land in a barrio known as the Toad, near a bog at the village bottoms. They crafted that two-room shack from cardboard, tarp, and plywood that could be scavenged from garbage dumps. They had more children. Enrique remembers nothing from those years but yelling, and his father beating his mother, and his mother having no idea where each day's food was coming from.

Then, a miracle. Enrique's father inherited all fifty acres owned by his parents, who had decided not to share any of it with their other children. With that, Enrique's father became a landowner and grew sugarcane, which, this being Mexico's populist 1970s, enjoyed new government price supports. With savings, he bought an old sugarcane truck. Property didn't soften Enrique's father. It inflated him with arrogance. Coming home drunk at night, he yelled at his kids and beat his wife more often. He spoke no words that weren't orders. When Enrique's mother asked her husband for money to run the household, he gave it with insults. His truck roared like a beast, and he rode around the village high in the seat, as if it were a fine mare.

One morning, when Enrique was eight, he was helping his father, who was hungover and working under the truck. His father called for his son to find him a tool. Enrique had no idea what the tool was. Under the truck, his father grew angry. Enrique spun about, searching without knowing what he was looking for. His father cursed him. Enrique began to cry in desperation. His father crawled out from under the truck. Enrique ran off. His father chased him down and beat him. Enrique had never beaten an animal the way he was beaten that day. He cried himself to sleep that night, angry that his mother hadn't defended him, hating life and his father.

He heard people say they were happy in their poverty. But Enrique never knew anybody poor who was anything but miserable. An unbridgeable river seemed to separate the Toad from the world. In the Toad, poverty pitted villagers against each other in a vicious battle for an upper hand. Enrique milked cows for another farmer. He was paid two liters of milk a day and ten pesos a week, and with it endured the kicks and insults from the farmer's son, who was his age. Once, when Enrique was sick, his mother took him to a hospital in Tepic. He stared at perfumed women, and men in new cars, and children with new clothes. The city was only a few miles from his rancho, but it seemed a distant land on the other side of that river.

Enrique grew older and went to school. There he learned to hate his teachers like his mother hated rain. They treated kids from the village's upper barrio with respect, but spoke sharply to the ragged children who came up from the Toad without food for lunch. To the upper-barrio kids, the teachers awarded prizes of candy and toys that no one from the Toad had a chance of winning. Some teachers forbade the Toad kids from going to the bathroom until they wet themselves. A few teachers showed up drunk; others didn't show up for weeks at a time. Enrique's father mocked him for not knowing his multiplication tables, but how could he know them with teachers like these?

Life held one thrill: His mother's brothers were up in Los Angeles working, which gave his family a connection that other kids envied. Villagers spoke of his uncles like far-off explorers and traded their latest news. Enrique didn't let on to his friends that his father never got along with these uncles. There had been a fight years before, in which his father had been knifed and two people on his uncles' side of the family died. His father married into the family but he and his brothers-in-law never liked each other.

Then one day news spread that an uncle was returning from the San Fernando Valley. Relatives thrilled at the gifts he would bring. That day, mothers washed their kids and lined them up in anticipation. The uncle, remembering the feud with Enrique's father, had gifts for everyone but Enrique, his sisters, and his mother. The children went home in tears of incomprehension.

Life improved only slowly. Somehow his mother saved enough to buy a cow and finally they were ranchers of a sort, and worked harder because of it. Enrique went to bed dreaming of life as a respected ranchero. For a while, he thought he glimpsed a future as a cop. Highway patrolman looked like an exciting job. But his father had no political connections to get him into the academy.

Besides, said his father, "I need an agronomist, not a patrolman. Remember, one day, this land will be yours. Your sisters will get married and go live with their husbands. You'll inherit the land and the house."

Enrique's father held that promise over him, and soon it seemed more like a threat. Enrique saw farmers like his father draining their lives into those fields. They remained the same ignorant, violent, cold men stuck in poverty, controlled by others. Escaping this fate became Enrique's greatest concern.

His urgency intensified when he spotted a girl. She was twelve and beautiful. Her father was a butcher in town. That placed her in the upper classes of the rancho, well above Enrique's station as the son of an alcoholic sugarcane farmer. She lived up the hill, which was more than just geographically above the Toad. The kids from that barrio had parents who owned stores, slightly better houses, and more land. They ruled the town playground and ran off kids from the Toad with rocks.

Enrique knew he could give this girl none of the life she, and her father, expected for her. But when he asked her to be his girlfriend, she accepted. Theirs was a chaste village romance, filled with kisses and hugs. For it to become more than that, Enrique knew he would have to get moving.

Then his mother went to California for a few months. She returned with gifts but also with the news that one of her brothers had been killed—by a police officer overstepping his authority, she said. People in the village accepted that story. His remaining uncles up north, whose anger at Enrique's mother for having married his father had subsided, sent Enrique his first clothes from America. Villagers viewed these men as heroes; some asked his uncles for help getting north. Enrique imagined his uncles were grand men in a place called Canoga Park.

His mother found work overseeing the village school's lunch program, so Enrique no longer went hungry at school. His father was elected treasurer of the local sugarcane farmers' cooperative. He oversaw the installation of the first village streetlights. It surprised Enrique to see his father so diligent about putting in village light poles while he brought so much darkness home.

Then junior high ended. Enrique attempted high school in Tepic. He spent two weeks there, each day without anything to eat for lunch, before he ran out of bus money and withdrew. The threat of a life in the fields now seemed frighteningly real. Toiling in the cane would never allow him to give his girl what she and her father expected for her. In the village, girls married young; though she was only thirteen, Enrique had no time to lose.

Plumbing was at last coming to the village. Now townsfolk could get drinking water from the faucet instead of from distant wells. Toilets would replace the hills. But Enrique thought only of his uncles in Canoga Park. So he made plans and he kept them to himself. He'd get to Tijuana, find a coyote to take him to Canoga Park. He had no address or phone number for his uncles, but surely they were so well-known that they'd be easy to find.

One day he walked through the village, greeted his friends, spent time with his girlfriend, and said farewell to no one. The next, he took a birth certificate and put on his best black jacket, one that his uncles had sent to him, a white collared shirt and blue pants, kissed his mother, and said he'd be back later that day. He went to Tepic and boarded Tres Estrellas de Oro, the low-cost bus line that over the years took north hundreds of thousands of Mexicans intending to cross.

He paid for the ticket with two hundred pesos he had swiped from his parents. He considered the money a loan so he wouldn't feel bad for taking it. He sat by the window for twenty-eight hours so he could see all the things he had never seen before.

It was 1989 and he was fourteen.

The Molecule

A ndy Coop very nearly spent his career watching paint dry.
The son of a machinist and school cafeteria worker, Coop
hailed from Halifax in Northern England. He finished his undergrad-
uate work in chemistry at Oxford University in 1991. He was given a
choice of where to continue his studies. At Cardiff University was a
professor whose specialty was the chemistry of paint. Industry at the
time was aiming to find a new paint that dried at a certain temperature. At the University of Bristol was John Lewis, who studied the
chemistry of drugs and addiction. In the 1960s, Lewis had discovered
buprenorphine, an opiate that he later helped develop into a treatment for heroin addicts.

Coop didn't remember giving the choice much thought. Drugs
sounded more interesting than paint was all, so off to Bristol and John
Lewis he went. It was there, in 1991, in a lab at Bristol that Andy Coop
encountered the morphine molecule—the essential element in all
opiates. In time, Andy Coop got hooked on the morphine molecule—
figuratively, of course, for he only once took a drug that contained it,
and that following surgery.

I looked up Andy Coop because I wanted to understand the molecule behind the story that consumed me.

Like no other particle on earth, the morphine molecule seemed to
possess heaven and hell. It allowed for modern surgery, saving and
improving too many lives to count. It stunted and ended too many lives
to count with addiction and overdose. Discussing it, you could invoke
some of humankind's greatest cultural creations and deepest questions:
Faust, Dr. Jekyll and Mr. Hyde, discussions on the fundamental nature
of man and human behavior, of free will and slavery, of God and evolution. Studying the molecule you naturally wandered into questions like,
Can mankind achieve happiness without pain? Would that happiness
even be worth it? Can we have it all?

"I might have loved paint," Coop told me. "But the conversation over evolution, heaven and hell, psychology—none of that matters when you're [studying paint]."

In heroin addicts, I had seen the debasement that comes from the loss of free will and enslavement to what amounts to an idea: permanent pleasure, numbness, and the avoidance of pain. But man's decay has always begun as soon as he has it all, and is free of friction, pain, and the deprivation that temper his behavior.

In fact, the United States achieved something like this state of affairs in the period this book is about: the last decade of the twentieth century and the first decade of the twenty-first century. When I returned home from Mexico during those years, I noticed a scary obesity emerging. It wasn't just the people. Everything seemed obese and excessive. Massive Hummers and SUVs were cars on steroids. In some of the Southern California suburbs near where I grew up, on plots laid out with three-bedroom houses in the 1950s, seven-thousand-square-foot mansions barely squeezed between the lot lines, leaving no place for yards in which to enjoy the California sun.

In Northern California's Humboldt and Mendocino Counties, 1960s hippies became the last great American pioneers by escaping their parents' artificial world. They lived in tepees without electricity and funded the venture by growing pot. Now their children and grandchildren, like mad scientists, were using chemicals and thousand-watt bulbs, in railroad cars buried to avoid detection, to forge hyperpotent strains of pot. Their weed rippled like the muscles of bodybuilders, and growing this stuff helped destroy the natural world that their parents once sought.

Excess contaminated the best of America. Caltech churned out brilliant students, yet too many of them now went not to science but to Wall Street to create financial gimmicks that paid off handsomely and produced nothing. Exorbitant salaries, meanwhile, were paid to Wall Street and corporate executives, no matter how poorly they did. Banks packaged rolls of bad mortgages and we believed Standard & Poor's when they called them AAA. Well-off parents no longer asked their children to work when they became teenagers.

In Mexico, I gained new appreciation of what America means to a poor person limited by his own humble origins. I took great pride that America had turned more poor Mexicans into members of the middle class than had Mexico. Then I would return home and see too much of the country turning on this legacy in pursuit of comfort, living on credit, attempting to achieve happiness through more stuff. And I saw no coincidence that this was also when great new numbers of these same kids—most of them well-off and white—began consuming huge quantities of the morphine molecule, doping up and tuning out.

I looked up Andy Coop, who chairs the department of pharmaceutical sciences at the University of Maryland in Baltimore.

What gave the morphine molecule its immense power, he said, was that it evolved somehow to fit, key in lock, into the receptors that all mammals, especially humans, have in their brains and spines. The so-called *mu*-opioid receptors—designed to create pleasure sensations when they receive endorphins the body naturally produces—were especially welcoming to the morphine molecule. The receptor combines with endorphins to give us those glowing feelings at, say, the sight of an infant or the feel of a furry puppy. The morphine molecule overwhelms the receptor, creating a far more intense euphoria than anything we come by internally. It also produces drowsiness, constipation, and an end to physical pain. Aspirin had a limit to the amount of pain it could calm. But the more morphine you took, Coop said, the more pain was dulled.

For this reason, no plant has been more studied for its medicinal properties than the opium poppy. As the mature poppy's petals fall away, a golf-ball-sized bulb emerges atop the stem. The bulb houses a goo that contains opium. From opium, humans have derived laudanum, codeine, thebaine, hydrocodone, oxymorphone, and heroin, as well as almost two hundred other drugs—all containing the morphine molecule, or variations of it. Etorphine, derived from thebaine, is used in dart guns to tranquilize rhinoceroses and elephants.

Tobacco, coca leaves, and other plants had evolved to be pleasurable and addictive to humans, Coop said. But the morphine molecule surpassed them in euphoric intensity. Then it exacted a mighty vengeance when a human dared to stop using it. In withdrawal from the drug, an addict left narcotized numbness and returned to life and to feeling. Numbed addicts were notoriously impotent; in withdrawal they had frequent orgasms as they began to feel again. Humans with the temerity to attempt to withdraw from the morphine molecule were tormented first with excruciating pain that lasted for days. If an addict was always constipated and nodding off, his withdrawals brought ferocious diarrhea and a week of sleeplessness.

The morphine molecule resembled a spoiled lover, throwing a tantrum as it left. Junkies I talked to, in fact, said they had an almost constipated tingling when trying to urinate during the end of withdrawal, as if the last of the molecule, now holed up in the kidney, was fighting like hell to keep from being expelled. Like a lover, no other molecule in nature provided such merciful pain relief, then hooked humans so completely, and punished them so mercilessly for wanting their freedom from it.

Certain parasites in nature exert the kind of control that makes a host act contrary to its own interests. One protozoan, *Toxoplasma gondii*, reproduces inside the belly of a cat, and is then excreted by the feline. One way it begins the cycle again is to infect a rat passing near the excrement. *Toxoplasma gondii* reprograms the infected rat to love cat urine, which to healthy rats is a predator warning. An infected rat wallows in cat urine, offering itself up as an easy meal to a nearby cat. This way, the parasite again enters the cat's stomach, reproduces, and is expelled in the cat's excrement—and the cycle continues.

The morphine molecule exerts an analogous brainwashing on humans, pushing them to act contrary to their self-interest in pursuit of the molecule. Addicts betray loved ones, steal, live under freeways in harsh weather, and run similarly horrific risks to use the molecule.

It became the poster molecule for an age of excess. No amount of it was ever enough. The molecule created ever-higher tolerance. Plus, it had a way of railing on when the body gathered the courage to throw it out. This wasn't only during withdrawals. Most drugs are easily reduced to water-soluble glucose in the human body, which then expels them. Alone in nature, the morphine molecule rebelled. It resisted being turned into glucose and it stayed in the body.

"We still can't explain why this happens. It just doesn't follow the rules. Every other drug in the world—thousands of them—follows this rule. Morphine doesn't," Coop said. "It really is almost like someone designed it that way—diabolically so."

Delivered Like Pizza

Denver, Colorado

In 1979, a young man fell into a job at the Denver Police Department. He was new in town, fresh from a broken engagement in his native Pueblo, Colorado.

Dennis Chavez never meant to be a cop. His family traced its roots back to a seventeenth-century Spanish conquistador. Four centuries later, Chavez's father was a steelworker in Pueblo.

Chavez, a big guy, played football at the University of Colorado for a couple years in the 1970s before leaving the school. He worked construction. Then a friend recently hired on at Denver PD told him the work was fun and urged him to take the entrance test. Chavez passed it and within a few months was at the Denver Police Academy.

Early into his first year on patrol, however, a training officer told his friend that Chavez was failing, probably the dumbest in the new recruit class and almost certain to wash out before the year ended. That irked. Chavez put in extra time studying laws and the municipal code, exercising and adding new energy to his street work.

In time, his interest in sports channeled into power weight lifting. He cut his hair in a flattop, with lightning bolts cut into the sides and his badge number on the back of his head. Steroids were legal then. He would buy bodybuilding dope from a doctor who visited the gym where he lifted. Soon he was spending twelve hundred dollars a month on steroids and supplements. He was six feet four, 250 pounds, and muscles bulged from him as if his body were a squeezed balloon. Dennis Chavez was a ferocious cat back then, shaking hands with an iron grip, clubbing friends on the shoulders when he saw them. He arrived at every 911 call like a pit bull, pulling for action. When he barked, "How you doing?" at friends, it sounded like a cross between an interrogation and a command. Even cops tried to avoid him.

He was obsessed with his job, which he took to mean arresting bad guys. A lieutenant once criticized him for not writing enough tickets.

As training officer to new recruits, the lieutenant said, Chavez wasn't showing them enough balance to his police work.

"That's not what I do," Chavez told the lieutenant. "I find felons."

He spent his first years on the force learning from a cop named Robert Wallis. Wallis was the department's version of a supercop. He made major arrests all the time. He and his partner were involved in more than a dozen shootings, which to Chavez meant that Wallis was always getting in the way of the worst bad guys. Wallis was a guy he wanted to emulate. Wallis taught him about prison tattoos, and recognizing the look of a guy on the lam in line at a downtown shelter. From Wallis, Chavez learned early on that most crime is connected to illegal drugs, so understanding that world was crucial to good police work.

Heroin particularly interested Chavez. Back then, Mexican American families controlled the trade in Denver. But as Chavez worked them and arrested them, he heard they were being supplied by men from a place in Mexico called Nayarit. The name meant nothing to Chavez, but for years it kept coming up. The Nayarits sold a substance he hadn't seen before. Heroin in Denver up to then had been all light-brown powder. This Nayarit heroin, however, was dark and sticky and looked like Tootsie Rolls or rat feces. They called it black tar and Chavez heard stories they cut it with boiled-down Coca-Cola.

As the years passed, meanwhile, what Dennis Chavez realized he loved most about his job was the deduction of crime. It was the immersion in it, finding the thread of a criminal and his MO. Once, a serial rapist was striking across Denver. Chavez had taken the statement of the last victim, a high school girl, who, in tears, grabbed his hand and made him promise that he would catch the guy. Victims said the rapist held a Buck knife to them as he assaulted them. Chavez charted the rapist's attacks—his times, dates, locations. He staked out the southeast Denver neighborhood where he thought the guy would hit next. One night he saw a man walking down an alley and just knew it was the guy. Then the man jaywalked. Chavez stopped him and arrested him for carrying a concealed Buck knife in his pants. Victims came to the station house that night and identified Chavez's arrestee as their rapist.

A few years into the job, Dennis Chavez woke one morning unable to see, his heart pounding like an overheated piston. His girlfriend took him to the hospital. A doctor told him he was going to have a stroke if he didn't let up.

"You can die young and good-looking, or years from now fat and happy," the doctor said.

Dennis Chavez opted for the latter. He backed off the steroids and coffee, and stopped power lifting. He took up aikido and long rides into the Colorado mountains on his Harley. Later, he founded a club of officers who rode motorcycles and raised money for charities.

He mellowed. His police work changed, too. His affinity for sleuthing didn't flag. But no longer the pit bull, he had to develop other skills. Among these was the cultivation of snitches and, with that, a personality that other people wanted to be around. Finding informants was not hard, really. He'd arrest a guy and tell him he could work off the case by setting up others. Eventually that could lead to cash payments to the informant. What was hard was managing the relationship, particularly when the informant went from working off his case to making a salary from it. The best snitches were the ones who stayed in it and would do anything for their handlers. These relationships required finesse and a soothing personality that let an informant know that Chavez liked him and would protect him. It meant going against the book from time to time—accepting Christmas presents, for example, and giving them in return.

Informants became particularly important when, in 1995, Dennis Chavez joined the narcotics unit of the Denver Police Department. He was bequeathed his first long-term informant by a sergeant leaving the unit. The sergeant introduced Chavez to a man immersed in Denver's Mexican heroin underworld.

Chavez never had much connection to Mexico. His father had forbidden Spanish in the house so his children wouldn't speak accented English. But Chavez could see the Denver drug world changing. Mexican American dealer families were going to prison, dying, moving away. Mexicans stepped into the void, and when that happened, Chavez began hearing about the state of Nayarit all the time. The heroin in Denver was all black tar now.

In the late 1980s, he saw guys from Nayarit walking around downtown selling heroin to anyone who'd walk up to them. He arrested many of them, and found Nayarit on a map, but it still didn't mean much. He saw them move into cars and drive it around to customers. Mexicans were arrested at the bus station with backpacks and a kilo or two of the drug. But Chavez still had no sense for how this fit together, if it did at all.

Until one day, when his informant said to him, "You know they're all from the same town, right?"

*   *   *

I MET DENNIS CHAVEZ at a Mexican restaurant in north Denver, where he told me the story of how he began tracking the Nayarit heroin connection. He said he was intrigued by what the informant told him— that all that he was seeing related to heroin in Denver originated in one small town in Mexico. He prodded the man for more.

What Chavez had been seeing on the streets, the informant said— the dealers, the couriers with backpacks of heroin, the drivers with balloons of heroin—all looks very random and scattered, but it's not. It's all connected.

They're all from a town called Xalisco. Ha-LEES-koh—he said, pronouncing the word. Don't confuse it with a state in Mexico pronounced the same way, but spelled with a *j*. The state of Jalisco is one of Mexico's largest and Guadalajara is its capital. This town, he said, spells its name with an *x*. The informant had never been there, but believed it to be a small place.

All these guys running around Denver selling black tar heroin are from this town of Xalisco, or a few small villages near there, the informant told Chavez. Their success is based on a system they've learned. It's a system for selling heroin retail. Their system is a simple thing, really, and relies on cheap, illegal Mexican labor, just the way any fast-food joint does.

From then on, Chavez sat with the informant, at bars and in a truck outside the man's house, as the informant talked on about these guys from Xalisco and their heroin retail system—which was unlike anything the informant had seen in the drug underworld.

Think of it like a fast-food franchise, the informant said, like a pizza delivery service. Each heroin cell or franchise has an owner in Xalisco, Nayarit, who supplies the cell with heroin. The owner doesn't often come to the United States. He communicates only with the cell manager, who lives in Denver and runs the business for him.

Beneath the cell manager is a telephone operator, the informant said. The operator stays in an apartment all day and takes calls. The calls come from addicts, ordering their dope. Under the operator are several drivers, paid a weekly wage and given housing and food. Their job is to drive the city with their mouths full of little uninflated balloons of black tar heroin, twenty-five or thirty at a time in one mouth. They look like chipmunks. They have a bottle of water at the ready so if police pull them over, they swig the water and swallow the balloons. The balloons remain intact in the body and are eliminated in the driver's waste. Apart from the balloons in their mouths, drivers keep another hundred hidden somewhere in the car.

The operator's phone number is circulated among heroin addicts, who call with their orders. The operator's job, the informant said, is to tell them where to meet the driver: some suburban shopping center parking lot—a McDonald's, a Wendy's, a CVS pharmacy. The operators relay the message to the driver, the informant said.

The driver swings by the parking lot and the addict pulls out to follow him, usually down side streets. Then the driver stops. The addict jumps into the driver's car. There, in broken English and broken Spanish, a cross-cultural heroin deal is accomplished, with the driver spitting out the balloons the addict needs and taking his cash.

Drivers do this all day, the guy said. Business hours—eight A.M. to eight P.M. usually. A cell of drivers at first can quickly gross five thousand dollars a day; within a year, that cell can be clearing fifteen thousand dollars daily.

The system operates on certain principles, the informant said, and the Nayarit traffickers don't violate them. The cells compete with each other, but competing drivers know each other from back home, so they're never violent. They never carry guns. They work hard at blending in. They don't party where they live. They drive sedans that are several years old. None of the workers use the drug. Drivers spend a few months in a city and then the bosses send them home or to a cell in another town. The cells switch cars about as often as they switch drivers. New drivers are coming up all the time, usually farm boys from Xalisco County. The cell owners like young drivers because they're less likely to steal from them; the more experienced a driver becomes, the more likely he knows how to steal from the boss. The informant assumed there were thousands of these kids back in Nayarit aching to come north and drive some U.S. city with their mouths packed with heroin balloons.

To a degree unlike any other narcotics operation, he said, Xalisco cells run like small businesses. The cell owner pays each driver a salary— $1,200 a week was the going rate in Denver at the time. The cell owner holds each driver to exact expenses, demanding receipts for how much each spent for lunch, or for a hooker. Drivers are encouraged to offer special deals to addicts to drum up business: fifteen dollars per balloon or seven for a hundred dollars. A free balloon on Sunday to an addict who buys Monday through Saturday. Selling heroin a tenth of a gram at a time is their one and only, full-time, seven-days-a-week job, and that includes Christmas Day. Heroin addicts need their dope every day.

Cell profits were based on the markup inherent in retail. Their customers were strung-out, desperate junkies who couldn't afford a half a kilo of heroin. Anyone looking for a large amount of heroin was probably a cop aiming for a case that would land the dealer in prison for years. Ask to buy a large quantity of dope, the informant said, and they'll shut down their phones. You'll never hear from them again. That really startled the informant. He knew of no other Mexican trafficking group that preferred to sell tiny quantities.

Moreover, the Xalisco cells never deal with African Americans. They don't sell to black people; nor do they buy from blacks, who they fear will rob them. They sell almost exclusively to whites.

What the informant described, Chavaz could see, amounted to a major innovation in the U.S. drug underworld. These innovations had every bit the impact of those in the legitimate business world. When, for example, someone discovered that cocaine cooked with water and baking soda became rock hard, the smokable cocaine known as crack was born. Crack was a more effective delivery mechanism for cocaine—sending it straight to the brain.

The Xalisco traffickers' innovation was literally a delivery mechanism as well. Guys from Xalisco had figured out that what white people—especially middle-class white kids—want most is service, convenience. They didn't want to go to skid row or some seedy dope house to buy their drugs. Now they didn't need to. The guys from Xalisco would deliver it to them.

So the system spread. By the mid-1990s, Chavez's informant counted a dozen major metro areas in the western United States where cells from tiny Xalisco, Nayarit, operated. In Denver by then he could count eight or ten cells, each with three or four drivers, working daily.

As I listened to Chavez, it seemed to me that the guys from Xalisco were fired by the impulse that, in fact, moved so many Mexican immigrants. Most Mexican immigrants spent years in the United States not melting in but imagining instead the day when they would go home for good. This was their American Dream: to return to Mexico better off than they had left it and show everyone back home that that's how it was. They called home and sent money constantly. They were usually far more involved in, say, the digging of a new well in the rancho than in the workings of the school their children attended in the United States. They returned home for the village's annual fiesta and spent money they couldn't afford on barbecues, weddings, and quinceañeras. To that end, as they worked the toughest jobs in America, they assiduously built houses in the rancho back home that stood as monuments to their desire to return for good one day. These houses took a decade to finish. Immigrants added to their houses each time they returned. They invariably extended rebar from the top of the houses' first floors. Rebar was a promise that as soon as he got the money together, the owner was adding a second story. Rods of rebar, standing at attention, became part of the skyline of literally thousands of Mexican immigrant villages and ranchos.

The finished houses of migrant Mexico often had wrought-iron gates, modern plumbing, and marble floors. These towns slowly improved as they emptied of people whose dream was to build their houses, too. Over the years, the towns became dreamlands, as empty as movie sets, where immigrants went briefly to relax at Christmas or during the annual fiesta, and imagine their lives as wealthy retirees back home again one day. The great irony was that work, mortgages, and U.S.-born children kept most migrants from ever returning to Mexico to live permanently in those houses they built with such sacrifice.

But the Xalisco heroin traffickers did it all the time. Their story was about immigration and what moves a poor Mexican to migrate as much as it was a tale of drug trafficking. Those Xalisco traffickers who didn't end up in prison went back to live in those houses. They put down no roots in this country; they spent as little money in America as they could, in fact. Jamaicans, Russians, Italians, even other Mexican traffickers, all bought property and broadcasted their wealth in the United States. The Xalisco traffickers were the only immigrant narcotics mafia Chavez knew of that aimed to just go home, and with nary a shot fired.

Denver became a Xalisco hub as their operations expanded, and probably no cop in America learned more about them than Dennis Chavez. By the time I met him, hundreds of arrests and sweeping federal indictments had not stopped them. They had spread like a virus, quietly and unrecognized by many in law enforcement, who often mistook Xalisco franchises for isolated groups of small-time dealers.

"I call them the Xalisco Boys," Chavez said. "They're nationwide."

Enrique Alone

Tijuana, Mexico

Chaotic Tijuana was the biggest city Enrique had ever seen. Thousands of people flowed like a river through the central bus station before crossing into the United States. The station roiled with humble, hungry folks from ranchos like his. Boys darted in and out of traffic, washing windshields for change. Men who'd tried to cross and were turned back had fallen into alcohol. They reminded Enrique of the drunks in the rancho.

Enrique slept on the bus terminal's chairs and wandered the city streets during the day. He found a coyote and asked the price to the place called Canoga Park. When he told the man he had no address for his uncles, but figured he'd just ask around, the coyote laughed.

"Canoga Park is huge. It's not like your rancho."

Still, he hung on in Tijuana, fearing to return home a failure. He washed in the bus station bathroom, every morning looking more like a Tijuana urchin. Finally, famished, his prized clothes filthy and stinking and his money almost gone, he dialed the village's telephone in tears. His departure was the talk of the rancho. Aunts and uncles crowded around the phone. On a second call, his hysterical mother answered. She gave him a number for uncles in Los Angeles who were coming for him. They arrived and arranged for him to cross the border posing as the son of a man with papers. Two mornings later, Enrique was sitting in an uncle's apartment in Canoga Park in the San Fernando Valley.

"Now," the uncle said, "I'll give you a thousand dollars and a suitcase and you'll go home."

"No, what I want from life you can't buy with a thousand dollars."

His uncles took him to eat and then to another apartment. One uncle opened a closet and there, like a glorious revelation, were dozens of pairs of Levi's 501s, with labels and price tags attached.

"Take what you want."

With that, the boy who had never had more than two threadbare pairs of pants now had his first new, tough dark-blue 501s. 501s marked his time up north. Much later he would remember the first time he bought a pair for himself in America, and then the first time he came home wearing 501s.

Back home, villagers, and Enrique himself, had always assumed his uncles were working hard in some honorable trade up in the great El Norte, one that paid enough to fund bountiful gifts every time they returned. Now they sat him down. One uncle pulled out a shoebox filled with golf-ball-sized chunks of a dark, sticky substance and balloons of every color.

"What's that?" Enrique asked.

"*Chiva*," his uncle said. Goat, the Mexican slang term for black tar heroin. "This is how we make our money."

Cora Indian campesinos grew the poppies in the mountains above Xalisco. They harvested the opium goo from the flowers and sold it to cookers whom Enrique's uncles knew. A newly cooked kilo of vinegary, sticky chiva would head north in a boom box or a backpack within a couple days, virtually uncut, and often hit L.A. streets only a week after the goo was drawn from the poppy.

As Enrique's uncle spoke, he rolled little pieces of the gunk into balls the size of BBs. He put each one in a tiny balloon and tied each balloon. Finally, he wrapped the telephone in a towel to muffle the ring. As Enrique was wondering why, the uncle plugged in the phone and the calls started coming and never stopped.

These are customers, his uncle explained over the ringing. We have guys out there driving around all day with these balloons. We give each caller a different intersection to meet a driver. Then we beep a driver the code for the intersection where that customer will be. We do this all day long.

"We wouldn't have told you had you not showed up," his uncle said. "But now that you're here . . ."

Enrique saw his chance. He begged to work for them. You're too young, said one uncle. You need to go to school. Or we send you home. But Enrique pleaded and finally the uncles relented. They put him to work driving the place most Angelinos refer to simply as the Valley.

The San Fernando Valley comprises 260 square miles, larger than Chicago, and contains the sprawling northern chunk of Los Angeles. At its west end is Canoga Park, a district of sixty thousand people, bisected by boulevards with palm trees. Classic, modest suburban ranch-style houses made of stucco line its residential streets.

For years after it emerged from citrus groves in the 1950s, Canoga Park and the Valley had been famously white, with only small islands of Mexican American barrios. But the mass migration of Mexicans to Southern California and the end of the Cold War changed the area. Defense contractors departed; so did many white people. Soon, districts of Los Angeles such as Van Nuys, Reseda, North Hollywood, and Canoga Park were largely Mexican. Those changes were beginning as Enrique arrived.

Though fourteen, Enrique was tall enough not to arouse suspicion behind the wheel. He drove the streets of the San Fernando Valley with his mouth full of tiny balloons, following beeps from his uncles. He learned where Canoga Park ended and West Hills began. He trolled those palm-tree-lined boulevards—Sherman Way, Roscoe, and Sepulveda—that were wider than the highways back home.

Those first weeks he remembered like a fairy tale, as if everything he had heard about America were true: money, clothes, and good food seemed as plentiful as the sunshine. At the apartment, he turned on a VCR and a porno film leaped to life. His uncles ate often at El Tapatio and Pocos, a seafood restaurant. They drank at the Majestic, a bar that Nayarit immigrants frequented; as long as Enrique was with them the waitresses served him beer. His idea of becoming a state trooper evaporated, as did any thought of school.

After a few months, the uncles installed Enrique in an apartment on De Soto Avenue and gave him the keys to two cars. He would run the business—roll the heroin into balloons, take calls, direct drivers on the street. The phone rang all day until he shut it down at eight P.M. As he turned fifteen, he was taking orders for five thousand dollars' worth of heroin a day. The apartment's closets filled with stolen 501s and VCRs and porno films that addicts exchanged for dope. Enrique no longer had to worry about his jeans fading when he washed them. There were always more. He showered with fragrant shampoo, and exchanged the village pond for the swimming pool at an uncle's house in a neighborhood full of Americans. His clients were nurses and lawyers—one of his best clients was a wealthy lawyer—prostitutes, former soldiers who'd been to Vietnam, old junkies from the barrio, and young cholos.

One day he was at an uncle's house and the phone rang. A caller from home. His uncle's face clouded.

"*Problemas*," he said, his hand over the mouthpiece.

Problemas—problems—the word seemed so nondescript. But in the ranchos of Mexico, it is a euphemism for tangled webs of murder and lawlessness. Problemas were shootings and feuds that grew from a chance word, a property dispute, the theft of a sister for marriage. Problemas kept rancheros poor and fleeing north to the United States. Some great amount of the migration to the United States was due more to problemas—escaping murder, fleeing feuds—than to simple economics and poverty. Problemas could empty a rancho in less than a generation. Sometimes a village would see the problemas die out only to be reignited by a chance meeting of old enemies on a bus or a street corner years later. Rancho dances in particular bred problemas. At dances, people drank, and sex and machismo roiled just beneath the surface. In some towns, the saying was *"Baile el viernes; cuerpo el sabado"* ("Dance Friday night, body Saturday morning"). A shooting at a dance could embitter a family against another for years. Keeping track of the bewildering history of conflicts became an essential ranchero survival skill.

Something like this had divided the family of Enrique's mother. Enrique never knew the cause of the feud between the two sides of his mother's family, nor why his grandparents had married if the problemas were so serious. But the feud would come and go like bad weather. The phone call that morning in Canoga Park brought news that it had come again. A mass shooting in the village. Two were dead, fifteen wounded. One side of his mother's family was to blame; the victims were mostly from the other side.

News of the shootings mainly served to remind Enrique of why he was in Canoga Park selling drugs. Back home, drug users were the moral equivalents of pedophiles. But drug sales were his pathway out of problemas. He saw dayworkers on Sherman Way, exploited, sometimes not paid—yet that wasn't treated as a crime. They tried to work the right way and look what happened. He wasn't forcing anyone to buy his dope. With that thought, and the problemas he was escaping, he felt peace. And the 501s didn't hurt either.

For seven months he worked for his uncles in Canoga Park. Finally, they packed him a suitcase and gave him two thousand dollars for all his labor and sent him home. He thought he was due more, but the rancho's ethos of poverty reigned, even in the San Fernando Valley: They could exploit him, so they did and he couldn't object. Heroin had not changed that. In fact, he thought his uncles remained cautious villagers in many ways. They had been in the San Fernando Valley for almost a decade. Yet they still ran their business for a few months, made some money, and shut it down, less afraid of the police than of what people back home would say.

Dozens of villagers welcomed Enrique home to his isolated rancho and the Toad, a few miles outside the town of Xalisco, Nayarit. The poor kid from the Toad was now admired as the only village boy to cross the border alone. He gave his money to his mother, keeping two hundred dollars. He bought a bottle of Cazadores tequila and the party that night was big. Older folks besieged him with questions. A few friends took him aside and asked for help finding the kind of work he was doing. He put them off, but saw that apparently word had spread more than his uncles had realized. He wanted to get back to California himself in a few months.

He was only fifteen and people were coming to *him* for favors. It was a luxurious feeling and he bathed in it. As the night mingled with tequila and took the edge off the stifling heat, the stereo played his favorite corrido, "El Numero Uno," by Los Incomparables de Tijuana.

Enrique pulled his Beretta 9mm and howled as he held it high and fired it into the air.

The Poppy

The story of the opium poppy is almost as old as man. Opium was likely our first drug as agricultural civilizations formed near rivers. Mesopotamians grew the poppy at the Tigris and Euphrates. The Assyrians invented the method, still widely used today, of slicing and draining the poppy's pod of the goo containing opium. "The Sumerians, the world's first civilization and agriculturists, used the ideograms *hul* and *gil* for the poppy, translating it as the 'joy plant,'" wrote Martin Booth, in his classic *Opium: A History*.

The ancient Egyptians first produced opium as a drug. Thebaine, an opium derivative, is named for Thebes, the Egyptian city that was the first great center of opium-poppy production. Indians also grew the poppy and used opium. So did the Greeks. Homer and Virgil mention opium, and potions derived from it. The expanding Arab empire and later the Venetians, both inveterate traders, helped spread the drug.

Early civilizations saw opium as an antidote to the burdens of life—to sorrow and to pain—and as an effective sleep inducer. They also knew it as lethally poisonous and intensely habit-forming. But its benefits made the risks easy to overlook.

In the early 1800s, a German pharmacist's apprentice named Friedrich Sertürner isolated the sleep-inducing element in opium and named it morphine for Morpheus, the Greek god of sleep and dreams. Morphine was more potent than simple opium and killed more pain.

War spread the morphine molecule through the nineteenth century. More than 330 wars broke out, forcing countries to learn to produce morphine. The U.S. Civil War prompted the planting of opium poppies in Virginia, Georgia, and South Carolina for the first time, and bequeathed the country thousands of morphine-addicted soldiers. Two nineteenth-century wars were over the morphine molecule itself, and whether China could prevent the sale on her own soil of India-grown opium. The drug provided huge revenues essential to the British Empire and was one of their few products for which the self-sufficient Chinese showed an appetite. That it lost two of these Opium Wars to the British explains China's infamous and widespread opium problem in 1900 where only moderate numbers of addicts existed in 1840.

In 1853, meanwhile, an Edinburgh doctor named Alexander Wood invented the hypodermic needle, a delivery system superior to both eating the pills and the then-popular anal suppositories. Needles allowed more accurate dosing. Wood and other doctors also believed needles would literally remove the patient's appetite for the drug, which no longer had to be eaten. This proved incorrect. Wood's wife became the first recorded overdose death from an injected opiate.

In the United States, more opium came with (newly addicted) Chinese immigrants, who smoked it in back-alley dens within Chinatowns in San Francisco and elsewhere. Opium dens were outlawed, and after Chinese immigration was made illegal, the practice of smoking opium eventually declined, too. Morphine replaced it.

Patent medicines with morphine and opium, meanwhile, were sold as miracle cures. These elixirs were branded with names evoking quaint home remedies. Opium was the active ingredient in, for example, Mrs. Winslow's Soothing Syrup, which was used to pacify children. These remedies were marketed aggressively in newspapers and popular media. Patent medicines sales exploded, rising from $3.5 million in 1859 to almost $75 million by the twentieth century.

In London in 1874, Dr. Alder Wright was attempting to find a nonaddictive form of morphine when he synthesized a drug that he called diacetylmorphine—a terrific painkiller. In 1898, a Bayer Laboratory chemist in Germany, Heinrich Dreser, reproduced Wright's diacetylmorphine and called it heroin—for *heroisch*, German for "heroic," the word that Bayer workers used to describe how it made them feel when Dreser tested it on them.

Heroin was first believed to be nonaddictive. Heroin pills were marketed as a remedy for coughs and respiratory ailments. With tuberculosis a public health threat, this was no small point. As junkies ever since have discovered, heroin is an effective constipator and was thus marketed as an antidiarrheal. Women used it, on doctor's orders, for menstrual cramps and respiratory problems. Doctors didn't have much else to prescribe for pain or disease. Thus addiction exploded—to a drug that people believed was safe because doctors said so.

This aroused U.S. public opinion, which forced the passage of the

Harrison Narcotics Tax Act of 1914. The law taxed and regulated opiates and coca-leaf products, while allowing doctors to use them in the practice of medicine. But it was transformed into America's first prohibition statute when police started arresting doctors for prescribing opiates to addicts. Addiction was not yet considered a disease, so an addict technically wasn't a medical patient.

Physicians soon stopped prescribing the drugs. People with real pain were left to endure. Addicts, meanwhile, turned to crime. "[Because the addict] is denied the medical care he urgently needs," one medical journal reported, "he is driven to the underworld where he can get his drug . . . The most depraved criminals are often the dispensers of these habit-forming drugs."

A government campaign demonizing "dope fiends" followed, aided by a compliant media. The addict was a deviant, a crime-prone, weak-willed moral failure. This idea stuck and informed the view of junkies for decades. The mythic figure of the heroin pusher also emerged. He supposedly lurked around schoolyards and candy stores, giving youths habit-forming dope, hoping for future customers.

With slight medical benefits compared to its high addiction risk, heroin ought to have passed into history. Instead, heroin replaced morphine on the streets. It thrived because it was tailor-made for dope traffickers. Heroin was easy to make, and cheaper than morphine. It was also more concentrated, and thus easier to hide and more profitable to dilute. The highs, and the lows, too, were quicker and more intense than those of other opiates. An addict craved heroin several times a day, and physically had to have it to function; so he was a terrific customer.

Traffickers and mafias made heroin's career. New York established itself as the country's heroin center in part because the drug's early manufacturers were located there. Once heroin was made illegal, it came clandestinely through the city's port from Europe and Asia. New York's immigrants sold it on the street: Chinese and European Jews, among them, and much later, Puerto Ricans, Colombians, and Dominicans. The logic of heroin distribution allowed New York to remain the nation's principal heroin hub through most of the twentieth century. While the drug came mostly from Asia, the Middle East, or Colombia, the drug was taken in at New York's port, distributed by endlessly replenished immigrant or black gangs, and from there sent up and down the East Coast and into the Midwest.

Marijuana, like wine, has been hybridized into endless varietals. But heroin is a commodity, like sugar, and usually varies only in how much it's been cut—that is, diluted—or how well it's been processed and refined. Thus, to differentiate their product, dealers learned to market aggressively, and New York City is where they learned to do it first.

Italians apparently led the way. In the 1930s, "an aggressive new generation of Italian gangsters began infiltrating the drug traffic, replacing other groups, notably the Jews," wrote historian David Courtwright in *Dark Paradise*, his history of opiate addiction in America. "Not only did the price increase, but the level of adulteration as well."

New York's Italians pioneered heroin pushing, giving free samples to new customers. Their weak dope made injecting it popular. Injecting heroin sent what little heroin was in the dose directly to the brain, maximizing euphoria. Injecting begot nasty public health problems—among them, later, ferocious rates of hepatitis C and HIV. (Mexican black tar added to them. Because tar is a semiprocessed, less-filtered form of heroin, the impurities that remain in the drug clogged addicts' veins when injected. Unable to find veins, addicts shoot it into muscles. "Muscling" black tar heroin, in turn, leads to infections, rotting skin, botulism, even gangrene.)

In the 1970s, East Coast heroin dealers, mostly blacks by then, began printing brands on glassine bags broadcasting the supposed potency of the drug inside, or the headlines of the day: brands like Hell Date, Toxic Waste, Knockout, NFL, Obamacare, Government Shutdown.

Over the decade the drug that square America despised became the choice drug of despised America: urban outcasts, wandering con men, homosexuals, pickpockets, artists, and jazz musicians populated the early heroin world. Underground classics such as William Burroughs's *Junky* described its nonconformist denizens, and mesmerized later generations intent on rebellion.

But heroin was never about the romantic subversion of societal norms. It was instead about the squarest of American things: business—dull, cold commerce. Heroin lent itself to structured underworld businesses. Addicts had no free will to choose one day *not* to buy the product. They were slaves to a take-no-prisoners molecule. Dealers could thus organize heroin distribution almost according to principles taught in business schools, providing they didn't use the product. And providing they marketed.

Stories about selling opiates quickly became tales of business models and the search for new markets.

Easier than Sugarcane

Xalisco, Nayarit

One afternoon in April 1996, a funeral procession left the village of Aquiles Serdán, in the state of Nayarit, Mexico.

Dozens of people trudged uphill, heading north to the town of Xalisco, the county seat, blocking traffic on the highway that also led south down to the beach resort of Puerto Vallarta. A banda—a brass band of trumpets, clarinets, bass and snare drums, and a massive tuba—serenaded the marchers with "Te Vas Angel Mio" ("You're Leaving, My Angel"). Men fired guns in the air and took turns shouldering the casket that contained the corpse of a man named David Tejeda.

He grew up a ranchero kid, better off than some by rural Mexican standards. But by the time he died, his Andalusians and quarter horses were the finest animals in the county. He was also a master horse dancer. Horse dancing is a popular pastime among northwest Mexican rancheros. It involves spurring and prodding the horse to prance and hop in time to a banda's staccato beat. At the county's annual Feria del Elote (Corn Fair), following the traditional horse parade that winds through Xalisco, David Tejeda would display his horse-dancing prowess to the admiration and envy of all.

Now, as the men from his family carried Tejeda's body to be buried, they also led his favorite animal—a white quarter horse named Palomo, saddled and riderless—and prodded it to dance as the banda played. For an hour, the procession moved up the highway, then over cobblestone streets to the Xalisco cemetery.

David Tejeda was among the first from Xalisco County to sell heroin in the San Fernando Valley. Just as important, he was among the first to publicly display what black tar heroin could do for a ranchero kid. He built stables and attached them to the large new houses he also built for his family.

I heard about David Tejeda well after I began piecing together the story of the Xalisco Boys. By then, what began on the day that I stood on the banks of the Ohio River in Huntington, West Virginia, had turned into an obsession with the rancheros from this one small town of Xalisco, Nayarit. Thousands of Americans were addicted to the tar heroin the Xalisco Boys sold that netted millions of dollars a month. I found nothing written about them, yet I could see they were changing drug use in many parts of the country. I wondered how they wound up in so many places: Memphis, Omaha, Myrtle Beach, Nashville, Indianapolis, and Minneapolis.

They reminded me, in fact, of another group I'd heard of—the Herreras. The Herreras were Mexico's first vast drug-trafficking ranchero family in the United States. They lived in and around a rancho known, aptly, as Los Herreras, an isolated, roadless place in the mountains of Durango, founded in the late 1600s and accessible for centuries only on horseback. Like so many from the ranchos of Mexico, they were actually a clan, made up of numerous intermarried families: Nevarez, Medina, Diaz, Villanueva, and Venegas were other last names. They intermarried with the Corral family from the rancho Los Corrales. Law enforcement estimated the clan comprised a thousand people, spreading across several ranchos in Durango, all involved in producing, transporting, or selling heroin.

The first Herreras appear to have intended to work legitimately when they arrived in Chicago sometime in the 1950s. But poppies grew well in the mountains of Durango. In time, they moved to heroin.

Much of the U.S. market was then supplied by Turkey, Afghanistan, and Southeast Asia half a world away, their dope coming through New York City. But after police dismantled the Turkish and European heroin network known as the French Connection in 1972, the Herrera clan grew into the most important source of heroin in much of the country, annually importing seven and a half tons of the brown powder known as Mexican Mud.

The Herreras were "not really a cartel per se. It was an old-time organized crime family," said Leo Arreguin, a retired DEA agent I tracked down who infiltrated the clan in the early 1980s. Most Herreras looked like auto mechanics, scruffy and unassuming, driving beater cars, he said. Arreguin used to buy from one Herrera who'd drive to the McDonald's meeting spot in a car so worn-out that it burned oil and left a smoke cloud behind. One of the clan, Baltazar Nevarez-Herrera, owned a beef slaughterhouse in Chicago. For a while, the clan shipped its heroin in small metal tubes they fed to cows in Mexico. When the cows reached Chicago, they were slaughtered and the tubes retrieved, Arreguin said.

The clan moved to Denver, Detroit, Dallas, Oklahoma City, Los Angeles, and many other towns. Each clan member was an independent entrepreneur, buying the family heroin. A Chicago police investigation into the Herreras estimated it took sixty million dollars in profits out of that town alone, funneling all that to Durango through shady currency exchange shops around South Chicago. The clan used its money, in part, to build parks and roads and other stuff that tends to endear villagers to narcos in the mountains of northwest Mexico.

Directing the clan was its patriarch, Don Jaime Herrera-Nevarez, a former police officer, who never left Mexico. It's said that he had something to do with the reason that a Mexican ounce of heroin—known as a *pedazo*, or piece—is actually twenty-five grams, and not twenty-eight, which is the normal measure of an ounce. (This difference has caused many disputes among buyers who, unaware of the difference, feel they're getting ripped off.) Legend has it that Don Jaime had a large spoon holding twenty-five grams that he used to scoop heroin. That became a standard ounce in the Mexican heroin world. I never learned whether this legend, recounted by several older DEA agents who tracked the Herreras, was true.

In 1985, Don Jaime, several brothers and cousins, and his son, Jaimito, along with dozens of other relatives, were busted. Many went to prison. That didn't end the clan's activities, but they didn't have quite the same power.

The shorter distances from Latin America to the United States, which allowed the region to remain more competitive in many agricultural commodities, eventually pushed out the Turkish and Asian heroin. Colombians began introducing their brown powder in the eastern half of the United States in the 1980s, along with their more famous cocaine. It was much cheaper than the white powder from Asia. Other Mexicans, especially the Sinaloans, began sending black tar heroin north to the western United States in the early 1980s, replacing the Mexican Mud. Even as the Herreras played a reduced supply role, heroin's price in America trended downward.

Black tar, the most rudimentary form of heroin, was especially cheap to make. With Mexico so close by, tar's price could keep dropping. This, as I found out, was crucial to the story I came upon as I discovered the Xalisco Boys' networks.

The Xalisco Boys seemed like a modern version of the Herreras, and as hard to get a handle on. I sifted through shards of information about their hazy underworld that came to me from indictments and interviews with addicts and cops, with prosecutors, DEA and FBI agents, and imprisoned Xalisco traffickers. Slowly a picture emerged of how a small town of sugarcane farmers grew by the early twenty-first century into the most proficient group of drug traffickers America has ever seen.

The first migrants from Xalisco settled in the San Fernando Valley— in Van Nuys, Panorama City, and Canoga Park. Many Xalisco migrants were there illegally, but worked legitimate jobs in construction, landscaping, and restaurants. However, by the early 1980s, a few families set to selling black tar heroin on Valley streets and in parks. The opium poppy grew bountifully in the mountains above Xalisco, and these families had relatives who mastered the folkcraft of cooking opium goo into black tar. Tar had the advantage of being moldable, like clay, and thus easy to shape into, say, the battery compartment of a boom box. Their tar was also potent and very condensed, and, as it was heroin, which addicts needed every day, it lent itself to retail, where the real profit was. The quantities needed were relatively small. A courier could take across a kilo in a purse, or strapped under clothing. Xalisco families living in Tijuana hired themselves out as these couriers.

The first Xalisco heroin traffickers mostly hailed from a single clan, many of whose members bore the last name Tejeda. Back in Xalisco County, the Tejeda clan spread across several ranchos in webs of cousins, sisters, uncles, brothers, and in-laws. The last names also included Sánchez, Díaz, Ibarría, Lizama, López, Navarro, Cienfuegos, Lerma, Bernal, García, Hernández, and others knitted together through blood, marriage, and rancho life—the children of farmers, who also raised sugarcane, coffee, corn, and cattle.

They were not the poorest of Xalisco's peon farmworkers. On the contrary, "they were people who had access to enough money to get up north, pay a coyote, and look for new kinds of work," said a Tepic professional I spoke with, who is from Xalisco. "Xalisquillo had many well-known sugarcane families. They were why Xalisco was first in production of sugarcane in the state of Nayarit. Their sons were the ones who started this [heroin business] in the eighties and nineties. These parents tried to teach the sons agriculture. The sons worked in the fields. It's really hard work. They didn't want to keep on doing what their dads did. They saw that [heroin] was a good business and so they began to leave. It's easier to make money in the business than to continue working in sugarcane."

In the early 1980s, before cell phones or beepers, these Tejedas would stand on the street or in some San Fernando Valley park. Buyers approached and the dealer would cut off a piece of heroin with a small knife.

That they lived in the San Fernando Valley, I suspected, made their story possible. They were far from the Sinaloans. Sinaloa is the state in Mexico where drug trafficking began. Sinaloans tend to be brash, brazen, violent. Other Mexicans hold them in something like awe. Sinaloans came to dominate the east side of Los Angeles County in the 1980s. The tiny suburbs southeast of Los Angeles—Paramount, Huntington Park, Bell Gardens, South Gate, and others—began as bedroom communities for ex-GIs from World War II, but by the 1980s these cities were solidly Mexican, and Sinaloan in particular. When that happened, these towns also became distribution terminals for Sinaloan drugs to cities across the United States. But the San Fernando Valley is far away, across hills in the northwest part of Los Angeles, and out there Sinaloans aren't as numerous. Other traffickers had room to expand.

Among the first Xalisco Boys to do so was David Tejeda. He was the oldest of six sons of a wealthy sugarcane farmer in the rancho of Aquiles Serdán. Wealthy by local standards, anyway. His family had land, cattle, horses, and houses, even before he went north to sell dope. David Tejeda was a light-skinned guy with a fondness for white cowboy hats and leather jackets with epaulets, in the style of the slain narco-balladeer Chalino Sánchez. Tejeda lived in Canoga Park and drank at the Majestic, the Van Nuys bar that was a favorite of Xalisco dealers like Enrique's uncles. He fought a lot, had a lot of girlfriends, and made a few enemies that way. But he gave jobs in the San Fernando Valley to poor kids from back home. A lot of people respected him for that.

"We all dreamed of coming up here to work for him," said one Xalisco trafficker I talked to in a U.S. prison. "I went to him and asked for work. I was like thirteen or fourteen. He said no, that I was too young. Many kids came and knocked on his door with the same request. I have cousins and friends who came and did work with him."

Los Angeles was a hive of gang activity during the late 1980s and early 1990s. In some neighborhoods, a different gang controlled every few blocks. Crack was big. Mobs of young men sold it by standing on L.A. streets. Gangs began levying taxes on these street dealers. About this time, the Xalisco Boys took their heroin trade off the street, out of the parks, and went to cars. Addicts were given a phone number to call. When they called, they were told where to meet a driver; the driver was directed to waiting clients by codes sent to them via beepers. Cars and beepers allowed a heroin crew access to a broader client base, and made the Xalisco Boys less obvious to police. In cars, dealers avoided gang taxation and the violence that accompanied the street crack trade.

With the rudimentary delivery model in place, business boomed. Word of the business spread around Xalisco. More young men arrived from the town. They copied the system. They called their new businesses *tienditas*—little stores. Owning a business was a narcotic itself for young rancho kids who had nothing. Some drivers learned the business with an established cell, then went out and opened their own. Each cell was an independent business, competing with others. Shootouts were unthinkable. Violence brought police attention; guns earned long prison time. Plus everyone knew each other from Xalisco, so violence would have created repercussions back home. A sell-and-let-sell ethos took hold and by the early 1990s, Xalisco heroin tienditas quietly crawled all over the Valley. As more people entered the business, profits dwindled. Police wised up and arrested several dealers.

About that time, in 1990 or maybe a year or two later, it appears, David Tejeda discovered Hawaii. He'd been selling to addicts who came over from Hawaii. Now he moved a crew of drivers there, and used those addict customers as guides to this new market where heroin fetched triple the price.

Slowly, others followed his lead and Xalisco dealers expanded. Before long, they also were in Pomona, San Diego, and Portland. Then in Las Vegas. Tejeda "was okay with others starting up their own tienditas. There's plenty for everybody, he thought," said another trafficker.

But that wasn't always true. Most cities then had a small universe of heroin addicts, who were usually old and poor. A crew new to town had to steal customers from the crews who were already there. The zero-sum game that ensued taught the Xalisco Boys the importance of branding and marketing. To keep customers, they learned to emphasize customer service, discounts, the convenience and safety of delivery. They had to ensure their dope was always good quality—meaning uncut and potent.

The competition for a limited number of addicts also kept them moving on through the 1990s in search of new, less-saturated markets. When they did this, they defied the norms of Mexican drug trafficking.

Most Mexican traffickers naturally followed the immigrants from their home states. This was astute and common sense, for no immigrant group has settled in such numbers in so many parts of America as Mexicans had by the end of the 1990s. Mexican immigrants were in rural areas where local police were often monolingual and understaffed. Those areas had cash-only businesses—Mexican restaurants and money-wiring services—that could be used to launder cash. By the 1990s, small towns and communities in rural Colorado, Georgia, and Arkansas, where Mexicans worked in meat plants, became major hubs for traffickers, places where they divided the dope loads they'd brought in and with which they supplied much larger towns. Mexican traffickers did this by following the immigrants. Thus by the 1990s, for example, it was possible for Sinaloan traffickers to find drug markets in many parts of America using Sinaloan immigrant communities as their point of contact and place to blend in. Michoacan traffickers did the same in the many U.S. regions where Michoacan immigrants became essential parts of the local economy.

But Nayarit is Mexico's fifth-smallest state, with barely a million people. Its migrants are few and have congregated mainly in Los Angeles and Reno. To find new heroin markets, the Xalisco Boys would have to move where they had no natural family or rancho connection. That's exactly what they did. Like Spanish conquistadors, venturing beyond the comfortable hometown networks became part of the Xalisco Boys' DNA.

To do this, though, they needed guides. Spaniards relied on Indians who hated the Aztecs to guide them across the New World to Tenochtitlán, the capital of the Aztec Empire, now Mexico City. Junkies did the same for the Xalisco Boys. The Xalisco Boys supplied these junkies' habits in exchange for help in moving into a new area, and in renting apartments, in registering cellular phones, and buying cars.

"You get one person to show you around and pass around the [phone] number and it's like bees to a hive," one imprisoned Xalisco Boy told me. "They all know each other. It's like having a scout. That's what happened in Las Vegas. A female addict there told some of the families, 'I know people in Tennessee.' So they went with her to Memphis. It became one of the biggest markets for a while."

They went to towns with large Mexican populations, where the Boys could blend in, and where no gang or mafia controlled the drug trade. But junkies got them there and found them their first customers. Junkies allowed the Xalisco Boys to expand far beyond where they might have had they only relied on Nayarit immigrant connections.

With faith in the addictive power of their dope, the Xalisco Boys harnessed these junkies who led them to rich new markets where almost no Nayarits lived, but where thousands of middle-class white kids were beginning to dope up on prescription opiate painkillers.

Junkies could track the telltale signs through the streets of a new city to the hidden customers that the Xalisco Boys might never find otherwise. Junkies knew the slang and could read looks of desperation.

Most important of all—and crucial to the expansion of the Xalisco Boys—was that junkies could navigate America's methadone clinics.

THE PAINKILLER KNOWN AS methadone was synthesized by German scientists in the effort to make Nazi Germany medicinally self-reliant as it prepared for war. The Allies took the patent after the war, and Eli Lilly Company introduced the drug in the United States in 1947. U.S. doctors identified it as a potential aide to heroin addicts.

That idea was taken up by Dr. Vincent Dole, an addiction specialist at the Rockefeller Institute in New York City. Methadone, Dole found, was the only opiate whose addicts did not demand increasing doses every few hours. Instead, they were happy with the same dose once a day, which could carry them through the next twenty-four hours. Methadone addicts could actually discuss topics unrelated to dope. This was not true of heroin addicts, whom Dole found tediously single-minded in their focus on the drug. Dole believed addicts could be maintained on methadone indefinitely, and that with one dose a day they could function as normal human beings. In 1970 in New York City, he opened the first methadone clinic for heroin addicts.

Dole believed that rehabilitation was dependent on human relationships—group therapy, 12-step meetings, and the like. But as a last resort for those who defied all efforts to kick the habit, methadone, Dole believed, could be a crutch, helping them through life.

President Richard Nixon permitted methadone as a treatment for heroin addiction, which plagued many soldiers returning from the Vietnam War. By the late 1970s, federally regulated methadone clinics were popping up around the country. These clinics quietly showed how a narcotic might be dispensed legally in a safe, crime-free environment. Methadone stabilized an addict and allowed him to find a job and repair damaged relationships. There were also no dirty needles, no crime, and addicts knew they couldn't be robbed at the clinics. What's more, methadone undercut and replaced the street heroin dealers' trade with a clean, well-lighted place for opiates; everyone was better off.

Methadone clinics opened before sunrise. One reason for this was that many addicts, looking for trades easy to enter, had become construction workers, carpenters, painters. They had to get to these jobs early. Methadone users were like ghosts, showing up early in the morning for years on end, drinking their dose, and silently going about their lives. In time, though, methadone became a battlefield between those who thought it should be used to wean addicts off opiates, and those, like Vincent Dole, who saw it as a lifelong drug, like insulin for diabetics.

One strategy or the other might well have worked. But the worst of both emerged at many clinics. Methadone was often dispensed as if the goal was kicking the habit, with small doses. But as methadone clinics became for-profit affairs, many cut the counseling and therapy that might help patients kick opiates altogether. Critics could be forgiven for seeing some clinic owners as drug dealers, stringing patients out for years, and charging twenty and thirty times what the drug actually cost, which was about fifty cents a dose. In 1990, the U.S. General Accounting Office reported that half the clinics were poorly managed, unaccountable, and provided little counseling or aftercare.

The result was that many methadone clinics maintained core populations of opiate addicts in cities all across the country, but on doses that were too small, and usually without much therapeutic support. Addicts who weren't given high enough doses craved another opiate later in the afternoon, after the clinics closed. They had to find their dope elsewhere, usually on the street, and thus remained tied to the heroin underworld. At clinics that combined low doses and insufficient rehab therapy, addicts took to using methadone and heroin interchangeably.

Methadone was a better alternative to weak powder heroin, which was more expensive and available only in dangerous housing projects or skid rows. But maintaining large numbers of people on any kind of opiate, particularly on low doses, made them easy prey for someone with a more efficient and convenient opiate delivery system. For years, though, no one could conceive of such a thing: a system of retailing street heroin that was cheaper than, as safe as, and more convenient than a methadone clinic.

But in the mid-1990s, that's exactly what the Xalisco Boys brought to towns across America. They discovered that methadone clinics were, in effect, game preserves.

*   *   *

METHADONE CLINICS GAVE XALISCO Boys the footholds in the first western U.S. cities as they expanded beyond the San Fernando Valley in the early 1990s. Every new cell learned to find the methadone clinic and give away free samples to the addicts.

One Xalisco Boy in Portland told authorities of a training that his cell put new drivers through. They were taught, he said, to lurk near methadone clinics, spot an addict, and follow him. Then they'd tap him on the shoulder and ask directions to someplace. Then they'd then spit out a few balloons. Along with the balloons, they'd give the addict a piece of paper with a phone number on it.

"Call us if we can help you out."

The value of each Xalisco heroin tiendita was in its list of customers. "This is how they would build and maintain it," said Steve Mygrant, a Portland-area prosecutor. "It was an ongoing recruiting practice, in the same way a corporate business would identify customers. They'd lose people along the way. So they were constantly engaged in this."

In time, most cells developed addicts they could trust, and some of these, in turn, helped tiendita owners expand to new cities in exchange for dope. Some of their junkie guides became legend down in Xalisco. In Cincinnati, I spoke with a girl in the Lower Price Hill neighborhood, home to transplanted Appalachians and overrun with heroin. She had been rustling up business for a series of Xalisco dealers intent on shaping a customer list as they came and went over the years. This girl was, in her own words, "a known quantity" down in Xalisco, a town she had never visited. Xalisco Boys who were just getting started in Cincinnati asked for her, looked her up, and pushed dope in her face wanting her help in establishing heroin routes throughout the Cincinnati metro area. It made kicking the habit almost impossible.

"They can't even say my name. But they tell them down there, 'Ask somebody for White Girl. Lower Price Hill.' One guy even came with a note with my name on it. Somebody had written my name and misspelled it," she said. "Over these years, I get out [of jail or rehab] and they're there looking for me. People will say, 'How do you always got this connection?' I don't know. It's not like I call Mexico and say can you send me a guy? But it's always there."

One prolific addict turned guide was a woman named Tracy Jefferson. Jefferson was a longtime drug user and manic depressive from Salem, Oregon. She hooked up with Luis Padilla-Peña, a Xalisco dealer in

Reno, Nevada, in 1993. Padilla-Peña had come to the United States in 1990 and found work in Las Vegas with the heroin crew run by a friend from the Tejeda-Sánchez clan. From there, he went off on his own. His big break was meeting Jefferson. Over the next two years, she helped Padilla-Peña and his family carve out heroin markets in Salem, Denver, Seattle, Colorado Springs, Oklahoma City, and Omaha—usually by enrolling herself in methadone clinics and giving away free black tar to the clinics' clients she met.

From Omaha, Jefferson said when she testified in federal court, she and the family were scouting Kansas City, St. Louis, and Des Moines. They would drop a town that didn't generate at least two thousand dollars in daily profit. For this reason, she testified, they passed on Cheyenne, Wyoming, and Yakima and Vancouver, Washington.

Another such guide was a kid from Mexico who grew up in Reseda. He didn't use drugs, but he had something else the Xalisco Boys needed. He was bilingual. He was from Mexico but was raised in the San Fernando Valley. In Reseda he met many Xalisco immigrants. In 1995, he was seventeen when a new cell leader hired him to work in Maui, Hawaii.

"None of them spoke English. That's why I was important to them," he said. "There were a lot of things they couldn't do. When I got there, I helped them expand."

By then, Hawaii had two Xalisco cells: one owned by David Tejeda, the other by a man named Toño Raices, who was from the small rancho of El Malinal in the hills near Xalisco.

Back in Xalisco, people say that Toño Raices aimed to be somebody in the drug world. Some say he envied David Tejeda. The story goes that Tejeda was owed four hundred thousand dollars for product by a man from the rancho of Pantanal who didn't want to pay. This man was backed up by Toño Raices.

One day in 1996, outside a Xalisco dance club, Tejeda met with his rivals. From there, they moved to a coffee warehouse Raices owned and, in a dispute over money, Tejeda was shot to death by Raices' men under a guayabo tree. No one was arrested. Vaqueros Musical, a local band, recounted Tejeda's death this way in a corrido:

> *He got a call, they say from a cellular.*
> *David, come to the Magueyes Bar and here I'll pay you . . .*
> *Thursday, 4th of April, 1996, they got him when he wasn't expecting it.*
> *They shot him point-blank with AK-47s.*

Three years later, Toño Raices was shot to death at the cemetery where Tejeda was buried. The way I heard the story, his enemies killed a boy who worked for him. At the boy's funeral, mourners paid city police to let them shoot guns in the air at the cemetery. But during the ceremony, state police arrived, presumably allied with the Tejedas. A shootout erupted between state police and armed mourners. A commandant died. So did Toño Raices. Vaqueros Musical recorded another corrido.

But David Tejeda's murder was the important one in the story of the Xalisco Boys and black tar heroin in America. His extended family had hundreds of relatives. He'd shown poor families they, too, could rise by selling heroin retail in the United States. Younger guys naturally went to him for advice. He supplied many of them as they expanded beyond the San Fernando Valley.

Tejeda's death had a strangely liberating effect on his extended family and other Xalisco crews. When he was alive, "a lot of people depended on him because he had everything going for him," said the kid from Reseda. "They didn't have to figure out how to do things for themselves. But once he was killed, they had to start doing things on their own. They didn't have nobody to depend on."

Forced now to become more intrepid, "everybody scattered everywhere."

Just a Phone Call Away

Portland, Oregon

In his forties, Alan Levine lost both legs to frostbite when he fell asleep drunk under an overpass in an Illinois snowstorm. Somehow he survived this and in time he migrated west, ending up in Portland, Oregon.

He was already a longtime heroin addict. Levine first used heroin at age twenty in New York and that first shot made him feel the way he wanted to feel the rest of his life—like the King of the World and the President of Everything.

All his life, Alan Levine loved drugs and the charge they gave him. But his lack of legs got in the way. He shuffled around on prosthetics. Usually, he procured dope from some house where he had a connection, or by wandering around the Old Town Chinatown neighborhood north of Portland's downtown, an arduous trek repeated three or four times a day. Levine hobbled along, driven by his addiction. Each time, he never knew what he was getting, or whether he would be robbed or arrested. He'd make it back to his motel, fix, and zone out until it was time to go look for more, surviving on panhandling and a monthly disability check.

In 1993, Levine returned to Portland after a year away. He heard that dealers had come to town who now delivered dope if you called in an order. Somehow Levine got their business card, though years later he couldn't remember precisely how. He had never known of a heroin dealer with a business card and a convenient number you could call.

With that card, well, Alan Levine might've just died and gone to heaven.

WAYNE BALDASSARE, MEANWHILE, WAS sure he was entering hell.

Baldassare was a cop who loved dope work. He'd been on the Portland Police Drugs and Vice Division since 1982. He loved the creativity the job required, that he had to use and care for informants. Each day was different: an undercover buy in the morning, a search warrant in the afternoon. The job required imagination, because the dealers were themselves endlessly creative.

For years, heroin was the easiest drug to work because it was sold out of houses. You arrested a junkie. Terrified of withdrawing in jail, he'd tell you how a dope house worked. The junkie would bring an undercover officer to the dealer. Then you busted the place.

But in about 1991, Baldassare saw all that change. Young Mexican guys, clean-cut, courteous, and looking quite out of their element, were driving the town in old cars, delivering heroin. "All of a sudden you got a dispatch center taking orders and calling these delivery guys," he said. "It made it very hard to get a good case. You were looking at hours of surveillance for five or six small bags of dope."

The delivery drivers did tours of six months and then left. If they were arrested they were deported, not prosecuted, because they never carried large amounts of dope. The cases were always light. Baldessare first figured they were small-timers. Later he realized that, quite to the contrary, they had learned how drug investigations worked: prosecutors prized cases with large quantities of drugs. Crack and methamphetamine were the priorities then, each measured in kilos. As camouflage, these Mexican heroin guys used just-in-time supplying, like any global corporation, to ensure they had only tiny quantities in their cars or apartments. This, too, was sophistication Baldessare didn't see in the heroin underworld.

Soon these delivery drivers crowded into Portland. Heroin prices dropped and Baldassare watched the drivers get wise. They drove in circles to lose the officers following them. It took four or five officers to tail one car. Up to then, Portland hadn't much of an aerial police service. One officer owned a four-seat Cessna and charged the city for gas when he used it for police work, which wasn't often. Now the airplane was pressed into regular service, with a pilot and an observer watching the heroin delivery car on the street below. Baldassare was the observer. Peering through binoculars from above, he radioed locations to his colleagues on the ground.

It was grueling work and went on for hours. Baldassare was one of the few officers who could peer through binoculars from the plane, as it went around in circles, without getting airsick. As the drivers tooled around Portland all day making deliveries, Baldassare spent ten, twelve hours a day in the plane, watching from twenty-five hundred feet in the air, stopping only to refuel. This was before GPS; nor were there cell phones to track.

"It was line of sight," he said. "If you looked away, you could lose them. So you picked your times to look away. If your neck was getting a kink in it, you had to choose when to massage it."

Above downtown, Baldassare could follow a heroin car for a half circle of the plane, then lose it behind a building as the Cessna completed its circle, hoping to pick up on a new go-round. Cars easily got lost under Portland's dense canopy of trees.

Before long, the department had to expand its air force. An air force was a luxury most police departments the size of Portland's can't afford, but which this new heroin system made necessary. The city hired another two pilots. Finally, the department bought a new plane with full-length windows for easier surveillance.

THEIR BUSINESS CARD WAS yellow. It had a phone number and an eagle with a snake in its talons, the emblem on the flag of Mexico. That was all. No names. No slogan. Call anytime, Alan Levine was told. One night, he did.

Give us twenty minutes, said the guy on the end of the line. To Levine's immense surprise, within fifteen minutes, a Mexican kid was knocking at his motel door. He was young and nervous and clean-cut. He looked like a farm boy. He spoke no English. But he had sixty dollars' worth of black tar heroin.

Levine had never forgotten the first rapturous feeling he got from heroin back in the 1960s. But through the years that followed, he also never felt that high again. Until, that is, he shot up black tar heroin that night. Levine called the number three times a day after that. The delivery guys changed often and he called them all Pedro. They were reliable. They arrived quickly. Now, instead of having to brave Old Town on his two fake legs, Alan Levine could sit in his motel room, aware that he was "just a phone call away from getting loaded."

The Mexicans were the only dealers Levine had encountered who never ran out of dope. In time, prices dropped to as little as five dollars a hit as these crews brought huge supplies of high-quality tar heroin to Portland and competed against each other. Yet he noticed that they never feuded. They gave him credit. They often gave him a little extra, avid to keep him as a customer.

One night, one of these kids, a driver as Alan Levine remembers it, tried to scam him, offering eighteen balloons for a hundred dollars when the deal, already long established, was twenty-five balloons.

Levine objected. Let's see what the boss says, the boy said. Levine got in his car and followed the driver across Portland. They came to a house. Out came a man Levine years later determined to be Enrique Tejeda-Cienfuegos, but whom he came to know then as El Gato.

Tejeda-Cienfuegos was from the village of Aquiles Serdán, a few miles south of Xalisco. He and his four brothers ran a heroin franchise in Portland. Levine knew nothing of this. He only knew that the delivery kid was trying to screw him and he explained this to El Gato that night. The boy now produced the twenty-five bags of heroin, saying in Spanish that this is what he offered Levine the whole time and there'd been some misunderstanding. El Gato was apologetic and gave Levine those twenty-five bags of heroin for free. Levine never saw that driver again.

El Gato "was evidently powerful," Levine remembered, when I spoke with him in a motel room near downtown Portland one night many years later. I tracked Levine down through his ex-wife because by then I realized the history of heroin was best told by addicts, the older the better. I sat in a chair while he, legless, sat in his bed, smoking constantly. Cigarettes gave his voice a growl as grizzled as his face and a strange chop to his jaws that sounded, when he spoke, as if he were chomping on a juicy steak. Sure enough, he knew the story of the Xalisco Boys' arrival in Portland as well as anybody, even if he knew them only as a rotating series of Mexicans he called Pedro. When I showed him a mug shot, he definitely remembered El Gato.

"When he spoke, they acted," he said. "He had some status. He took a liking to me because I paid on time. After that, they'd come and say, 'Gato said to give you this; Gato said to give you that.' They called me Liver because I told them I had hepatitis C and I didn't want to share needles."

El Gato later gave Levine a Buck knife, perhaps feeling he could use some protection. Levine realized he was worlds away now from how heroin had operated for so long.

"You didn't have to leave your house. Dealing with those people was paradise. You could nickel-and-dime them, too, when they got there. They were eager for the green money."

Levine had never known any dealer to give away free drugs to get people hooked, or to keep addicts from getting clean—the kind of mythical pushers the government and the media had invented amid the "dope fiend" scare. Until he met the Xalisco Boys.

"This marketing technique *was* about that. They knew what they were doing. They were marketers."

Enrique Adrift

A Rancho in Nayarit, Mexico

The morning after Enrique's big homecoming party, following his return from Canoga Park, his mother was happy and his father held his tongue. California gave Enrique a new option. If his father mistreated him, he'd leave again. So they ate together as a family and tried to forget past misery now that their new Northerner, as they called him, had come home.

The problemas between both sides of his mother's family grew worse. The shootings didn't stop. Most of his grandfather's relatives had to leave. Relatives of his grandmother dominated the barrio. But Enrique felt his experience up north elevated him above this petty world. He spoke to both sides. He could think of nothing but California. His life would be different and this he believed was entirely due to El Norte and heroin. Yet, he still had only a skinny horse that he thought looked more like a dog. His California sojourn had left him little to offer his girlfriend. He wanted a rematch with California; that's how he looked at it. A test of wills. No one would use him again. His uncles, he saw, made some money and then backed out of the business for a while for fear of village gossip. Enrique was more afraid of poverty.

Other kids were now going north the way he had. The retail system that Xalisco immigrants were devising in the San Fernando Valley allowed even the humblest to do more than just dream. It was also ending his rancho's dismal isolation. For years, when cars passed through, villagers would hide, fearing it was a child kidnapper. Girls covered their faces when someone brought out the first video cameras at a party. But as men went north to sell dope and returned with money, they brought with them a feel for the outside world and an enhanced vision of what was possible. Everyone could have his own business, be his own boss. The Xalisco heroin system was a lot like the United States in that way. America fulfilled the promise of the unknown to rancheros, and an escape from humiliation for Mexico's poor from villages just like Enrique's. The Xalisco heroin system did it faster. Plus it was risky and this beckoned farm boys who saw they had nothing to lose and everything to gain. By risking a lot, they added to their status back home.

After a few months, in about 1991, one of Enrique's uncles called from the San Fernando Valley and offered him work with good pay. This time Enrique arrived confident and brash, proud of his worldliness, no longer the scared village kid.

He saw immediately why his uncles had called him. More heroin dealers from Xalisco had followed the lead of the pioneers and crowded into the San Fernando Valley's already-proven market. Competition intensified. Prices were dropping.

By this time, the families who would make heroin their lives' work were established in the Valley. Of course, David Tejeda and his brothers were there. Beto Sánchez and the Sánchez clan were growing big. So, too, were Beto Bonque and his family, as well as the Bernals. The Langaricas—brothers Julio, Chuy, and Tino, whose father was a witch doctor back in Xalisco—had cells, as did their cousins, the Garcia-Langaricas, Polla and Macho. There were others as well; one family had Pasadena to itself.

Each family had two or three cells going, and each cell had at least a couple drivers working shifts from six A.M. to noon and noon to six P.M. every day. At night, they met at apartments and rolled heroin into balloons for the next day. It was not a glamorous business. You were there to work, said the family bosses, who paid each driver six hundred dollars a week and wanted every hour accounted for. The job of heroin driver resembled sweatshop work. The cell owners changed the drivers in and out, moving them into apartments and out again six months later, switching cars even more frequently, and ordering drivers to hand out beeper numbers to junkies on the street along with free samples. By the early 1990s, the San Fernando Valley was like a convention, a reunion of people from Xalisco County. Everyone wanted in.

One dealer, known as El Gato, from the village of Aquiles Serdán, was especially aggressive. El Gato didn't care what people said about him back home. Enrique admired that. El Gato wanted people to know that in his house, hunger was a thing of the past. El Gato came home with clothes, cars, ice chests full of American beer, and guns of various calibers.

"El Gato is everywhere and it won't be easy to run him out," his uncle said.

His uncles promised Enrique more money and a new truck in Mexico if he did well. With another driver, Enrique, properly inspired, patrolled the streets of the San Fernando Valley like the state trooper he once wanted to be—now looking for addicts. He'd give them a free sample and a phone number. Within a few weeks, Enrique raised the daily take to five thousand dollars.

Then, early one morning, police raided an uncle's house. The other uncles had looked to this man for leadership. In the weeks that followed, Enrique saw his remaining uncles falter. Gang members robbed their drivers and they did nothing. Several times clients put knives to Enrique's throat. He spit the balloons into their hands, remembering a saying from his father: "Die for what's yours, but not for what's others."

More people arrived from Xalisco to sell the chiva. The heroin networks multiplied. El Gato's workers began leaving him to start their own cells. There wasn't much El Gato could do. Any retaliation in Canoga Park would cause issues back home, and bring LAPD attention. A friend Enrique knew from Xalisco came up and started his own network. Just started the cell right there in the Valley. Then El Gato surprised everyone. He took a junkie and chiva and opened a heroin cell down in San Diego. Before long, Enrique heard, El Gato had one going up in Portland as well. David Tejeda had that store going in Hawaii. These kinds of moves rocked the Xalisco heroin world in the San Fernando Valley. Above all, they showed the Xalisco Boys that they could find new markets, that the system could succeed far from the Valley's Nayarit enclave.

Enrique, a kid of sixteen now, watched all this. As the business floundered under his uncles' weak leadership, he and a friend bought a car and rented an apartment on the sly. For a while, without his uncles' knowledge, he ran his own heroin tiendita on the side. But then a gang member robbed him, took his dope, and cut him. His uncles discovered his side business. They beat him for his temerity, gave him eighteen hundred dollars as payment for his months of work, and packed him off to Nayarit.

With that, the one escape from a life of sugarcane farming seemed closed to him forever. His return to the rancho was greeted less enthusiastically this time. His sisters smiled at the gifts, but he felt their disappointment. He had no other options. He went to work again in the fields with his father, who smirked and mocked him. As if to show up his son, his father installed a satellite dish outside the family shack. In Mexican ranchos at the time, satellite dishes, standing fifteen feet high, were one way a family showed neighbors that it had arrived. Didn't matter if some days it got no reception, the towering pole and broad dish made a statement. His family had no decent bathroom, Enrique wryly observed, but it had a satellite dish. Still, his father was happy, so the family was relieved.

One day the land would be his, his father reminded him. Enrique should get used to that idea. But even that was years away. Without heroin, Enrique couldn't imagine a life where he controlled his own decisions.

Harvest time came with heat and humidity that felt like boiling soup. Enrique made fifty pesos a load trucking the towering stacks of cut cane to the mill. In the fields from three A.M. to six P.M., the heat sapped him, his legs buckled, and he arrived home every night looking like he had been tossed in a bag of charcoal, thinking to himself, "I'm leaving my soul in these fields."

Searching for the Holy Grail

Lexington, Kentucky

On New Year's Day 2013, I steered a rental car through the snow-covered rolling hills just north of Lexington. The land there is divided into horse farms, and black four-board fencing provides simple and clear outlines to the pastures. As my car loped hypnotically past these farms and trees laden with mistletoe, I came to a lonely two-lane county road known as CR 1977. CR 1977 rises over small hills, curves, and then deflates as the hills bottom out. The road cuts past a farm to the north, home to a dozen studs, stallions, and broodmares. It passes the Masterson Equestrian facility, a large park for horses.

Then it bends and reveals a collection of stern, tall brick buildings set well back from the road. The compound could pass for a nineteenth-century factory were it not for the towering stadium lights that clarify the situation. The Federal Medical Center, as it's now known, is home to seventeen hundred prison inmates.

I got out of my car. Prison officials had denied my request to see its innards. So 150 yards was as close as I was getting to one of the strangest monuments in the story of American opiate addiction. When it went up in 1935, this federal fortress was known as the Narcotic Farm. The Roosevelt administration deemed it a "New Deal for the Drug Addict."

Under the Harrison Act of 1914, thousands of addicts were convicted as criminals and streamed into prisons, where their drug seeking disrupted life in the institutions. The government built the Narcotic Farm to house them.

It was a rare place—both a prison and a treatment center—that for forty years reflected the country's schizophrenic approach to opiates and drug addiction. During years when much of the country was segregated, blacks and whites, gays and straights, Latinos, Italians, Irish, Chinese, men, and women from across America shared a thousand acres in Kentucky—with only heroin in common. Many were serving prison sentences; others, like beat writer William Burroughs, checked themselves in to kick the habit.

The Farm stressed outdoor work as addiction therapy. Inmates milked cows and raised tomatoes and wheat, and supplied the institution with food. There was a canning plant, a radio repair service, and a dental lab making false teeth. Administrators felt recreation was therapy. Addicts played basketball and tennis; the Farm had a golf course, a bowling alley, and basket-weaving classes.

In the 1940s, off in New York City, Charlie Parker turned swing jazz inside out. Hundreds of younger New York musicians worshipped the alto saxophonist and turned to heroin hoping to play more like Bird, who died addicted in 1955, his body and his art corroded by junk. Many of these musicians went to prison. A virtual generation of bebop's young punks in dark glasses came to the Farm: Sonny Rollins, Lee Morgan, Howard McGhee, Elvin Jones, Chet Baker, Tadd Dameron, Jackie McLean, Sonny Stitt, and many more. They jammed for hours, formed bands that were never recorded, and played shows for the Farm's inmates and Lexington hipsters who were allowed to attend. A Farm jazz band once played on *The Tonight Show Starring Johnny Carson*.

I encountered the story of the Narcotic Farm as I sought to understand how, decades later, a Mexican village came to sell heroin across the country and in places where the drug had once been virtually unknown. The threads of these stories, I came to believe, ultimately connected.

For years the Farm was the world's foremost center of addiction research, for reasons that predated the institution itself. World War I had again demonstrated to doctors the merciful painkilling benefits the morphine molecule provided. Fresh, too, in their memory were heroin's first decades, which showed just as clearly that addiction too often bedeviled those who used opiates. Try as they might—with strategies as varied as farm work, group therapy, or prison—rehabilitation specialists never graduated much more than 10 percent of their addicts to true opiate freedom. The rest relapsed, slaves, it appeared, to the morphine molecule. This seemed a shame to scientists and physicians. Was mankind really doomed to not have it all? Couldn't it have heaven without hell? Couldn't the best scientists find a way of extracting the painkilling attributes from the molecule while discarding its miserable addictiveness?

In 1928, what would become known as the Committee on Problems of Drug Dependence (CPDD) brought together the country's best researchers to do just that. John D. Rockefeller Jr. organized it using money his father had set aside. The CPDD promoted cooperation among drug researchers in government, academia, and industry. German science used this kind of collaboration to come up with some of the world's best drugs. But German drug supplies to America ceased during World War I. After the war, American scientists concluded that the country was vulnerable because U.S. drug research was random and haphazard.

The CPDD funded chemists and pharmacologists, academics and industrial scientists, toward the goal of finding a nonaddictive pain-killer. Novocain, invented in 1905, avoided the need for addictive cocaine in dentistry. Why not a morphine substitute? Such a drug could cleanse doctors' image as clueless dealers of dangerous drugs that they'd earned by widely prescribing heroin in the early 1900s. Academics, meanwhile, hoped for a new era of modern scientific research applied to medicinal drugs. Law enforcement hoped a nonaddictive pain reliever would lessen the fallout from its attempts to rid the country of opium.

Researchers called this drug the Holy Grail and the search for it would take the rest of the century and beyond.

The CPDD set up a laboratory at the University of Virginia to create these new drugs. Another lab formed at the University of Michigan, to test new drugs on animals. Now all that was needed was a place to test the new drugs on humans, a place where drug addicts were in ready and huge supply.

In 1935, the U.S. Narcotic Farm opened.

The Farm contained a section known as the Addiction Research Center (ARC). For decades, the ARC tested on inmates every major opiate that Committee-sponsored chemists produced: Dilaudid, Demerol, darvon, codeine, as well as Thorazine and many tranquilizers and sedatives. Experiments at the Farm showed that methadone lasted longer and spared junkies the severe highs and lows of heroin that spurred their frenzied attempts to score. Thus, they concluded, metha-done could act as a replacement for heroin.

The ARC had a staff of psychiatrists, biochemists, physiologists, pharmacologists, lab technicians, and four guards. They studied every aspect of morphine's interaction with man. ARC research developed the first quantitative scales for measuring degrees of addiction, severity of withdrawal, and the addictiveness of many drugs. For four decades, heroin and morphine addicts with long sentences would volunteer for studies because they were given dope. After the studies ended, the subjects were given a six-month rehabilitation to ensure they were no longer physically dependent.

As American science organized to search for the Holy Grail of a nonaddictive painkiller, the Farm made this research possible and kept hope alive. Researchers viewed their mission simply: to prevent another heroin; prevent another highly addictive drug unleashed on the country without proper study. With this, they justified experimentation on inmates. "The ARC saw itself as safeguarding public health on a global scale by preventing addictive compounds from destroying the lives of thousands," wrote Nancy Campbell, J. P. Olsen, and Luke Walden in *The Narcotic Farm*, a fascinating book on the institution.

The research at Lexington generated hundreds of scholarly articles and amounted to the only serious study of addiction in the world at the time. The World Health Organization relied on it for data. Addiction study emerged there as a scientific field, and ARC staff were the first to conceive of addiction as not a character failing, or a crime, but rather a chronic brain disorder. The ARC was shut down in the 1970s, when the U.S. Senate's Church Committee, investigating the Central Intelligence Agency, found that the ARC had done experiments with LSD on inmates at the behest of the CIA. With that, an era ended. The Farm was transformed into the prison and hospital that it is today.

But for forty years, all the drugs created in the CPDD's search for the Holy Grail were tested on inmates at the Narcotic Farm in Lexington, Kentucky.

Early on, the UVA laboratory's first director, Lyndon Small, synthesized a drug he called metopon. Metopon had some of morphine's painkilling attributes but was slightly less addictive. Metopon fell short of the idea the CPDD pursued. Yet it was taken as proof that a morphine-like painkiller that was not addictive—that elusive Holy Grail—might be found someday.

This goal urged on the next generations of drug researchers, and in time helped fire a cadre of revolutionaries seeking a better way to treat pain in America.

The Pain

THROUGH MOST OF THE twentieth century, doctors treating the terminally ill faced attitudes that seemed medieval when it came to opiates. Docs who prescribed the painkillers were treated as virtual outlaws. Parsimony described how drugs were distributed. Several doctors' signatures were often required even for small doses as dying people writhed in the most indecent pain. Treatments for pain came in strange concoctions. One was called the Brompton cocktail—a combo named for the English hospital where it was used: morphine, cocaine, Thorazine, honey, gin, and water—which read to me like a concoction some street junkie would come up with, but which I'm told was pretty effective.

In the 1970s, attitudes slowly began changing. In England, Cicely Saunders, a nurse and researcher, opened a hospice that treated terminal cancer patients with opiates. Under Saunders, St. Christopher's Hospice in London was the world's first to combine care for the dying with research and clinical trials. St. Christopher's was inspired by the idea that patients should be treated for pain without the drugs also destroying their personalities. Saunders's employee, Robert Twycross, began experiments that showed enormous benefits from using opiates on dying cancer patients. St. Christopher's promoted opiates, sometimes at high doses, to relieve the pain of the dying. Saunders and Twycross believed it inhumane to do otherwise. If people were soon to die, what did it matter if they were addicted? Wasn't pain relief and a dignified death more important? At St. Christopher's, dying patients were given opiates regularly, whether they were in pain or not.

The Queen honored Saunders with damehood.

Dame Cicely and Twycross worked hard to change minds, though this took longer in the United States, where decades of opiate demonization made doctors wary. Twycross once said that exiting a plane in New York City, he "could smell the fear of addiction in America."

In 1972, a British company called Napp Pharmaceuticals developed a controlled-release formula, known as Continus, that the company first put to use with an asthma medicine. One day Twycross suggested to some Napp reps that their company might use Continus to develop a timed-release morphine pill. Napp eventually did so, and this proved important to this story. It offered doctors a new tool for treating pain in dying patients. Napp, also, is owned by Purdue, the laxative manufacturer that Arthur Sackler and his brothers had purchased in the 1950s.

Meanwhile, a Swedish cancer physician named Jan Stjernsward was put in a position to change pain treatment worldwide. Stjernsward was made chief of the cancer program for the World Health Organization in Geneva in 1980. He'd spent time years before in a Kenyan hospital, where he witnessed acres of cancer patients dying in agony. The third world lacked the resources to treat cancer. With morphine, Stjernsward felt, patients could at least spend their last days pain-free. But doctors refused to use it, fearing addiction.

Now, as WHO's new cancer chief, Stjernsward remembered Kenya. He set about establishing norms for treating dying cancer patients with opiates, primarily morphine. Ten-milligram morphine pills cost a penny apiece. This would allow, Stjernsward believed, the same care the world over to people who were leaving life as to those who were entering it.

He met Vittorio Ventafridda, who ran a foundation in Milan that was the first in Italy to provide pain treatment to terminally ill patients. Lunching with Stjernsward one day in the cafeteria of WHO's Geneva headquarters, Ventafridda wrote out on a napkin simple principles for treating dying patients with opiates. It was a ladder of treatment. Increasingly powerful drugs, including opiates combined with nonopiates, should be used if pain did not subside. This was a radical idea at the time.

Stjernsward later gathered most of the world's few experts in pain treatment—sixteen in all—in a medieval castle in Milan to shape a world health policy, and brought that napkin with him.

The ladder that Ventafridda outlined at lunch that day enshrined the idea that opiates should be used to deal with terminally ill patients on whom nonopiates did not work. This was a humane approach, particularly in countries where few had access to cancer treatment. WHO published a book in more than twenty languages laying out simple pain treatment steps, which came to be known as the WHO Ladder. Within it, morphine was deemed "an essential drug" in cancer pain relief.

WHO went further. It claimed freedom from pain as a universal human right. The Ladder was accompanied by a concept relevant to our story that moved public and medical opinion. It was this: If a patient said he was in pain, doctors should believe him and prescribe accordingly. This attitude grew from a patients' rights movement that sprung in part from the Nuremberg Trials, where Nazi doctors were found to be experimenters who disregarded patients' autonomy, and later from the 1960s counterculture that suspected the motives of all established institutions, medicine included.

With the WHO Ladder, doctors' concern over the use of opium-derived drugs began to ease. They were, after all, remarkably effective at knocking down pain, which was now a human right. Worldwide morphine consumption began to climb, rising thirtyfold between 1980 and 2011.

But a strange thing happened. Use didn't rise in the developing world, which might reasonably be viewed as the region in most acute pain. Instead, the wealthiest countries, with 20 percent of the world's population, came to consume almost all—more than 90 percent—of the world's morphine. This was due to prejudice against opiates and regulations on their use in poor countries, on which the WHO Ladder apparently had little effect. An opiophobia ruled these countries, and still does, as patients are allowed to die in grotesque agony rather than be provided the relief that opium-based painkillers offer. India, a major opium producer, has minute per capita consumption of morphine (0.12 milligrams per capita a year in 2011), due mostly to a government bureaucracy that taxes the drug heavily.

In 1985, members of the International Association for the Study of Pain met in Buenos Aires. While there, the pain specialists visited a hospital where a neurosurgeon told them that opiates were allowed only for those undergoing surgery. He was forced every year to perform a thousand cordotomies for those with chronic pain—severing the pain and temperature nerves in a patient's spine.

"It was appalling. That was more than all the cordotomies done annually in the U.S. and Europe," said Dr. John Loeser, who was on the tour from his multidisciplinary pain clinic at the University of Washington.

Experiences like these seared doctors who were interested in pain management. Also on tour that year was Dr. Kathleen Foley, from New York's Memorial Sloan Kettering Cancer Center. Foley began her career in the 1970s, during the last years of the opiate dark ages, when doctors used these drugs under only the most controlled circumstances.

By the 1980s, Foley, a devout Catholic, had become a voice for these dying cancer patients, and an advocate for treating their pain with opiates. In 1981, she transformed pain treatment for cancer patients at Sloan Kettering, bringing together researchers to study pain and clinicians to provide pain treatment—the first pain group of its kind.

As time went on, Foley, however, took her advocacy of opiate treatment a step further. Opiates should not be confined to just cancer or postsurgical patients, she believed. They should also be used, she argued, to treat patients with pain that did not grow from a disease, injury, or surgery: pain that was chronic but equally life mangling—bad lower backs, knee pain, and others.

As I followed my story, I came to realize that this idea, alighting on the realities of American medicine and medical marketing of the 1980s and 1990s, eventually connected to why, years later, men from a small town in Mexico could sell so much heroin in parts of the country that had never seen it before.

In 1984, a young doctor came to Sloan Kettering for a fellowship under Foley. Russell Portenoy had grown up in Yonkers and developed an interest in biology as a child. A dapper and articulate man, Portenoy attended Cornell University, then medical school at the University of Maryland. He did a neurology residency at Albert Einstein College of Medicine.

Portenoy worked among Sloan Kettering cancer patients for almost two years. During the 1980s and 1990s, he and Foley helped midwife a new specialty in American medicine. Palliative care—treating the pain and stress of the seriously ill—grew from a variety of influences: the hospice movement of Cicely Saunders and the idea, then surprisingly uncommon in medicine, that death should be dignified. Palliative care involved far more than just drugs. It included psychological, spiritual, and family counseling. The new discipline gave Russell Portenoy "the talking points I needed to mold my work life," he once wrote. As an emerging discipline, palliative care appealed to a bright young doctor interested in staking out his own ideas. Comforting the seriously ill and dying touched on the altruistic reasons why anyone would enter medical school in the first place.

What's more, it challenged him. Just knowing a symptom didn't mean he understood the patient. Portenoy wrote later that he found himself forced to study the profound psychosocial and spiritual impact of advanced illness. He was forced to learn, for example, how to tell a family of a loved one's life-threatening illness. Palliative care, he came to believe, was guided by moral issues of patient autonomy and respect for cultural and individual differences. Decisions were made with the input of the patient and family. This was very different from how medicine had treated serious illness and pain. Watching people struggle with pain, and talking to families who faced the loss of a loved one, gave Portenoy a touch of idealism, a bit of the crusader pushing up against conventional wisdom.

IN FACT, THE 1980S were good years for a young doctor with pain as his focus doing battle with conventional wisdom. Researchers had come to new understandings of how pain happened in the brain. The work of Cicely Saunders in England was dissolving the old bugaboos about the prohibition on using opiates in the United States. Medical advances were extending the lives of cancer patients in some cases from months to years. These treatments were themselves painful, and thus many more patients required attention for their pain.

In 1984, Purdue Frederick produced one solution. It released MS Contin, a timed-release morphine pill—the product of that conversation Robert Twycross had with the Napp Pharmaceuticals reps in England years before. MS Contin was intended for cancer and postoperative patients.

In Salt Lake City, a doctor named Lynn Webster had been studying new techniques for acute pain at Holy Cross Hospital. One day in 1989, a woman named Dorothy had surgery on her lung. During surgery Webster inserted in Dorothy's back an epidural catheter with an injection of pain medicine. Through the catheter Webster gave her small, continuous doses of opiate anesthetics. Epidurals had been used in labor and delivery, but new research showed epidurals could be used for other things. They could, Webster reasoned, allow him to gain more localized pain control with less medication than the typical intravenous or muscular injections.

In fact, Dorothy left surgery awake and coherent, unlike typical post-op patients, who were prostrate and completely sedated. Word spread through the hospital. She asked for coffee, stood up, and raised her arms—to the shock of hospital staff. "Nobody's done this before at the hospital. All these doctors and nurses are standing in the doorways," remembered Marsha Stanton, a nurse who worked with Webster at the time. "She drinks her coffee and she's fine. She's not nauseated, which usually they are."

Webster, and then others, energized by new possibilities, began treating more patients with this kind of pain control.

To Russell Portenoy, these were revolutionary times. It was cruel not to give pain-relieving opiate drugs to dying cancer patients or those emerging from surgery. Soon this was no longer a controversial opinion in America. Terminal patients no longer had to die in agony. The pendulum was swinging toward more humane pain treatment.

It thrilled him, Portenoy said later, to be able to relieve the crippling pain he saw in patients. He viewed pain management as "a white-hat" profession, made possible by pharmaceutical companies' innovations. Their powerful new pain relievers seemed far less addictive because through their timed-release formulas they eased relief out to the patient over many hours.

Now, to the patient crushed by pain, "the pain-management specialist who knows what he or she is doing can go in there and find a way to offer something that—it doesn't provide comfort, it provides hope," he said later. "I believe in drugs. I think pharmaceuticals are a great gift to humankind."

Pain and the Pro Wrestler

Seattle, Washington

John Bonica was born in Sicily, grew up in Brooklyn, and began lifting weights at age eleven. In college in Long Island and New York, he was a star collegiate wrestler. He earned his way through college and medical school as a pro wrestler. This career continued after he joined the U.S. Army before World War II. When a higher-up told him that pro wrestling was unbecoming of an officer, he donned a mask to hide his identity and became the Masked Marvel, touring with carnivals and wrestling as many as twenty people in a day. He met his future wife, Emma, at a pro wrestling match.

Pro wrestling also proved important to his future work. It partly disabled Bonica and bequeathed him lifelong chronic pain from torn hip joints, shoulder injuries, multiple rib fractures, and excruciating cauliflower ears "like two baseballs" that required plastic surgery.

"Working 15 to 18 hours a day," he told *People* magazine in 1977, kept the pain at bay.

Watching his wife go through searing pain in childbirth in 1943 set Bonica on his career as an anesthesiologist. He trained hundreds of anesthesiologists in the U.S. Army Medical Corps. After the war, he became chief anesthesiologist at Tacoma General Hospital and wrote a classic textbook, *The Management of Pain.*

Bonica opened America's first pain clinic when he was appointed chief of anesthesia at the University of Washington School of Medicine in 1960. Pain could only be salved, Bonica believed, when many disciplines within medicine, and beyond, were applied. The clinic pioneered an approach to pain that had patients see as many as fourteen specialists, who would then work out a therapy that a patient would be asked to follow in his daily life. Bonica's multidisciplinary approach was complicated and required a lot of the patient, but was often effective.

Bonica retired in 1977. His successors, Drs. Bill Fordyce and John Loeser, expanded the Center for Pain Relief at the UW medical school.

The clinic used occupational and physical therapists, psychologists, social workers, and others to treat pain. Patients spent three weeks in the clinic and left with medical and life strategies for controlling pain, such as exercise and diet—a bio-psycho-social approach, in the term Loeser coined.

"We were trying to teach [patients] that they were the ones who controlled whether they were well or not well," Loeser said. "The patient has to do the work. Chronic pain is more than something going wrong inside the person's body. It always has social and psychological factors playing a role. Physicians have traditionally ignored such things."

The UW pain clinic set itself against trends in medical marketing. Those Valium ads that years before insisted that one pill could solve a patient's problems were wrong, researchers at UW believed, at least where pain was concerned. Pain was complicated.

But "there is a philosophy among many patients—'I'm entitled to be free of pain,'" said Loeser. "People are entitled to health care. Health care should be a human right. Pain management must be a part of health care. But they are not entitled to pain relief. The physician may not be capable of providing them with pain relief. Some problems are not readily solvable. A patient is entitled to reasonable attempts to relieve the pain by reasonable means. You're not entitled to pain relief any more than you're entitled to happiness.

"But usually the patient says, 'I come to you, the doctor. Fix me.' They treat themselves like an automobile. People become believers in the philosophy that all I need is to go to my doctor and my doctor will tell me what the problem is. That attitude has been fostered by the medical community and Big Pharma. The population wants to be fixed overnight. This is the issue we addressed with chronic pain patients. They have to learn it's their body, their pain, their health. The work is done by them."

Bonica's protégés at the University of Washington were suggesting a comprehensive approach to treating pain, in which opiates played only a small role. By the early 1990s, hundreds of clinics in America followed the UW model. Yet, almost from the beginning, insurance companies balked. In time, they stopped funding crucial parts of multidisciplinary treatment that weren't strictly medical: physical, occupational, and psychological therapy, in particular. Loeser and his staff battled them incessantly. He would show the companies that the patients became healthier, and this saved the companies money in the long run. "But the people making the funding decisions have nothing whatsoever to do with health," Loeser said. "They were more and more restrictive in what they would pay for."

Thus doctors were increasingly deprived of some crucial tools to treat that pain just as patients were taught to believe that they had a right to pain relief.

The Man Comes
Los Angeles, California

The Man had come out of the west dusty and wizened. His grandfather, whose name he bore but whom he never knew, had two women, two families—one in Phoenix, the other in New Mexico. His father's half brother, whom he never knew, was murdered by Pablo Acosta, a weed smuggler and the first Mexican drug lord.

In 1939, the Man's father moved the family from New Mexico to California. The agricultural town of Brawley in California's Imperial Valley was a pit stop for Depression migrants taking the southern route into the Golden State. His parents worked on the Brawley farm of a relative, and during this time the Man was born. They then moved to Fresno, where his father became a farm labor contractor.

His parents separated when he was thirteen. He went with his mother to Van Nuys in the San Fernando Valley of Los Angeles. They found a house in the Van Nuys barrio, a place without sidewalks or much police presence. This being the 1950s, Mexican Americans, in the Valley's sea of white people, rarely ventured out of their barrios unless it was to go to work. Families in Barrio Van Nuys owned their homes. The men were employed in the lower rungs of the movie industry or as city and county workers, paving roads, landscaping public buildings. They hung out after work at the neighborhood store and drank beer under pepper trees.

The Man dropped out of Van Nuys High, got his diploma at a continuation school. By then he was also trafficking—cutting up pounds of weed and selling joints in the neighborhood. When pills—whites, reds, bennies—became the fashion, he drove to Tijuana, stayed all weekend, bought jars of them, and tripled his money back in Van Nuys. He liked to think that he was something of a shot caller among his generation. He was nineteen. About then he started using heroin. Many of the young men in Barrio Van Nuys used it and most of them died young.

He became a steamfitter later, and had other jobs, two marriages, and children, but mostly he was, as he put it years later, a "drug merchant." He liked to see himself as sticking it to the Establishment, living outside the law. He served several prison terms; it usually took less than forty-eight hours of freedom before he was shooting up again. Not much mattered to him but the drug. He bought houses for his family, his kids. Mostly, though, money was to be used to get more dope. About the only other thing that held his interest for so many years was gambling on NFL games.

What bedeviled him was a reliable source of heroin supply. His sources had always been difficult to maintain. People were always going to jail, or he was. Or they died. Either way, it was always a battle to find consistently good-quality heroin in large amounts.

In the 1970s, he met a guy, a relative of a lieutenant of Ernesto "Don Neto" Fonseca. Fonseca was a grizzled Mexican drug kingpin who later gained infamy, and a life prison term, for his part in organizing the Sinaloa drug cartel. Fonseca's nephew, Rafael Caro Quintero, joined him behind bars for arranging the torture killing of DEA agent Enrique "Kiki" Camarena in 1985.

The Man and his contact took the train down to Mexico to buy a kilo from Fonseca. They met the legendary capo in the hotel he built in downtown Culiacán, the sweltering capital of Sinaloa, the birthplace of Mexican trafficking.

"I'm gonna give you this kilo and see what you guys can do with it up there," Fonseca told them. "I'd like to open a market up there. You guys do right and I'll keep supplying you."

For four months, they did Don Neto right and he kept sending them kilos. Then they were arrested and the Fonseca connection disappeared. The Man found other sources in Mexicali, which didn't last long either.

But all that was years ago.

When I met him, the Man was slowed by a liver problem. His eyelids often hung at half-mast. Years of trafficking, gambling, and spiking his veins had sapped him, in his seventies, of any real mirth. He never read novels, only nonfiction. His laugh issued from him as a dry chuckle, thin as cardboard.

But when he was in his late fifties, he had happened on a scheme that would, in his eyes, make his life worthwhile. It involved bringing black tar heroin to new people and places east of the Mississippi River. He had blown into these cities across America like a wind, a different name in every town, in old used cars that were gray or beige. He left behind a drug that would change these places, and bring misery to thousands of families.

Through the 1990s, that drug, in turn, transformed the small Mexican town of Xalisco, Nayarit, a place he would come to view as his own, where he would buy property and keep a woman. He was a contemporary of David Tejeda, whom he knew, though not well. Tejeda was among the pioneers to ignite the first stage of the Xalisco heroin expansion in the early 1990s. The Man began the second, in 1998. So, after I tracked him down, I visited him often and listened to him talk about the past. He held the answer, I came to realize, to how black tar heroin crossed the Mississippi River to stay.

He liked to think himself a hero to the young men from the small town of Xalisco, Nayarit, whom he recruited and taught to retail the drug. "I'd have fathers and mothers come ask me for work for their sons, knowing exactly what they were going to do, exactly what I did," he said one day in the living room of his Central Valley home. "These are people who are dirt poor. They see all these other young kids with new trucks, building houses, mothers and fathers driving around in a half-nice pickup. Then the kid's bugging them, 'I want to go up north.'"

Initially, the market they sold to was older addicts like him—the heroin underworld that had survived since the 1970s, when the drug was last popular. But as it happened, illicit use of another drug—a pharmaceutical called OxyContin—was creating a vast new market for heroin among middle- and upper-class white people. Folks with money. When he heard about OxyContin, he began to follow it, knowing that if he did, he would soon have a market.

The relentless Xalisco retail delivery system evolved as it fed on this ever-growing base of customers addicted to OxyContin in America and on the deep frustration of young, landless working-class men in Mexico. These men did not form a cartel. They could not. The envidia—small-town jealousy—and the wild-bronco attitudes that rule Mexican ranchos prevented grand organizations from forming. "Families cannot work together," the Man told me. "We're real envious of each other."

But precisely because they could not, their heroin system became pernicious and successful. It aroused the entrepreneurial spirit of rancheros, young and driven, as it harnessed a cheap and addictive product to the power of small-scale free-market capitalism. The system marked a radical departure in the way Mexican traffickers sold and profited from dope, and it challenged U.S. law enforcement.

"We didn't start the heroin-dealing business. We just used a different method," the Man said. "We weren't a cartel. We were all different cells. Everybody's their own group. There's the boss of each little group. They all work individually. There's some heavy dudes; some who are mediocre and some who are trying to make it. Some go bust. Some got a lot."

The Revolution

IN 1986, RUSSELL PORTENOY, then thirty-one, and his mentor, Kathy Foley, published what became a declaration of independence for the vanguard of pain specialists interested in using opiates for chronic pain, though Portenoy hardly intended it as such.

Other researchers had been issuing papers saying that many chronic-pain patients using opiates invariably ended up addicted. Portenoy and Foley hadn't seen that. They reviewed the cases of thirty-eight of their cancer patients with chronic pain who used opiate painkillers. Only two grew addicted, and they had histories of drug abuse. The rest functioned well and most of them without pain, to boot.

Portenoy and Foley wrote a paper reporting those observations and submitted it to a medical journal called *Pain*. Opiates themselves were not inherently addictive, the authors suggested; a lot depended on the people taking them.

Cited among the footnotes supporting the paper was a letter to the editor, by Jane Porter and Dr. Hershel Jick out of Boston, in a 1980 edition of the *New England Journal of Medicine*. It was headlined "Addiction Rare in Patients Treated with Narcotics."

The idea in the *Pain* paper, Portenoy said later, was that "these drugs have certain characteristics, which, when interacting with a certain kind of brain, can lead to bad outcomes; but it's not inherent in the pill such that everybody given that pill becomes an addict."

From that gradually grew the idea that opiates might be prescribed not only to people dying from cancer but to others, perhaps those with chronic pain, a far more controversial idea. The paper warned against prescribing them for patients with a history of drug abuse. In later interviews and research, Portenoy made clear he believed a doctor needed to spend a good deal of time with each patient, delving into his or her medical and family history. He described a questionnaire a doctor should give to patients to determine the risk of addiction in each individual. He proposed two famous extremes: a teetotaling seventy-plus-year-old woman with bleeding ulcers and osteoarthritis, and a twenty-something kid who's smoked weed for several years, has tattoos on his back, and suffers chronic pain in his knees from surgery a year before. The former was at far less risk of opiate addiction than the latter. Yet most of the decisions a family doctor had to make—for family docs were on the front lines in prescribing pain relievers—were far more complicated. What about the forty-year-old construction worker, with a brother in jail, who in his early twenties drank a lot, but who is successfully raising a family and suffers from chronic back pain?

That *Pain* paper, which Portenoy believed would be forgotten, was instead feverishly debated. With Foley and Sloan Kettering's name on the paper, it convulsed the consensus against the limited use of opiates. Portenoy was attacked personally. Treating chronic pain with opiates went against so many long-held medical beliefs. The drugs were dangerous and addictive, many felt, when used that way. One researcher wrote to *Pain* claiming Portenoy and Foley did not understand the nature of pain.

"The anger that that paper generated, and people buttonholing me at conferences and telling me that I was a bad guy and stuff that makes that even sound good," Portenoy later told an interviewer. "It was really an interesting time to live through."

Against this vehement reaction, Foley and Portenoy viewed themselves as warriors on patients' behalf, cracking a tired prohibitionist dogma that had outlived its usefulness, particularly as technology and drugs advanced.

Nodes of support for their position emerged around the country.

One was Salt Lake City. Lynn Webster's acute-pain service at Holy Cross Hospital was only part of it. Pain researchers and clinics congregated in Utah seeking other ways of treating pain patients. The state's Mormon population stayed put, so clinicians could do a study on a group of people, followed by another five years later, and five years after that with the same people. Moreover, while many Utahans, as Mormons, didn't consume caffeine, nicotine, and other drugs, the clandestine use of prescription pills, primarily painkillers, had taken hold, giving clinicians ample opportunity to study addiction.

Among the people eager for a new approach to pain treatment was Webster's nurse, Marsha Stanton. Stanton was raised a Christian Scientist, but went to nursing school. She grew into her career in the

1960s and 1970s, years when physicians and medical instructors insisted on the chary use of opiates, no matter the patient. "We were all—nurses, pharmacists, physicians—taught: Don't overdose, don't overdose. You give the smallest amount of medication over the longest period of time because you don't want to give a patient too much, for fear of addiction."

But during the 1980s, medications and technology were making new treatment possible. Old attitudes began to fade. From Utah, Webster, Michael Ashburn, Perry Fine, Brad Hare, and Richard Chapman emerged as pain clinicians and thought leaders, along with Portenoy and others in New York. Soon a critical mass was reached and an effervescent pain-management scene developed in Salt Lake. This new Salt Lake pain vanguard held monthly meetings that attracted a hundred people at a time to listen to speakers, discuss new techniques in pain management, and put the old days behind them.

"Salt Lake City became one of the meccas for the new and innovative kinds of things," said Stanton. "We were interested in better patient care. What we had done for all these years wasn't working. I remember lecturing many, many times and saying I feel so badly that I treated patients so poorly for so long. But we have the technology now that we didn't have before."

An idea advanced that pain counteracted opiates' euphoric effect and thus reduced the risk of addiction. In a statement on its website, the American Pain Society claimed that risk of addiction was low when opiates are used to treat patients in pain. There appeared to be no ceiling on the dose of opiate painkillers a pain patient might take. Pain, the APS went on, acted against the tendency of opiates to stop the lungs from breathing. Thus, withholding the drugs "on the basis of respiratory concerns is unwarranted."

Changes in attitudes and techniques in pain treatment were coming quickly. Anesthesiologists found a new role in medicine. Before, anesthesiologists left the patients after surgery. Now they could accompany patients through days or weeks of postoperative recovery, tending to new techniques, such as the epidural that Lynn Webster had given Dorothy. More anesthesiologists became pain specialists. Specialists required nurses. American Society for Pain Management Nursing formed in 1990, funded largely by the Baxter company, and within a couple years had more than two thousand members.

In 1996, the president of the American Pain Society, Dr. James Campbell, said in a speech that "if pain were assessed with the same zeal as other vital signs are, it would have a much better chance of being treated properly. We need to train doctors and nurses to treat pain as a vital sign."

The American Pain Society trademarked the slogan "Pain: The Fifth Vital Sign" and used it to promote the idea that doctors should attend to pain as routinely as to the other vital signs.

In 1998, the Veterans Health Administration made pain a "fifth vital sign"—another gauge of a patient's baseline health, along with pulse, blood pressure, body temperature, and respiration. The Joint Commission for Accreditation of Healthcare Organizations (JCAHO)—which accredits sixteen thousand health care organizations in the United States—did the same. Hospitals were now to be judged on how they assessed, and treated, a patient's pain. The California legislature required hospitals and nursing homes to screen for pain along with the other vital signs. The state's Board of Pharmacy was by then assuring members that "studies show [opiates have] an extremely low potential for abuse" when used correctly.

From all this, the idea took hold that America was undertreating pain. Tens of millions of people, surveys reported, were in pain that wasn't being treated. Pain's undertreatment was viewed as an unnecessary epidemic, for medicine now had tools to treat it. A 2001 survey of a thousand people living at home with pain due to a medical condition reported: Half couldn't remember what it felt like to not be in pain, 40 percent said pain was constant, and 22 percent said they suffered severe pain. Only 13 percent had seen a pain specialist.

Doctors and medical associations, however, were worried. Prescribing these drugs might lead to addiction. They demanded legal clarity. So, beginning with California, states passed laws exempting doctors from prosecution if they prescribed opiates for pain within the practice of responsible health care. Numerous states approved so-called intractable pain regulations: Ohio, Oregon, Washington, and others.

Soon what can only be described as a revolution in medical thought and practice was under way. Doctors were urged to begin attending to the country's pain epidemic by prescribing these drugs. Interns and residents were taught that these drugs were now not addictive, that doctors thus had a mission, a duty, to use them. In some hospitals, doctors were told they could be sued if they did not treat pain aggressively, which meant with opiates.

Russell Portenoy, meanwhile, was made director of the Pain Medicine and Palliative Care department at Beth Israel Medical Center in New York City—the country's first such department at a major hospital. From this vantage point, and with funding from several drug companies, he pressed a campaign to destigmatize opiates. The drug company Baxter and others produced intravenous patient-controlled analgesia (PCA) pumps, allowing patients to administer their own pain-killer with the push of a button. In Tulsa, Oklahoma, two pediatric nurses—Donna Wong and her colleague, Connie Baker—sought a way of assessing pain in children who had trouble describing what they felt. Wong was incorrectly diagnosed with leukemia as a child, and subjected to painful operations without the aid of analgesics. She became a nurse. In the 1980s, with the smiley face fad in recent memory, the women devised a series of six faces a child could point to. The chart begins with a smiling face and ends with a tearful, grimacing face. The Wong-Baker FACES scale is now a standard in gauging pain in children. There are other versions for adults. Patients are asked to quantify their pain according to a scale—numbered from 0 to 10, 10 being worst. These scales were highly subjective, but they were about the only pain-measurement tools medicine had to offer.

Crucial implements in the revolution were Press Ganey surveys. Designed by a physician and a statistician, the surveys gauged patient satisfaction with their doctors. The surveys were a reasonable idea. They became widely used at U.S. hospitals in the 1990s as patient rights grew paramount and the JCAHO began aggressively measuring how hospitals treated patient pain.

Through all this, patients were getting used to demanding drugs for treatment. They did not, however, have to accept the idea that they might, say, eat better and exercise more, and that this might help them lose weight and feel better. Doctors, of course, couldn't insist. As the defenestration of the physician's authority and clinical experience was under way, patients didn't have to take accountability for their own behavior.

All this happened in about a decade. In a country where doctors once feared opiates, a culture of aggressive opiate use was emerging by the mid-1990s. This had support from several quarters: pain specialists and medical school professors, the JCAHO, the drug companies, even hospital lawyers, and so on. Ideas cross-pollinated at the pain conferences that now sprouted around the United States—supported by the pharmaceutical companies that had new medications and technologies to sell. Like-minded people met and questioned old therapies and authorities. At the core of this culture was the idea that these painkillers were virtually nonaddictive when used to treat pain.

Proponents of this approach tried to embed it with nuance. The VHA cited patients' homelessness, PTSD, injuries, and substance abuse in advising that "the complexity of chronic pain management is often beyond the expertise of a single practitioner." Primary care doctors should consult pain specialists and multidisciplinary pain clinics. One paper in the International Association for the Study of Pain called pain assessment not an isolated event but an "ongoing process," which evolved with new evidence and patient input.

"The fifth vital sign" was a "concept, not a guide for pain assessment," one report read. Along with the pain number scale, a doctor ought to ask numerous questions about a patient's pain history, the pain's location, severity, impact on daily life, as well as the patient's family history, substance abuse, psychological issues, and so on. In fact, pain was really *not* a vital sign, after all, for unlike the four real vital signs it cannot be measured objectively and with exactitude. The National Pharmaceutical Council advised that "the manner in which information is elicited from the patient is important. Ideally, the clinician should afford ample time, let the patient tell the story in his or her own words, and ask open-ended questions."

Time was the key. Chronic-pain patients took more time than most to diagnose. Problem was doctors had *less* time. Just as patient rights were emphasized and surveys were circulating asking them to judge their doctors' performance, patients were in fact losing their most precious medical commodity: time with their doctors.

With the managed care movement of the 1980s and 1990s, insurance companies cut costs and reduced what services they'd pay for. They required that patients give up their longtime physicians for those on a list of approved providers. They negotiated lower fees with doctors. To make up the difference, primary care docs had to fit more patients into a day. (A *Newsweek* story claimed that to do a good job a primary care doctor ought to have a roster of eighteen hundred patients. The average load today is twenty-three hundred, with some seeing up to three thousand.)

"The way you're reimbursed in a day, if you actually take the time to treat somebody's pain, you'd be out of business," one longtime family doc told me. "By the model you're stuck in, you can't do it. The hospital will get rid of you. If you're by yourself, you can't pay for your secretary."

So as the movement to destigmatize opiates and use them for chronic pain gained energy, the seeds of discontent were already being sown. These drugs were advertised mostly to primary care physicians, who had little pain-management training and were making their money by churning patients through their offices at a thirteen-minute clip. Not much time for nuance. Not much time for listening, or for open-ended questions that might elicit long and complicated answers. On the contrary, just as Valium helped doctors deal with anxious patients in the 1960s, opiates helped a harried doctor with what was now the largest drain on his time: chronic-pain patients. As the movement gained strength from new drugs and devices, the crucial ingredient in pain management—the amount of time a doctor could spend with each patient—fell. Digging through all this, I found at least two studies that showed that prescribing of all kinds rose as doctor visits shortened. Not surprising. As every doctor knows, nothing cuts short a patient visit like a prescription pad.

The Press Ganey patient surveys, it turned out, had an unintended effect in this context. It was to subtly pressure doctors to write unnecessary scripts for opiates. A doctor reluctant to write them was more likely to get a poor patient evaluation. Too many bad scores and a hospital began asking questions.

"I get raises, and keep my job, based on whether I'm keeping my patients happy," said a nursing supervisor I spoke with. "When the Joint Commission surveyed us they looked through charts looking at pain. They were looking at other things, but pain was the number one thing. They just hammered and hammered on pain. You had to control everybody's pain. The [Press Ganey] scores were one way they measured how the doctors were doing."

And there was another problem. No one had done serious, long-term studies of whether opiates actually were nonaddictive when used by such patients. Years later, in fact, there still is no evidence of how many chronic-pain patients can be successfully treated with opiates without growing dependent, then addicted. Determining who is a good candidate for opiate treatment is a mystery, and particularly difficult when doctors have no pain-management training and only thirteen minutes with each patient.

The new pain movement pushed past these doubts. It acquired a quasi-religious fervor among people seared by the nontreatment of pain of years past. A pendulum began to swing. The cruelty of earlier times discredited those who might question the emerging doctrine of opiates for chronic pain. Pain specialists working toward a new day felt gratitude to pharmaceutical companies for developing the drugs and devices that made possible the humane treatment of pain. Among them was Purdue Frederick, which in 1991 formed an associated company,

Purdue Pharma, that in turn grew into a leader in timed-release pain medications. Purdue was unknown to the public, but well-known to pain specialists. It was leading the way with new tools in pain treatment, MS Contin above all, but with other drugs on the way. The company also had attempted to control theft by developing a database to aid law enforcement investigations into pharmacy robberies.

"For those of us doing pain management, that was the ultimate; Purdue was *the* company," Marsha Stanton said. "They had done everything right. They'd blown onto the market. They had supported the clinicians, supported the education. They had done everything we thought they should have."

Purdue, in particular, funded pain researchers, many of whom saw the company as an innovator and ally. This included Russell Portenoy. Portenoy, in turn, spoke frequently and with passion at conferences of primary care doctors, urging them to consider new approaches to pain that included opiates, and timed-release opiates in particular.

Years after his *Pain* paper, suggesting that pain patients treated with opiates might not be at risk of addiction, Portenoy said it was based on "weak, weak, weak data" and called it "a little paper [that] turned into an important paper."

Nevertheless, with that 1986 paper, a debate among researchers broke wide open. That debate quaked medical practice and changed the lives of people oblivious to these discussions going on in the corridors of hospitals and medical academia. The great new question of pain management was: Can opiate painkillers be used without risk of addiction by chronic-pain patients, who would live for years, in the same way that these drugs were now used on patients dying of cancer?

With crusaders' confidence, and fed in part by the discovery of what was increasingly called a "report" in the *New England Journal of Medicine* coauthored by a Boston doctor named Hershel Jick, more and more people—especially Dr. Russell Portenoy and salespeople from the little-known pharmaceutical company, Purdue Pharma, which was about to release a new painkiller—answered yes.

All About the 501s

Boise, Idaho

From what Ed Ruplinger could tell, there was nothing dumb about Polla.

Polla was a Mexican in his midforties. He was about five feet nine and the type of guy who could have easily grown heavy had he not gone to the gym, which he did a lot. Polla was trim, conservative, respectable, and looked to the world like a small businessman. He had a wife back in Mexico who nagged him about doing the books, about making sure the flow of inventory was reliable, and that his salesmen weren't abusing their expense accounts out in the field.

Polla's real name was Cesar Garcia-Langarica. He was in the black tar heroin business and he was from Xalisco, Nayarit, on Mexico's Pacific coast. It was 1995 and Ed Ruplinger was a narcotics investigator with a drug task force in Boise, Idaho.

Polla's young workers were both the source of his profits and the bane of his existence. Motivating them while he was out of town took most of his working hours. He did this without threat or coercion, and handled their misadventures with patience, it seemed to Ruplinger. When one of them crashed into a sign outside the complex where Polla had rented them an apartment, he appeared at the manager's office the next day with money to pay for the damage. Ruplinger heard this story from the apartment complex manager.

Through the 1990s, the Xalisco system had refined through trial and error. The Boys compared notes at barbecues back in Xalisco and slowly a set of rules evolved that was passed along like folklore. One rule: no violence. At the time, the best-known drug gangs, the Bloods and Crips, shot it out over crack cocaine on street corners in towns far from Los Angeles, garnering police attention wherever they went. Watching all this, the Xalisco Boys quietly began to expand nationwide by doing exactly the opposite. Polla was part of that 1990s expansion and one place he showed up was Boise.

Ruplinger's interest was first piqued when the drug unit suddenly began arresting Mexican drivers tooling around town selling heroin in balloons they kept in their mouths. They were easy to spot and bust, particularly with the help of addicts who, once arrested, were terrified of withdrawing in jail. As Dennis Chavez had seen in Denver, and as drug agents elsewhere would later discover, Ruplinger noticed that these Mexican drivers often had only a small amount of heroin and no weapons. So they never did much jail time. But it struck Ruplinger's best police nerve that whenever he could determine where they were from, it turned out they were from a state in Mexico called Nayarit. What's more, these guys were replaced within a couple of days. After a while, Ruplinger realized it didn't matter how many Nayarit heroin drivers his task force arrested, more drivers filled the open slots.

Anybody could have taken the case, but Ed Ruplinger alone set about trying to answer the questions that arose as the Ada Metro Narcotics Task Force arrested more and more of these drivers. Who was behind them? he wondered. It was way too organized. This could not be unique to Boise, which was no one's natural choice of a place to start up a drug-dealing enterprise. It had to have started somewhere else.

Ruplinger had been puzzling this out for a few weeks, and not getting very far, when he first noticed Garcia-Langarica's name. It surfaced on the apartment records of these drivers, or the cars they drove. One day, Ruplinger watched a driver swing by an apartment building and pass a trim fellow some money. Here, clearly, was the boss, Ruplinger thought.

Yet the first time Ruplinger and his colleagues followed Polla, the suspected ringleader walked into a Mexican restaurant and took his place as a cook behind the grill. The man Ruplinger took for a heroin kingpin appeared instead to be a simple cook and not worth the unit's time. But Ruplinger's hunch proved correct. A month later Garcia-Langarica quit the job. From then on, when Polla was in town, he spent all his time supervising his heroin drivers.

Polla's drivers had been operating for a while and seemed to have Boise to themselves. Then a sharp-eyed postal inspector, just before Christmas 1996, came upon a package that alerted a drug-sniffing dog. Inside was a Santa Claus doll and inside the doll was black tar heroin. The local narcotics task force, which included Ruplinger, had the parcel delivered to the apartment it was addressed to. A Boise drug team burst in and found four well-dressed, middle-aged Mexican men sitting around a card table already breaking up the heroin into small packets. They, too, were all from the state of Nayarit—last name of Tejeda.

The Santa Claus bust actually marked the beginning of the end of Polla's dominion over Boise. Ruplinger figured that word of Boise had spread among the Nayarit heroin traffickers, and crew after crew descended on the town to compete with Polla and what he had set up in Idaho's capital. One of Polla's former drivers ran a new cell, Ruplinger was amazed to note. He had gone back to Mexico, then returned to Boise with his own drivers, a dispatcher, and a supply source to compete head-to-head with his former boss.

"Polla was one of the founding fathers. He comes in and sets it all up," Ruplinger said, when we met in Boise. "The word gets out back home. Then every operative in Nayarit ends up moving in."

MUCH LATER, AS I continued to piece through the story of the Xalisco Boys, I met a woman who said she was married to one of the drivers who worked for Polla back in the mid-1990s. Polla, she said, started in the San Fernando Valley, but competition pushed him to move his cells to Pomona and Ontario, forty miles east of Los Angeles. His drivers often hung out at her mother's restaurant in Pomona, she said. There she met one of Polla's drivers, married him, and had children with him. They visited Xalisco twice.

When we met, she told me that her now ex-husband had helped start a cell for Polla in Salt Lake City in the 1990s, then broke off and began competing with him; her brother-in-law helped open Boise for Polla, then also started his own cell there in competition with his ex-boss.

At the time, the cities had only small populations of heroin addicts, people scrounging every day to get their fix. A stagnant market left only one place to get customers. "We were just poaching from Polla," she said. "We would make the balloons bigger to attract [his] customers. Then we'd give specials, six for a hundred dollars instead of just five. It was a back-and-forth competition. 'Don't go with them. We can give you a better deal.'"

But as we talked, what she told me about her ex and his family intrigued me even more. He came from a family that had land and farm animals; they grew sugarcane and made cheese. They were middle-class by the standards of Mexican farm communities, she said. I expected most of these traffickers had come from the dirt-poorest families. That was true of the drivers, particularly those who came later, she said, but most of the heroin pioneers of Xalisco County were the sons of farmers who were pretty well-off, again by Mexican agricultural standards. They had some money to invest. With resources also came broader horizons of what was possible and what they wanted, or expected, from life.

Selling heroin was just easier than growing sugarcane; it was more adventurous, and involved more cash. It gave them the means to build better houses, and this set off a construction boom across Xalisco County that employed dozens if not hundreds of construction workers by the end of the 1990s. The houses went up in a few months, not in a decade. No house in downtown Xalisco had rebar extending from the top of it. That was the difference between Xalisco and every other Mexican immigrant town. Xalisco had notably less rebar.

Then she said something strange. After building their houses, and providing for their families, what the guys she knew from Xalisco, Nayarit, seemed to want most of all were Levi's 501s.

Levi's 501s were the pantswear gold standard for men in Mexico's ranchos in the 1990s. They were very expensive in Mexico. One thing that made the Xalisco Boys' retail system so popular, and young men eager to work in it, was that the system provided a way to accumulate quantities, large stacks, of 501s very cheaply. That was because U.S. junkies soon learned these dealers' tastes and offered endless supplies of shoplifted 501s in exchange for their daily dope. Before long the junkies took orders according to size and color and traded them two for one: two pairs of 501s for one twenty-dollar balloon of black tar.

While she was married into the Xalisco world, "it was more about the jeans than anything," she told me. "From day one, any opportunity to barter for jeans—they'd take it. They had stacks of jeans. They'd bring back home exactly the sizes people wanted."

This thirst for Levi's 501s, she said, is part of what propelled the Xalisco system as it began to expand out of the San Fernando Valley and through the western United States in the mid-1990s. Back in the ranchos, nothing said that a man had moved up in the world like walking around in public in dark-blue 501s. Seeing others in brand-new Levi's 501s, meanwhile, inspired many youngsters—who had only thin, cheap jeans, if they had any at all—to hire on as drivers.

The more I asked about Levi's 501s as fuel to the expansion of the Xalisco heroin networks, the more people had to say about it.

"I once brought home fifty pairs of Levi's, in suitcases, which I took with me coming down on the bus from California," said one Xalisco trafficker who worked crews from San Fernando Valley to Columbus, and eventually was made manger of a crew in Denver as well. "I'd get them from clients who'd steal them from Sears. Many dealers like me were bringing back big quantities of Levi's. I'd give them away to friends and my family. But then after a while they started demanding them. `Send me this, send me that.' Then they wanted shirts, tennis shoes. They wanted everything."

Levi's 501s were, in fact, part of a larger keep-up-with-the-Joneses competition that heroin revenue fueled back in the small town. Very quickly, the families got caught up in this. Around town, the gossip would start weeks in advance: So-and-so's coming home with gifts and then we're going to kill a cow and he's going to pay for the banda. Every trafficker's return was like Christmas Day as relatives lined up for gifts, especially those jeans. Some traffickers came pulling trailers full of clothes.

"The family wants more and more and more, so the guys start feeling the pressure," the ex-wife I interviewed told me. "'Give me, give me. You need to provide for me.' Their own family starts thinking they deserve this. My ex's sister was demanding, 'You need to give me this, or you need to give me that.' Whatever's yours is mine. My ex used to send all kinds of clothes home. First it was 501s, but then later it was 'I want Guess jeans,' then Tommy Hilfigers."

Just as an addict couldn't choose not to use dope, these men couldn't *not* return to sell it. Up north, they slept on the floors of apartments, unwilling to invest even in a mattress, awaiting the day when they could go home bearing gifts. Once back in Xalisco, she said, they walked the town the object of other men's envy, paying for the banda and the beer, and surrounded by women. And no driver ever wanted to miss the Feria del Elote in August. "That's when you get to show off the most," she said. "It's like a kid going to Disneyland for the first time. They walk around with their chest out. Everybody looks at them."

I imagined their *mu* receptors jolted in endorphins.

"They live for it. They save their fricking pennies for it," she said. "It's a euphoria. They get high on it. They're in fantasyland, in a dream where they think they're the kings. Until the money runs out."

Thus with an addict's energy and single-mindedness, she said, the Xalisco Boys sought new markets with higher profit margins, awaiting the chance to go back home, the kings of their dreamland for a week or two. Only the self-centeredness of addiction, she said, explained how farm boys from a traditional and conservative small town could sell a product, anathema to their parents, to sad-eyed, vulnerable junkies and not be tormented.

"I used to work in a laboratory where they did research on animals, and have to kill them," the ex-wife said. "The way you deal with that is you disassociate yourself from that animal. You don't let it get to you. You put up that barrier. That's what they do. They do that with people."

ED RUPLINGER STRUGGLED TO keep up as more crews started up in Boise. He created timelines and flow charts of connections between Polla and drivers and other U.S. cities. Others in the unit thought he was crazy. When had Boise figured in any kind of international narcotics conspiracy? Plus so many Hispanic names wearied the mind.

Ruplinger got permission to run wiretaps on Polla's phones. The extent of Polla's business then grew clearer. He had crews in Portland, too, and in Salt Lake City and Honolulu. Salt Lake did more business than Boise. Ruplinger heard Polla complain that he left Denver because it got so he couldn't make any money there with crews from his hometown competing for the same addicts. New cells took his clients and to win them back he had to lower his prices.

Ruplinger marveled at how massive and connected the Xalisco network was. Polla's heroin store practiced just-in-time supply, with women as mules every couple weeks bringing up a pound of heroin at a time. Keen to keep competitors at bay, Polla insisted that his drivers provide excellent customer service. Once when a driver reported a customer complaint of a bad batch of dope, Polla promised to make it right; the driver delivered better-quality stuff to the client the next day. When Ruplinger heard that, he felt he was watching the expansion of some new scary thing, as if he were all alone in a lab where a virus had escaped its test tube.

One day, Ruplinger heard one of the drivers tell Polla that he was afraid of delivering to the nearby town of Caldwell because the gangs there scared him. Polla told him he'd handle it. The conversation stayed with Ruplinger, who had worked in Southern California and knew that the gangs in tiny Caldwell were but faint echoes of gangs elsewhere. What kind of drug crew was this that was scared of the wannabe gangs of Caldwell, Idaho?

Every narcotics agent in the 1990s had the Bloods and Crips crack warfare as a precedent, and the Colombian cocaine cowboys in Miami before that. The Nayarits weren't that way. With faith in their addictive product, they didn't need to shoot it out for territory. These drivers knew each other, and would stop to chat or meet for lunch. Even as they competed and drove down each other's prices, they did so in peace. They went out of their way to avoid attention. It helped that the drivers had no investment in how much they sold, and that they didn't use. There was no incentive for them to cut their dope. They didn't make any more money if they cut it than if they sold it as it came. They were employees, guys on a salary, with their costs covered and a stipend of several hundred dollars a week. The last thing they wanted was violence.

In two years, from 1995 to 1997, Boise's minor market had a half-dozen crews selling heroin like pizza. But that wasn't all. From the wiretaps, Ruplinger heard Polla call Phoenix, Ontario, El Monte, Salt Lake, Portland, Billings, Las Vegas, Honolulu. If Boise had a half dozen, how many crews must Denver have? What about Portland? Las Vegas? The heroin cells were like ants in a garden: You didn't see them unless you got close enough and knew what to look for. Then, even when you stamped them out, more came to take their place.

It was 1997. Well before most other cops in the country, Ed Ruplinger was figuring out how to see the ants.

The Landmark Study

BY THE 1990S, IT would have alarmed Dr. Hershel Jick, out in Boston, to know that his letter to the editor of the *New England Journal of Medicine*, which he had long forgotten, had become a foundation for a revolution in U.S. medical practice. This was wildly beyond anything Herschel Jick intended when he penned it.

But that's what happened. The revolution extended to hospitals, medical clinics, and family practices across the country.

It's unclear who retrieved the Porter and Jick letter from obscurity. But it appears to have been cited first as a footnote in Kathy Foley and Russell Portenoy's 1986 paper in *Pain*. In time, the paragraph became known simply as Porter and Jick. That shorthand, in turn, lent prestige to the tiny thing and the claim attributed to it: that less than 1 percent of patients treated with narcotics developed addictions to them.

That "less than 1 percent" statistic stuck. But a crucial point was lost: Jick's database consisted of *hospitalized* patients from years when opiates were strictly controlled in hospitals and given in tiny doses to those suffering the most acute pain, all overseen by doctors. These were not chronic-pain patients going home with bottles of pain pills. It was a bizarre misinterpretation, for Jick's letter really supported a contrary claim: that when used in hospitals for acute pain, and then when mightily controlled, opiates rarely produce addiction. Nevertheless, its message was transformed into that broad headline: "Addiction Rare in Patients Treated with Narcotics."

Others began citing its purported claim. Marsha Stanton remembers citing Porter and Jick frequently in educational seminars that she gave through the 1990s to doctors and nurses on pain treatment: "Everybody heard it everywhere. It was Porter and Jick. We all used it. We all thought it was gospel."

A lot went into making it so. Porter and Jick appeared in that bible of scholarly and journalistic rectitude, the *New England Journal of Medicine*. Medical professionals assumed everyone else had read it. But only in 2010 did the *NEJM* put all its archives online; before that, the archives only went back to 1993. To actually look up Porter and Jick, to discover that it was a one-paragraph letter to the editor, and *not* a scientific study, required going to a medical school library and digging up the actual issue, which took time most doctors didn't have. Instead, primary care docs took the word of pain specialists, who pointed to Porter and Jick as evidence that opiates were far less addictive for chronic-pain patients than previously thought. Not that primary care doctors needed much encouragement. Chronic-pain patients, desperate for relief, could be insistent, rude, and abusive to staff, and took a lot of time to diagnose and treat. Physicians had a mantra: "One chronic-pain patient can ruin your whole day." Now a solution was at hand.

That single paragraph, buried in the back pages of the *New England Journal of Medicine*, was mentioned, lectured on, and cited until it emerged transformed into, in the words of one textbook, a "landmark report" that "did much to counteract" fears of addiction in pain patients treated with opiates. It did nothing of the kind.

In a 1989 monograph for the National Institutes of Health, physicians from Harvard and Johns Hopkins urged readers to "consider the work" of Porter and Jick, which showed "clearly" that fear of addiction in those with no past drug abuse didn't justify avoiding opiates, since the "study" showed that addiction among patients "given these drugs in a hospital setting was extremely low." One researcher, writing in 1990 in *Scientific American*, called Porter and Jick "an extensive study." A paper for the Institute for Clinical Systems Improvement called Porter and Jick "a landmark report."

Then, the final anointing: *Time* magazine in a 2001 story titled "Less Pain, More Gain," called Porter and Jick a "landmark study" showing that the "exaggerated fear that patients would become addicted" to opiates was "basically unwarranted."

For years in medical schools, Marsha Stanton recalled, "I clearly remember instructors saying, 'Don't overdose, don't overdose, don't overdose. Don't make these patients addicted.' But now here's this statistic: Look, oh, it's in print. It's gospel. I used [Porter and Jick] in lectures all the time. Everybody did. It didn't matter whether you were a physician, a pharmacist, or a nurse; you used it. No one disputed it. Should we have? Of course we should have."

Everyone knew of opiates' painkilling benefits. But how *addictive* were they? That was the question. Most doctors figured history and experience showed that the answer was: very. Porter and Jick, as it was cited, suggested otherwise. So did Dr. Portenoy: Depending on the patient, he believed, these drugs might be used to great advantage.

Portenoy was a pain-management pioneer. In addition to his Beth Israel appointment, he was an editor in chief at the *Journal of Pain and Symptom Management*, an editor at *Pain*, and on the editorial board of other medical journals. He would write numerous books, textbooks that students used in medical school. He was quoted often in newspapers. Above all, Portenoy took his message on the road to the kinds of association conferences where new ideas in medicine are proposed: the International Association for the Study of Pain, the American Pain Society, the American Academy of Pain Medicine.

All of this helped create, by the mid-1990s, a new conventional wisdom that science had advanced and now knew that opiates wouldn't addict a pain patient. Addicts and pain patients were two different things. "With addicts, their quality of life goes down as they use drugs," one leading pain doctor, Scott Fishman, told *New York* magazine in 2000. "With pain patients, it improves. They're entirely different phenomena."

This spelled bad times for the more complicated multidisciplinary approach to pain. Why, after all, was all that effort necessary if pain patients could be given pills with little risk of addiction? Patients, too, were hard to motivate when the treatment required behavior changes, such as more exercise. Pills were an easier solution. Multidisciplinary clinics began to fade. Over a thousand such clinics existed nationwide in 1998; only eighty five were around seven years later.

Out in Seattle, Dr. John Loeser and his staff soldiered on at the University of Washington's Center for Pain Relief, expanding on the ideas of John Bonica. But as insurance companies stopped paying for pain services, the university's medical center eliminated them. In 1998, Loeser resigned in disgust. The university eventually moved the historic clinic to a basement. There it remained, a game preserve of sorts for a few multidisciplinary holdouts who kept their heads down. A plastic surgery unit moved into the space the pain clinic once occupied.

Use of opiates, meanwhile, changed medical thinking. Usually, a patient demanding ever-higher doses of a drug would be proof that the drug wasn't working. But in opiate pain treatment, it was taken as proof that the doctor hadn't yet prescribed enough. Indeed, some doctors came to believe that a pain patient demanding higher doses was likely to be exhibiting signs of "pseudoaddiction," looking for a dose large enough to kill the pain—the cure for which was more opiates.

Two doctors writing in 1989 in the journal *Pain* coined the term to describe the case of a seventeen-year-old suffering from leukemia, pneumonia, and chest pain and asking for opiate painkillers, which physicians had misdiagnosed as addiction. One of the authors, J. David Haddox, later went to work at Purdue Pharma as vice president for health policy. The other, David Weissman, later described what doctors ought to do in cases of pseudoaddiction. Build trust and "aggressively" increase the dose of opiates until pain was relieved, Weissman wrote.

For all I know, pseudoaddiction may well be a real syndrome. But its importance to this story lies in that it helped nourish a growing body of thought that there was conceivably no limit to the amount of opiates a patient might need. Doctors might prescribe hundreds of milligrams a day. Certainly according to the widely accepted misinterpretation of Porter and Jick at least, there was minimal risk.

"No physician would simply go on with the same unsuccessful treatment, but that is what happens with opioids," said Loeser. "Patients come and say, 'That's great, Doc, but I need more.' The doctor gives them a higher dose. Then, three months later, they say the same thing, and so on. The point is if it were working, you wouldn't need more."

Nevertheless, a movement was born, radiating out from a simple one-paragraph statement in 1980. Other documents were used as well. Portenoy and Foley's own 1986 paper about thirty-eight patients—citing Porter and Jick—was among them. So, too, was a 1982 survey of supervisors at ninety-three burn units that found no patients growing addicted to opiate painkillers, and a 1977 study of drug dependency in patients with chronic headaches. But it appears that none was cited, nor misinterpreted, as often as Porter and Jick.

Dr. Hershel Jick, meanwhile, kept plumbing his ever-expanding patient databases. They could be, he believed, a source of clinically based information about drugs and their effects, something mankind had never possessed. He produced papers on a wide variety of topics: whether oral polio vaccines caused a collapsing of the bowels in children; whether certain oral contraceptives caused blood clots in women; and on the origin of a mumps epidemic in England.

All the while, his 1980 letter was sparking a movement.

"It's an amazing thing," he said, many years later. "That particular letter, for me, is very near the bottom of a long list of studies that I've done. It's useful as it stands because there's nothing else like it on hospitalized patients. But if you read it carefully, it does *not* speak to the level of addiction in outpatients who take these drugs for chronic pain."

Enrique Redeemed

Xalisco, Nayarit

O ne day in the fall of 1993, a tall, slender, light-skinned man in new cowboy boots and a cowboy hat low over his eyes boarded a bus in Nogales, Sonora, and headed south to his home in Nayarit.

Enrique wore a new pair of dark-blue Levi's 501s. His hat cost five hundred dollars, his boots a thousand dollars—at a western wear shop in Phoenix, Arizona. He had another fifteen thousand dollars in cash in his right pants pocket. His bus wound out of Nogales and down Mexico's Highway 15 that runs parallel to the Pacific coast. He sat wary of his surroundings, even when the driver put on a movie starring the comedian Cantinflas. He didn't watch it. He kept a hand on his right pants pocket and didn't dare sleep.

The bus trip amounted to his redemption. Months before, as Enrique toiled in the sugarcane fields with his father and despaired of ever finding a way out of his poverty, he suddenly received, and accepted, an offer to work in Phoenix. A cell boss needed a driver for his heroin store.

On his last day of work as a sugarcane farmer, he arrived at the sugar mill black from the soot and dust of the field, as if he'd stepped out of a coal mine. He took his bags of sugarcane and threw them as hard as he could onto the pile.

"The next job I have is going to be for love of the work, not for need," he promised the foreman.

The next day he kissed his mother and took a bus to Arizona.

This was his chance. The San Fernando Valley, with his uncles working, would always limit him. He went to Phoenix eager to show his abilities. In a week he knew the streets, and before long was running the store himself—cutting up the heroin, answering the beeper, and driving to deliver the balloons to the clients. His customers were mostly professional women: lawyers, nurses, a prostitute or two. He soon raised the store's daily take from twelve hundred to three thousand dollars. He worked from eight A.M. to nine P.M., grabbed a hamburger at a drive-through, and was at home by ten P.M. to balloon up the heroin for the next day. He didn't have time to clean his apartment or his clothes and he made five thousand dollars that month.

One day, his suppliers in Phoenix told him the boss would be arriving that night from Xalisco. This man impressed Enrique. He had a permit and could cross the border legally whenever he wanted. He was there to meet with his workers.

As Enrique headed home that night, his beeper buzzed. He found a pay phone. The big boss wanted McDonald's—a fish sandwich—before the meeting. Enrique scurried to get the food and returned to the apartment. He walked in as two gunmen had his boss and his suppliers in their underwear and on their knees in the bathroom.

The invaders had found two ounces of heroin, jewelry, and some cash. Yet when they demanded more, and placed a gun to his head, Enrique kept silent. That morning, he had packed tens of thousands of dollars in stacks of cash, but had no time to do anything with it. He put it at the bottom of a trash bag overflowing with the detritus of his fast-food diet—old french fries, pizza crusts, used paper plates, and soda cans. If he told the gunmen about the money, it would look like he'd set it all up. So he took their pistol-whipping in silence and they left with only five thousand dollars and those ounces of heroin, while at the bottom of that garbage bag was another eighty thousand dollars they didn't get.

The boss, a grateful witness to this kid's loyalty, pulled him off the street and gave him two heroin drivers to supervise. Enrique worked harder. Business boomed. He sent money to his family to begin building a house for himself. When telephone service finally came to the Toad, he paid to make sure his family had a line installed in their house.

Three months after the robbery, Enrique was ready to return home. He bought his boots and hat, and boarded that bus with the fifteen thousand dollars in his pocket and his eyes wide-open. Below the bus, he had stowed duffel bags bulging with clothes, jewelry, shoes, and VCRs. For so long he had sought this magnificent return. He thought of his uncles in California who had sent him home with so little after working for so long. They hadn't the spine to make the business what it could be, or the vision to see what he was capable of. His new boss had vision; Enrique felt elated to have broken from the small world of his rancho.

The clothes he brought home were Levi's 501s, Guess, Tommy Hilfiger, and Polo—measures of his success. His dad would have to remain silent. At fifteen, Enrique had been helping his family survive; now, at eighteen, the heroin he sold in Phoenix allowed him to take over the job full-time.

His family gathered him up at the bus station in Tepic. They drove him down the highway, through Xalisco, into their rancho. There, across the road from his childhood home, stood his new house, under construction and paid for with the money he had sent. It had two bedrooms, a full kitchen, a garage with an automatic door, a roof through which the rain never came, and a bathroom that was indoors. He felt at that moment that everything was possible, and he wanted to cry.

Later, in his room with his mother, he pulled the cash out of his pocket and more from his sock. It fluttered onto the bed.

"Did you rob someone?"

"No," he said, smiling broadly. "It's mine."

He noticed she didn't ask how he got it. He was sure she imagined.

That night he would always remember was the first time his family had more than enough to eat. He brought out shirts, dresses, toys. His youngest sister called him Dad.

The Arizona heroin business—and his loyalty during the robbery—won him new friends and, soon, invitations to parties in Xalisco thrown by the top heroin cell bosses. They had new cars and big houses. He felt ashamed of his petty dreams of a year before. In this world men dreamed big.

For the next two years, he split his time between his village and Phoenix, running his boss's heroin crews on the streets. He bought a used black Mercury Cougar. He took his girlfriend and his family to El Sarandeado, El Diamante—Tepic's best restaurants. He put his sister through college; she was the first in her family to graduate from college. He went into bars and restaurants and didn't think whether he could afford it. Freedom was what he felt, mostly. His mother no longer asked her husband for money to feed the family, nor endured his blows and insults in exchange. His father no longer had to depend on the mill to pay him.

Over the years, merchants in town had learned many ways to put down the farmers who drew a living from the sugarcane and coffee and who constantly asked for credit. Now, for the first time, the baker smiled when Enrique's mother entered his shop and spoke warmly to her; he waved to Enrique's father when he passed.

That year at the Feria del Elote, Enrique and a friend who worked with him in Arizona owned the central plaza in Xalisco. The Saturday of the fair, they paid a banda three thousand dollars to play all night. They drank and offered alcohol to anyone who showed up. They only stopped because Mass at the cathedral was about to begin on Sunday morning. Xalisco had never seen that before from a couple guys from a rancho. Usually rancheros would save all year to pay for only one hour of banda music in the plaza. But heroin did that: it made everyone equal.

It did not, however, endear Enrique to his girlfriend's father, who was happy to sell his meat to his mother but didn't want an uneducated kid from the Toad, a chiva dealer, for a son-in-law. When Enrique was a boy, the butcher had been friendly. But since Enrique took up with his daughter, the man never spoke to him and Enrique learned to keep his distance.

In time, returning occasionally to Phoenix, and then a stint in Portland, then back home again, Enrique began to feel unsettled. His salary wasn't bad but his expenses had risen now that he was spending so much time among all those new friends. He was limited. He could see what was on the other side of that river that he felt divided the Toad from the world, but he couldn't make it across as a worker.

His ambitions were greater now. He had a car, but wanted a new one. He had a new house, with tile floors; he had piles of clothes and money, but it wasn't enough to retire on. He'd taken orders all his life and wanted to know how it felt to be the boss.

He was twenty-two, time to get married. His girlfriend's parents would never allow it. She was still in high school.

So, one day in 1996, he took ten thousand pesos, a thousand dollars, and his Beretta 9mm and filled the Cougar with gas. He went to his girlfriend's school and drove her off to Puerto Vallarta, stealing her from her parents. It was the village way of marrying against the parents' wishes. When she realized what was happening, she put up a fight at first, with lots of conditions, all of which he agreed to. He took her to the Hotel Krystal, which he remembered later for the first valet service he'd ever used. When they returned, in the eyes of the rancho, they were as good as married, no matter what her parents said.

He took her to his new house to live. Then he set off to Albuquerque, New Mexico, where he had heard black tar heroin would find a market, and he a future.

We Realized This Is Corporate

Portland, Oregon

D r. Gary Oxman never forgot what he learned from the Bloods and Crips.

In the 1980s, Blood and Crip gangs moved out of Los Angeles in search of new markets for crack cocaine. Their turf war over L.A.'s crack market had turned parts of the city into war zones. Heading north up Interstate 5, one place they landed was Portland, Oregon. By the mid-1980s, the City of Roses was awash in crack and crack houses. Drive-by shootings and murders soared. So did rates of syphilis.

Oxman was hired at the Multnomah County Health Department in 1984. One day, he spoke to a teacher in a black neighborhood, who explained what was taking place: Bloods, Crips, crack, crack houses, sex for drugs. Hence the syphilis epidemic he was seeing. Oxman and his colleagues studied the outbreaks, and eventually wrote a research paper on the problem, showing that a dozen or so people actively trading sex for crack had triggered a syphilis outbreak.

Federal indictments sent dozens of crack-slinging gang members to prison in the late 1980s. This calmed the syphilis epidemic in Multnomah County. By then, Oxman had learned to listen to the community and also that when it came to drugs, a few people could create a public health catastrophe.

In the spring of 1999, Oxman found himself one afternoon in a meeting with Sharron Kelley, a Multnomah County commissioner, in downtown Portland. It was budget season. Oxman, a thin, fit fellow with curly hair, a mustache, and a goatee, was now the chief health officer for Multnomah County.

Heroin addiction was rampant and the hepatitis C virus was spreading across Portland, Kelley said. How would the Health Department like some money to pay for treatment and services for hep C patients?

That money would help a great deal, he said. Thousands of people were now infected with the virus.

Kelley went on about the treatment and services the county lacked and that Oxman might put in place. As the meeting wound down, Kelley added, "Oh, by the way, there's this advocacy group in the community called RAP, comprising drug users in recovery. A lot of their friends who are still using are dying of heroin overdoses. Can you do an epidemiological study on that?"

Oxman replied, "Sure."

RAP—the Recovery Association Project—was a union of recovering heroin addicts organized by a local nonprofit called Central City Concern. Central City had long run detox centers for alcoholics and drug addicts. By the mid-1990s, with the decline of the black gangs' control of the crack trade in Portland, the numbers of CCC detox patients was falling quickly. Center directors actually wondered how long they'd be in the detox business.

"Then, all of a sudden, something happened. We were getting all these people addicted to heroin," said Ed Blackburn, now the director of Central City. "You were seeing young people. We were used to seeing forty-year-old heroin addicts at the detox center. Then we were seeing twenty-three-year-old heroin addicts. This was 1994, 1995. We'd been detoxing heroin addicts for years, but it was always pretty stable: five to ten percent of our patients. Then it went up. By 1996 to '97, it was over fifty percent heroin."

The Xalisco boys were now all over Portland.

Blackburn is a follower of Saul Alinsky, the legendary community organizer in Chicago, who trained politically marginalized groups in pushing politicians to respond. As heroin surged, Blackburn used a federal grant to train recovering addicts in using their stories and experience in politics. He hired a couple of them and they spent time at the detox centers recruiting others to join RAP. Before long, hundreds of newly recovering addicts organized. They began going to city and county meetings demanding services and funding.

One of them was the legless addict, Alan Levine. By 1998, Levine had been using the Xalisco Boys' delivery system daily for five years and it had lost its allure.

"You know Joe Camel—that cigarette ad strategy aimed at young people?" Levine said. "That's what these guys were doing. They were aiming at the young people. The kids could snort it, smoke it, eat it, mainline it. All of a sudden we had a network of high schoolers who were addicted to heroin. Heroin became a lot more potent and a lot more deadly. There were more and more heroin deaths to the point where I stopped using heroin and I started working against it."

Levine and others hit the streets and soon RAP had hundreds of members. From there, they turned to pushing elected officials to fund treatment for addicts. Levine was eventually put on the governor's Council on Drug Abuse, and a county drug planning committee.

In Portland a class of earnest activists and nonprofit executives had emerged over the decades advocating on behalf of the disenfranchised and speaking an anesthetized and politically correct language. To this activist class, the RAPsters were like battery acid. RAPsters were street rabble with lives like open sores. They were blunt, uncensored, and not too polite. Blackburn trained them to tell their stories—which often didn't fit in the neat world of heroes and villains that the professional advocates preferred. Alan Levine could be particularly graphic at public meetings, with his two stumps and an eloquent growl spinning tales of a debased life spent vainly seeking that first high that made him feel like the President of Everything.

RAP put together a mentor system: An addict leaving jail while detoxing would meet a former addict who took him to get housing and food, and help him avoid old friends and situations. With that, and given the enormous numbers of new addicts created by the cheap and reliable supply of the Xalisco Boys' heroin, "the sheer numbers of people getting sober skyrocketed" as well, Blackburn said.

Many joined RAP. They spoke openly of their addiction. They orchestrated large meetings with elected officials designed to maneuver politicians into supporting increased funding for, say, recovery housing. RAPsters spoke with a special urgency about heroin overdose. They could see what others had not: that heroin overdose deaths were surging on the streets. Their friends were dying and they cast around for a politician to listen.

One who did was Multnomah County commissioner Sharron Kelley. Thus Gary Oxman ended up in 1999 with the task of studying and explaining the county's raging bout of heroin overdoses, which was something, as it turned out, that Oxman at first could not find at all.

DURING THESE YEARS, A California transplant named Kim Ellis was badly addicted to heroin. Xalisco Boys were everywhere, blending in to Portland's growing Latino immigrant community. She never knew where they were from. She called them worker bees—the guys who delivered her heroin whenever she called. Some of them she got to know.

"We're everywhere," one told her. "As soon as I go home to Mexico, there's my brothers and my cousin waiting to come up and take my place."

Most drivers were between seventeen and thirty years of age. To poor Mexicans like them, the image of America included money, big cars, the Dallas Cowboys, Bruce Willis movies, McDonald's, and, especially, American girls. But they worked every day and hibernated in bare apartments at night. All they were ever going to know of the great and mythical United States was what they saw delivering heroin. The only girls Xalisco drivers were going to meet were their female junkie customers. They were farm boys, not thugs or cartel killers. They were polite, raised among the conservative traditions of the Mexican small town, and awed by America. They never used their product and some of them were sweet and courteous.

For female junkies, hardened by daily exposure to the worst of human nature, this occasional dose of tender attention was welcome. "Every single guy I encountered, they were personable guys," Ellis said. "It came to the point where there was a human element, a relationship that started. Once I was in the car I no longer saw them as people who were making money helping me with my demise. They were just people. When it was time to get clean I missed that relationship. It became really hard to hate them."

This was part of why the Xalisco Boys succeeded. To their customers, many Xalisco Boys were not like typical heroin dealers, who were addicts as well, cold and conniving. Some of the boys became friendly with their addict customers. Even through the language barrier, they were personable, sometimes charming.

Empathy for her Xalisco dealers made it doubly difficult for Ellis to kick heroin, which she did years later. "In order to kick, I had to hate them. If I held on to one thing that was good, even if it was twisted good, I'd hold on to heroin," she told me. "The last worker bee I had was falling in love with me. He never tried anything but always asked me if I could go out to dinner. I picked up on the fact that these guys were not going to riddle my body with bullets and dump me somewhere. They'd ask, 'Ever want to go dancing or something?' They're real people trying to survive in their car and they're meeting others, like me, who are trying to survive in their addiction. Even now, as much as I hate heroin, I don't hate those guys who were my dealers."

*   *   *

GARY OXMAN WENT TO the state's Vital Records Department, considered the gold standard by public health researchers looking into death trends. Believing the RAPsters were probably on to something, he was surprised when he did not find records of large numbers of overdoses. He went to the county medical examiner's office. The office kept lists of each year's accidental deaths. From those he culled the reports of drug-related deaths, and from them, in turn, came up with a large stack of reports of deaths due to drug overdoses. Yet on his first cursory viewing, he still didn't see many that were heroin overdoses.

Intrigued, Oxman and a team of researchers pored over these death reports in the basement of the medical examiner's office for the next three months. And there he saw the problem. Each autopsy physician had different ways of describing a heroin overdose. One used "acute intravenous narcotism." Another used "narcotics overdose." There was "polydrug overdose," though not officially listing heroin. Another used, simply, "heroin overdose." The numbers had been growing steadily, hidden in the tall weeds of inconsistent language.

Eventually, he tallied more than a hundred heroin overdoses a year since 1996. He dug further into the files, reading all the overdose reports back to the early 1990s. What he and his team found astonished Oxman. There was no sudden spike in heroin deaths, as RAP believed. It was scarier than that. Deaths had been marching straight up for almost a decade and no one had noticed. Multnomah County had 10 heroin overdose deaths in 1991, about the time the Xalisco Boys arrived, and ended 1999 with 111—a 1,000 percent increase in eight years.

"By the time we discovered it," Oxman said years later, "it wasn't a new wave at all."

Unbeknownst to anyone, heroin overdoses had become Multnomah County's second cause of accidental death among men twenty to fifty-four years old—after car crashes.

"This level of heroin overdose deaths is considered epidemic," Oxman and his team wrote in a report to the county commission in December 1999. Oxman put together a team of public health workers and sociologists to interview street addicts over the next year. Heroin in Portland had never been cheaper, more available, or more potent. For twenty dollars, a beginning heroin user could stay high all day.

"The story, as we heard it, was of a marketing strategy [for heroin] that had changed from selling to a small number of addicts who had expensive habits and toward a large number of addicts with cheap heroin," said Oxman.

BY THE LATE 1990S, a few lone cops around the western United States, like Dennis Chavez and Ed Ruplinger, were beginning to see that the Xalisco Boys were far more than scruffy independent street dealers.

As time went on, these officers formed a kind of club—one that many of them didn't know they belonged to—of law enforcement intrigued by what they were seeing and what this could be. Generally, because heroin was not then any jurisdiction's top drug priority, this club attracted dogged investigators who waded through thickets of Spanish aliases, trusting their own hunches and undaunted by arrests that yielded only a few grams of heroin. On the contrary, once these cops understood the Xalisco Boys' system and reach, they realized that the small quantities of dope seized were even *more* ominous than large seizures. It meant that a vast network of traffickers had figured out what defined a successful drug bust for U.S. narcotics agents, their bosses, the media, and the public: large amounts of dope, money, and guns. It meant they had rules and practices in place so they'd never be caught with any of that. And they did this relentlessly, over and over, across the country.

In Portland, Oregon, one of these cops was an FBI agent named Paul "Rock" Stone, who, like many of his peers, didn't quite understand what he was seeing at first. A voluble, hard-charging agent, Stone grew up in California's Central Valley and was a Merced police officer before joining the bureau. In April 1999 he transferred from a violent crimes unit to the squad investigating narcotics organizations in Portland.

One case he encountered early on was from an informant who said he was buying heroin from Mexicans—two guys with baseball caps in an old car. These street dealers were selling tenth-of-a-gram heroin doses that when tested by the FBI came up 80 percent pure. Street dealers don't *ever* consistently sell addict-ready doses that pure. The traditional heroin trade made it impossible. In the typical heroin supply chain, the drug moves from wholesalers through middlemen down to street dealers. Every trafficker who handles the dope steps on it— expands the volume by diluting it—before selling it. Usually by the time heroin makes it from the poppy to the addict's arm, it's been sold a half-dozen times, stepped on each time, and is about 12 percent pure.

FBI and DEA tests always showed that. Stone would have passed the case to local police but for the fact that "you don't have street-level addicts getting a balloon of 80 percent heroin." Fatal heroin overdoses he found were surging, so Stone kept at it.

He tracked calls made from the phones taken from these street dealers. With the phones came another revelation. They were calling cities across the country: Los Angeles, Phoenix, Denver, Columbus. And down to a place called Nayarit, Mexico. Something else: The numbers they called in these cities were turning up in cases the FBI had under way across the country.

"A street-level guy selling a tenth of a gram should not hit a half-dozen FBI multiagency cases in other cities and other states. It just does not make sense in our world," Stone said.

He formed a task force with the DEA and the Portland police. They tapped the dealers' phones and pagers. Stone marveled at their system's sophistication. Dispatchers sent pages to drivers that baffled investigators. Something like 181*2*3*0 would show up, for example. Later, informants taught the investigators that the first number was a north–south street, many of which are numbered in Portland; the second number was a code drivers memorized for a major east–west street: 1 was Burnside, 2 was Halsey, and so on; the third number was code for the number of blocks away; the last number was either 0 or 5: north or south, respectively. So 181*2*3*0 told the runner to meet the addict three blocks north of the intersection of 181st Street and Halsey.

Sources revealed why dealers didn't step on the heroin. "It's because they're salaried," Stone said. "The runners are up here, nephews of the regional sales manager, and just coming to do a job, paid five hundred dollars a week. They didn't care what the potency was; they made the salary no matter how much they sold."

Salaried employees were unheard-of in the drug business.

"We realized this is corporate," Stone said. "These are company cars, company apartments, company phones. And it all gets handed to the next guy when they move on."

In Portland alone by then, nine cells were delivering heroin, each with at least three cars and drivers rotating in and out of each of them. Stone had been to Mexico for work and vacation, but hadn't heard of Nayarit. Sources told him the runners were all from a small collection of villages that weren't on most maps: Testerazo, Pantanal, Aquiles Serdán, Emiliano Zapata, and the town Xalisco. The same last names kept popping up, too: Tejeda, Sánchez, Cienfuegos, Diaz, Lerma, Bernal, and others.

As Stone learned more about Nayarit, he realized the opium was produced in the mountains by the families of these same dealers—so they were an amalgam of wholesalers and retailers, each cell a small business, producing its own heroin, and sending it to the United States and selling it by the tenth of a gram on streets of cities like Portland—controlling their own distribution from flower to arm. Between the mountains and the street was not a phalanx of dealers, each making a profit by diluting the dope. "There was no one in between what would normally be step one and step seven but them."

Stone did some math. Each tenth of a gram sold for about fifteen dollars. The cells were grossing $150,000 from each kilo. Informants told him that it cost about two thousand dollars to produce a kilo of black tar heroin in Nayarit. In Portland, their overhead was cheap apartments, old cars, gas, food, and five hundred dollars a week for each driver. Profit per kilo, Stone figured, was well over a hundred thousand dollars.

With enormous flexibility on price, they could sell heroin cheaply and with unprecedented potency. Because they competed among each other, their prices dropped. Beginning in about 1991, the loose network of Xalisco heroin cells had arrived, cornered, and then saturated Portland. The result was the decadelong rise in overdoses that Gary Oxman had found—a relatively small group of people creating a major drug plague.

BY 1999, THE XALISCO Boys had been in Portland, Oregon, for almost a decade and brought the price down to where "you could maintain a moderate heroin habit for about the same price as a six-pack of premium beer" per day, Oxman told me years later. "The economy was booming, and there was a huge number of addicts, most of whom were functional. Most of the users went to work high, had a habit [while] working at jobs."

Overdoses, and not burglaries and robberies, became the new barometers of the city's heroin problem. Oxman hired an advertising firm to organize focus groups of addicts and design a campaign to reduce the deaths. Oxman's department had matchbooks printed with messages urging addicts not to shoot up alone, and, when a friend was overdosing, to "dial 911, stay and help. If you can't stay . . . still dial 911, [then] ditch and dash."

By 2001, using modern advertising and RAP's rabble on the streets, the black tar heroin overdose deaths that began when the Xalisco Boys came to town had fallen by more than a third. And for a while, with nothing else priming the market, those overdoses stayed down.

Purdue

OxyContin is a simple pill. It contains only one drug: oxycodone, a painkiller that Germans synthesized in 1916 from thebaine, an opium derivative. Molecularly, oxycodone is similar to heroin.

OxyContin riffed off an earlier Purdue product: MS Contin. MS Contin was Purdue's first foray into pain management using the Continus timed-release formula invented by Napp in England. MS Contin sent morphine into a patient's bloodstream continuously—hence Contin—over several hours. To accomplish this, MS Contin came in large doses of morphine: 15, 30, 60, 100, and 200 mg. Purdue marketed it to cancer patients and people just out of surgery, and MS Contin apparently served them well.

Likewise, OxyContin contains large doses of oxycodone—40 and 80 mg typically—wrapped in a timed-release formula that slowly sends the drug into the body over several hours. It has legitimate medical uses, and has assuaged the pain of many Americans, for whom life would otherwise be torture.

But OxyContin came out in 1996, which was a very different time in American medicine than 1984, when MS Contin appeared, or its story might have been similarly pedestrian. In the 1980s, few people in medicine accepted prescribing a strong opiate for chronic pain. By 1996, however, the opiate revolution wrought by the pain crusaders had been changing minds in American medicine for a decade. More insurance companies were reimbursing for pills, but not for therapy that was not strictly medical. Pain was now considered a vital sign, measured by a subjective scale between 1 and 10, and treated aggressively.

Later, Purdue officials would say that what happened with OxyContin surprised them because MS Contin hadn't been abused. That wasn't entirely accurate. Detectives in Ohio I spoke to remembered that MS Contin was stolen and abused. Doctors were conned into prescribing it to drug addicts in some cities, but not others—in Cincinnati but not in

Columbus, for example. But certainly abuse of MS Contin was sporadic and never hit the levels that its cousin, OxyContin, would attain.

To promote OxyContin, Purdue hired William Douglas McAdams for the first time. While Arthur Sackler was alive, he didn't allow the firm to work for Purdue, said Win Gerson, then the president of the firm. But Sackler had died in 1987 and the ad firm now got the Purdue contract. In preparing OxyContin for sale, Purdue thought it was just an extension of MS Contin, Gerson said. "There was nothing that suggested in reading the data that five minutes after you marketed it the kids would learn how to break it down," Gerson told me. "[Purdue] followed the model of the drug they had, which was MS Contin. They absolutely thought that OxyContin would not be addictive."

But MS Contin wasn't sold as a virtually risk-free panacea for chronic pain. Other opiate painkillers had been confined to small doses and combined with acetaminophen or Tylenol to make them hard to liquefy and inject. These drugs were Vicodin, Lorcet, Lortab, Percocet, and others. Yet even those were abused. Moreover, no one had imagined that a pill containing a drug similar to heroin would be marketed almost like an over-the-counter drug. But by 1996 American physicians were tenderized to accepting opiates for chronic pain. Undertreated pain was an epidemic and physicians now had the duty, the calling, to relieve it using the new tools and drugs the pharmaceutical companies were inventing.

Indeed, some pain crusaders saw Purdue's continuous release mechanism as the Holy Grail that the Rockefeller Committee had sought, and that had eluded researchers, testing drugs at the Narcotic Farm, for decades. If a nonaddictive drug couldn't be found, perhaps a new method for administering opiates would lead to less addiction. OxyContin theoretically parsed out oxycodone in a way that did not cause the intense highs and lows that caused addiction. This was an exciting possibility. All that testing at the Narcotic Farm in Lexington might not have been in vain after all. Science might finally have come up with a way to provide merciful pain relief without the torment of addiction—albeit not in the way that researchers originally imagined.

"We went from not having very potent drugs . . . to an oral morphine form and to a pharmaceutical industry that wanted to promote it," Kathy Foley said in an oral history interview in 1996, the year OxyContin was released. "So we, for the first time, then, had a marketer and a distributor for a drug that we had, and an educator. We knew then that oral morphine was effective. We can get away from these silly elixirs and cocktails into tablets that people take once or twice a day, and we're into a revolutionary field of pain management . . . It was the drug-delivery device that changed, not the drug, and with that the whole mentality, 'Well, now that we have this drug, we can treat pain.' Really extraordinary."

This possibility was indeed extraordinary. Up to then, pain patients spent most of their day thinking about pain, or the pills they needed every two to four hours to keep it at bay. Clock watching, it was called. Two OxyContin a day was better. That became a main selling point. The advantage was hardly trivial. Two pills a day allowed a pain patient's life to recommence.

FDA examiner Dr. Curtis Wright, supervisor of the agency's team that examined Purdue's application, thought OxyContin might well possess addictive side effects and thought its only benefit was to reduce the number of pills a patient had to take every day. "Care should be taken to limit competitive promotion," Wright is quoted as writing in an FDA report by the *New York Times*'s Barry Meier in his 2003 book on OxyContin, *Pain Killer*. Wright later left the FDA to work for Purdue.

In 1995, the FDA approved OxyContin for 10, 20, and 40 mg pills. Later, it added 80 and 160 mg pills. Despite the high doses of oxycodone loaded into each pill, the FDA bought the idea that by creating fewer surges of euphoria and depression OxyContin would be less addictive—the Holy Grail, at last.

The FDA approved a unique warning label for OxyContin. It allowed Purdue to claim that OxyContin had a lower potential for abuse than other oxycodone products because its timed-release formula allowed for a delay in absorbing the drug. "No other manufacturer of a Schedule II narcotic ever got the go-ahead from the FDA to make such a claim," Meier wrote. "It was a claim that soon became a cornerstone of the marketing of OxyContin."

The warning label also inadvertently told addicts how to abuse the pill, warning patients not to crush the tablets because that would release "a potentially toxic amount of the drug." That was like an invitation to a junkie. A 2003 U.S. GAO report on the company's OxyContin marketing efforts, requested by members of Congress, found that the FDA didn't realize that "the drug could be dissolved in water and injected."

From the start, Purdue promoted OxyContin far beyond the cancer and postsurgical patients to whom it marketed MS Contin. Purdue positioned OxyContin as the opiate of choice in the World Health

Organization's Ladder of pain management. The company aimed to convince doctors to aggressively treat noncancer pain, and prescribe OxyContin for moderate pain lasting more than a few days. OxyContin ought to be used for bad backs, knee pain, tooth extraction, headaches, fibromyalgia, as well as football, hockey, and dirt-bike injuries, broken bones, and, of course, after surgery. This was a vast new market for an opiate painkiller. U.S. back pain patients alone numbered some thirty-five million people; the total number of cancer patients were a fifth of that.

To get there, Purdue had to answer doctors' first doubt: Isn't this stuff addictive?

As Arthur Sackler had done with Valium in the 1960s, Purdue set about promoting OxyContin as virtually risk-free and a solution to the problems patients presented doctors with every day. The company urged salespeople, meanwhile, to "attach an emotional aspect to non-cancer pain so physicians treat it more seriously and aggressively." Many pain patients suffered badly. Purdue urged doctors to believe that Oxy was the drug to "start with and stay with." The doctors needn't worry because the oxycodone was released slowly over many hours. Thus, OxyContin did not create the steep highs and lows that created cravings.

This message went out mostly to primary care doctors, whose sole pain-management training was usually at medical conferences, listening to the pain crusaders, who bore the news that opiates had been "shown" to be addictive in less than 1 percent of pain patients.

A former Purdue sales manager for West Virginia, William Gergely, said that the company urged its salespeople to emphasize the safety of OxyContin. Gergely declined my request for an interview. But in 2003, he told the *South Florida Sun Sentinel*: "They told us to say things like it is 'virtually' non-addicting. That's what we were instructed to do. It's not right, but that's what they told us to say . . . You'd tell the doctor there is a study, but you wouldn't show it to him."

In *Pain Killer*, Barry Meier describes at length Purdue's sales techniques and training. The company put its sales reps through several weeks of training. One question they addressed concerned the risk of addiction to pain patients when treated with narcotics. "The correct answer was 'less than one percent,'" Meier wrote.

The Man and the Nayarit

Northern Nevada

By the early 1990s, the Man was doing time at the Northern Nevada Correctional Center, a medium-security prison in Carson City.

White inmates ran the yard; blacks were also a force. But the prison's Mexican population was small and vulnerable. They were mostly illegal immigrants and first-time inmates, wary and quiet, and spoke no English. The Man, bilingual all his life, became their spokesman.

Blacks and whites had their own large gardens, watered by underground pipes, where they could grow vegetables, melons, and other food. Mexicans had nothing. He lobbied for a plot where Mexicans could grow their food. Prison officials gave them a piece of land, but it had no water.

He met with the warden. "What's the point of having land with no water?" he told her. "You're mistreating my people."

The warden let them extend a water pipe out to the garden. From then on, the Man got a cut of whatever the Mexicans harvested from the garden.

He kept on. On the Fourth of July, the whites fired up large grills where they barbecued ribs and roasted corn on the cob. There was nothing for Cinco de Mayo. The Man lobbied the warden and the Mexican inmates soon had the kitchen for a half day on May 5, and the gym after that for a party. They invited the guards and their wives, and the inmates taught the wives to dance *la quebradita*, with banda music blasting from the boom boxes they set up. The Man gave a speech, thanking the warden for acknowledging the Mexican inmates and their holiday.

He organized soccer games with teams from outside. He played on the inmates' baseball team. The prison was made of barracks and he had a corner in one where he lived, and a table on which he played dominos and cards. There, he began to hang out with a guy from the small Pacific coast state of Nayarit in Mexico who was doing time for transporting cocaine.

Turned out, the Nayarit had come to the United States illegally at eighteen to work derecho—the right way. An uncle had taken him and his brothers to Yakima to pick apples for a time. He then made his way down to the San Fernando Valley, which had the largest community of people from his town in the United States.

One of them, a cousin, was by then selling heroin from an apartment in Panorama City, a district of Los Angeles in the San Fernando Valley. From the cousin, the Nayarit learned the trade on the street. Then he fell in with some guys sending cocaine to Nevada and was arrested and went to prison.

In prison, the Nayarit had no money. The Man cooked and shared his food with him. The Nayarit, meanwhile, told him an intriguing tale.

He was, he said, from a town called Xalisco, near the Nayarit capital city of Tepic. In the mountains above Xalisco, he said, opium poppies grew abundantly. Cora Indians sold the flowers' goo to people in his town. Cooking the opium goo into black tar heroin was a folkcraft that a few families in this town had mastered. They supplied relatives in the San Fernando Valley. Since he'd been locked up, the Nayarit said, his cousins had expanded to Honolulu, Phoenix, and Portland, too.

Problem was, the Nayarit said, his family spoke no English, and didn't understand the addict world. So they missed markets and opportunities. You're bilingual. You're American, he said. You've been on methadone and know the clinics where they congregate. Right now you're just an addict, the Nayarit told him. You've had to depend for supply on wherever you can find a source. I can supply all the dope you need. We could get rich like you wouldn't believe. You, me, my family, my brothers. Reno, Denver, Salt Lake, and Hawaii. These are big markets.

"He had a broad vision of what this could mean for his town," the Man told me years later. "I grasped it, took a hold of it, and took off with it. I give him credit for having the vision in seeing that I could help out, that I could do a lot for them. I knew about the addict in the United States. With what I knew here, we could combine and scratch each other's back. We were just talking about the western states then."

And not even all the western states, for he would not go to Texas and Arizona. The Man had spent years in California prisons, where Latino inmates had long feuded with those from Texas and Arizona. He considered those states backwaters of ignorance, and though heroin was big there, he never considered them potential markets.

He paroled to Reno in 1993. A few months later, the Nayarit appeared at his door. He had been deported, but had returned. He walked in bursting with ideas. Back home, he saw his cousin and others who said they had a system. It was 1993, and pagers were the rage. The Nayarit described his cousin's system. It worked like this: Addicts called a number. The operator would then page a runner with a code for where to deliver the addict his dope. His cousin hired Xalisco kids to come up and run the dope around to the junkies. Most of these drivers were relatives, from poor families that farmed sugarcane, work that was hot, hard, and led nowhere. Hundreds of these young kids back home— poor, whose fathers owned a few acres and never got ahead—burned to move beyond sugar, and up the social ladder.

"They'll work hard for a salary and they won't cheat you," the Nayarit said. "They're happy for the work."

Over a lifetime of heroin use, the Man had never heard of anyone working drugs for a salary. But he saw the ingenuity in the system. Up to that point, heroin had always been sold by dealers from some apartment or house. Eventually, cops would raid the house, so dealers were constantly moving, and having to let their customers know their new addresses. But with pagers, dealers could operate from cars, the Nayarit told him. Buyers didn't have to expose themselves by going to an address, or a skid row, to buy their heroin. They need only keep a telephone number handy and the heroin could be brought to them. With consistent supply from Nayarit, the system offered addicts reliability, convenience, and safety.

In Reno, not long after that, the new partners started their first heroin store. They worked out the kinks, selling mostly to veteran dope fiends. It didn't earn much—about a thousand dollars a day. But soon more guys from the village were clamoring for work; some started their own crews, saturating the market. To make money selling heroin by the tenth of a gram, you needed volume. The only way to do that was to expand to other markets.

With their Reno store still operating with the kids from Xalisco, the Nayarit and the Man moved on to Salt Lake, found a motel, and discovered that Salt Lake City had a load of old dope fiends. Still, it was a clean town. The Man had to hand it to the Mormons: They did run a clean town. Plus Salt Lake had a lot of Mexicans, so they could blend in.

Soon they were selling out. The Man sent for more dope from Reno. The Nayarit called down to Xalisco and two kids arrived in Salt Lake ready to work. They set up a cell that he claims continues to this day, run by the Nayarit's brother-in-law.

From Salt Lake City, with two tienditas in place, they took a vacation. They flew to Mexico with thirty thousand dollars and, with his partner as a guide, the Man arrived for the first time in the town of Xalisco in the small state of Nayarit.

Swing with OxyContin

Southern Ohio

In 1997, in the town of Chillicothe, in southern Ohio, Phillip Prior, a family physician at a local hospital, began to notice salesmen from a company called Purdue Pharma making regular appearances.

The salesmen would arrive every few months to provide docs an elaborate lunch of steak, salad, and dessert. They had slides and graphics that presented the startling idea that the company's new drug, OxyContin, was virtually nonaddictive. Less than 1 percent of patients ever grew addicted, they said in their presentations.

This claim startled Prior because OxyContin contained large doses of the opiate called oxycodone. Prior had attended medical school in the early 1980s, where he had learned opiates were generally to be avoided. He'd remembered a study that concluded that daily usage of 30 mg of oxycodone was enough to cause withdrawal.

The Purdue sales campaign contradicted "what we had learned in medical school. I was trained that they were dangerous, addictive [drugs] and only effective for a short period of time," Prior said. "We were very hesitant to use narcotics because they're dangerous. It flew so much in the face of what we were trained—about narcotics being a last-ditch effort for dying cancer patients, and not to be used for nonmalignant pain."

But the salesmen had charts and graphs supporting the idea that because OxyContin was a timed-release medication that patients felt fewer of the strong highs and deep lows that led to addiction. Thus, the salesmen insisted, it could be prescribed to people with chronic pain in their backs, knees, or other joints, chronic pelvic pain, or fibromyalgia, or to women after giving birth.

"It was a very effective presentation," Prior said. "It really did make you doubt your feelings about what you'd been taught in medical school."

They came through often—six times in 1997 to his hospital alone, Prior remembered, and held hundreds of meetings in the southern

Ohio area, all with the same message. The OxyContin sales campaign mounted by Purdue Pharma was legend, and manifest in it was the spirit of Arthur Sackler and his focus on direct contact with physicians.

Purdue had its salespeople dig in on doctors who its data showed were already heavy opiate prescribers. To expand the numbers of prescribers, sales reps also visited nurses, pharmacists, hospices, hospitals, and nursing homes. The physician call list used by Purdue sales reps began at thirty-three thousand, then rose to more than seventy thousand doctors nationwide. Purdue's sales force tripled to more than a thousand as OxyContin gained momentum.

During these years, the company was hardly alone in this. The decade of the 1990s was the era of the blockbuster drug, the billion-dollar pill, and a pharmaceutical sales force arms race was part of the excess of the time. The industry's business model was based on creating a pill—for cholesterol, depression, pain, or impotence—and then promoting it with growing numbers of salespeople. During the 1990s and into the next decade, Arthur Sackler's vision of pharmaceutical promotion reached its most exquisite expression as drug companies hired ever-larger sales teams. In 1995, 35,000 Americans were pharmaceutical sales reps. Ten years later, a record 110,000 people—Sackler's progeny all—were traveling the country selling legal drugs in America.

They crowded into doctors' offices and hospital corridors. Pfizer, that tiny chemical concern that had hired Sackler a half century before, was now the world's largest drug company, with blockbuster drugs like Viagra, the antidepressant Zoloft, and the best-selling drug ever, Lipitor, an anticholesterol drug. Pfizer was at the forefront of putting Sackler's ideas into practice. Its sales force grew to thirty-eight thousand people worldwide—twelve thousand in the United States alone. Doctors complained they were getting visits by three Pfizer reps a day. The industry called it "feet on the street," with mobs of salesmen calling on doctors to get them to change how they prescribed. But Pfizer was only the leader in an industry obsessed with blockbuster drugs and convinced that more salespeople was the way to get doctors' attention in a crowded market. A pharmaceutical Wild West emerged. Salespeople stampeded into offices. They made claims that helped sell the drugs to besieged doctors. Those claims also led years later to blockbuster lawsuits and criminal cases against their companies.

Purdue increased the sales quota of OxyContin needed to make bonuses. Even so, salespeople surpassed every goal. In 1996, Purdue paid one million dollars in bonuses tied to Oxy sales, and forty million dollars in bonuses five years later. Some Purdue reps—particularly in southern Ohio, eastern Kentucky, and other areas first afflicted with rampant Oxy addiction—were reported to have made as much as a hundred thousand dollars in bonuses in one quarter during these years. Those were unlike any bonuses ever paid in the U.S. pharmaceutical industry. Veteran drug salespeople say that in most drug companies, a bonus for a stellar *year* is thirty thousand dollars; companies can predict how well its drugs can sell, and raise goals on drugs doing well to avoid paying such whopping bonuses. So Purdue was apparently underestimating the amount these folks could sell every year, and/or the drug, combined with the pain revolution and the idea that it was essentially nonaddictive, was virtually selling itself. Whatever the case, the bonuses to Purdue salespeople in these regions had little relation to those paid at most U.S. drug companies. They bore instead a striking similarity to the kinds of profits made in the drug underworld.

It was a good time to be a Purdue salesman.

In 2002, the Pharmaceutical Research and Manufacturers of America, a pharmaceutical trade group, and the U.S. Department of Health and Human Services put out voluntary guidelines on marketing opiate painkillers. Attempting to restrain the massive pharma sales force, they admonished companies from offering inappropriate travel, meals, and gifts to get doctors to prescribe certain drugs, and from paying excessive consulting and research fees to doctors. The guidelines prohibited giving away merchandise not related to health care.

But that was in 2002. For Oxy's first six years, Purdue was not limited by much.

Purdue offered OxyContin coupons to physicians, who could in turn give them to patients for a onetime free prescription at a participating pharmacy. By the time Purdue discontinued the program, thirty-four thousand coupons had been redeemed.

Doctors received OxyContin fishing hats, stuffed toys, coffee mugs, golf balls, and pens with a chart converting a patient's dose in other pills to OxyContin. *Swing Is Alive,* a CD the company gave out, urged listeners to "Swing in the Right Direction with OxyContin" and featured ten big-band tunes, including Count Basie's "One O'Clock Jump" and "Boogie Woogie Bugle Boy" by the Andrews Sisters. Pads of message paper with the OxyContin logo were given to doctors so they would be "reminded of OxyContin every time they get a phone message."

Many of these methods—premiums, trips, giveaways—were time-tested strategies that grew from the revolution Arthur Sackler began and were refined over time by many pharmaceutical companies. Only this time, the pill being marketed contained a large whack of a drug virtually identical to heroin. The DEA later said that no company had ever used this kind of branded merchandise to market a so-called Schedule II drug (Schedule II is a federal designation for drugs with accepted medical uses, but a high potential for abuse resulting in dependency).

Purdue held some forty pain-management and speaker-training seminars. The company recruited physicians for its national speakers bureau to talk about the use of oxycodone—and by implication OxyContin—to doctors and nurses at medical conferences and hospitals. These conferences took place in Boca Raton, Florida, and Scottsdale, Arizona, and some five thousand physicians, pharmacists, and nurses attended in the five years the seminars were offered.

Purdue also made continuing medical education (CME) an important part of its campaign. By the 1990s, CME had been around for a decade but had grown largely dependent on drug company funding. The companies shelled out hundreds of millions of dollars, usually from their marketing budgets, to fly medical practitioners to resorts. There, the companies plied them with dinners, golf outings, and spa treatments while sending them to seminars on a medical issue, led by specialists that the companies often suggested. Often the conclusion was that a drug the companies made was a solution to a medical problem. Hardworking doctors, furthermore, weren't eager to go to unappealing places; but they flocked to resorts like Scottsdale for their CME, expecting to be catered to by wealthy drug companies.

Significant education, of course, usually did take place. Most medical professionals wouldn't have sat through the simple hawking of drugs. But the conflicts of interest were palpable. During those years, "CME was often a clandestine marketing tool for drug companies," said one seminar organizer who remains in the business. "Golf, dinner, wine and dine doctors and you will win these guys' hearts and minds, or at least some of them."

In 2004, the Accreditation Council for Continuing Medical Education wrote new rules aimed to "brighten the line" between pharmaceutical companies and the seminars. The rules now prohibit pharma company influence on content and speaker selection, as well as limitations on how grant funding can be used. Drug company funding for the seminars has since dropped off and several of the major medical education companies left the business. Now a lot of CME is online, where the risk of improper influence through resorts, dinners, and golf outings is removed.

But prior to that, Purdue sponsored CME seminars, particularly on new techniques for pain treatment, which often urged the use of unnamed timed-release opiates; not coincidentally, OxyContin was the only such pill on the market. The U.S. General Accounting Office reported that the company helped fund more than 20,000 education programs. These often included ways for physicians to get CME credits at state and local medical conferences.

Russell Portenoy was a frequent Purdue speaker and an eloquent one. He stressed the complexity of pain treatment; pain sometimes required a multidisciplinary approach, he said. But he also insisted that chronic pain was frequently best treated with long-acting opiate painkillers.

"It wasn't like Portenoy came up with these concepts to benefit Purdue. He sincerely believed that these were miracle drugs for chronic pain," said the CME seminar organizer, who worked with the doctor and the company. "But had Portenoy not had Purdue's money behind him, he would have published some papers, made some speeches, and his influence would have been minor. With Purdue's millions behind him, his message, which dovetailed with their marketing plans, was hugely magnified. He was a godsend for Purdue. All you need is one guy to say what he was saying. The others guys who are sounding a warning about these drugs don't get funded. They get a journal article, not a megaphone."

Video was another medium Purdue used to apparently great effect. In 1998, Purdue sent out fifteen thousand copies of a video about OxyContin to doctors around the country without submitting it to the FDA for review, contrary to the agency's regulations. *I Got My Life Back: Patients in Pain Tell Their Story* told of the pain relief enjoyed by several patients.

Two years later, Purdue sent out another twelve thousand copies of an updated version of *I Got My Life Back*, showing patients talking about how OxyContin changed their lives. It included information on the 160 mg version of the pill, and made "unsubstantiated claims regarding OxyContin's effect on patients' quality of life . . . and minimized the risks associated with the drug," according to the GAO's 2003 report on the company's OxyContin promo campaign.

A doctor in the video again made the claim—erroneously lifted from Porter and Jick—that narcotic painkillers were shown to cause addiction in less than 1 percent of patients.

In addition, the company sent out fourteen thousand copies of a video intended for doctors' office waiting rooms—*From One Pain Patient to Another: Advice from Patients Who Have Found Relief*—encouraging patients to report their pain to physicians, and aiming to relieve concerns about taking opiate painkillers, claiming again that the pills caused addiction in less than 1 percent of patients.

Purdue funded pain societies and websites promoting pain treatment. These organizations appeared to be informational, but were funded by pharmaceutical companies. Partners Against Pain was founded in 1997 to offer consumers information about pain treatment options, including OxyContin, and providing a list of doctors around the United States who treated pain. One Purdue-funded website, FamilyPractice.com, offered doctors listings of free continuing medical educational programs on pain management.

The American Pain Foundation, a Baltimore organization that promoted the use of opiates for both acute and chronic pain, was funded by Purdue. The foundation organized e-mail campaigns to media outlets it accused of biased reporting on opiates and pain treatment. ProPublica, an investigative journalism nonprofit, reported that the foundation sided with Purdue in a 2001 class action case brought by Ohio patients who claimed to have become addicted to, or dependent on, OxyContin. (The APF would disband in 2012 as a U.S. Senate committee announced it was investigating the group's role in promoting the use of opiate painkillers.)

Purdue donated money for website development to established groups, such as the American Chronic Pain Association and the American Academy of Pain Medicine.

The company was widely criticized for its campaign. Eventually, it would be prosecuted criminally. Yet Purdue's marketing couldn't have found an audience without the pain crusaders who tenderized the terrain for years before that, convincing primary care doctors that in this new age opiates could be prescribed to pain patients with virtually no risk of addiction. In many cases, hospital lawyers advised doctors that patients could sue them for not adequately treating their pain if they didn't prescribe these drugs. Had that not happened—had there been no insistence that pain was undertreated and that pain was now a fifth vital sign—OxyContin would likely not have found the market it did.

By 2003, more than half of the prescribers of OxyContin nationwide were primary care doctors, who had little pain-management training and were under pressure to get patients in and out of their offices. Oxy prescriptions for chronic pain rose from 670,000 in 1997 to 6.2 million in 2002. Those for cancer pain rose from 250,000 to just over a million over the same time.

Phil Prior soon noticed colleagues prescribing OxyContin for chronic ailments—back and knee pain, for example, or the fibromyalgia that the salesmen had mentioned.

In southern Ohio, few people had ever come to drug treatment strung out on opiates. By 1998, however, Chillicothe and the surrounding towns were awash in hundreds of patients addicted to OxyContin. Indeed, patients would go to doctor after doctor with stories of pain and requests for more of the new drug. Dealers who sold meth or cocaine on the street started pushing Oxy. Addicts learned to crush it and snort it, or inject it, obtaining all twelve hours' worth of oxycodone at once.

Seniors realized they could subsidize their retirement by selling their prescription Oxys to younger folks. Some of the first Oxy dealers, in fact, were seniors who saw the value of the pills in their cabinets. "It's like hitting the Lotto if your doctor will put you on OxyContin," Prior said. "People don't even think twice about selling."

OxyContin sales shot up. They surpassed Purdue's goals every year, until they exceeded one billion dollars in each of 2001 and 2002. Rampant abuse accompanied those sales figures. News reports coined the nickname "hillbilly heroin" and chronicled the devastation caused by addiction to OxyContin. How many addicts began as recreational users and how many had once been pain patients was never quite clear.

Not far from Chillicothe, at West Virginia University in Morgantown, Dr. Carl "Rolly" Sullivan watched his drug rehabilitation clinic fill with OxyContin addicts. Alcoholics had been the clinic's stock-in-trade. But West Virginia towns now teemed with opiate addicts to the point where alcoholics couldn't find a bed at Sullivan's clinic. He was seeing people on spectacular doses of OxyContin every day—300 mg and more. He couldn't tell the difference between them and a heroin addict.

"Purdue and the pharmaceutical industry were saying that addiction in OxyContin is really rare," said Sullivan. "The incidence of addiction was far higher than they indicated. But there was an enthusiasm for using [opiates] that was not borne out by science."

As news reports recounted rising OxyContin abuse and addiction, Purdue called Sullivan and asked him to speak to its sales reps. Twenty of them met Sullivan at a hotel in Charleston. He saw they were concerned. He spent a couple hours with them, describing the foot traffic at his clinic, the amounts of their drug that addicts, some of them former pain patients, were consuming.

"We were told this was safe," said one sales rep.

Sullivan brought along a woman from his clinic recovering from addiction to OxyContin. One sales rep asked her how long she would need to score OxyContin on the street outside the hotel.

"About twenty minutes," the woman replied. "But that's only because I don't drive."

Sullivan thought the visit sobered the sales reps, who'd been charging hard into doctors' offices for five years by then. But he noticed that Purdue kept selling OxyContin the way it had. The pill now made up 90 percent of the company's annual revenue.

Six months later, the woman Sullivan brought to the meeting died of an OxyContin overdose.

The Man at Home

Xalisco, Nayarit

The state of Nayarit lies along 180 miles of Pacific Ocean coastline, and stretches inland into the western Sierra Madre Mountains.

In the centralized politics of Mexico, Nayarit was an afterthought. Following Mexican Independence, the small territory remained part of the state of Jalisco for a century. Even when it was separated from its larger neighbor, Nayarit remained a military district. Only in 1917 was it made autonomous—becoming the fifth smallest of Mexico's thirty-one states. Its population didn't top one million people until 2010. The state is surrounded by some of Mexico's behemoth states; Zacatecas and Durango are nearby. Sinaloa, the state streaking up the coast north of Nayarit, is the birthplace of Mexican drug trafficking. Tiny Nayarit rarely made the news.

Just south of the state capital of Tepic lies the town of Xalisco. Originally, the town spelled its name with a *j*—Jalisco. To avoid confusion with the state, town officials changed the spelling to Xalisco, and many residents refer to it as Xalisquillo—Little Xalisco.

Xalisco is bisected by a road that heads out of Tepic and south eighty miles into the resort of Puerto Vallarta. Xalisco's San Cayetano Catholic Church was built in 1812, and this looks to be about the age of the cobblestones that stud the narrow street around the town's central Plaza Hidalgo.

The municipio, or county, of Xalisco, with a population of 49,000 people, comprises a necklace of small villages surrounding the county seat. To the east is Pantanal, with its view of the Sangangüey volcano, and where authorities placed Tepic's airport. To the south, along the Puerto Vallarta highway, is hilly Testerazo, followed by Emiliano Zapata, where a bust of the Mexican revolutionary marks the entrance to town. Farther south is Aquiles Serdán. There are other villages—La Curva, El Malinal, Adolfo López Mateos, El Carrizal.

The Man arrived here for the first time in August 1993 and found a humble place, looking like so many other Mexican small towns. Xalisco's plaza held a basketball court and bandstand, and was surrounded by a market, a small city hall, a few clothing stores, an ice-cream shop. Old men in straw cowboy hats and sandals gathered to kibitz about town life. The trucks were few and old, and the houses were narrow—row houses that opened right onto the sidewalk. Outside the town center was undeveloped land that separated Xalisco from the capital city a couple miles north.

Early August is the time of the town's Feria del Elote—the Corn Fair. Like Xalisco itself, the fair the Man attended was picturesque but humble, with basketball and soccer tournaments pitting neighborhood and village teams against each other. There were modest carnival rides, cotton candy, a horse parade, and every night bands, for hire by the song, played in the plaza.

That year, he and the Nayarit and others who were dealing heroin in the United States sponsored soccer teams in the fair's tournament for the first time. The Man sponsored the team from La Talega, a neighborhood on Xalisco's south end, buying them uniforms and balls, then betting with the Nayarit and other dealers on who would win. The loser paid for six hours of banda music in the plaza that night.

Once only legitimate businessmen—large landowners often—spent heavily at the fiesta. But as the new heroin traffickers grew in numbers and in confidence, they never missed a feria and the chance to relax and spend money ostentatiously.

Their free spending boosted Xalisco's economy. People watched who was spending a lot, with an arch of an eyebrow at a new truck or recently purchased house or the guy who was suddenly paying the banda in the plaza. The fair became a kind of convention for tar heroin traffickers in the United States. At parties around town, they would show off, talk about how well they were doing, share tips on avoiding cops, or complain about the arrest of a trusted driver.

The Man never missed a Feria del Elote after that. In 1996, he bought a half-built house from a woman whose bank-robber husband was doing fifty years in prison in Sinaloa. He added on to it, with grass in the front yard, resembling houses in California. He added a bar, a music room, wide hallways, and two bathrooms. He met a woman and they shacked up. Every year, after the fair was over, the Man returned to the United States.

In Reno, he hung out in the sports betting room of the Cal Neva Casino, where he sated his other addiction: gambling on NFL games. There he met a card dealer, a large, husky black man named Daniel. Daniel and his wife were longtime heroin users from Columbus, Ohio. Daniel, it turned out, loved black tar heroin. It was a revelation. Back east there was nothing like it. In Columbus, any heroin they could get was weak powder, stepped on to the point where it qualified as bunk. An addict had to spend a hundred dollars or more daily just to not get dope sick.

Daniel took the Man aside one day at Cal Neva.

"You should take this out to Columbus, man," he said. "You'd become a millionaire. There ain't nothing like this out there. I got an uncle I could hook you up with."

He thanked Daniel.

"I didn't even think of Columbus until he put a bug in my ear," he told me many years later.

Meanwhile, his woman in Nayarit was complaining that he was taking the risks, running everything in the United States. The Nayarit was back in Mexico doing nothing and getting money he didn't deserve, she said.

"You know what it's like once you get a woman involved," he later told me. "She said, 'You're doing everything. I don't see him doing nothing.'"

He had to admit that keeping track of businesses in Portland, Reno, Salt Lake, Hawaii, and Denver was distracting. The small details of retailing drove him nuts: keeping the kids working hard and not straying into partying; replacing a seized car in Denver or a driver arrested in Portland. When two drivers in Hawaii killed their cell bosses, the Man claimed the bodies at the request of the family and sent them back to Mexico.

He wanted a break. His friend pleaded with him.

"You're breaking up when we're going strong," the Nayarit told him. "We're doing good."

"It's time I got out on my own."

It was 1997. The Man was fully integrated into Xalisco, thinking of the town as home now. He owned property there. He had a woman, livestock, and respect. In the plaza, parents whose sons he had hired came up to him and shook his hand. One even gave him a pig, another a cow. He now had the contacts to bring in his own supply up north.

The Man contacted Daniel, that card dealer in Reno, who produced a telephone number for his uncle, Chuckie, in Columbus.

"Call him," Daniel said. "He'll help hook you up with everyone you need."

The Man returned to Xalisco. He bought a house near the beach in San Blas, Nayarit's main tourist town. He relaxed for six months. But no money was coming in and his woman was spending a lot. So, after six months of kicking back, he returned to the United States in 1998, thinking it was now time to expand east. He looked at a map and saw three cities in a row: Indianapolis, Dayton, and Columbus. He figured he would try his luck.

On June 11, 1998, he flew into Indianapolis and found a cheap motel off Washington Street, the hooker stroll on the east side of town.

"Watch out, man," said the motel clerk as he checked in. "There's a tornado comin'. Stay away from the window and look for a place to get low."

The Man had never seen a tornado. He watched with special concentration that afternoon as the sky got dark and a wind attacked. The wind blew the rain sideways and it hit his window like volleys of BBs; it was not cool, like the rain in California, but eerily warm. Then a massive dark funnel a quarter-mile wide, roaring like a jet plane, came right down Washington Street. He watched it rip roofing off a Pizza Hut, and shred a day-care center. A man parked his car and scurried his family indoors. A moment later, the car was gone. They found it three blocks away.

The tornado was one of eight that tore through central Indiana that evening. No one died. Still, it was an unsettling introduction and the Man never felt right in Indianapolis after that.

The next day, he bought a used car—a brown Cadillac Cimarron, a model so poorly conceived and designed that many marked it as a seminal event in the decline of Detroit. But it didn't stand out and cost only two thousand dollars.

Camping out in front of the town's methadone clinic, he gave away samples of his dope and soon had a client list of desperate junkies avid for the black tar they'd never seen before. Then one day cops stopped him after seeing a couple exiting his Cimarron near the clinic.

"We've got reports you've been dealing heroin."

"Check the car," he replied. "I got no drugs. I was just dropping them off"—he nodded in the couple's direction—"'cause they needed a ride."

The cops found nothing. But they told him, "We have a photograph of you and your car. Every time we see you, we're stopping you."

So he moved on to Dayton, with a kid he brought in from his Reno store. They hooked up with a dealer, a black guy retired from Delphi, the GM auto-parts company, who seemed to know every addict in town. Sure enough, no one in Ohio had seen this kind of dope.

But he never forgot Daniel's message and the promise of Columbus. One sunny summer day, after they had been in Dayton a couple weeks, he left the kid with the Delphi retiree and he drove to Columbus. He found a motel off Highway 70 west of town, and called Daniel's uncle, Chuckie.

They met at the town's methadone clinic off Bryden Road the next morning. The clinic was a hive of illegal dope trading. Almost anything a user wanted was for sale. He gave Chuckie a few free samples and his beeper number.

That afternoon, Chuckie called.

"That's some killer stuff you got," he said. "I gotta whole buncha people want some of that."

The Man drove back to Dayton and pulled up stakes.

"We were selling a lot," he told me. "But the thing I didn't like in Dayton was we were dealing with a lot of blacks. I don't deal with blacks if I don't have to. In the long run they'll rip you off. They'll hurt your kids. They'll pistol-whip you."

Columbus had more white people, it appeared, and a large community of Mexicans in which to mingle. He pointed the Cimarron east again to the vast expanses of central Ohio and the state capital, surrounded by large white suburbs and highways—close to four states and the put-upon region of Appalachia—where up to that point no one had seen much heroin.

What's OxyContin?

Portsmouth, Ohio

One Friday shortly before Christmas in 1997, a reporter from the *Portsmouth Daily Times* called Ed Hughes. Hughes ran the Counseling Center, Portsmouth's lone addiction-treatment clinic. The reporter asked if he could come to the staff's party to write a story about staying sober over the holidays.

Hughes agreed. The reporter interviewed some of the staff, asking especially about the younger clients. Midway through the party, the reporter took Hughes aside.

"What's OxyContin?"

Hughes hadn't heard of it.

"Some of your clients say they're using it."

The next Monday, Hughes began calling around. His staff told him the drug had started showing up recently, that it contained a large amount of oxycodone, and that users had learned to crush it and snort it.

He called colleagues at treatment centers in northern Ohio, describing what Portsmouth was seeing. No one in Cleveland, Akron, Columbus, or Cincinnati knew anything about OxyContin. Had Hughes made calls into the rest of Appalachia, he would have heard a far different story, one that resembled what was just getting started in Portsmouth.

But at the time, he said, "we didn't realize that we were essentially on the cutting edge of a crisis."

Around that time, Karen Charles and her husband, Jerry, were making plans to move their flooring shop into a building on Biggs Lane in South Shore, Kentucky, across the Ohio River from Portsmouth.

The Charleses knew that a doctor named David Procter had a practice at the beige metal building next door. In the months after relocating, they saw his business was a lot larger than they'd figured. The traffic, in fact, kept growing. It seemed like no other doctor's practice they knew. Procter's waiting room could no longer accommodate the crowds. Procter's clinic often stayed open well past its posted business hours. People parked along little Biggs Lane all day long waiting to see him.

"They'd eat two meals in their cars," said Karen.

Many patients were from other counties, even other states. Karen Charles remembers Missouri and Arkansas license plates. Unsavory folks, most of them. They blocked access to the Charles Flooring parking lot. A fight once erupted between Procter clients and a truck driver blocked from making a delivery. On another occasion, someone called in a bomb threat and police evacuated the clinic, along with the Charles's flooring shop and nearby houses. Karen Charles never dared enter the Procter clinic, but she heard he was selling OxyContin.

"It changed everything around here," she said years later. "It was something else—something I hope to never be around again. I talked to him a few times. I don't know how he expected us to run a business. Little old ladies are not going to come in a store with such riffraff hanging around."

A reporter from the *Portsmouth Daily Times* eventually wrote a very different story from the one that ran after that Christmas party. The story talked about a new trend in addiction in southern Ohio and neighboring states: opiates, primarily oxycodone, delivered most prominently in that new pill called OxyContin.

About a week after the second story ran, Ed Hughes received a telephone call from a lawyer representing Purdue Pharma. The caller threatened to sue the Counseling Center if Hughes ever said in print that OxyContin was addictive. This startled Hughes, who wasn't quoted as saying that OxyContin was addictive. The Counseling Center was mentioned in the *Daily Times* story, but it was the young clients who said they were addicted to the drug. He wondered how the company, based in Connecticut, had spotted the story in the tiny newspaper.

"Something big was going on," he said. "How did they know that article showed up in the *Portsmouth Daily Times* unless they were tracking that kind of information?"

The Counseling Center that Hughes ran had begun in a small house seventeen years earlier. Hughes, a recovering alcoholic, felt rehabilitation really involved rebuilding an enslaved person. He believed recovery was possible only with a multidisciplinary approach to treating the addict—"a continuum of care," Hughes said. An addict in treatment needed a 12-step program, but he also needed help finding housing, with writing a résumé, and with finding child care and clothes for job interviews. These services had to be close by. Addicts usually had no car, no driver's license, and no gas money. Hughes had seen people go back to drugs because they hadn't been able to get to a court date or an appointment with a doctor or a probation officer.

By the late nineties, the Counseling Center had moved into a large new building for outpatients. It also had a small house for men and the only rehab residence in Ohio for female addicts with children. The Center had room for all the alcoholics and cocaine users who came to it. About the time of that Christmas party in 1997, Hughes figured he would spend the next year consolidating and improving the Center's internal workings, rather than expanding to meet the area's need. That had been accomplished, he thought.

Not even close. Portsmouth was about to become ground zero of an almost viral explosion of opiate use and abuse. By the spring of 1998, Oxy addicts were everywhere, mostly young and white. "It was like a wildfire," Hughes remembered.

This drug scourge had a different origin from others he had seen. In Portsmouth, it began with what came to be called pill mills, a business model invented in town, but growing from the aggressive nationwide prescribing of opiates, particularly OxyContin. A pill mill was a pain-management clinic, staffed by a doctor with little more than a prescription pad. A pill mill became a virtual ATM for dope as the doctor issued prescriptions to hundreds of people a day.

"There were doctors putting a lot of this stuff out on the street," Hughes said. "There were long lines. This form of marketing the drug to a drug-addicted people, I don't think that had been done before."

Smack Clans in the Sanctuary

Chimayo, New Mexico

Jim Kuykendall grew from classic Drug Enforcement Administration lineage. His uncle, Travis Kuykendall, retired as assistant special agent in charge of the DEA's El Paso office. His father, Jaime Kuykendall, worked for Customs and Border Patrol in the 1960s, running the Texas-Mexico border fighting the then-incipient drug gangs. His father's christened name was James, but he grew up in the small Texas border town of Eagle Pass and married a Mexican woman. Embracing both cultures, he was known as Jaime.

The Kuykendall brothers joined the DEA when it formed from several federal agencies in 1973. Jaime Kuykendall opened the DEA's office in Guayaquil, Ecuador, shortly thereafter. Jim Kuykendall spent much of his youth there, thinking his dad was some kind of James Bond, but not really knowing what it was that his father did.

In the 1980s, Jaime Kuykendall moved to Mexico. He was Guadalajara station chief for the DEA in 1985 when traffickers kidnapped, tortured, and murdered his agent, Enrique "Kiki" Camarena, a killing that was covered up by Mexican government officials in league with traffickers. The murder traumatized the new DEA and intensified its focus on Mexico. The episode was the topic of a classic book, later made into a movie, called *Desperados*, by journalist Elaine Shannon. Jaime Kuykendall wrote his own book on the Camerena episode, *O Plomo o Plata? Silver or Lead?*

In college in Texas, Jim Kuykendall first studied journalism; but then, working as a campus police officer, he switched his major to criminal justice. One night he had dinner with a DEA agent, an old drinking buddy of his father's.

"Think about applying to the DEA," the agent told him.

Other federal law enforcement agencies, the DEA man said, controlled their people from above to an almost stifling degree. Oversight limited the freedom an agent had in conducting an investigation. In part because of the kind of work the DEA did, individual agents had unmatched control over cases and could make them as big as their own abilities dictated. Unlike local policing, DEA agents had the chance to travel and live abroad, and the department would prize an agent like Kuykendall, fluent in Spanish.

That sounded like an adventure. Not long after graduating in 1987, Jim Kuykendall applied to the agency where his father and his uncle were living legends.

He did tours in Beaumont, Texas, and Bogotá, Colombia, before returning to the United States in 1998. He was stationed in Albuquerque, New Mexico, the senior agent in the office. By that point in his career, Jim Kuykendall had seen that his father's buddy was right: A DEA agent could make a difference, aided by the enormous power of the federal government's conspiracy laws. These statutes allowed the government to charge a person for involvement in a criminal enterprise even if there was no immediately incriminating evidence—no drugs in an apartment when the cops searched, for example. Wiretap cases were about what was happening at that moment. The conspiracy cases Kuykendall grew to prefer had more to do with what had happened in the past. They did not depend so much on dangerous undercover buys or finding a suspect in possession of lots of dope. Instead, they required agents to go back through the record, cobble together witnesses and reports of past arrests, showing a pattern of, say, a group selling drugs over many years.

Defense attorneys criticize conspiracy cases at times as too broad, sweeping up, for example, everyone a defendant contacts. But Kuykendall found that conspiracy cases appealed to his inner journalist. Conspiracy cases required telling a story. Using conspiracy statutes, an agent learned part of the story of a criminal enterprise as he made a case, then flipped the defendants and came back with more arrests and learned the whole story, or at least most of it. Telling the full story of a criminal enterprise had a lot to do with justice Kuykendall came to believe, for little of what these enterprises really were was apparent on the day of a bust.

Jim Kuykendall had made several cases like this in his career, and as he settled into his job in Albuquerque he would make another up in the small town of Chimayo, New Mexico.

Chimayo, with a population of less than four thousand people, was founded five hundred years ago by Spanish conquistadors. It is twenty-five miles from Santa Fe, in the verdant Española Valley.

The town is known for several things. It is the Lowrider Capital of the World. Residents are obsessed with the dressed-up, low-slung cars. Chimayo's cherry-red heirloom chiles are powerful and their seeds have been passed down through generations of growers. A small adobe church in Chimayo, built in 1816, attracts thousands of pilgrims and tourists a year. The milk chocolate soil around the church is said to cure illnesses. Some twenty-five tons of it is sold each year to people who rub it on their bodies or simply keep it in small plastic cases. Every night Chimayo residents venture into the hills, dig up more soil, and deposit it at the shrine. Every Good Friday, thirty thousand pilgrims come to the small adobe Santuario de Chimayo, as the church is known, some walking from Albuquerque, ninety miles away.

But the town is also known for an illness the soil hasn't cured. Chimayo has the highest rate of heroin addiction in America. When people discuss heroin addiction in Chimayo, they tend to talk of it in terms of a culture, something passed down through generations. Entire Chimayo families are addicted, beginning with the grandparents or even great-grandparents.

This had been true for many years when Jim Kuykendall, a few weeks into his job, called Chris Valdez, a New Mexico State Police narcotics officer up in the Española Valley.

When Valdez was growing up in the area, this illness was known but hidden. By the time he became a cop, though, heroin was about all Valdez ever saw. Several families, whose ancestors had been in the valley since the 1600s, sold the heroin. In the cloistered world of tiny Chimayo no one could touch them. Addict burglaries and car break-ins, meanwhile, grew worse every year.

For decades, Chimayo addicts had subsisted on powder heroin that Valdez assumed came from Asia somewhere. It had been cut often and was weak. Then sometime in about 1997, Mexicans arrived and began providing potent and cheap black tar heroin. Chimayo dealers wouldn't let the Mexicans sell in town, but they were happy to buy this new product wholesale, and parcel it out to their customers. That's when things seemed to unravel fast. With almost unlimited supply, users who'd controlled their addiction used far more. People stole wantonly. And those who had lived for years on weak powder heroin began to die on the strong black tar.

Not long after moving to Albuquerque, Kuykendall went up to the valley and Valdez drove him around. The police officer pointed out the mobile homes of heroin dealers—double- and triple-wides being especially prized among valley residents. Chimayo was an insular place, Valdez said. Cops were hated but needles were everywhere and overdose deaths were rising steadily. Few homes kept a stereo or television for long.

Three clans dealt heroin: the Barelas, with Felix its patriarch, and his many brothers, several of whom were strung out; there was Josefa Gallegos, whose son, Brian, lived in a shack out back behind her house, his arms rotting from tar heroin injections; finally there was "Fat Jose" and Jesse "Donuts" Martinez and their relatives.

These families had the nicest mobile homes and best lowriders. Felix Barela's lowrider was the finest in the valley—a dark-purple Thunderbird known as the Wizard. The dealer families loved Harleys, too, another prized possession in Chimayo. Felix Barela also had several fine racehorses, including Red Hot Mag, the state's best quarter horse. Each clan ran virtual convenience stores of dope, with fifty to a hundred addicts coming every day, some three times a day.

As the death toll rose through 1998 and into 1999, families of dead addicts, joined by priests from a New Mexico order known as Hermanos los Penitentes, began protest processions through the mountains to the santuario. They bore signs with the names of people who had died from overdoses, or been killed by burglars.

Kuykendall left shocked by the problem. Still, it appeared to be a local, not federal, issue—retail street dealing, it seemed to him.

A few weeks later, though, Valdez called. Get up here tomorrow, he said. There's a meeting of a Chimayo Crime Prevention Organization. People are mad.

That night, Kuykendall walked into the Rancho de Chimayo restaurant, and was startled to see congressmen, judges, the head of the New Mexico State Police, and city councilmen, along with Bruce Richardson, the board of the Chimayo crime prevention group.

Richardson spoke. Criminal clans ran the valley and children were finding used syringes.

"You have done nothing," Richardson told the officials that night.

He brought forward a large pickle jar filled with used syringes. The public officials gave what Kuykendall considered elected-official responses, appeasing no one.

He drove home to Albuquerque that night. The politicians' presence told him that they knew things were bad. He had always told younger agents to focus on the biggest dealer wherever they were stationed.

That dealer may not be Pablo Escobar, he would say, but the biggest dealer in a small town is still a problem to that town.

The next day, Kuykendall opened a case against Chimayo's three heroin clans.

Liberace Shows the Way

Portsmouth, Ohio

By the end of the 1990s, Dr. David Procter was one of the few people doing well in Portsmouth, Ohio.

He had himself a $750,000 mansion, with a swimming pool, African art, and two seven-foot bronze storks. He owned a Mercedes, a Porsche, and a red Corvette—rare possessions in the Ohio River valley.

In the late 1980s, the Kentucky Board of Medical Licensure investigated patient complaints of unethical practices against him. Board agents found that he prescribed opiates aggressively and often without much diagnosis, or follow-up. He was found to have violated no Kentucky medical regulation and retained his license, but was placed on probation. In fact, the state records reflected a doctor who prescribed the drugs often yet discontinued them just as frequently, who consulted other physicians and urged his chronic-pain patients to use exercise or physical therapy to control their pain. David Procter seemed to be searching for solutions to what ailed his patients.

A decade later that had changed. A nurse in California once told me, "When you deal with people who are in pain all day long, after a while you get worn down."

Something like that happened to David Procter. More patient complaints in the 1990s prompted a second state investigation. By then, those records show, he regularly prescribed Valium, Vicodin, the sedative Soma, Xanax, and a steady regimen of Redux diet pills—all with almost no diagnosis or suggestions for other treatment, such as physical therapy. Nor was there any discussion of improving diet as a way to lose weight and reduce pain. As I read the Licensure Board investigative reports, it seemed that many years in deindustrialized America seeing vulnerable people and manipulative people who used drugs and the government dole to navigate economic disaster had corroded any medical ethics Procter once possessed.

So I went to Portsmouth to see if I could learn more about the doctor whom locals called the Godfather of the Pill Mill, the man who had started the first business and showed others how it was done.

No one in Portsmouth had forgotten David Procter, though he was long gone by then. Some remembered him fondly. Many said they had gone to his clinic and waited in long lines for dope prescriptions.

One of them was Kathy Newman, who in 1996 was a high school cheerleader and the daughter of a contractor. Kathy had just graduated from Portsmouth High School when she broke ribs in a car accident. The emergency room in town was wary of prescribing more than ibuprofen for pain. You should go see David Procter, her friends said: He'll give you something that works.

Kathy drove to the South Shore clinic and walked into a madhouse. The room was packed; people were standing in the aisles, tense and greedy with anticipation. After three hours, she got in to see the doctor. Procter prescribed her Vicodin and spent a half hour telling her that she would probably have back and hip pain for the rest of her life, and thus would need this prescription for that long as well. Newman went along with it, not sure what to think.

"I'm scared to death. I'm so young and afraid that I was going to be on this the rest of my life," she said.

In fact, those Vicodins led to a fourteen-year addiction that eventually had Newman shooting up OxyContin and getting pill prescriptions from a half-dozen doctors around town. Years disappeared in zoned-out addiction. She once found herself in an abandoned farmhouse with people she didn't know, unaware how she got there. A pit bull ran through the living room, chased by an enraged rooster.

The pain-treatment revolution had many faces and these mostly belonged to well-meaning doctors and dedicated nurses. But in the Rust Belt, another kind of pain had emerged. Waves of people sought disability as a way to survive as jobs departed. Legions of doctors arose who were not so well-meaning, or who simply found a livelihood helping people who were looking for a monthly government disability check as a solution to unemployment. By the time the pain revolution changed U.S. medicine, the Ohio River valley had a class of these docs. They were an economic coping strategy for a lot of folks. They charged cash for each visit and were quick with the prescription pad, willing to go along with whatever the patient claimed was pain, wherever the patient claimed he had it. Then along came OxyContin.

If heroin was the perfect drug for drug traffickers, OxyContin was ideal for these pill mill doctors. The drug had several things going for it, as far as they were concerned: First, it was a pharmaceutically produced pill with a legal medical use; second, it created addicts, and not just among those who looked to abuse it, but among many who came in search of pain relief. Every patient who was prescribed the drug stood a chance of soon needing it every day. These people were willing to pay cash. They never missed an appointment. If diagnosis wasn't your concern, a clinic was a low-overhead operation: a rented building, a few waiting rooms, some office staff. And bouncers. These clinics did require bouncers. They also required a physician with a DEA registration number that permitted him to prescribe federally designated Schedule II narcotics like OxyContin. Prescriptions for Schedule II drugs had to be written each month by a doctor for a patient, who had to come to the office in person. That meant a monthly-visit fee from every patient—$250 usually. And that kept waiting rooms full and cash rolling in.

Among the very first docs in America to figure out the potency of OxyContin as a business model was David Procter in Portsmouth, Ohio. He believed all his patients. Not only that, he encouraged them to believe in imaginary pain.

"Injured people start going to him and he gives them this new wonderful medicine: OxyContin," said Lisa Roberts, a public health nurse in Portsmouth, who had worked with Procter years before at a hospital where he had privileges. "Soon they're getting addicted. They'd say my pain's getting worse and he'd increase the dose. I started seeing people I know, who are hardworking decent people, acting all bizarre, rolling cars, stealing."

Danny Colley, who grew up in Portsmouth's rough East End neighborhood, watched Procter's gradual corruption. Procter had been his family's doctor when he was a child. At twenty, now fully involved in the drug world, Colley visited his former doctor's clinic. Procter was the first cash-only doc around and was by then prescribing Xanax and Lortabs for everything. Later, he became the first to prescribe OxyContin for Colley. His clinic was full.

"He was the one guy and he was burning it down," Colley said. "When he gave me my Lortabs, he said put these under your tongue and let them melt—do not snort them. When I got my first Oxys, he told me to be careful but that I could snort those. His exact words. He gave me the same thing he said he was taking. He's giving me the dope I need so I'm not sick. I thought he was my dude! I thought he was looking out for me. I thought it was the coolest thing ever."

Colley went to Procter after being injured on a job. "He got workers' comp to pay for my medicine for a year and a half," Colley said. "He was helping with that. He had a photographic fucking memory. We all thought he was the smartest person in the world. He was brilliant, but he was a crook."

Local doctors took a cue from Procter. Dr. John Lilly opened in downtown Portsmouth. He had lines out the door, too. After that, things opened wide.

Kathy Newman noticed it wasn't just the unscrupulous docs. It seemed every physician in town was under the influence of opiates' remarkable painkilling potential. Anyway, she could find no doctor in Portsmouth offering a pain solution that didn't involve opiates.

"They'd be, like, 'Well, let's try you on Lorcet tens.' 'Oh, that didn't work for a month? Let's move you on to twenties,'" Kathy Newman said. "Within three months of me telling them that Vicodin fives aren't working anymore, I was on Oxy twenties, paying cash all the way."

Doctors prescribed those drugs. The other truth, though, is that opiates were all most patients demanded in southern Ohio by then.

FIFTY MILES AWAY, AN addict who sometimes went by the name of Jeremy Wilder saw easy money and grabbed it.

Wilder, a tall, lanky guy with a heavy Appalachian drawl, was raised downriver from Portsmouth in the one-stoplight town of Aberdeen, situated between two power plants in Brown County.

Jeremy was a union carpenter. But he grew up around the kind of moral ambivalence that characterized life in the small Ohio River valley towns as the Rust Belt took shape. The easy money got the better of him.

In 1995, Jeremy heard that Dr. Fortune Williams had been hired by David Procter to start up a clinic out in Garrison, Kentucky. Williams was the first doc Jeremy went to as he emerged as one of the first pill dealers in his county. He paid Williams $250 for the visit and $200 more for prescriptions that included OxyContin. Jeremy later found a doctor in Williamsburg, Ohio, and another in Portsmouth to supply him with pills as well.

I met Jeremy as I traveled the heartland of the opiate plague, bisected by the Ohio River. Through him, I realized that as the pain revolution spread, powered by OxyContin, the area once starved for health care had seen doctors descend on it like locusts.

By the mid-1990s, Jeremy Wilder was the biggest pill dealer in Aberdeen while still working carpentry jobs in Cincinnati and around southern Ohio. He had a window in his house to which users in the area literally beat a path.

At first, Jeremy didn't use the drugs he sold. But one night at a party he broke down and snorted an Oxy. That was it. Soon he was selling to support his habit. Then, in Cincinnati one day, he couldn't find Oxys. A neighbor of his Cincinnati connection could get something else: black tar heroin. Jeremy balked. He wanted no part of heroin. But the next day, he couldn't take the dope sick anymore. The guy phoned a Mexican, who brought over small balloons of black tar heroin. Jeremy never took the pills again.

For the next two years, he barely existed. He drove daily to Cincinnati to buy pills from a woman and his tar from the Mexicans. He sold the pills to pay for the heroin he used. For a while each balloon he bought from the Mexicans came with a paper attached and a phone number. Call anytime. He never forgot that. He guessed they were just starting out. He was new to heroin and wondered if all traffickers marketed like that, but figured they did not.

In late 1998, Jeremy Wilder, from the town of Aberdeen in rural Brown County, was among the first in southern Ohio to make the transition from OxyContin to heroin.

He was not the last.

ABOUT THAT YEAR, REPORTS from the Kentucky Board of Medical Licensure's second investigation into David Procter began telling strange tales. He was losing all control, manipulating damaged and addicted women for sex.

One upset Kentucky medical inspector, who reviewed dozens of Procter patient records during the late 1990s, used terms like "gross incompetence," "negligence," and "malpractice." Procter, the inspector wrote, didn't even record a patient's height, weight, pulse, or temperature. "Dr. Procter's records are extremely poor and I am unable to tell what exactly was prescribed in each visit from his notes," he wrote.

Of a second Procter patient: "There is significant lack of evidence of evaluation and alternative treatment to this patient except for the use of controlled substances."

And a third: "There did not appear to be any type of practice of medicine involved except the description of symptoms by the patient and the doctor writing for controlled substances. I do not believe this constitutes the practice of medicine."

Patient complaints prompted the investigation. Among them three women reported they repeatedly had sex with Procter in his office at his insistence in exchange for prescriptions. One said Procter pushed her to have sex with him, threatening not to give her an office job or help with her husband's workers' compensation claim if she did not allow him to lick her vagina, though her toddler son was in the room when he did it. Another went to Procter for depression that grew from an abortion she had had at eighteen. On the first visit, she said, Procter told her to write a letter outlining all her problems, which they would review. With each visit, she would write a letter about her emotional problems, which he would review, and then have sex with her. After a few such visits, the letter reading was dispensed with and Procter got straight to the sex. On the last of twenty visits, she took a drug overdose in his office and he had a nurse drive her home. After that, she told investigators, she entered drug rehab.

In November 1998, Procter had a car accident. He claimed it left him with short-term memory loss, unable to practice medicine. People were skeptical. Some suggested Procter used the injuries as a ruse, saying he could no longer remember where certain patients' records were, or how he had treated them. Either way, he relinquished his medical license to the state of Kentucky, but kept his pain clinic open. He hired doctors from across the country to staff it—docs for whom the job of wantonly prescribing opiates was the only one available.

In the hollowing out of small-town America, the pill mill doc was a kind of a coup de grâce. In so many towns, locally owned businesses had expired. Family diners were replaced by Applebee's and town hardware stores by Home Depot. Then ersatz pain physicians replaced family docs and became about the only health care some towns had. Around northern Kentucky and southern Ohio, Procter's docs were initially hailed for coming to the area. In truth, they were vinegar in the mouth of a crucified region.

In the three years following his car accident, Procter hired fifteen doctors. They arrived with histories of drug use, previously suspended licenses, and mental problems, ready to prescribe while working for Procter for twenty-five hundred dollars a week. Some of these doctors stayed. They learned the business. Then they left to set up their own pain clinics in nearby small towns, taking with them office staff trained by Procter. One Kentucky lawman dubbed him "Ray Kroc," for the man who spread McDonald's restaurants nationwide. Procter's business model spread like a virus, unleashing unstable doctors on a vulnerable region.

Dr. Frederick Cohn worked for Procter before relocating to an abandoned supermarket in the town of Paintsville (pop. 3,400) in eastern Kentucky, where he saw as many as 146 patients a day, three minutes each, while lines formed outside. Cohn had preprinted prescriptions for various narcotics, including OxyContin, Lortab, Soma, and Xanax. He prescribed the same pills in the same amounts over and over throughout the day, no matter the patient's complaint— 2.7 million pills in one year.

Dr. Steven Snyder worked for Procter for several months in 1999 before leaving to start his own pain clinic. Snyder once had his medical license suspended in Indiana and Florida for drug use. He was a long-time drug user. But in 1997, apparently unaware of his past, the state of Kentucky granted him an osteopath's license. While working for Procter, Snyder was addicted to Lorcet and was injecting OxyContin while writing narcotics prescriptions ten and twelve hours a day. He told a DEA investigator that he often split prescriptions with patients, supplying his habit and that of his wife.

Dr. Fortune Williams worked for Procter before moving to Garrison, Kentucky, where he worked in a clinic owned by Nancy Sadler, a former Procter employee. On some days, he saw patients for ninety seconds at a time, and issued forty-six thousand controlled-substance prescriptions—for a total of 2.3 million pills—in nine months.

Dr. Rodolfo Santos worked in Procter's clinic for a while, during which time at least one of his patients died. An investigator wrote that Santos displayed "gross ignorance, gross negligence, gross incompetence" and "a level of care that I would not find acceptable in a first year medical student." Santos said he knew he was dealing with addicted patients who lied, and scammed drugs from him, but that he was trying to educate them. "Who will help them?" he told an investigator.

As the pain revolution spread across the country, so, too, did pain clinics—places where people in pain went for treatment, most often in the form of the opiate painkillers that were now accepted in modern medicine. The pain clinic became a business model, repeated over and over, and many were legitimate. But the business also attracted doctors who were unethical or compromised from the start. Even doctors whose intentions were honorable occasionally had their scruples worn out and warped by the temptation and constant pressure from pain patients and drug-seeking addicts. In either case, many clinics became places where doctors dispensed prescriptions like candy for cash, and became known as pill mills.

Once these businesses got going, they didn't just prescribe opiate painkillers, such as Vicodin or OxyContin. There also emerged in the wake of

David Procter a taste in the Rust Belt and Appalachia for the class of psychoactive drugs known as benzodiazepines. Valium was the first benzo, but Xanax bars were the most popular. As Procter showed his clients, benzodiazepines combined with opiates were especially potent and addictive. Both were depressants and very dangerous when taken together. But addicts grew to love the two together as benzos seemed to enhance the euphoria of the opiates. The combined prescription of opiates and benzos was a hot ticket at pill mills in Portsmouth and elsewhere.

I asked a detective, seasoned by investigations into many of these clinics, to describe the difference between a pill mill and a legitimate pain clinic. Look at the parking lot, he said. If you see lines of people standing around outside, smoking, people getting pizza delivered, fist-fights, and traffic jams—if you see people in pajamas who don't care what they look like in public—that's a pill mill. And that's what popped up all over Portsmouth, growing from David Procter's first clinic.

Procter, meanwhile, gained the DEA's attention. The agency launched an investigation into Plaza Healthcare. Procter pleaded guilty to conspiring to distribute prescription medication; then he fled to Canada with a Cincinnati bail bondswoman who was neither his wife nor his mistress, a few days before he was to be sentenced. They were captured at the Canadian border with forty thousand dollars and plane tickets to the Cayman Islands. His lawyer, Gary "Rocky" Billiter, aided the escape.

Procter was returned to Kentucky, where he had already testified against Drs. Williams and Santos in court in return for a lighter sentence in his own case. He eventually served eleven years in prison. Santos and Williams also went off to prison, as did Cohn and Snyder and Billiter.

With that, the era of the pill mill owned by doctors from out of town drew to a close in Portsmouth, Ohio.

David Procter ended up at the federal prison and hospital in Lexington, Kentucky, that once was the Narcotic Farm. I wrote to him there, toward the end of his sentence, asking to hear what he had to say about Portsmouth, pills, pain clinics, and his legacy. He declined and a year later was released.

As the pain revolution was taking hold across the country, however, Procter and his physician progeny showed a beat-down region a brand-new business model. Before long some of the first locally owned businesses in years opened in Portsmouth, known to folks in town as the "pain managements."

The Man in the Heartland

Columbus, Ohio

The city of Columbus, Ohio, in many ways is a fine replica of the United States.

Its income and age distribution, its racial demographics and diversity of opinion, make Columbus a microcosm of America, and one that marketers especially prize. There's a large white population, and moderate numbers of blacks. Unlike other parts of Ohio, Columbus has sizable immigrant groups—from Mexico, Somalia, Nepal, and other parts of Asia—who flocked to town to fill the low-end service jobs. A large college-student population at Ohio State and other schools has kept it vibrant and edgy.

No place, apparently, represents the country more faithfully and for that reason Columbus, Ohio, has been known as "the test-market capital of the United States" for several years now.

These days it's no longer Peoria but Columbus that marketers use as a barometer of America. White Castle and Wendy's and more than a dozen other fast-food chains headquarter there. Many companies have used the town to gauge interest in new product offerings, placing them in stores in Columbus first before rolling out those products nationally. McDonald's tested its McRib in Columbus, and Wendy's and Panera have tested prototype stores there as well. Taco Bell's BLT Tacos were tested in the Columbus market. R. J. Reynolds tried tobacco in the form of a mint that did away with secondhand smoke. Giant Eagle's massive Market District supermarket in Columbus tests a variety of concepts, among them the sale of wine by the glass.

"If you raked America together, in the center you'd find Columbus. And I think that's really what makes us a unique test bed, as opposed to being average," a spokesman for the Columbus Partnership told CBS News in a story in which the reporter concluded, "What they choose in Columbus today may very well determine what you will buy tomorrow."

By the end of 1998, the Man was proving that true of black tar heroin as well. For the bounties of Columbus, he discovered, were indeed ample.

A metro area of close to two million, Columbus wasn't Youngstown or Cleveland; it had no organized mafias or armed gangs controlling the drug underworld. It was connected by freeways to regional markets as far east as Wheeling, West Virginia, and south to Lexington and eastern Kentucky. There was Cincinnati to the southwest. Plus all around it were suburbs and farm towns with money. Columbus always was a highly educated community, with a service, not industrial, economy. As parts of the state went into something like permanent recession, in Columbus the suburbs spread and the malls stayed busy.

All this the Man saw upon arriving in the summer of 1998, which seems to be the first time Mexican black tar heroin made a large and sustained appearance east of the Mississippi River.

Up to then, the Colombian powder was all Columbus dealers could get, usually by driving to New York City—then diluting it before sale. "They were stepping on it five or six times," the Man said. "Addicts would buy a hundred-dollar bag twice a day just to get well. They'd buy a forty-dollar bag of mine and stay well all day."

Mexico's proximity and his connection to the Nayarit poppy supply and Xalisco cookers meant he got the heroin quickly, cheaply, and unadulterated. Enormously potent dope could be sold at scarily low prices. This gave black tar a competitive advantage over heroin from Colombia, Mexico's main heroin competition, and, of course, what little arrived from Asia.

He immediately sent for two more kids from Xalisco—so now he had three. He brought out a woman from California who rented two apartments in her name: one for the workers and one for him.

He found a car lot with an amenable owner. Every two months he switched cars. He exchanged an old Honda Accord for a Prelude and that for a Civic and then for a Camry—white, beige, gray. He ran two shifts of drivers: eight A.M. to three P.M. and three P.M. to nine P.M. They devised codes for places to meet the addicts: 1 was a Burger King, 2 a Kmart parking lot.

He tutored his new Xalisco Boys. Never leave the house with anything in your pockets. Take only what you can swallow if you get pulled over. And never carry a gun. An illegal who is arrested gets deported; an illegal with a gun gets ten years.

Some of them still dressed as they had back home, with cowboy boots and belt buckles. "Go to the stores downtown," he told two of them one day. "Look at how they dress the mannequins at JCPenney's. Buy clothes like that so you blend in with the people here."

He insisted they send money home weekly. Most didn't need to be told, and religiously sent money to Mom via Western Union. Those who didn't, he knew he would be hearing from their parents. For some kids, he sent the money to their parents' house himself.

Sell to whites; that's where the money is, he told them. Steer clear of blacks. He didn't have to insist too strongly on this point, either. His runners came with their own ideas forged by the negative view of black people common in Mexican culture that was, in turn, reinforced by the stories of returning immigrants who lived in Compton, Watts, and South Central Los Angeles, where powerful black gangs terrorized vulnerable Mexicans. So the Xalisco Boys stayed away from black neighborhoods, and this was one reason why, as their system expanded, Nayarit black tar was primarily sold to, and used by, whites.

Otherwise, he had a live-and-let-live attitude. The U.S. market was large enough and tar heroin was addictive enough. It never occurred to him to sell wholesale. Retail, he made almost triple what he would have made selling heroin wholesale. He had a bunch of poor ranchero kids down in Nayarit eager to drive around with tiny balloons in their mouths—so his risk was minimal, and they were only deported when arrested because they usually prssessed such small quantities of dope. Selling small quantities allowed him to get the most money out of the dope he got up from Mexico. Plus, as he hired more of these men, his standing in Xalisco improved and he got respect every time he returned.

Columbus had been at the bottom of Ohio's heroin distribution chain. At the time the Man arrived, heroin in Columbus was at most 3 percent pure, old addicts told me, and even that was hard to get. For years before his arrival, in the entire city of Columbus, Ohio, heroin was sold at precisely one street corner: Mt. Vernon Avenue at North 20th Street.

The city instead had always been a pill town. Pills were easier to trust than low-grade heroin. "The advent of black tar heroin in this community suddenly put a much purer-grade heroin on the streets of central Ohio," said Ronnie Pogue, cofounder of Columbus's lone methadone clinic, CompDrug. "The hunger for heroin, which had always been there, immediately saw an upward spike, because you also saw a spike in the overdose rate."

Columbus had the only methadone clinic for hundreds of miles around. Long before the Man arrived, the region's opiate addicts had been traveling into Columbus to score whatever they could find in front of the clinic. As word spread of the high quality of black tar, these pilgrims became some of his first clients—users from Zanesville, Toledo, Chillicothe, from northern Kentucky and western West Virginia. Some of his best clients were from Ashland, Kentucky, who had bought for years in front of Columbus's methadone clinic. They bought his tar and went back to Ashland and sold it for triple.

Black tar became the talk of Columbus's drug underworld. It was the most powerful heroin anyone had tried. Plus the Mexicans soon had a delivery driver in each area. With that, heroin found its way to suburban kids. "They broke this city down into 'Domino's: thirty minutes or less,'" one veteran addict told me. "When you're dope sick, that makes a big difference. Then, every time you found them somebody new, it was a free balloon. Usually it was seven balloons for a hundred dollars. But if you brought them enough people and were spending with them, you could get as many as thirteen balloons for a hundred dollars."

With addicts transformed into a new sales force, the Man was soon making so much money that he had to concentrate less on running the cell and more on getting cash back to Mexico. He formed a network of young women. A tailor in Los Angeles made them corsets with pockets that held a hundred thousand dollars in cash. He sent the women on airplanes to El Paso where they crossed his money to Ciudad Juárez and from there back to Xalisquillo. For more than a year, he sent two girls a month back to Mexico with a hundred thousand dollars in pure Columbus, Ohio, profit tucked in their corsets.

His product was coming in from a man named Oscar Hernandez-Garcia, a member of the Tejeda clan who operated a heroin supply business out of his apartment in Panorama City in Los Angeles. Hernandez-Garcia, known as Mosca (Fly), had developed a business as a wholesaler, supplying black tar to Xalisco cells from Portland and Phoenix to Columbus and Hawaii.

The Man used Federal Express to bring the product from Mosca's apartment in California. He would go to California, and buy a small electric oven from Target or Kmart, open the back of the oven, stuff it with tar heroin, then take it to FedEx for packaging. Police didn't often search a package that FedEx prepared. He sent the ovens to a pliant Columbus addict who lived in the basement of his senile parents' home, and paid him in heroin.

With Columbus humming along, he looked for new markets.

One addict, a kid named Mikey, told him people in Wheeling, West Virginia, would go crazy for black tar. Mikey introduced him around Wheeling. There, the Man made a startling discovery.

Mikey introduced him to a woman in her late thirties, a heroin addict. She showed him a bottle of pills, wanting to trade them for his tar. OxyContin, the pills were called, she said. He'd never heard the name and turned her down. But it struck him that she drove a new Dodge Durango and owned a house. He'd never known a longtime heroin addict who had a house and new SUV. So he listened to her. OxyContin, she told him, contained a pharmaceutical opiate, a prescription painkiller similar to heroin. He got to know the woman better. Turned out she traveled the area buying these pills cheap from seniors, then sold them to Oxy addicts in the hills of Appalachia. She bought her daily heroin with the money.

He couldn't have known it then, but, arriving in 1998, he had happened onto the biggest metro area in a five-state region where, two years into the Purdue Pharma promotional campaign, opiate addiction was exploding due to abuse of this new drug called OxyContin. By his own good fortune, not far away was Portsmouth, Ohio, where scandalous pain clinics were just starting to follow the lead of Dr. David Procter into a new business model of writing prescriptions for millions of these pills to long lines of addicts. Meanwhile, the pain revolution was in full swing in U.S. medicine. Specialists were urging well-meaning doctors everywhere to prescribe opiate painkillers for pain, convinced that when used this way they were all but nonaddictive.

Central Ohio, in other words, was about to be a great place to be a heroin dealer.

His black tar, once it came to an area where OxyContin had already tenderized the terrain, sold not to tapped-out old junkies but to younger kids, many from the suburbs, most of whom had money and all of whom were white. Their transition from Oxy to heroin, he saw, was a natural and easy one. Oxy addicts began by sucking on and dissolving the pills' timed-release coating. They were left with 40 or 80 mg of pure oxycodone. At first, addicts crushed the pills and snorted the powder. As their tolerance built, they used more. To get a bigger bang from the pill, they liquefied it and injected it. But their tolerance never stopped climbing. OxyContin sold on the street for a dollar a milligram and addicts very quickly were using well over 100 mg a day. As they reached their financial limits, many switched to heroin, since they were already shooting up Oxy and had lost any fear of the needle.

Black tar was potent, far cheaper, and his delivery system made it easier to get than the pills. Plus tar could be smoked—didn't have to be injected, which attracted kids to whom needles were at first anathema. The way he saw it, every Oxy addict was a tar junkie in waiting, and there were thousands of new Oxy addicts. All he had to do was work it.

His Nayarit brothers might never have figured this out. Like many Mexican immigrants who lived in Spanish-only enclaves, they were oblivious to subtle trends in the American society and culture in which they lived. As traffickers, they cared only to sell their dope and send money home. Drivers were short-timers all, on salary, there for six to nine months, holed up in apartments, and knowing only a few words of English ("no credit" or "fifteen minutes"), exchanged with desperate addicts who spoke no Spanish. Discovering emerging markets required an English speaker who understood the street.

Landing in Columbus just as the region around it was becoming ground zero in America's opiate epidemic, he could see opportunities developing simply because, he told me once, "I could talk to the white people."

His arrival was a fateful coincidence. Other traffickers might have filled the eventual demand for heroin created in this region where prescription pill abuse got bad first. Later, many did. But few were so ready to take advantage of it, so aggressive in their marketing, and so quickly replenished as the Xalisco Boys and the Man who brought them there.

Wheeling taught the Man that new markets were now everywhere the pills were. With the Boys working his store in Columbus, he found a place in Carnegie, Pennsylvania, a suburb of Pittsburgh, and close enough to service other towns like Steubenville and Wheeling.

He also eyed Nashville. Its Mexican population was growing, nearing eighty thousand people. The town, he heard, was swamped in OxyContin. He set up one of his Columbus drivers, along with a new kid up from Xalisco, in a store that was soon booming. Choose the right town and you can't miss, he thought to himself. The Nashville store covered his expenses for the expansion he eyed throughout the mid-South.

At the urging of another addict, he took a trip down to Virginia, through Roanoke, Richmond, and Newport News. It was another large market, but the federal government had too many installations there. Langley and a naval base made him nervous. He went through

Chattanooga, Tennessee—a town with a lively underworld, but too small. Mexicans in cars would stand out. He drove down to Pensacola and Jacksonville, but left.

"Florida is dominated by Colombians and Cubans and Puerto Ricans. That kind of race, they ain't got no understanding," he said. "Kill, kill, kill—they think they can solve everything by killing. I wasn't gonna kill nobody over drugs. I'd probably be buried the rest of my life in prison."

He nixed Philadelphia, too. It had a huge heroin market, but it was run by the Mafia and street gangs. He didn't even consider New York or Baltimore. It was crazy to think that a bunch of Mexican farm boys could break in there. Why would they want to? The country was full of towns like Columbus—wealthy places with growing numbers of addicts and no competition.

So the contours of the Xalisco heroin nation took shape, based largely on the territory the Man carved out by avoiding the biggest cities where heroin markets were already controlled, and by following the OxyContin.

He tried to keep his eastern tienditas a secret to his Nayarit friends. When he went back to Reno or Los Angeles to arrange deliveries, he always told friends that he was working in New York City. But in a small town like Xalisco, people talked. After a year in Columbus, his drivers went home for the Feria del Elote and started bragging about the great heroin market they were working up in central Ohio. By the fall of 1999, two more crews were in Columbus. One belonged to a former driver, now venturing out on his own. Two more followed. A kind of "Go east, young man" ethos took hold among the Xalisco Boys. The price of heroin in Columbus fell. No crew leader could cut his dope unless he wanted to lose his clients. So the product stayed strong even as it got cheaper.

Competition, as always, attuned the Xalisco crews to customer service. They even crossed the city to keep a customer, and gave away free dope to any client hinting at quitting.

One woman I met lived twenty-five miles outside Columbus and at one point she hadn't called to buy for three days. A Xalisco Boy called her.

"Señorita, why haven't you been buying recently?"

"I don't have any money," she said.

He drove out to deliver fifty dollars' worth of heroin to her, for which he required no payment. No, it's free, he said.

"He wanted to keep me using, and buying from him," she said. She did both.

A year or so after the Man settled in Columbus, he drove to Charlotte looking for bigger profits. Addicts told him he would make a million there. No one there had seen anything like black tar heroin. Heroin, in fact, had only a small market in Charlotte. He met junkie contacts at the town's methadone clinic and gave them free samples. Soon, business boomed again. He pulled a driver out of Columbus and another out of Nashville and they set up the black tar heroin franchise in Charlotte.

A couple weeks later, the Sánchez family, from the ranchos near Xalisco, arrived. They had an addict guide of their own—a big Native American fellow. The Sánchezes owed their expanding heroin empire to addicts. Addicts had guided the family out of San Fernando to Las Vegas, then to Memphis and Nashville and from there to Charlotte. The Man didn't know them, only knew of them. They were cousins of the late David Tejeda, from the rancho of Aquiles Serdán, down the road from Xalisco. Now they were in Charlotte, too.

It was bound to happen. It was a free market, after all.

Bodies Are the Key to the Case

Sante Fe, New Mexico

In Chimayo, the heroin clans' dominance went back years. It didn't matter that members of these clans had all been arrested, as had their workers. The problem was, Chris Valdez told Jim Kuykendall, that none had done much prison time; then always returned home. The families grew stronger with each demonstration of impunity. Still, the old cases interested Kuykendall. Drugs had been seized in each case. A historical record of the clans' control existed throughout those cases. Kuykendall saw there was a story to be told. Witnesses, people in prison now—users or low-rung workers who could talk about the clans—had been there when the cops barged in on one family or another. Plus those who'd died from heroin overdoses could speak from the grave, if only their loved ones would talk. Their stories might tell best of all how deeply the clans' power resided in Chimayo.

To Jim Kuykendall, all this history was important, for it formed a story of the clans' control that might become the basis of a federal conspiracy case. He formed a team of local cops and targeted the main heroin-dealing families in Chimayo, and in particular Felix Barela, who said he made his money from cutting firewood.

A short while later, Kuykendall briefed top federal agents and prosecutors. The FBI wanted to contribute agents to go up on wiretaps. Kuykendall resisted. Wiretaps were unnecessary. "The key to the case are the bodies," Kuykendall said. "They each tell a story. There's a story behind who these people are, where they bought their drugs, and how they died. We need to tell that story."

He got the medical examiners' reports of dozens of overdose cases and divided them among the investigators. They fanned across the Española Valley, interviewing families of the deceased. Years before, as black tar heroin accelerated the valley's decay, each dead junkie had been viewed as one less problem. No one had cared enough to interview their families. But the families were integral to the Chimayo heroin tale, Kuykendall believed. Addicts, even those well into adulthood, often returned to live with their parents once they lost their jobs, houses, and spouses. Parents lived in torment, as their children stole from them, slaves to the morphine molecule. It turned out many parents and siblings, unable to withstand the torment that would ensue if they refused—and afraid that if they let their family member borrow the car that it would never be seen again—had driven the addicts to their dealers' houses.

These parents, it turned out, were eager to talk. They greeted the investigators with tears and hugs; they recounted watching helplessly as their kids fell apart. One mother, in tears, pinched Kuykendall's cheeks as she made him promise he would get the people who sold her child heroin. These parents said the Barela family, as the school year approached, would hand out lists of what clothes their children needed. When they wanted new televisions or stereos, they'd let the addicts know. Soon junkies would be plying them with newly stolen pants for their kids.

One afternoon, Kuykendall went to visit Dennis Smith, a man in his seventies whose son, Donald, had died. Donald Smith had moved back to live with his father after a fight with his girlfriend over his heroin use.

Sitting with Kuykendall, the elder Smith said that on the trip home from an outing one night his son had demanded they return to Chimayo so he could buy heroin. He threatened to jump from the car if his father didn't turn around. Dennis Smith said he drove his son back to the Barela compound—a place where he had taken him several times before. The elder Smith turned the car around and headed back to the Barelas' for his kid's dope. He found his son's corpse in the trailer in the back of his property the next morning.

One resident, George Roybal, told the detectives that he often took his disabled brother, Ernie, to buy dope from the Barelas and the Martinezes. Another, Lynette Salazar, told them she took her son, Armando, to a clan house, as she had done often, to trade auto supplies for a hit of dope, and from this Armando died later that day.

Kuykendall flew to Montana to visit a woman who had driven through the valley one fall. Enchanted with its natural beauty, she decided to stay. She moved in right next to a member of the Martinez clan. At first, she told Kuykendall, she believed her next-door neighbor—Jesse "Donuts" Martinez—was a Boy Scout leader from all the youths who would visit the house all afternoon. Soon, though, she saw kids with belts around their arms. Her young son began finding syringes in the yard. She called the cops and began noting every car that pulled up—thirty a day sometimes. She spent a year watching junkies coming in and out, shooting up in the backyard in full view of her window. She called police repeatedly; finally she gave up and moved to Montana.

In the end, the case against the clans involved relatively few under-cover drug buys. It revolved instead around testimony of people whom Kuykendall and the agents had tracked down. The families and friends of the dead told their stories to a grand jury, with Kuykendall finishing up to recount the history of heroin in the valley and the clans' control. The grand jury indicted thirty-four people, including Felix Barela, Josefa Gallegos, "Fat Jose" Martinez, and his brother "Donuts."

At six A.M. on Wednesday, September 29, 1999, a five-mile caravan of law enforcement officers rolled into Chimayo as three helicopters buzzed like dragonflies across the skies. They seized land and motor-cycles and Felix Barela's beloved lowrider, the Wizard. Two months later, they seized his prized sorrel racehorse, Red Hot Mag, which his trainer had secreted out of the state, but brought back to race at the SunRay racetrack in Farmington. After the horse won the eighth race, Kuykendall and his agents stopped the jockey leaving the track, produced a judge's order, and confiscated the horse. They went to the track office and seized the twenty-two thousand dollars in prize money as well. They later auctioned Red Hot Mag for fifteen thousand dollars.

Fifteen acres of the Barela compound, where hundreds of addicts once used to buy, was deeded to the Boys and Girls Club. Without land, the clans had no base of operations. Even after leaving prison, they did not return to Chimayo.

But the story of the Chimayo clans is important to our own because months before that bust, in April 1999, as Jim Kuykendall and his newly deputized agents sifted through the clans' history, a body turned up in Santa Fe. A twenty-one-year-old Mexican kid named Aurelio Rodriguez-Zepeda, from the small town of Xalisco in the state of Nayarit, was found in the trunk of a car beaten and bloody.

The town of Xalisco, Nayarit, meant nothing to the agents at the time, other than it ironically happened to be the sister city to nearby Taos, New Mexico. Nor was the kid's murder especially intriguing. But the car in which Rodriguez-Zepeda was found was registered to Josefa Gallegos, the heroin matriarch of Chimayo. So they stuck with it.

As it happened, Rodriguez-Zepeda was found with a cellular phone.

The agents plugged the numbers found in the phone into a federal law enforcement database. One number turned up as connected to another heroin case that the FBI was investigating in Phoenix.

Kuykendall called the FBI in Phoenix and spoke to an agent named Gary Woodling.

Woodling had a strange story to tell. He was part of a group of agents tracking black tar heroin traffickers from the state of Nayarit, Mexico. From Phoenix, these traffickers had set up retail heroin cells across the United States in mid-major towns. Three Nayarit brothers ran the Phoenix cell and seemed to have decided that wherever US Air flew from Phoenix would make a good heroin outpost. These were not the traditional drug hubs of, say, Philadelphia, Miami, or Chicago. Instead, Woodling said, Nayarits were going to towns like Boise, Salt Lake, Omaha, Denver, Pittsburgh, even Billings, Montana. A local narc in Boise named Ed Ruplinger, in fact, had already run a sizable investigation into some of these guys, Woodling told him.

Kuykendall and his agents went back and combed the subpoenaed phone records for the heroin clans of Chimayo. From the records, it seems that when the clans wanted to order supplies they called a central number—apparently a dispatcher. This dispatcher, the records show, then quickly called the number for Aurelio Rodriguez-Zepeda. It seemed the dead kid was some kind of black tar deliveryman, being sent regularly to supply the Chimayo dealers.

Kuykendall and the agents had long assumed that those who supplied the Chimayo heroin clans were an isolated group of Mexican dealers who had stumbled into the fertile heroin terrain of the Española Valley. Woodling dispelled this notion. As the investigation into the Gallegoses, the Barelas, and the Martinezes drew to a close, and five miles of police cars streamed into Chimayo that day in September 1999, Kuykendall and his investigators knew they were onto something bigger.

Enrique on Top

Santa Fe, New Mexico

Robert Berardinelli knew a good thing when he saw one. When the Nayarit Mexicans came to town, this was, to him, a good thing.

A balding man in his fifties from a family that owned a funeral home in Santa Fe, Berardinelli was a heroin addict. He'd been addicted to the morphine molecule since back in 1969. He'd smuggled pot from Mexico in the 1970s and done some prison time. He'd been desperate to get off dope for years, tried methadone, but it didn't help. For most of his addiction, he purchased his dope from various Santa Fe street dealers. This was risky. His family had been active in public service in Santa Fe for most of the century; Berardinellis had served as judge, city councilman, postmaster, and county treasurer. For him to be hustling hits of heroin on the street from people he didn't always know exposed him to arrest and his family to shame.

But a lot changed back in the summer of 1997, he later told the detectives, when a group of heroin traffickers from the Mexican state of Nayarit showed up in Santa Fe, led by a guy who occasionally went by the name Enrique.

HEROIN HAD TAKEN ENRIQUE a long way from the Toad.

On the plane out of the Yuma airport heading to New Mexico, on the day that he watched those migrants rounded up, Enrique knew this trip was his moment, the one he had waited for. He'd been through childhood poverty, sold dope as a kid in the San Fernando Valley for uncles who underpaid him, then sold for that boss in Phoenix. He was married and had a lot to prove. He knew the business and was confident in his abilities as a salesman and motivator of people. Now, in 1997, he was heading off to start his own heroin cell.

Before leaving home, he asked his parents for their blessing.

"I don't know if I'll be returning," he told them.

Watching *la migra* roust those dusty immigrants from the Yuma airport put something of a closure on the last nagging qualms he had about selling chiva.

He arrived in Albuquerque, intending to make it the site of his first heroin business. But early on, he met an addict from Santa Fe who said construction workers in that town were heavily addicted. He paid the guy five thousand dollars for an introduction to some addicts. He found Santa Fe wide-open—no gangs, no competition. There, he set up the heroin cell that had been his goal for almost half his life by then.

He brought in kids from his village. Right off, that felt good—to be an employer, a benefactor. He taught them how to drive, how to package heroin in balloons. He taught them the streets. He paid them six hundred dollars a week, plus all expenses, including the coyote's fee to cross them into the United States. Soon his cell was selling balloons around Santa Fe. He returned to Nayarit.

He employed almost two dozen kids over the next three years, from the poorest ranchos. They worked harder, didn't steal, and were grateful. Some wanted to work for a bit and then return home to party. Others, as he had, wanted their own business and would work for him only as long as it took to gain experience and capital. Either way, he saw their serious moods as he sent them off to go drive for him in northern New Mexico. Some pretended to joke around, but he knew it was a bluff. He knew how much was riding on their trips—a truck, a piece of land, a girl, the threat of many years in prison.

Xalisco Boys were church mice in the United States. That ended as soon as they got home. They were young men and wanted to party. Enrique liked to think of himself as a guy who took care of his employees, because he had been there himself. He took them to El Queros strip club in Vallarta, all expenses paid, or to beach resorts in Nayarit. No sugarcane farmer was ever going to get into one of those places.

Meanwhile, he hired his mother a maid. He paid for a sister's quinceañera—the traditional Mexican coming-out birthday party for a fifteen-year-old girl. He paid for another to attend college. In a speech at her graduation party, she thanked her brother for all he had made possible. He took his family to fine restaurants in Tepic where they nervously rubbed elbows with the city's middle classes.

He would look around these restaurants and realize that chiva had finally allowed him to cross that river that separated his rancho from the world.

"At least I'm not going to die wanting to know what's on the other side," he told himself.

Enrique bought the land where he and his father were born. He hired men to help his father in the field.

Seeing his son with some cocaine one day, his father took Enrique aside. Be careful with that stuff, he said. Don't use it. He admitted he had been a drunk for too long. It was the first time he had spoken to Enrique as a father should to his son.

"That's all fine," Enrique said. "But why didn't you speak to me like this before?"

His father said nothing.

"You have to change," he upbraided his father. "No more yelling."

Rancho fathers didn't speak to their children, but instead resolved every problem with blows or orders. Heroin changed that in Enrique's house.

Still, there were headaches, the kind every small businessman faces. Enrique was constantly having to set up apartments for his guys in Santa Fe, getting them new cellular phones and Nextels. When a cop stopped one of his drivers, that car was useless. Finding new workers wasn't that hard; many men knocked on his door back home asking for work. But making sure they were trustworthy, then getting them up north and trained—that was a chore, and costly, too. He lived in the rancho but was always returning to Santa Fe to supervise, make changes, corral his workers, and get them straight.

From Santa Fe, he soon discovered the huge heroin market in tiny Chimayo, twenty-five miles north. He was content to supply the clans. With his black tar, the town that had endured decades of heroin addiction began to cave in. Two percent of the population—eighty-five people, veteran addicts many of them, who had lived for years on weaker heroin—died of black tar heroin overdoses over the next three years.

ENRIQUE'S NETWORKS CHANGED HEROIN in Santa Fe, too.

Now all Robert Berardinelli had to do was call a number. These new Mexicans had a delivery service just for heroin. Like pizza.

For years before they arrived, the dope was brown powder sold by junkies, who would dilute it; quality varied widely week to week. But the Nayarit guys didn't cut their heroin; they were always careful to deliver only balloons containing a standard weight of black tar heroin, which was uniformly potent. Most surprising, they didn't use their product. Every heroin dealer Berardinelli had known up to that point was a user, prone to cutting his dope. But these guys couldn't care less about using; they seemed interested only in making money.

"I always dreamed of that: 'I'm going to get clean and make some money doing this,'" Berardinelli said. "Every junkie I knew had that plan and never did it. These guys were fulfilling every addict's dream."

To Berardinelli and the street dope fiends, those Nayarit balloons became a brand every bit as dependable as a Coke can or a Holiday Inn sign. You always knew what you would find inside.

One day the Mexicans asked if Berardinelli could find them a car. They would pay him in heroin to put it in his name. So Robert Berardinelli undertook another life, that of facilitator for a cell of Xalisco, Nayarit, heroin dealers. He charged them three grams to put the car in his name, and another two grams to insure it.

Then the jobs multiplied. They asked him to wire their money back to Mexico, and he did. He put their pagers and phones in his name—and was paid in heroin. Occasionally, he would get a call from police telling him that a car registered in his name was being used by Mexicans who were stopped for speeding. He'd retrieve the car—and the Mexicans would pay him in heroin. When they asked him to find an apartment for a driver, he charged them a gram to find the place, two grams to fill out the lease application, and a gram and a half to put the utilities in his name.

Meanwhile, drivers rotated through every three months. "They'd be taught the routes," Berardinelli told me when I tracked him down fourteen years later in Santa Fe. "They'd come up and make money and they'd be gone and you may never see them again. Some would be back six months later. They were just kids trying to make money—the American Dream kind of deal. They said they were from Nayarit. They talked about how little money they'd make back home and how great it was that they could come and get away with this and help their families. Back home, they were doing farm labor, any damn thing they could get without a lot of education."

At a car lot once, Berardinelli met Enrique, who appeared to be the boss. He wanted to trade a Nissan for a Cadillac. Berardinelli signed the purchase agreement and Enrique gave him five grams of heroin.

Berardinelli spoke a little Spanish. Over nine months, Enrique visited him often, usually with a request—to put a car or a cell phone in Berardinelli's name. He always came with free dope. Berardinelli remembered Enrique liked to play the tough guy at first, and usually came with an entourage of three or four. But he lightened up when he discovered Berardinelli was an old smuggling hand. Berardinelli told them stories of crossing weed southeast of El Paso in airplanes driven by former Korean War pilots. He offered them Cokes, since apparently they didn't drink. He never saw them high.

"Because of the way this business model ran, it was so much more relaxed," he said. "There wasn't that element of fear in it. The dope was never cut; you got what you paid for. For a dope fiend like me, it was just really nice.

"I go from struggling every day to cop my drugs to having all the dope in the world, and all I have to do is put my name on a bunch of documents. They were giving me all this dope to do things I said I'd never do—buy them automobiles, rent apartments. When you're strung out on that shit, you just don't think properly. Reason goes out the window. You compromise your moral compass. All I had to do was call them and they'd give me whatever I wanted. My addiction got worse and worse. Like it did for a lot of people in northern New Mexico when they got here."

Heroin Like Hamburgers

Los Angeles, California

One day in January 2000, a hundred federal agents and police officers from twenty-two cities gathered at the DEA office in Los Angeles.

Paul "Rock" Stone came in from Portland. Jim Kuykendall came in from Albuquerque. Others came in from Hawaii, Denver, Utah, Phoenix, and elsewhere to discuss a tangle of investigations into black tar heroin traffickers across the United States. These investigations had once seemed separate things, as if heroin dealers had independently sprouted in Maui or Denver. But in 1999, DEA agents in Los Angeles had received information that a heroin dealer in San Diego was being supplied by a couple out of an apartment in the Panorama City district of the San Fernando Valley. Agents obtained a warrant for the Panorama City couple's phone records.

Oscar Hernandez-Garcia and his wife, Marina Lopez, were from Xalisco, Nayarit, it turned out. Agents learned that Hernandez-Garcia was calling numbers all over the United States from that apartment. They got a wiretap. They heard him arranging shipments of black tar, usually packed into the innards of electric ovens. Among the people Hernandez-Garcia spoke to frequently was the Man, who needed product for his stores in Columbus, Nashville, Wheeling, and Charlotte. They discussed the packages en route; occasionally, the Man, speaking English, followed up with Federal Express on packages that had gone missing.

The list of cities Hernandez-Garcia called grew long. With each new city, the agents contacted counterparts in those towns.

At DEA headquarters in Arlington, Virginia, a supervisor named Harry Sommers watched these heroin cases mount all over the country. Sommers's job was to coordinate far-flung DEA investigations as they expanded. The Nayarits got his attention simply because of the number of cities involved. Most of the cases appeared to be pretty small-time, involving a few ounces of heroin at the most. What was new, though—what caught Sommers's eye, besides the expanse of the cases—was that the heroin was far stronger than typical street-level dope, but it was being sold cheaper than ever. Plus the dealers were all from Nayarit, and as the cases poured in, they seemed to be everywhere in America.

They were even in Boise, Idaho, which surprised Sommers. A while before, Ed Ruplinger had put an end to his case and arrested a half dozen of Polla's drivers and couriers in Boise. Polla—Cesar Garcia-Langarica—was in Los Angeles at the time. A federal prosecutor wasn't interested then in pursuing the case to California or other places where Ruplinger had tracked the trafficker's cells. Polla presumably now lives in Nayarit; an indictment awaits him in Boise should he return to the United States. But at the time, Ruplinger never could get anyone to see that Boise was only a small part of a large web.

By 1999, though, that attitude was changing.

Sommers in Washington had never seen a system like this. These Xalisco heroin cells competed, yet borrowed dope from each other when supplies ran low. They were all connected, but the connections were easy to miss if you looked at each case individually. "You had to see it from the macro point of view," Sommers said.

He organized the January meeting of investigators at the DEA's L.A. office, and dubbed the operation Tar Pit.

That meeting made graphically clear the national scope of the Xalisco Boys for the first time. In Portland, the Tejeda-Cienfuegos brothers were already the focus of something called Operation Nytar. In Hawaii, there'd been a rare case of violence among workers at the cell David Tejeda had started years before. It had been run by two of his cousins, who were murdered in 1997 by their drivers whom they hadn't paid. In Phoenix, the FBI was onto several brothers, the Vivanco-Contrerases, who had stores in Arizona and other states, and sometimes supplied Enrique in Santa Fe. Oscar Hernandez-Garcia supplied them all, and many others, from that Panorama City apartment. He had brothers who were veteran heroin cookers down in Xalisco and kept him stocked.

At the L.A. meeting, an agent from each city got up and described the local investigation, what each was seeing. It was the same story over and over: Drivers would spend a few months working, tooling around mid-major cities of America with mouths full of balloons. Drivers were caught with only small amounts of drugs and thus were usually deported without even doing much jail time. The cells practiced just-in-time supplying, like a global corporation. They presumed that anyone asking to buy more than a few grams was a cop.

"It was eerie how uniform [the stories] were from town to town," said Rock Stone. "What we were seeing in Portland is what L.A. is seeing is what Denver is seeing. These [Xalisco Boys] are following exactly the same playbook. You couldn't help but feel how corporate these guys are, how standardized they are. It's like McDonald's, where you get the same burger in Louisiana as you get in California."

Yet no single person called the shots. Rather than one large organization, the thing appeared to agents to be an agglomeration of cells, each run by small entrepreneurs, each with employees, all of whom knew each other through rancho connections in Xalisco County. Hernandez-Garcia may have supplied them all, but that didn't mean he gave orders. Nor were their profits funneled to him. His tapped phone calls made that clear. He was just a wholesaler; they were retailers relentlessly focused on the bottom line and achieving efficiency through technology just like any other business. The evolution of Nextel push-to-talk phones by the late 1990s was one example. It allowed bosses to monitor their drivers and make sure they were working through the day.

In the room that day in Los Angeles, Jim Kuykendall listened and thought back to that first meeting in Chimayo a year before, amazed at what it had led to. The whole thing was like a web, and thus more flexible and resilient than the rigid hierarchies of so many Mexican drug-trafficking organizations.

And it all led back to that little town in one of Mexico's smallest states.

Tar Pit

Panorama City, California

"You're cheating on me, you bastard," a woman yelled into the phone at her husband in Mexico.

Marina Lopez was mad. Here she was in that run-down apartment, packaging dope all day. Her husband, Oscar Hernandez-Garcia, was philandering down in their hometown of Xalisco and now Marina was hearing the gossip all the way up in Panorama City.

The argument escalated.

"That's it, woman!" Hernandez-Garcia yelled into the phone. "I'm not coming back. I'm staying down here."

Unbeknownst to the couple, narcotics agents were listening in. The marital spat sent jolts across the country to the highest levels of American law enforcement.

It was June 12, 2000. By now, the case dubbed Operation Tar Pit reached across more of the United States than any other drug investigation in the country's history. The bust was set to take place three days hence. At the top of the indictment, the lead defendant, the guy around whom the case was built, was Oscar Hernandez-Garcia, wholesaling heroin across the country from his Panorama City apartment.

The June 15 bust date had been set weeks before by officials at the U.S. Department of Justice in Washington, who had the job of coordinating dozens of law enforcement agencies in cities across the country. But it almost required the presence in the United States of Oscar Hernandez-Garcia. And now it appeared that a marital tiff was going to keep him in Mexico. Given icy relations between the two countries regarding criminal extraditions, he might forever be out of the reach of U.S. justice.

Lisa Feldman, the federal prosecutor in charge of the case in Los Angeles, got on the phone to officials in Washington.

"We can't change the date," she was told.

"But he's my lead defendant."

"We've got too many resources committed. Sorry. It's gotta happen then."

For the next three days, Feldman and the agents waited on edge to see whether Oscar and Marina would make up. They did. Oscar Hernandez-Garcia got on a plane to Los Angeles. Hours later, a SWAT team hit their apartment. They found dope in the dishwasher and money in a container of baby formula. At the same time, federal agents and local cops swarmed into apartments in Cleveland and Columbus, in Salt Lake City and Phoenix, and Maui, Hawaii.

In Portland that morning, 108 officers met at a cavernous conference room at a north Portland hotel to discuss how they would hit eighteen residences and another fifteen cars. Rock Stone stayed up most the night listening to Xalisco Boys wiretaps, fearing he would miss something. By then, he had tracked these Nayarits to twenty-seven cities in twenty-two states—a massive yet diffuse corporation of drugs designed to resemble a motley collection of street dealers, and unlike any narcotics network he had ever known.

At six A.M. in southwest Albuquerque, Jim Kuykendall and other agents burst into a two-story adobe-style house where Enrique then lived with a girlfriend and her children. They arrested another half dozen of his drivers.

Later, Kuykendall sat down to talk with Enrique. "He just portrayed himself as a poor guy from small-town Mexico trying to make a buck—as if there was nothing too wrong with what he was doing," Kuykendall remembered. "A family guy looking out for his family and his kids. I'd talked to too many of the girls he'd slept with to believe that. He was a farm boy . . . and a midlevel trafficker."

Enrique spent the next thirteen years in a U.S. federal prison.

Across the country that day, 182 people were arrested in a dozen cities in Operation Tar Pit. Agents seized relatively small quantities of drugs and cash: sixty pounds of heroin and two hundred thousand dollars. Yet Tar Pit remains the largest case—geographically and in terms of manpower used—the DEA and FBI have ever mounted jointly.

"This is the first time we've seen a criminal drug-trafficking organization go coast-to-coast, also hitting Alaska and Hawaii," DEA administrator Donnie R. Marshall said at a press conference.

The bust reflected the spread of Mexican immigration. Mexican immigrants were now coast-to-coast, too. They formed the working classes in North Carolina, Alaska, Idaho, Minnesota, and Nevada. Mexicans were the largest influx of foreign-born labor to the American

South since slavery. They were in the biggest cities and were revitalizing parts of heartland America. The only locally owned new businesses in many rural towns were those that Mexicans started, and it was common by 2000 to find Mexican restaurants in Mississippi or an out-of-the-way burg in Tennessee.

This also meant Mexican traffickers had more places to blend in. That wasn't true even five years before. But by the late 1990s, as Mexican immigration was now virtually nationwide, Mexican drug networks national in scope were now possible, too. Such a thing was unprecedented in the history of U.S. organized crime. Not even the Italian Mafia had done it, but Operation Tar Pit showed that the Xalisco Boys had.

They were a new kind of drug trafficking in America. The Xalisco Boys weren't the General Motors of drugs. They succeeded because they were the Internet of dope: a network of cells with no one in charge of them all, with drivers rotating in and out, complementing each other as they competed for every junkie's last twenty bucks, yet doing this without guns, shutting down their phones fast as a website at any hint of law enforcement's approach.

Back in Xalisco that August, the Feria del Elote was dead. Bandas came to town and left empty-handed. Most cell owners left for Guadalajara, believing they were on some DEA or FBI list. The Man went on the lam, and returned to Xalisco just before the feria. "The town dried up," he said. "Nobody was coming to the plaza."

He was arrested in South Carolina two years later and sent to prison. The case against him was based mostly on wiretaps of his conversations with Hernandez-Garcia and with FedEx tracking the whereabouts of those packages of ovens stuffed with black tar heroin.

In Portland, Rock Stone would put together two more operations against the Xalisco Boys targeting a video store and a bridal shop that funneled crew money home to Nayarit, and sold the Xalisco networks their indispensable cell phones and pagers. He found an apartment that had 155 cars registered to it and shut that down, too.

Along the way, though, he came to a sobering conclusion. It wasn't just that the Xalisco runners were endlessly replaced. It was that even if Stone kept attacking management levels of these Nayarit heroin crews, the managers, too, would be replaced quickly. He'd never seen this in narcotics. Informants told him the Tejeda-Sánchez clan alone—with the Lermas, Diazes, Bernals, Cienfuegoses, Hernandezes, Garcias, and the rest—were more than two-hundred-deep back in Nayarit, and any of them could rotate in to a heroin crew in Portland as a regional sales manager or cell supervisor.

Not only that, though. On the horizon hovered a specter even more disturbing than rotating squads of heroin-franchise upper management, bizarre as that idea might seem. As Tar Pit took place, out of the east was swelling a wave of opiate abuse creating vast numbers of new addicts as it swept west across America.

PART II

Two-Thousand-Year-Old Questions

Boston, Massachusetts

One spring day in 2000, Dr. Nathaniel Katz left his Boston pain clinic and crossed the Charles River to a hotel in Cambridge. Awaiting his arrival were three hundred physicians and researchers attending a conference on infectious diseases.

Katz had been a practicing pain specialist for almost a decade. He'd agreed to speak to the conference on how to manage pain in AIDS patients. He walked through the Royal Sonesta Hotel in his best suit, a name tag affixed, and a carousel of slides under his arm.

"I was nervous. A pretty young woman was there. I was half noticing her. She comes up to me and says, 'Dr. Katz?' I'm thinking, great, my first fan and she's a pretty young girl. I'm ready for adulation. 'Nathaniel Katz?' she says. That's right, I say. She says to me, 'I've been waiting for ten years to tell you this. You killed my brother, Peter.'"

Nathaniel Katz had grown up in a Coney Island apartment near the elevated tracks. His parents, Eastern European Jews, survived the Holocaust and came to New York City in 1948. His father worked as a chemist with the city's transit authority. Katz finished high school at sixteen, college at twenty, and went on to medical school. By 1986, he had graduated and was interested in studying the nervous system. He did a three-year fellowship in neurology. He had no tutelage in pain management. No one did in medical school. "Just because it's a problem every doctor faces every day," he said, "doesn't mean that it's something you would run into in medical school."

He was surprised, as a young neurologist, to find pain everywhere. Back pain, neck pain, headaches, muscle pain, pain associated with MS, Parkinson's, or strokes. Patients virtually clawed at his lab coat for help in managing their pain.

"I kept on seeing these patients and not knowing what to do with them," he said.

As it happened, Katz got his training in the first years of the debate within American medicine over opiates and pain. Everywhere people quoted the notion, pried unwillingly from Hershel Jick's one-paragraph letter years before, that less than 1 percent of pain patients who were prescribed opiates developed addiction.

By the time Katz was well into his medical training, a new conventional wisdom on opiates had emerged. It went something like this, Katz remembered: "It was not only okay, but it was our holy mission, to cure the world of its pain by waking people up to the fact that opiates were safe. All those rumors of addiction were misguided. The solution was a poppy plant. It was there all along. The only reason we didn't use it was stigma and prejudice. Once it became 'clear' that pain patients weren't going to become addicted, now we were liberated to use that solution that had been in hand the whole time.

"My fellowship director even told me, 'If you have pain, you can't get addicted to opiates because the pain soaks up the euphoria.' Now you look back and it sounds so preposterous. That's actually what people thought. You can think what you want in the face of ten thousand years of reality."

But, young and dutiful, Katz prescribed opiates. Sure enough, some patients did well on the drugs—as his instructors said they would. But he noticed that just as many did poorly. They were running out of the drugs before the month was up, asking for more.

"The real problems were things I couldn't see. What was that patient doing with the medication when they left?"

Then Katz met Peter. Peter was incontinent and had numbness in his legs, the result of an injury to his lower spinal cord. Peter was also unemployed and an alcoholic.

At the time, pain specialists and addiction specialists rarely crossed paths. Even today, despite a national movement to treat pain with addictive drugs, the two specialties, remarkably, still don't have much contact; there are no joint conferences where the two specialties might meet.

So despite Peter's history of substance abuse, Katz prescribed opiates. Before long, Peter was asking for more before the end of the month. Katz hesitated. But Peter was a loquacious fellow. He charmed the doctor and each month walked out of Katz's office with more medication.

"I was faced with the dilemma that prescribers have," Katz said. "What is the nature of the problem? If it's an abuse problem, the patient's not going to tell you."

Before Katz had a chance to find out, Peter died from an overdose of the medication the young doctor was prescribing. His death was a turning point for Nathaniel Katz.

"He was dead and I liked him and I wanted to help him."

Katz had two questions: Are opiates safe when used to treat chronic pain? Are they effective in treating that pain? Katz searched the medical literature and found nothing.

"There's not a shred of research on the issue. All these so-called experts in pain are dedicated and have been training me that opioids aren't as addictive as we thought. But what is that based on? It was based on nothing. I felt I've just uncovered the problem of our age, and of 500 B.C.: What are the risks of opioids? There was no answer to those questions, despite the fact that people have been asking them for twenty-five hundred years."

BY THE 2000S, THE American pain revolution was complete.

Most of the country's hundred million chronic-pain patients were now receiving opiate painkillers, as it was accepted on faith that virtually none of them would grow addicted. They usually weren't receiving prescriptions from pain specialists. Their prescriptions came instead from general practitioners with little time and little training in pain management—the kind of docs Purdue Pharma targeted in its sales campaign. Doctors prescribed pills for wisdom teeth extraction, carpal tunnel syndrome, bad knees, chronic back pain, arthritis, and severe headaches. Football and hockey players were given them for separated shoulders. People were sent home with bottles full of ninety Vicodin or sixty OxyContin pills. In many cases—patients recovering from surgery—a half-dozen pills might have sufficed, but doctors often wanted to avoid further patient visits. Why not prescribe more if the pills were now virtually nonaddictive when used for pain?

Americans were enjoying an era of amped consumer spending based on massive debt and towering real estate values that appeared to rise endlessly. It was a time when the country seemed a dreamland where the old rules, constraints, and knowledge no longer applied. At the same time a culture of opiate use grew from a medical revolution that believed these narcotics now could be used to treat pain without fear of addiction—that the old rules, constraints, and knowledge, in other words, didn't apply.

Worldwide pharmaceutical opiate production rose steadily. But it was the United States, the country where the Englishman Robert Twycross once smelled "the fear of addiction" as he stepped from an airplane, that now consumed 83 percent of the world's oxycodone and fully 99 percent of the world's hydrocodone (the opiate in Vicodin and Lortab). "Gram for gram," a group of specialists wrote in the journal *Pain Physician* in 2012, "people in the United States consume more narcotic medication than any other nation worldwide."

Drugs containing hydrocodone became the most prescribed drugs in America (136 million prescriptions a year, as I write), and opiate painkillers the most prescribed class of drugs. U.S. sales of opiate painkillers quadrupled. Sales of oxycodone—the drug in OxyContin, but also sold in smaller-dose generic pills—rose almost ninefold between 1999 and 2010.

A rising sea level of opiates spread to every corner of the nation. Before long, a black market for pills emerged larger than anything the country had seen. OxyContin very quickly had a street price: a dollar a milligram—so forty dollars or eighty dollars per pill. Between 2002 and 2011, 25 million Americans used prescription pills nonmedically. Amid all this, opiate abusers began to get younger. In a 2004 survey by the U.S. Substance Abuse and Mental Health Services Administration (SAMHSA), 2.4 million people twelve years or older had used a prescription pain reliever nonmedically for the first time within the previous year—more than the estimated numbers using marijuana for the first time. The pain-pill abuser's average age was twenty-two.

Overdose deaths involving opiates rose from ten a day in 1999 to one every half hour by 2012. Abuse of prescription painkillers was behind 488,000 emergency room visits in 2011, almost triple the number of seven years before.

Generic methadone, for years strictly an addict-maintenance drug, suddenly started killing, too. As media reports of OxyContin abuse and overdoses spread, some doctors began prescribing methadone for pain instead. Most doctors knew that methadone remained in the bloodstream for up to sixty hours. An addict on methadone could lead a daily life without the gnawing cravings every few hours of the far-quicker-acting heroin. Thus some doctors figured that methadone was an equally long-lasting painkiller. Plus methadone was generic and cheap; insurance companies covered it. Methadone prescriptions more than quadrupled—from under a million in 1999 to 4.4 million in 2009 nationwide—mostly for headaches and bodily pain.

Many doctors, however, didn't understand that methadone, while it was long-lasting and therefore effective as a maintenance drug, was not a long-lasting *painkiller*. It relieved pain for only a few hours. So patients took more and more of it through the day to get pain relief. The drug built up in their bodies, causing overdoses. As methadone prescriptions rose, so did overdose deaths involving methadone—from 623 in 1999 to 4,706 in 2007.

A decade after OxyContin's release, meanwhile, 6.1 million people had abused it—that is to say, 2.4 percent of all Americans. In macro terms, these were small numbers. But through history, illicit drug scourges have always involved a tiny minority of Americans. Baltimore, with a robust heroin market dating back decades, is considered the country's heroin capital—with the DEA and the city's health department estimating that roughly 10 percent of the city's residents are addicted. The crack epidemic, at its height, involved fewer than half a million users a year nationwide, according to SAMHSA estimates.

But, as with crack cocaine, the numbers of new opiate addicts by the 2000s *were* enough to throw hospitals, emergency rooms, jails, courts, rehab centers, and families into turmoil, especially in areas where abuse was new.

Subsequent studies showed that almost all those who ended up addicted to OxyContin had already used a small-dose opiate pain reliever—Vicodin, Percocet, Lortab—which contained nonopiates such as acetaminophen or Tylenol. These pills were the first tentative steps doctors took in managing patients' pain as opiates became de rigueur. From there, some patients grew addicted.

Street addicts had for years used Lortab or Vicodin. But in large amounts, the acetaminophen in these pills damaged an addict's liver. Plus, in many areas, heroin was not available, or was so weak and expensive that addicts avoided it. What all that meant was that for a long time people who abused these small-dose painkillers didn't often progress beyond them, and they rarely died from them.

But in 1996, timed-release OxyContin arrived—in doses of 40, 80, and, for a while, 160 mg of oxycodone. OxyContin often served as an addict's bridge between these milder opiate painkillers and heroin.

OxyContin contained only oxycodone, and much more of it. When Vicodin or Lortab stopped being enough, when legitimate patients asked for more, doctors now had OxyContin, at ten times the strength. And for those already addicted, not only did OxyContin pack a bigger dose, it was easier to liquefy and inject than the milder pills. All you had to do was suck off the timed-release coating; you didn't need to separate out any Tylenol or acetaminophen. Oxy habits easily grew to 200 to 300 mg daily, quantities rarely possible with Lortab or Vicodin without causing massive liver damage.

What happened next was what the Man figured would happen when he first encountered OxyContin in Wheeling, West Virginia. Heroin use crept higher. Addicts' tolerance to OxyContin rose. Many stopped snorting the pills' powder and started injecting it for the stronger rush. Their habits hit hundreds of dollars a day. They were now fully hooked on the morphine molecule and no longer fearing the needle. They saw no reason not to switch to the far cheaper heroin. Others went to heroin much earlier because not only was it cheaper but it could be smoked, too, and they could tell themselves that they didn't need to inject it, which was true while their tolerance was low.

Either way, a government survey found that the number of people who reported using heroin in the previous year rose from 373,000 in 2007 to 620,000 in 2011.

Eighty percent of them had used a prescription painkiller first.

But all this took years to become clear.

Collision: Ground Zero

Columbus, Ohio

In another era, it's possible that Operation Tar Pit might have dismantled, or permanently crippled, the heroin networks from the tiny county of Xalisco in Nayarit, Mexico.

But because they weren't like typical top-down drug organizations, the Xalisco Boys' networks coughed and sputtered but did not die. The cell owners remained in Mexico and reconstituted their U.S. operations. Experienced drivers, meanwhile, used the vacancies Tar Pit created to start their own cells. Santa Fe hasn't been without a Xalisco tiendita since Enrique started it in 1997. Wholesale suppliers multiplied in the vacuum left when Oscar Hernandez-Garcia and his wife went to jail. Competition lowered prices and expanded the supply of tar heroin headed to the United States. Meanwhile, more young men raised their hands to fill the driver slots. Most important, they were now recruited from families unrelated to Xalisco's first heroin clans. These new heroin workers had watched the families in the Tejeda clan prosper and wanted in on the business. Their entry into the business expanded the available heroin workforce and kept labor costs low. Soon, the Feria del Elote was bursting with traffickers and bandas once again.

Up in the United States, the Boys no longer had to rely on the limited universe of older junkies. A younger and much larger population of heroin users was emerging—casualties of the nation's pain revolution. This synergy between pills and heroin happened first in one place. OxyContin's popularity was spreading west just as the trafficker I call the Man brought Xalisco black tar heroin east. They collided in central and southern Ohio. Roughly drawn, the region with Columbus to the north, and including parts of West Virginia and eastern Kentucky to the south, became the barometer for all that followed elsewhere in the country.

*   *   *

AMONG THE FIRST TO take its full measure was a doctor named Peter Rogers, who in 2003 was at Nationwide Children's Hospital in Columbus, in the adolescent medicine department. Tall, thin, and spectacled, Rogers had specialized in addiction for almost twenty years by then. He'd treated kids on cocaine and crack. He'd seen them on meth, scratching scabs and grinding their teeth. He'd seen youths on ecstasy, LSD, pot, and as full-blown alcoholics. But before one evening in February 2003, Peter Rogers had never seen a teenager addicted to heroin.

Rogers was at home that night when a nurse called. A sixteen-year-old girl was in the ER with her parents. The girl was shivering and throwing up. It was heroin withdrawal, her parents said. The nurses didn't know what to do.

Rogers drove in, certain that it couldn't be heroin, and not sure what he would do if it were. The girl was small and blond and looked like a cheerleader. But she had track marks up her arms. Her face was pale and worn. She had diarrhea, and pains in her legs, stomach, and back.

"She said she'd started with pain pills she got from her friends. The pills got a little expensive. Boyfriend was a heroin user and he injected her with heroin for the first time," Rogers remembered. "She used for a while, then she'd run out of money. Her parents realized something was really wrong. She told them."

As it happened, two months before, Rogers had taken a course in Cleveland in how to detoxify people addicted to opiates. He never thought he would actually use the information.

"I called the physician who taught the course. He said he had not seen any adolescents using heroin, but he gave me some ideas. I plugged her into an IV, hydrated her, gave her something for her nausea. I learned a lot from her."

This first heroin addict was from the wealthy suburb of Powell, a fact that surprised Rogers almost as much as learning that she was only sixteen.

"Where do you get your heroin?"

"From Mexicans."

"Where do you find them?"

She named a neighborhood not far from Children's Hospital that white girls from Powell did not frequent.

Rogers kept her in the hospital for three days. He spoke to her parents. She had admitted she was a heroin addict and was now detoxed, the parents said, so she was fine and could go home. Rogers had a different view, one learned from years as a recovering alcoholic himself. If she doesn't get long-term treatment, she is not going to stay sober, he told the parents. She's going to die, end up in jail, or be a chronic underachiever.

"They didn't believe me," Rogers said. "A few months later, the parents called. They said she's using heroin again. I saw her again, readmitted her. I think they were getting the message."

Once he admitted that girl to detox that night in 2003, it seemed to Rogers as if floodgates opened somewhere. Word spread among addicts that you could go to Children's and get detoxed. Peter Rogers watched the new opiate epidemic emerge out of nowhere and file through his clinic. Hundreds of kids. They were all white, suburban kids from well-to-do homes. Most were girls. One was a tennis champ. Another was the daughter of a Columbus cop. One was the daughter of a thoracic surgeon; there were several children of doctors, in fact.

All had started with pills. Many said they'd seen friends die. They had no idea where else to go. "The first kid showed up and word got out. I noticed that we got a lot of kids during that first six months from a place called Lancaster [a Columbus suburb]. It turns out these kids were coming to Columbus, buying heroin, going back to Lancaster."

Rogers was an early witness to heroin's new mainstreaming. The drug had for years appealed to rebellious kids from a seedy urban corner of America's counterculture. "I remember at eleven and twelve years old seeing pictures of [Sex Pistols bass player] Sid Vicious and thinking he's the coolest," one twenty-six-year-old recovering addict, a musician, told me. "Sid Vicious, [New York Dolls' guitarist] Johnny Thunders, Lou Reed, and William Burroughs, but also Charlie Parker. It was punk and jazz that made heroin so sexy and appealing, exciting and dangerous and subversive and not the norm. Then I saw the football players and the cheerleaders getting into it. These are people I turned to heroin to get away from."

To the suburban kids hooked first on pills, heroin fulfilled the dream of the adventures they'd never had in their quiet towns. Part of heroin's new appeal was that it kept them at the edge of a hazardous yet alluring dreamland. Finding dope every day could take them on a wild ride through worlds they hadn't known existed, which, however scuzzy or harrowing, left them with fantastical stories that awed their peers.

"You're as much addicted to going and buying it as to going and using it," one addict said. "You feel like James Bond. It's a crazy fantasy."

By the end of that year, Nationwide Children's Hospital, which had never admitted a teenage heroin addict that anyone could remember, had protocols for treating them. Rogers asked them all where they got the heroin: Mexicans, they said. Rogers called Columbus police. An officer told him they knew that Mexicans were selling the dope. We arrest them, the officer said. In a day or two, another comes in and takes their place.

Meanwhile, Rogers said, "I was living at the hospital. I was taking care of these kids. None of the other physicians really knew how to treat this. We were not ready for this. It was a whole new phenomenon. I called all over the country. What we were doing in Children's Hospital in Columbus was not something that anybody else was doing that I could find. We kept treating these kids. They kept coming in."

Rogers battled with insurance companies, who had apparently never heard of treating heroin addiction in teenagers. A couple years in, he gave a speech at the annual meeting of the American Academy of Pediatrics in Boston, describing what he was seeing to a sparse and bewildered audience.

"They weren't seeing any of this. They were thinking, 'Why do we need to learn about this?'"

Canaries in Coal Mines

Portsmouth, Ohio

For years after it closed, David Procter's Plaza Healthcare clinic would be known as the "boot camp for dirty docs." But Procter's influence went far beyond the unscrupulous doctors he brought to town. Instead, he showed Scioto County that starting a pain clinic was easy. Given an opening in Ohio state law, all you had to do was lease a building and hire a doctor who had a DEA permit to write prescriptions for Schedule II narcotics.

Pain clinics were now sprouting up across America as the opiates became commonly used for chronic pain, and the undertreatment of pain was identified as a public health problem. Not all pain clinics were pill mills. But as opiates became the principal treatment for pain, the pain clinic was often prone to abuse. It attracted patients relentlessly demanding drugs. Doctors found it hard to maintain standards. Some clinics were never legitimate, but many others started with good intentions and were simply pushed off course by patients' constant demands.

No place in America had more of these shady clinics per capita than did Scioto County, Ohio. Over the first years of the new century, a local junkyard owner, an attorney, a prison guard, an ex-bailiff, and a couple of convicted felons, as well as several doctors, all opened clinics, hiring doctors with permits to write the prescriptions and see patients at a rapid clip. Jody Robinson cashed in his car stereo shop to open a pain clinic through which he became, according to a later indictment, one of the region's biggest pill distributors.

Portsmouth became America's pill mill capital. The clinics were some of the only locally owned businesses to form in decades in Scioto County. People said the area's entrepreneurial spirit had drained from Portsmouth. In a twisted way, the pill mill showed that locals could still be as entrepreneurial as anyone. Billboards for pain clinics greeted travelers along the highways entering town. Drug dealers and users for miles around came to Portsmouth to stock up on pills.

One key to the pill mill explosion was the discovery of locum tenens lists, a clearinghouse for doctors around the country seeking temporary employment. Many of these doctors were desperate. They had license problems, or couldn't get malpractice insurance, or were alcoholics. These were the docs Procter had hired. Now other clinic owners did the same and quacks flocked to Portsmouth. Tracy Bias, a convicted felon, opened three pain clinics and hired doctors from New Mexico, Michigan, and Iowa, as well as two from other parts of Ohio.

Clinic staffers or locum tenens doctors found work at a pain clinic, learned the business, and then went out on their own. Soon, plain old drug dealers got in on the scam. Kevin Huff, a longtime marijuana dealer, set up a trailer alongside a highway in Chillicothe, Ohio, hired a nurse, and sold so many pills that he had shoeboxes full of cash lying around his home.

Several of the new clinic entrepreneurs had worked for David Procter. Nancy Sadler worked for Procter and then ran Fortune Williams's clinic. After Williams went to prison, she and her husband, Lester "Ape" Sadler, set up their own pain clinics. Procter's onetime attorney, Gary "Rocky" Billiter, opened a pain clinic as well.

After Procter's arrest, his employees Denise Huffman and her daughter, Alice Huffman Ball, opened Tri-State Health Care and Pain Management. A DEA investigation later found that people would drive for as many as ten hours to the Huffmans' clinic, pay two hundred dollars in cash to sit with a doctor and get a prescription for OxyContin, Lortab, Percocet, and other pain meds. The mother and daughter hired temp-agency doctors and threatened those who refused to prescribe pain medication. Several physicians left immediately.

In April 2003, the Huffmans solved their labor issues when they hired a Chicago chronic-pain specialist named Paul Volkman. Volkman was so prolific that the Huffmans had to open their own pill dispensary in the back of Tri-State after local pharmacies refused to honor his prescriptions. This pharmacy was somehow legal under Ohio law.

By September 2005, Volkman had written prescriptions for a million pills of various kinds. Another million pills were deemed missing due to the lack of any records kept by him or the Huffmans. A DEA investigation estimated that Volkman and the Huffmans took in some three million dollars from patients paying two hundred dollars a visit, and who lined up well before the clinic opened. The Huffmans paid staffers in pills, but staff also accepted bribes (in pills usually) to move patients up in line. Volkman rarely performed anything resembling a diagnosis.

Instead, he met with patients briefly, asked them a few questions—one of which was whether they were undercover law enforcement officers. He often ordered urine tests, but ignored them when they showed high levels of opiates. He had one patient sign a "death waiver," in which the patient acknowledged he might die from taking what Volkman was prescribing. At least twelve patients did die while Volkman worked for the Huffmans. He later opened his own clinic in Portsmouth, then in Chillicothe, and six more patients died.

For a couple months, Volkman even had a clinic in a house on a residential street in Portsmouth's Hilltop neighborhood. "He was in one of the bedrooms," said one addict. "The front room was the waiting area, and the kitchen was where you got your blood pressure checked out. He wrote me some crazy amounts of medication, 480 pills one month. No MRIs, no CAT scans, no nothing."

There were other pill mills. Volkman and the Huffmans were only part of the story in Scioto County.

But not many in the country paid much attention to what was developing in and around Portsmouth. The area was abandoned—by politics and power, and even by many who once lived there. Plus those who remained behind, who were the first to get caught up in the gathering storm, were complicit in their own degradation, so no one paid them much attention.

Folks like those from the Lucasville Bottoms.

I WAS POKING AROUND southern Ohio, trying to understand all this, when I encountered a lawyer named Joe Hale.

Hale has silver hair, a baritone voice, and a Marlboro Red always at the ready. By 1999, he had been a defense attorney for fifteen years in Scioto County. A country boy from the oak of Appalachia, Hale had a client list that was mostly court appointed. The money wasn't great, but it kept him busy and in the courtroom.

One place Hale made a lot of his money was Lucasville. Lucasville is a small town a few minutes north of Portsmouth along Highway 23. It has a prison that holds Ohio's death house, where death row inmates are executed. Across the street from the prison is a high school. Lucasville also includes a couple stoplights, a gas station or two, and a few failed restaurants. But to Joe Hale, Lucasville was the Bottoms.

The Lucasville Bottoms are flatlands that flood every decade or so when the nearby Scioto River rises. The rest of the time, the Bottoms provide cheap housing, most of it of the single-wide mobile home variety. Many of its residents are on federal disability. Many of them are small-time criminals. Joe Hale had defended hundreds of Bottoms residents through his career on charges of drug possession, domestic violence, and drunk and disorderly.

The Bottoms are a clannish place, but Hale became well-known there. He got used to the rhythms of the Bottoms, which revolved around government checks on the first of the month. People rarely visited a doctor, and when they did, it was to guys like David Procter, who accepted cash.

In the late 1990s, as David Procter was heavily prescribing OxyContin, a client named Tony Blevins showed up to do some work on Hale's house with a bottle of pills. Blevins called them OCs. He offered Hale a few. Hale had no interest in the pills, but he noticed that several of his usually energetic construction workers were like zombies. He came to find out people in the Bottoms were crushing the pills and injecting them. Most Bottoms denizens didn't know how to do that. A profession called "shooters" thrived in the Bottoms for a while. For a free hit for themselves, shooters would inject users who were new to the needle.

"Over the next three, four, five months, [Oxy] was all you heard about," Hale said. "Some people were very experienced, very well-known, with years as drug users; they started overdosing and dying. Because they were people with criminal records and never made a contribution to society, nobody gave a damn."

This had been going on for a while, to Hale's growing alarm, when in April 1999, Jack Burton paid him a visit. Burton was the unofficial godfather of the Lucasville Bottoms, influential among many families, rumored to be involved in crime. A gaunt fellow, Burton drove a white sedan and in it, slunk down behind the wheel, he cruised the Bottoms.

Burton's daughter, Jackie, had just died of an OxyContin overdose. Hale had defended Jackie Burton after a couple barroom brawls that landed her in court. The first time Jackie Burton was shot up with OxyContin, she nodded off and the shooter who injected her wasn't paying attention. She was probably dead for an hour before anyone noticed.

Now Jack Burton was in Hale's office asking what he could do about the company that made the drug.

"Jack," Hale told him. "You're asking me to take on a major pharmaceutical corporation." He turned Burton down. But months passed and the deaths in the Bottoms mounted. Hale kept thinking.

"This is a lawsuit that could mean a lot of money," he said.

In May 2001, Hale filed what is believed to be the first Oxy-related wrongful-death lawsuit against Purdue Pharma, on behalf of Jackie Burton.

"Purdue Pharma has unleashed a pharmaceutical atomic bomb into the free flow of commerce with absolutely disastrous consequences that they should have foreseen," he told the *Portsmouth Daily Times*.

A Cincinnati law firm eventually joined Hale's case, preparing it as a class action lawsuit, and asked Hale to find more plaintiffs. Hale found petty thieves and able-bodied disability recipients—people whose already dysfunctional lives had been further mangled by opiate addiction.

Several months later, the Cincinnati firm withdrew from the suit. "Nobody told me that a class representative shouldn't have a bunch of felony convictions," Hale said. "And that there were all these ideals that these class action plaintiffs were supposed to have."

The Bottoms sure didn't produce anyone that a TV camera or jury would find sympathetic. After a few court hearings with him at one table and six or eight well-dressed Purdue attorneys on the other, Hale dropped the suit. But he always saw the Lucasville Bottoms as an early warning sign that Ohio and the country ignored at their peril. A Purdue Pharma press release later noted that the company had won every suit filed against it. That didn't surprise Joe Hale.

"By the time you were in a position to have a lawsuit against Purdue Pharma, you were already likely to have fucked up so badly that you wouldn't work as a class action plaintiff," he said as we drove around the Bottoms one spring day, down lanes of narrow mobile homes and junked cars.

But that's how it was as the opiate epidemic took shape in southern Ohio beginning in the late 1990s. Portsmouth, the Lucasville Bottoms, and other forgotten places of America nearby acted like the canaries in those now-shuttered Appalachian coal mines. Just no one in the country listened much until more respectable types sounded the same alarm and famous people died.

Fifty, Hundred Cases a Month

Olympia, Washington

The state of Washington's workers' compensation system is one of only five in the country that hold monopolies on insuring workers. The state insures two-thirds of all Washington's 1.2 million workers; it oversees the rest, workers at companies large enough to insure themselves.

Thus Labor and Industries—as the system is known—generates enormous amounts of data about worker injuries and deaths. As narcotic painkillers became accepted treatment for chronic pain, workers with on-the-job injuries were mightily affected. Almost alone in the country, L&I, in a three-story glass building off in Tumwater, Washington, far from Portsmouth and the Lucasville Bottoms, sat atop a mountain of data affording a broad vista of what was forming.

Seeing it all, however, would require someone with an abhorrence of disorder.

That described Jaymie Mai.

Mai grew up in postwar Vietnam, the child of a South Vietnamese navy seaman imprisoned in a communist reeducation camp. In 1978, her mother took her six children aboard a small fishing boat with seventy-five other people. They floated aimlessly, besieged by Thai pirates, on a boat crammed with people retching violently, until a Malaysian merchant ship happened by and took them aboard. A year later, Mai and her family were on a plane to Seattle and a new life.

Mai got a pharmacy degree at the University of Washington. She worked as a pharmacist at various hospitals. In 2000, wanting to start a family and looking for more predictable hours, she took a job as L&I's chief pharmacist, overseeing the cases of workers receiving prescription drugs for injuries.

She came to the job agnostic on the then-increasing use of opiates in medicine. In the hospitals where she worked up to then, opiates were used for broken legs or following surgery, which she believed appropriate.

Mai possessed an intense need for order. Sloppiness and unanswered questions were anathema. She cleaned her house a lot because it helped her destress and think things through, while restoring order. She loved to garden, as much to instill order as for the love of plants. She prized roses and planted them outside the new house that she and her husband bought when she was hired on as L&I's chief pharmacist.

She would need them. One part of her job involved ensuring doctors were documenting whether the new opiate painkillers were helping to reduce patients' pain and improve their ability to function. Otherwise, why should the state keep paying for the drugs? There, she saw for the first time how the drugs were used for chronic pain, and grew alarmed.

"It was automatic: 'You hurt? Let me write you a prescription for opioids,'" she said. "They were treating patients with opioids and the patient would come in with more complaints of pain a month later and they would up the dose. 'See me next month.' I could see in the medical record that the provider wasn't checking to see if the drug was even helping them. The patient would come in every visit complaining of more pain. Nobody ever said, 'Wait a minute. Time out. Let's figure out what's going on.'

"Fifty, a hundred cases a month. But there's no attempt to document if the drug was working, one, or, two, if they even are appropriate candidates to receive opioids. Did they try a nonopioid first?"

Then, six months into the job, Mai noticed some of these workers began dying from these very painkillers. This didn't happen. Workers whose original complaint was a sprained back or knee did *not* die. Yet one case after another crossed her desk—all overdosing. In Washington in a typical year fifty or more workers died, but these were from accidents—electrocutions, falls, etc.—or from cancers like asbestosis. Now workers with back sprains were dying as well.

She went to her boss, L&I's medical director, Dr. Gary Franklin.

"What should we be doing about them?"

Gary Franklin had been an opiate skeptic from the start. He had a master's degree in public health and several years as a professor of neurology and preventive medicine at the University of Colorado. He took the job as L&I's medical director in 1988 as the crusade to destigmatize opiates in medicine was getting under way.

Soon, doctors advising L&I were quoting Porter and Jick on the percentage of pain patients addicted when prescribed opiates. "Not more than one percent. They'd say, 'We don't think they're addictive as we used to think,'" Franklin said.

In 1999, Washington, through a state medical commission, removed legal sanctions for doctors for prescribing narcotics in the course of acceptable medical practice—its own intractable pain regulation.

"It meant there's no ceiling on dose, that the way to treat tolerance is to increase the dose," Franklin said.

Now, two years into these state regulations allowing more liberal prescribing, his new chief pharmacist was in his office telling him she was seeing opiate-overdose deaths of workers with bad backs. Franklin still had questions. Were these workers dying from recreational abuse of opiates, or pills they'd been prescribed?

"We didn't want to overcall the deaths," Franklin told me. "Doctors had spent so much time getting people to use more opioids. I knew we were going to take a hit if we said people are dying of prescription opioids."

More information was needed: death certificates, coroner autopsy reports, the drug prescriptions for each person who died. Over the next two years, in a back room on L&I's second floor, Mai pored over cases of workers dying from opiate overdoses. Finding them was the first task. Some 266 people in the workers' comp system had died since 1995. Mai whittled this down to 60 where drugs were mentioned, and ordered the doctors' records, the death certificate, and the autopsy reports for each.

Finally, in 2005, in a paper published in the *American Journal of Industrial Medicine*, Franklin and Mai reported that forty-four people with chronic pain in Washington's workers' comp system had died due definitely, probably, or possibly to prescription opiate use between 1995 and 2002. Most had died after 1999, the year the state's intractable pain regulation was written. Most were men; most were under fifty years old. They had come to workers' comp with non-life-threatening ailments—lower back pain or carpal tunnel syndrome, say—for which they were prescribed Schedule II opiates, and were dead a short while later.

Mai and Franklin also found that prescriptions for the strongest opiates more than doubled. Prescriptions for much milder pain relievers dropped or remained the same. This was also strange. Normally, doctors would be expected to start out with the milder drugs. But faced with patient pain, doctors were going right to the heavy artillery, and that meant, beginning in about 1997, OxyContin.

Franklin and Mai's paper was the first time anyone in the country had documented the deaths associated with the new prescribing of opiates for noncancer pain.

They wrote to workers' comp doctors telling them this was happening. They got phone calls in return from people outraged that the state might be preparing to take away their meds. But then directors from Washington's Medicaid and the Veterans Administration got on the phone. They were also finding opiate overdose deaths on the rise.

Mai and Franklin called Jennifer Sabel. Sabel is an epidemiologist at the state of Washington's department of health and had just begun studying deaths from injury and violence, including fatal drug overdoses. Mai and Franklin asked whether the surge in opiate-overdose deaths was taking place not only among Washington workers but across the state's population.

Sabel said she'd look.

Junkie Kingdom in Dreamland

Portsmouth, Ohio

Finally, inevitably, Dreamland closed.

This happened in 1993. Jaime Williams had sold it years before. The new owners couldn't keep up the pool and the population was no longer there to support it. More people had pools in their backyards. Dreamland stood empty for two years. Residents organized to save it, but there were fewer of them now since Portsmouth had lost its steel mill and shoe factories. The city could have bought it but dallied. The owners made a deal with a developer who wanted to put in a shopping center. Dreaming of tax revenue as budgets shrank, the city council let it happen. Before anyone could sue to stall the deal, the developer brought in bulldozers late at night and crippled the pool by knocking out its filtration system.

Over two months, the bulldozers tore out the lockers and the diving boards, filled in Dreamland and covered it in blacktop. Longtime Portsmouthians couldn't bear to watch. An O'Reilly Auto Parts and an AT&T cellular store now stand at the edge of a massive asphalt parking lot that once was Dreamland.

Tax revenue from Dreamland never much materialized. Instead, the Dreamland debacle fed the idea that city hall contained a bunch of dullards.

As the town's decline intensified, Portsmouth opted for a strong mayor, a form of government usually reserved for large cities. It would save the town the cost of a city manager. But the mayors had no experience in, or time for, running a town's complicated daily affairs. One mayor was a grocery store clerk. Predictably, basic municipal governance was abandoned. Trash-pickup schedules grew undecipherable. Unlit parks became prostitution hives. Police, with few officers, gave up. City politics became a street brawl and recalls grew common. City council meetings were left to gadflies infected with a debilitating negativity: Nothing would work, so why try?

For years, the town had a protector in Vern Riffe Jr. Riffe ran a political machine from his post as the powerful Democratic speaker of Ohio's House of Representatives. A son of Portsmouth, he was a prolific fund-raiser. He funneled tax money into the town and other forgotten parts of Appalachian Ohio. He had Shawnee State University built in Portsmouth. As Portsmouth's benefactor, Riffe was a beloved figure. Yet he was part of a larger culture of dependence that Portsmouth had trouble shaking. "Everybody was looking for some outside source to come in and save us," said Scott Douthat, a native son and professor of sociology at the university.

After Dreamland closed, the town went indoors. Police took the place of the communal adult supervision that the pool had provided. Walmart became the spot to socialize.

Opiates, the most private and selfish of drugs, moved in and made easy work of a landscape stripped of any communal girding. Kids used to get together for beers and bonfires by the river and talk all night. Bonfires seemed to fade away once the pills came around.

The factories and the shops on Chillicothe Street were replaced by the clinics David Procter pioneered, which found cheap space in the town's abandoned buildings. Pill mills were about the only locally owned businesses to open.

By the new millennium, Purdue Pharma's promotion of OxyContin and the crusade to liberalize opiate prescribing were seeing their first noxious effects across southern Ohio, West Virginia, and eastern Kentucky. Portsmouth for a while had a pill mill for every eighteen hundred residents.

"My daughter was addicted," said Lisa Roberts, the city's public health nurse. "A judge's kid became addicted. A mayor's kid became addicted. A police chief's kid got addicted. The kids who came from excellent families got addicted."

It seemed like an evil lottery, a massive brainwashing. One by one people succumbed. After a while, Roberts could recognize the look, say, in an old friend she hadn't seen for a while. "They're coming over to your house [with] these big elaborate stories to get money off you," she said. "It's like watching people being picked off one by one by one."

Slaves to the morphine molecule, the generation born into the town's decline set about tearing Portsmouth apart. You could see them trudging like zombies along Highway 52, which ran through Portsmouth, on missions to placate the molecule. They ripped air conditioners out of houses for the copper wire inside. They stole manhole covers. They took large spools of copper wire from behind the school district office. They stole their children's Christmas presents.

Until finally, alone down on the Ohio River, Portsmouth became a kind of junkie kingdom and pills became currency, more valuable than cash. To a degree unlike any other town in America, a raging, full-blown OxyContin economy developed.

DVDs, refrigerators, dentist visits, cable TV installation, Tide detergent, tools, clothes, and children's school supplies—pills bought them all in Portsmouth, Ohio.

AMONG THE FIRST LOCAL entrepreneurs to emerge was Mary Ann Henson, a pretty blond woman who grew up middle-class. Her adoptive parents cherished her and were very religious. She didn't recall so much as a beer in her refrigerator growing up. She was a cheerleader at East Portsmouth High School and in the fall of 1990 she was the school's homecoming queen. It was a bittersweet moment, as nobody knew she was two months pregnant. She started using pills not long after leaving home with her newborn daughter at the end of her senior year.

"I thought I knew everything," she said. "I was eighteen."

Mary Ann ended up strung out, on welfare, with food stamps and a Medicaid health-insurance card. For a while she had a boyfriend who broke into pharmacies with a group of friends. Her boyfriend went to prison and Mary Ann was strapped for cash.

One day, a friend asked, "Hon, ain't you been to the doctor?"

The woman took her to a doctor named John Lilly. Lilly had followed David Procter's lead and opened the area's second pain clinic. Lilly was in downtown Portsmouth. His clinic lines stretched around the block. Lilly asked Mary Ann to lift one knee, then the other, and the visit was over. He prescribed her a month's worth of Lorcet and Xanax. Mary Ann gave half the pills to the woman who paid for her visit and kept half. The woman then took her across the river to David Procter for the same charade. Mary Ann sold her pills and a business was formed. She began going to Lilly and Procter.

Pill abuse was a minor subculture back then. Abusing Vicodin or Lortab was hard work. They contained only small doses of opiates, and included acetaminophen or Tylenol to discourage their abuse. People who used them usually developed serious liver problems from the acetaminophen. But they didn't often overdose on the weaker pills. Once OxyContin arrived, however "it went from people strung out on dope to people strung out and dying on dope," said one Portsmouth addict who by then was taking so many Lortabs that he permanently damaged his liver.

In Portsmouth, OxyContin did something else: It turned pill scamming into big business for the town's generation of decline. Mary Ann bought the MRI results of a person with a sprained lumbar. She scanned the pages into a computer, and used the MRI repeatedly, changing the name on it over and over. Next, she recruited street addicts. She paid them to go to the doctor, each armed with that MRI in their names. The docs of Portsmouth charged $250 cash per visit. In time, Mary Ann was driving several addicts at a time to one clinic one day, and another group of addicts to another clinic the next, waiting while they got their prescriptions.

Usually, each addict left the clinic with scripts for ninety 80 mg OxyContins—three a day, for a month. The doctor also prescribed 120 generic oxycodone 30 mg pills and 90 Xanax bars. Mary Ann took half of the haul in exchange for driving the addict to the clinic and paying the $250 doctor's fee.

This became a classic business model in Portsmouth and elsewhere. Thousands of people procured dope and made money this way.

The weak link in this pill scam was pharmacists. Many local Portsmouth pharmacists soon caught on and wouldn't fill prescriptions from notorious clinics. So addicts crowded into cars, driven by dealers like Mary Ann, and set off rummaging through rural towns for hours looking for willing pharmacists. The whole time they talked about dope like gold miners about all they were going to do with their pills this time. This time, they vowed, they weren't going to use them. Rather, they were going to sell them and accumulate some cash. Then *they* would be the ones to drive junkies to clinics and pay their visits. Those dreams evaporated on the long ride home as they snorted or injected their pills and were left again with nothing.

Once a pharmacist was found, another problem presented itself: how to pay for the prescription. The price of each patient's prescribed drugs was between eight and twelve hundred dollars. Paying cash was certainly an option. But for junkies, and even for dealers with more discipline, coming up with that kind of money was hard. And so the Medicaid card entered our story.

The card provides health insurance through Medicaid, and part of that insurance pays for medicine—whatever pills a doctor deems that the insured patient needs. Among those who receive Medicaid cards are people on state welfare or on a federal disability program known as SSI (Supplemental Security Income).

In Scioto County, annual SSI applicants almost doubled in the decade ending 2008—from 870 to 1,600. An untrained observer of Portsmouth's bleak economic landscape might have understood; jobs, after all, were scarce. People needed money and that check helped. That was true, but by then pills and pain clinics had altered the classic welfare calculus: It wasn't the monthly SSI *check* people cared so much about; rather, they wanted the Medicaid card that came with it.

If you could get a prescription from a willing doctor—and Portsmouth had plenty of those—the Medicaid health insurance cards paid for that prescription every month. For a three-dollar Medicaid co-pay, therefore, an addict got pills priced at a thousand dollars, with the difference paid for by U.S. and state taxpayers. A user could turn around and sell those pills, obtained for that three-dollar co-pay, for as much as ten thousand dollars on the street.

Combined with pill mills, the Medicaid card scam allowed prolific quantities of prescription medication to hit the streets. The more pills that sloshed around the region, the more people grew addicted, and the bigger the business grew, and the more people died. The Oxy black market might never have spread and deepened so quickly had addicts been forced to pay for all those pills with cash at market prices.

MORE ISOLATED PARTS OF Appalachia had other stories to tell about OxyContin, stories not connected to pill mills, but just as related to economic decline, and thus to SSI and Medicaid cards.

In hilly Floyd County, Kentucky, a hundred miles south of Portsmouth, the story had to do with mining. When the deep mines were working years ago, Floyd County had a lot of jobs. A man would work down in the mines for twenty years, pay into his disability—a federal program known as Social Security Disability Insurance (SSDI)—and be out of the mines with black lung by age forty-five with a monthly check large enough to support a family. That became a life strategy in Eastern Kentucky.

But when the deep mines closed, strip mines took their place, using far fewer workers. Those who worked weren't so easily injured. They didn't qualify for workers' compensation. As jobs disappeared, so did the disability income people could receive. Eventually, entire families grew up on SSI, which paid only a few hundred dollars a month. SSI, however, *did* come with a Medicaid card, and that made all the difference when OxyContin appeared.

"Twenty years ago they were drawing SSDI and full workers'

comp—say, eighteen hundred dollars a month," said Brent Turner, the commonwealth prosecutor for that part of eastern Kentucky, whose career began in 2000, just as OxyContin became a business for impoverished families across Appalachia.

"The checks were higher because they'd go work in the mines and pay into their [SSDI] disability. Now we've got people who aren't working, who are drawing SSI, maybe five hundred dollars a month. We've got people who have kids and wives and the whole family trying to survive on five hundred dollars. I'm not making excuses for them. Many haven't had a job. But it is what it is. When you don't work, and never have had a job, or paid into the system, you don't qualify for much. We have boatloads of people who qualify only for SSI. You wouldn't believe the number of people we see, twenty or thirty years old, have never had a job and are drawing checks since they were teenagers.

"That was one of the driving factors when pills exploded. We can talk morality all day long, but if you're drawing five hundred dollars a month and you have a Medicaid card that allows you to get a monthly supply of pills worth several thousand dollars, you're going to sell your pills."

As the pain revolution took hold, "decent family docs were real liberal about prescribing them," Turner said. "You have the easy availability of all these narcotics and you put it all together and they just exploded. When it comes to pills, it's the aggregation of all those small-time people is what's killing everybody. If the only people we incarcerate are Scarface, we won't incarcerate anybody. It's a cultural thing and everybody's doing it."

Much like the Xalisco heroin system, OxyContin didn't have kingpins. Instead, the market was moved by a bunch of small-time operators relying on newly relaxed attitudes regarding pain pill prescribing, a new pill with a huge whack of dope, and the Medicaid card. Medicaid cards had been around for years. With OxyContin, they became licenses to print money.

"WE ALWAYS ASSUMED THAT Purdue Pharma knew that so many people [in the area] had Medicaid cards," Lisa Roberts, the Portsmouth city nurse, told me. "And that's why they marketed OxyContin so hard around here."

Whether the company knew that, Purdue did have information on the doctors who prescribed drugs most liberally. Many of them were in areas, not coincidentally, where the numbers of welfare and federal disability recipients were comparatively high—like southern Ohio and eastern Kentucky.

Every pill Mary Ann Henson harvested from the addicts whom she took to a pain clinic she could sell for a dollar a milligram—eighty dollars for one Oxy 80 mg pill, in other words. At those prices, and taking half the pills from each addict, she could make five thousand dollars from each patient she took to a doctor. She sold the pills from her house with her husband, Keith Henson. Years later they remembered their operation resembling a McDonald's drive-through. Four people on the porch waiting while ten more were doing business in the living room.

Portsmouth once had the industrial ingenuity to invent the shoelace machine. Now it invented the modern pill mill. The clinics and OxyContin made Portsmouth, Ohio, a destination again. People flocked to the pain clinics from southern Ohio, eastern Kentucky, West Virginia, and Indiana. People in line to see John Lilly ordered pizza while they waited. They drank beer and snorted pills and puked in the bushes. Fortune Williams, out in Kentucky, hired security guards to direct traffic. From her flooring shop next to David Procter's clinic, Karen Charles watched fistfights among patients in line.

Those lines were the addict Internet. News spread along the line about what doctor prescribed which drugs, who had a car stereo for sale. It may have been in those clinic lines where OxyContin first emerged as an economic currency in Portsmouth, Ohio.

Addicts of the morphine molecule valued dope above everything, including children and cash. Pills could not be altered or diluted. Pills held their value, and that value was printed on each pill. It helped that OxyContin came in 40 and 80 mg pills, and generic oxycodone came in 10, 15, 20, and 30 mg doses—different denominations for ease of use as currency. The pill mills acted as the central banks, controlling the "money supply," which they kept constant and plentiful, and thus resisted inflationary or deflationary spikes.

By the late 1990s a critical mass was achieved and for about a decade the value of most goods in Portsmouth, and many services, was measured in pills.

Armed robbers in Portsmouth hit dealers' houses, took the pills, and ignored the cash. Mary Ann once bought a car with OxyContin. She paid an off-duty cable TV worker in pills to install service. She paid a dentist visit with pills. She ransomed Keith from drug-addicted kidnappers with pills. She bought steak and diapers and laundry detergent with pills. Shoes for pills. Purses for pills. Perfume for pills.

Crucially, pills also bought children's love. Junkies, whose main relationship was with dope, could briefly emerge from the fog to buy their children the toy, video game, or bracelet they coveted with pills—usually buying it off a shoplifter.

Part of the economy was a pulsing network of people putting out feelers—kind of a junkie Craigslist.

"Someone says, 'Hey, I'm looking for a chain saw,'" Mary Ann said. "Then some guy comes by with a chain saw. You buy the chain saw for an oxycodone thirty you paid almost nothing for [thanks to your Medicaid card], and you call the other guy and sell him the chain saw for a hundred dollars cash."

Something like that had evolved with Lorcet years before, but on a tiny scale. OxyContin, with so much dope in each pill, bought big stuff. Stone-cold, teeth-gnashing, mainlining junkies like Mary Ann now had big-screen TVs and computers, nice furniture and power tools.

Even urine leaked into the OxyContin economy. As authorities scrutinized Scioto County doctors, some clinics began requiring occasional urine tests. Probation officers always wanted them. So a black market in clean urine emerged, in which the fluid was exchanged like water in the desert. Addicts bought false bladders they strapped to their stomachs with tubes leading down into their pants. Neighbors of one pain clinic near downtown got used to people knocking on their doors asking if they wanted to sell their urine. Outside the pill mills stood people who charged in pills to pee in a cup, promising clean urine as they chugged water. Veteran clients would crumble oxycodone into the purchased urine, because doctors wanted to see that patients had no drug in their system other than what they prescribed. Kids' urine was coveted for its purity and was worth an Oxy 40 in Portsmouth for several years.

Meanwhile, a sophisticated opiate class system emerged. At the top were the people who never used, but sold pills and bought anything a junkie brought in.

The late Jerry Lockhart was one of the elite. He lived on a promontory dubbed OxyContin Hill in West Portsmouth. Lockhart also took people monthly to see pill mill doctors, paid for their visits, and then took half the pills they were prescribed. These people were street rats—the lowest in the opiate class system.

Street rats were addicts who could never accumulate the capital to pay for their own doctor's visit, much less anyone else's. They scavenged scrap metal or stole lawn ornaments from front yards. They had a million hustles to get well through the month. The town had hundreds of street rats, and more crowding in from elsewhere on day trips to Portsmouth pill mills.

The relationship between street rats and distributors like Lockhart resembled sharecropping. One way street rats made it through the month was to ask dealers like Jerry Lockhart to front them pills. By the time their monthly doctor's appointment rolled around, they owed most of what they were going to be prescribed. "If we were getting a hundred and eighty of them, we already owed him a hundred," another addict said.

I talked to an addict named Donnie. In the Marines overseas, Donnie had been badly wounded, for which he was given morphine. He carried the taste for opiates with him when he returned to Portsmouth, which by then was bathing in them. As an Oxy addiction took hold, Donnie began selling his garage tools. He figured he sold almost all those tools to Jerry Lockhart.

During the month, he went frequently to Lockhart for pills. Lockhart would give him two, expecting four after the doctor's visit. By his doctor's visit, Donnie usually owed Lockhart almost all of what he was going to be prescribed.

Lockhart traded pills for stolen goods, which he sold out of a large garage on his property. He gave addicts pills for their food stamp cards and bought groceries with the cards. One addict said he gave Lockhart his card and didn't see it again until Lockhart died two years later. An addict who said he worked for Lockhart told me Lockhart built virtually his entire house with material purchased with Lowe's gift cards. All these cards came via merchandise addicts stole from the store: They returned the shoplifted stuff for gift cards; then they brought the cards to Lockhart for pills.

Shoplifters, in fact, were the wandering peddlers in Portsmouth's junkie kingdom, providing the goods central to daily life in the OxyContin economy and taking only pills in payment. They stole groceries or tampons or detergent or microwaves on order.

Shoplifters' importance to the OxyContin economy grew, in turn, from a new and indispensable rural institution.

In Portsmouth, as in much of rural America, most of what there is to buy is sold only at Walmart. In this case, the Walmart is in the neighboring town of New Boston, on the land where the coke plant once stood, and the smokestack remains. Everybody shops and socializes there.

I live in Southern California, a market that Walmart has not penetrated as completely. When I lived in Mexico, the Walmarts were only in Mexico City's far-off suburbs. I entered my first Walmart in 2003 while visiting a southwest Kansas meatpacking town for a story about a high school soccer team. I came with a set of embarrassingly naïve images of what I expected from southwest Kansas. Few areas had contributed so many icons to Americans' history: pioneers, cattle trails, family farms, Dodge City, and even the Wizard of Oz. All of it pivoted around, I imagined, the Main Street of small-town America.

I instead found ghost towns. My footsteps echoed down small-town Main Streets. On one, a pharmacist left a note in the window of her store. She had enjoyed serving the town, she wrote, but couldn't hang on anymore and she hoped they'd understand why she was leaving like all the rest. She left no forwarding address.

Walmart was often the only place to buy most of life's essentials in these heartland towns. Strolling their Walmarts, I imagined its aisles haunted by the ghosts of store owners who once sustained small-town America. On one aisle was the departed local grocer, down another the former hardware store owner, next to that, the woman's clothier or that long-gone pharmacist.

So maybe I should not have been surprised to learn that in Portsmouth's OxyContin economy, when the new rural junkies needed to get well, like everybody else, they turned to Walmart.

Before OxyContin, it wasn't much to scrounge up four or five bucks to buy a Lorcet or a Vicodin to get well.

"You could find that in your couch," said one addict.

Then Oxy came around, with its large dose of dope, high cost, and much stronger withdrawals. Suddenly dope-sick junkies needed a place where they could quickly come up with two hundred dollars in merchandise to sell.

"The more money you need to get the pill, the more product's got to be had," said Keith Henson, Mary Ann's husband. "You could go to Walmart and spend a half hour in there and get enough for a pill or two."

Of course, users could also con loved ones; they sold dope themselves; they broke into gun shops or robbed drug dealers. Lashed on by the morphine molecule, they did that and a lot more. But for many, the enormous blue retailer drew them like a magnet. Barred from your local Walmart? Another was twenty-five miles away in almost any direction.

Some large though immeasurable amount of the merchandise supporting addiction, as the opiates settled on heartland America, was mined from the aisles of Walmart, where Main Streets had gone to die.

In Portsmouth's Oxy economy, junkie shoplifters had to be flexible. On any given day, they might get orders for boys' shoes and a power saw and car stereo speakers and a T-bone steak. Once upon a time, that might have meant visits to four shops on Chillicothe Street. No longer.

"Walmart has such a big variety," said Angie Thuma, a former nurse who stole from Walmart for years as a street addict. "I had people I would sell [shoplifted items] to on a daily basis. Everything was in one spot. If you need men's clothes, it was at Walmart. If you needed shoes, I stole hundreds of pairs of shoes from Walmart. It was everything a person would want in one store."

Walmart also regulated prices in the OxyContin economy. Shoplifters got half the value in pills of the price tag on the item. If there was no price listed on say, a Black and Decker circular saw an addict was offering, Keith Henson said, "You'd call Walmart and do a price check. 'I'm looking for this [Black and Decker] circular saw. How much do them run?' They'd tell you. 'It's sixty-nine ninety-nine.'" Keith would pay roughly half that in pills—usually an oxycodone 30—for that circular saw the addict was offering.

Of course, prices were subject to a junkie's desperation. This was pitiless commerce. Mary Ann once offered a junkie an oxycodone 15 for a pair of stolen Nike Jordan basketball shoes because the guy was too dope sick to go find another buyer. She bought a refrigerator from a family with children for three 30s. But generally, if a shoplifter stole a bag of diapers, Tide detergent, DVDs, and a power sander, worth about two hundred dollars at Walmart, he had a reasonable expectation that a dealer in town would pay him half the value in pills: an OxyContin 80 and an oxycodone 20.

It helped that Walmart employees displayed little love for the store and its famously low wages. Some workers were strung out themselves. Some greeters were too old to recognize what was happening. Either way, a lot of Walmart workers had no hankering for a junkie face-off.

"They're making ten dollars an hour," said a veteran booster I met in Portsmouth. "They can see the look in our faces, 'Don't get in our way.' Every now and then you find one with a cape. One who's trying to get that manager position. The tough guy's going to try. But when I'm in withdrawal, I'm tougher."

The opiate scourge might never have spread as quickly had these rural areas where it all started possessed a diversity of small retailers, whose owners had invested their lives in their stores, knew the addicts personally, and stood ready to defend against them.

Walmart allowed junkie shoplifters to play Santa to the pill economy, filling dealers' orders for toys and presents in exchange for dope. Angie Thuma supplied a half dozen dealers with all their Christmas presents for several years running, and gifts for her kids as well. (As it happened, Christmas Day was big for dealers, who opened for business awaiting junkies wanting to exchange for pills the gifts they—or their children— received.) "For a couple months before each Christmas, I couldn't steal enough," Thuma said. "Even if I went several times a day, I didn't have enough arms to get everything they wanted."

It was not only drug dealers who bought the lifted merchandise. Many in the town's depressed, minimum wage economy were avid for a deal and didn't care too much where it came from. Some of Angie Thuma's best clients were middle-aged women raising their grandkids, who couldn't get by on the salaries they earned.

But by and large, it was dealers who fueled the shoplifting trade and prodded the boosters to new ingenuity. As dealers prepared their kids to return to school in August, shoplifters fanned out armed with long order lists of clothes with kids' sizes in shoes, shirts and pants, and school supplies. One kid I talked to wheeled flat-screen TVs through a Walmart tire shop, which rarely had much supervision, and had a door with no alarm. Line a purse with aluminum foil and the sensors of any merchandise you put in it wouldn't activate the alarms as you exited Walmart.

Thuma drove other boosters to Walmart, who'd go in the store and find a large box containing a child's outdoor plastic slide. They wheeled it to a secluded area of the store and emptied it. Then they would tour the store filling the now-empty box with DVD players, Xbox consoles, headphones, Tide detergent pods. They would pay the twenty dollars that the slide cost, and wheel the box to the exit. When the alarm invariably went off, they would show the elderly greeter the receipt and be waved out. Some electronic malfunction, no doubt, honey.

Another veteran Wal-Mart booster told me he would wear very baggy clothing, with long-john underwear underneath, taped at the ankles. He'd walk through the store stuffing merchandise in his long johns, which would balloon out, though nothing would show under his baggy pants and shirt. "I walked out of there, it looked like I was four hundred pounds," he said.

People in Portsmouth opened stores in their apartments, specializing in certain products, most of which they stole from Walmart: garden supplies, tools, automotive equipment. One recovering addict told me he visited the apartment of a woman who stocked everything a baby needed. "She had a bedroom you could go into set up like a store, diapers in one corner, baby food and formula, clothes on a dresser like a display table," he said. "Then she'd have boxes of high chairs and strollers. She would go into Walmart to steal shit; or she'd have people go in there with orders and they'd deliver it to her."

Walmart, for a long time, did not require a receipt for returned goods. Anything stolen could be returned for a gift card for the full value of the merchandise. Dealers bought those cards for half their value in pills. A five-hundred-dollar Walmart card was worth three OxyContin 80s—for which the dealer had paid a few dollars with the Medicaid card scam. A vast trade in Walmart cards kept Portsmouth's army of pill dealers in household necessities.

A Walmart receipt, meanwhile, could get you cash. Junkies scoured Walmart parking lots for discarded receipts. They'd steal the items on a receipt, flashing the paper at the greeter as they left. Then they'd return the merchandise, with the receipt, and exchange it for cash.

AMID THIS MADNESS, THE sons and daughters of Portsmouth's business owners, the children of sheriff's captains and doctors and lawyers, saw a future in OxyContin. Some regarded pills as a grassroots response to economic catastrophe—the way some poor Mexican villagers view drug trafficking. Dealers who could not have found a legitimate job in moribund Portsmouth bartered pills to support themselves and feed their kids. Some remodeled dilapidated houses. Others bought cars or trucks.

"When six months ago there were kids going to school with shoes falling off their feet, and now they have new shoes, we feel that's an accomplishment," Mary Ann said. "Our parents had all this opportunity. Portsmouth was a booming place then, [with] a bus system and trolley and jobs that lasted. We were raised with a sense of pride for our town. But when we get out into the real world there's nothing to be proud of. We can't help our town. So when we found a way to help our town, we did—which in turn backfired on everyone, of course."

Down in Xalisco, Nayarit, black tar heroin lifted sugarcane farmers to the status of local merchants. In Portsmouth, middle-class pill addicts made choices that plunged them into the underclass. They ended their education with high school. They had kids too young and weren't married when they did. Before long, they were pocked and penniless on the street.

But as a generation of kids wasted away in postindustrial Portsmouth, their parents were unable to *not* give them gas money to get to some new job that never existed. They couldn't bring themselves to *not* pay their bail or electric bill.

When some of these kids died, mortified parents told neighbors that their son had a heart attack, or their daughter had died from injuries sustained in a car accident.

It took a full decade before a Portsmouth mother was able to reject pretense and be the first in the state to say publicly that dope killed her son.

A Criminal Case

Southern Virginia

In August 2001, about the time Jaymie Mai was discovering how many injured Washington workers were dying from painkiller overdoses, and reports of widespread OxyContin abuse were circulating through Appalachia, John Brownlee took the job of U.S. attorney for the western district of Virginia.

The office is a small one, with only twenty-four attorneys. But it was located near the gathering opiate storm.

Brownlee had a sterling Republican Party pedigree. His father had once been secretary of the army. Brownlee was in the army reserve and continued to perform his reservist service while U.S. attorney. He was being mentioned as a possible future governor of Virginia, or a state attorney general.

Years later, after all that transpired, when Brownlee was in private practice and those possibilities were no longer being discussed, I spoke with him at some length by telephone.

During his years as U.S. attorney, he said, people were dying of overdoses across the states of Kentucky, West Virginia, Ohio, and southern Virginia. Other prosecutors' offices were indicting notorious pill mill doctors, David Procter among them. Brownlee's office jumped into the fray with the controversial prosecution of a Roanoke doctor named Cecil Knox, who state records showed was a prolific prescriber of OxyContin.

From there, Brownlee said, he decided to take a broader view of what was going on.

"We looked at this and said we should take a look at the company marketing this stuff," he said. He subpoenaed all Purdue's records related to marketing OxyContin. The records numbered in the millions of pages and e-mails. Federal employees took up residence in a conference room on a floor of Purdue headquarters in Stamford, Connecticut, and copied company files for months.

Brownlee said the records showed how the company was training salespeople to sell OxyContin as if it were nonaddictive and did not provoke withdrawal symptoms. Physicians, therefore, could feel comfortable prescribing it for many kinds of pain.

"One of the pieces of evidence that was looked at were 'call notes.' The company had a process in which salesmen would go to a doctor, then summarize what was discussed. That went back to a central clearinghouse. Once we were able to see those, we began to see a pattern of conduct. Is this a few rogue guys or is this more of a corporate policy? It became clear that this was more than a few rogue [salesmen]. They were trained to sell the drug in a way that was simply not accurate. That was some of the best evidence of misbranding.

"It was an extremely high percentage of sales reps in various states who were making these allegations. This was done in all fifty states. That's when you rise to corporate culpability."

By the fall of 2006, John Brownlee was prepared to file a case of criminal misbranding against Purdue Pharma, the maker of OxyContin.

"Took Over the OxyContin Belt"

Columbus, Ohio

Forget you have children.

This advice was given to Mario, an illegal immigrant, by his new boss from Xalisco, Nayarit. Mario was preparing for what turned out to be a short career as a dispatcher for a black tar heroin cell in Columbus, Ohio, a few years after the Man brought the drug there.

"Forget that people may do to your kids what you're doing to the children of others," his new boss told him in a restaurant one day. "Otherwise you won't sleep."

"And," he added, "don't let the clients die. Care for them. They're giving you money."

Mario had worked for several years as a mechanic in Portland, Oregon. Many of his clients then were heroin runners in Portland from Xalisco, Nayarit, or villages nearby. He sold them two or three cars a week. They offered him work in their networks, which he declined at first. Then a series of financial problems made him reconsider. So one summer he accepted a job with the Xalisco man he called his "boss" and they drove to Columbus.

"I spoke some English. I was clean. I had ID, good credit to rent an apartment. I rented one there; they paid the rent," he told me.

He earned five hundred dollars a week as a dispatcher, taking telephone orders from a roster of users. The network's sales grew to more than two thousand dollars a day. His boss returned to Nayarit, and waited for workers like Mario to send the money home. Mario woke in his bare apartment each morning, took phone calls all day, directed the drivers, but rarely socialized with them. He hated needles, but he lived far from the effects of what he was selling.

"I never saw anyone inject himself," he said. "I never saw people get sick from lack of dope. I never knew how people got sick. I never knew anything of the people who died. Had I known, I'd have left it."

The drugs arrived regularly from Nayarit. It did not come in truckloads, as he imagined it would, like on those television shows. Rather, it came with couriers carrying a kilo or two at a time. Ant-like, he thought. His boss shipped it from Nayarit to Pomona, California, where it was cut up and sent in smaller quantities to Columbus and other cities. The boss hired workers from Xalisquillo whose families he knew, so he knew the network would send its profits back to him every month. His boss himself had once worked as a runner in another network before going out on his own. He knew all the dealers and drivers in Columbus. Mario made trips with his boss to Nashville and Charlotte to arrange supply deals with other networks.

He dispatched drivers around Columbus for four months until the day the police barged in and he went to prison.

"Nayarit doesn't have a cartel," he said. "It's people acting as individuals who are doing it on their own: micro-entrepreneurs. They're always looking for where there's more money, places where there's no competition. There are thousands of small networks. Anyone can be boss of a network."

BECAUSE OF THAT, THE Xalisco Boys had succeeded by the mid-2000s in avoiding virtually every town Americans traditionally associate with heroin. No Xalisco Boy ventured to Baltimore or Philadelphia or Detroit. No Nayarit sugarcane farm boy was going to shoot it out with armed heroin gangs in New York City. They didn't have to. Midsize metro areas had legions of new young customers and no worrisome gangs or mafias. The Xalisco Boys' ranchero farmboy roots and unbeatable retail system led them to areas of least resistance, now tenderized to heroin by the widespread prescribing of legal opiate painkillers.

"They went," said one cop I met, "and took over the OxyContin Belt in America."

The Xalisco Boys, in fact, were hardly the country's only heroin dealers. Detroit, Baltimore, Philadelphia, and New York had drug gangs who'd controlled the trade for years. Nor were the Boys the only Mexicans trafficking in black tar heroin. Northern California was controlled by traffickers from the Tierra Caliente, a humid and notoriously violent part of west-central Mexico; no Xalisco Boy ever stepped foot in Northern California. Sinaloans controlled the Chicago and the Atlanta markets, both of which were major distribution hubs; the Boys for sure weren't going there.

Yet all these gangs were known for their violence and gunplay. To me, that made them almost passé—like Wild West gunslingers. None of them controlled the drug from its production in Mexico to its sale by the tenth of a gram on streets across the United States. The Xalisco Boys did. They were dope traffickers for a new age when marketing is king and even people are brands.

Purdue branded OxyContin as the convenient solution to disruptive chronic-pain patients. The Xalisco Boys branded their system: the safe and reliable delivery of balloons containing heroin of standardized weight and potency. The addict's convenient everyday solution. The one to start with and stay with.

Like Purdue, but quite unlike traditional heroin dealers, the Xalisco Boys didn't sit around waiting for customers to come to them. They targeted new ones using come-ons, price breaks. They followed up sales to good clients with phone calls that amounted to customer satisfaction surveys. Was the dope good? Was the driver polite? Drivers would travel across town to sell a fifteen-dollar balloon. Addicts learned to play one crew off another. "The other guy was giving me seven balloons for a hundred dollars; you're only giving me six." The effect was to keep the addict not only using but drumming up more customers to get bigger discounts.

Meanwhile Xalisco dealers were constantly monitoring good customers for signs that any of them were trying to quit. Those addicts got a phone call, then a driver plying them with free dope. One Albuquerque addict told me this story: He called his Xalisco dealer, whom he considered his friend, to say he was going into rehab. Good idea, the dealer said. This stuff's killing you. An hour later the dealer was at the addict's door with free heroin. Now that you're quitting, the dealer said, here's a going-away present as a way of saying thanks for your business. The addict kept using.

A woman in Columbus told me her dealer welcomed her home from jail with a care package of several balloons of tar heroin to get her using again.

The more astute among the Xalisco traffickers realized that they owed much of their success to prescription opiates. A few had heard of OxyContin. Most of the Xalisco Boys I interviewed, though, had not. They were oblivious. They knew nothing of the history of heroin in America. They didn't know how their customers came to the drug, that they were now selling to a historically new clientele, customers no one expected to be using the drug. Why would they? They spoke no English and holed up in Spartan apartments when they weren't driving, and thus had little feel for the United States. They weren't sociologists.

Most weren't about to converse with the addicts about how they got into dope. To them, the less face time with addicts, the better. They were quick-hit artists. They were selling well and didn't care why.

But their delivery system and cold-blooded marketing, combined with an enormous and growing clientele newly addicted to pills, were the reasons for their success. By the 2000s, these ranchero farm boys, from a county of just forty-five thousand people in a state most Americans couldn't find on a map, had become the most prolific single confederation of heroin traffickers in the United States, aggressively seeking new markets while supplying dope in at least seventeen states, including unexpected places where heroin was all but unknown before they showed up.

The Final Convenience

Charlotte, North Carolina

Few parts of the United States benefited more from the economic expansion that began in the mid-1990s than Charlotte, North Carolina. Its metro area, which includes part of northern South Carolina, grew fastest of any metro region between 2000 and 2010.

NationsBank of Charlotte acquired Bank of America in 1998 and the city became B of A headquarters. New York retirees, in turn, flooded the town and Charlotte learned what a bagel was. Six other Fortune 500 companies appeared, as did NBA and NFL franchises, and a silver skyline. Charlotte's metro area includes almost fifty golf and country clubs. The town's southern end absorbed the better-off newcomers, who transformed it from cow pastures to a sprawl of McMansions and shopping malls in less than a generation.

Latino immigrants came for the jobs, too. Attracted to the state by agriculture and pork slaughterhouse work, they filled in fading North Carolina rural towns, then moved to the more stable work in Charlotte. The city's Latino population grew faster than any in the country.

Prescription pill use rose in Charlotte just as it did across the country with the pain revolution. In time, that meant more opiate addicts. For years, heroin in Charlotte was powder brought in from New York, uniformly weak and sold solely by young black men on a few streets off Statesville Avenue in the north part of town. Their clientele was limited to the modest numbers of addicts in the metro area.

The Statesville area was where, in the early 1990s, Brent Foushee got his training as a young narcotics officer.

In his younger days, Brent Foushee spent two summers selling Bibles in Mississippi and the coal-mining regions of eastern Kentucky. It was, he thought later, the kind of work that stunted one's growth as a human being. He was awful at it. As he sold the New King James version, he endured occasional lectures from Pentecostals who favored the original King James and believed the new version to be heresy.

In Pikeville, in a mining region of Kentucky, a place Foushee came to regard as the end of the world, he lived in a trailer park. His neighbor was the owner of a coal mine who was hiding out because his workers had gone on strike and he was running the mine with nonunion labor.

Yet Foushee came to believe that it was there, selling the Bible, where his training as a narcotics officer began. A natural introvert, he had to force himself to knock on the doors of people he didn't know and keep talking.

Years later, he joined the Charlotte Police Department. Early on, his narcotics sergeant ordered him to make a heroin buy on a street near Statesville Avenue. Foushee had three weeks earlier been there on patrol, in uniform.

"They're going to know I'm a cop," he said.

"Naw, don't worry. Just do it," said the sergeant. "You'll be all right."

So that afternoon, in plainclothes, his hair now longer and unkempt, Foushee walked onto the street. Whistles and hoots sounded the alarm.

"Five-oh! Five-oh!" the dealers called, the street code for "Cop!"

Foushee approached a dealer, doing his best to look strung out.

"I need something, man," he said.

"You a cop, dude," the young dealer said.

"No, man, I ain't a cop. I'm sick. I need something."

"You a cop, motherfucker."

"No, no, I ain't."

"Who that, then?"

The dealer pointed into some woods fifty yards away and to Foushee's partner, a large man trying to hide behind a sapling.

"Dude, that's my fucking brother! He's watching me to make sure I don't use his shit after I buy it. Man, you going to sell me this or not?"

Sure enough, the dealer sold him the smack.

Keep talking, Foushee learned. Like a salesman. If you're talking you're still alive. Talk was the undercover cop's great gift and Foushee came to rely on it in times of stress. The kid wasn't stupid, Foushee thought later. He was just begging to be persuaded, letting greed control his better judgment. Street dealers made money on each sale and thus wanted to be convinced. Talk long enough, desperately enough, and you could usually get them to sell to you. Talking and convincing people, using his wits, were what selling Bibles trained him to do.

But Foushee also noticed that very little of what he learned selling Bibles and buying dope applied once the Xalisco Boys arrived in Charlotte. Within years of the Man's first visit to Charlotte, the Xalisco Boys were crawling all over the town. Foushee watched as heroin got cheaper, more potent, more available. The market for the Statesville dope got real thin. Unlike the dealers near Statesville Avenue, these Mexican guys drove cars. Even if you did speak Spanish, which Foushee did not, you couldn't talk with them, because the deal took place in a matter of seconds and they were gone.

Before the Xalisco Boys, department policy forbade an undercover cop from getting into a dealer's car alone. But the Xalisco Boys never sold outside their car. So one day, Foushee called the number and was told to park at a shopping center. Soon, a small red four-door car passed with a Mexican at the wheel. The driver raised an eyebrow. Foushee pulled out after him.

He followed the red car into a residential neighborhood and through several streets until it pulled over. Foushee radioed his location to his backup and walked over to the driver's window. The guy's car was immaculate. In the heroin world, most cars Foushee had seen were strewn with festering food, crumpled cigarette packs, and grimy clothes. But here was an older car, a heroin delivery vehicle, without a speck of trash. He handed sixty dollars to the driver, who spit three balloons into his hand, gave them to Foushee, and drove off. Foushee stood in the street and watched him go, saliva-covered balloons in his hand, feeling witness to a revolution. He later wrote a thesis on the Xalisco system for a master's degree in criminal justice.

In time, the Xalisco Boy drivers proved easy to bust. But the cells were all but impossible to eradicate. Prison sentences that North Carolina imposed for heroin trafficking of seven to twenty years barely affected them.

This especially bothered Sheena Gatehouse, who became chief of the drug unit at the Mecklenburg County district attorney's office as the Xalisco system spread. Gatehouse had joined the prosecutor's office just out of law school. She spent her first years prosecuting misdemeanors and small drug cases, usually marijuana. She left to become a defense attorney and handled the first of the region's OxyContin abuse cases— her clients being the children of doctors. In 2009, she returned to the prosecutor's office.

Black tar heroin dominated the caseload. The Xalisco Boys were relentless, and what made them so was that the workers, the drivers, were disposable. The bosses didn't seem to care how many got arrested. They always sent more.

Addicts were overdosing and dying around Charlotte. Gatehouse's office instituted a new rule: no easy deals on heroin cases. Twenty-year sentences grew common. Yet this didn't affect the Xalisco system, or the prevalence of their heroin. The price kept dropping. Balloons containing a tenth of a gram started at five for a hundred dollars, then went to ten for a hundred. Finally, by 2011, you could buy fifteen balloons of potent Xalisco black tar heroin for a hundred dollars—$6.50 a dose, about the price of a pack of Marlboros—in Charlotte, North Carolina, a town that barely knew the drug a few years before.

One bust in 2012 made her question the approach. Cops spent months buying from Xalisco drivers. The investigation involved a dozen officers. Finally, they busted the drivers and a dispatcher. They also took down some addicts, seizing their cell phones. Three days later, those confiscated phones started ringing: Xalisco dealers were calling; the store was back in business, they said, with new drivers up from Mexico. Officers hadn't even finished processing the evidence from the bust and the store was running again.

The drivers were not career thugs, as far as Gatehouse could tell. They were farm boys hoping for a better day through black tar. Sheena Gatehouse went back and forth on the wisdom of the tough approach. The damage they did clearly required it. But, she said, "we're sending a farm boy away for twenty years and have had no impact."

More kids back home clamored for the chance to replace those just arrested. What's more, each bust seemed to provide an opening for more crews, so that one busted crew was replaced not by just one but sometimes by two. With competition, addicts had more numbers they could call and Xalisco customer service kept improving.

At the Carolinas Medical Center, Bob Martin saw the change as well. Martin, a former New York cop, came to Charlotte in 1996 for a job as director of Substance Abuse Services at CMC. During his first years, when he heard of a big heroin bust, he threw up his hands. His beds were certain to fill with junkies checking in to ride out the drought.

But by the early 2000s, whenever police corralled a dozen Xalisco heroin dealers, Martin saw no new flood of addicts rushing to his beds. There was no drought. The bust didn't affect the area's supply of heroin.

"No matter how many million-dollar busts you guys do," he told the officers, "it doesn't show up on our radar."

Martin also noticed an entirely new kind of junkie.

Half of CMC's patients addicted to opiates now had private health insurance. Martin studied the zip codes where they lived and found that they came from the town's wealthiest neighborhoods—Raintree, Quail

Hollow, Mint Hill—in south Charlotte that had once been cow fields. These areas were also home to nine country clubs and the region's best shopping malls.

It was as if these guys from Xalisco had done market research to discover new heroin markets. This thought also occurred to a Charlotte undercover police officer who went by the name of Jaime. He had been working narcotics at the Charlotte Police Department since 2007— black tar heroin mostly, buying from Xalisco dealers hundreds of times.

Jaime believed that the Xalisco Boys looked for towns where kids had cell phones, money, and cars and where a lot of people were addicted to prescription painkillers. At first, he saw they were almost sadistic the way they talked down to desperate junkies, leaving them waiting, and insulting them when they finally showed up. But in 2009 that changed. After Jaime bought from them, crew bosses called to ask: Was the service good? Was the runner rude? Once, a crew boss called to apologize for a late driver. He had a lot of customers, he said. And he was going to get on his people to be more prompt.

After another buy, Jaime's phone rang.

"We've heard from others that that batch wasn't as good," the guy said in halting English. "What did you think? If it was bad, I want to tell the guys we got it from that we don't want that stuff anymore."

Jaime had no choice but to go along.

"Yeah, man, it was crap. Really bad."

"We'll make it up to you."

At the next buy his dealer gave him an extra balloon, and apologies.

Jaime attributed the new attitude to competition among the Xalisco crews in Charlotte. Other higher-ups in Xalisco, he figured, were imposing the quality control of a Fortune 500 company. Their service was better, he noted, than many legitimate retailers.

Meanwhile, though supplies of heroin were unrelenting and addicts were everywhere, Jaime saw no outrage in Charlotte. He spoke to the parents of one junkie after another. As soon as he said the word "heroin," their minds crashed to a halt. They couldn't conceive of their children on heroin. For every symptom, the parents had an answer. Did they see burned aluminum foil around the house? We thought he was burning incense. Was he slurring his speech? He was getting over the flu. Were his grades falling? He was going through a phase.

Jaime spoke to the city's Drug Free Coalition, which was focused on alcohol and marijuana.

"No," he told them. "Heroin is the real problem."

He and Gatehouse spoke to a group of headmasters from Charlotte's best private schools, hoping it would ignite a local crusade. It didn't.

Despite spreading addiction, no parent in Charlotte, of the dozens he spoke to, came forward to warn school groups, churches, the media. Heroin touched the families of doctors, ministers, bank executives, and lawyers, but they retreated from it, crushed by grief and the drug's stigma. How a son died with a spike in his arm was not what you talked about at the country club. A half-dozen reporters asked Jaime for contacts with parents who had lost children. He would plead with the parents to come forward and tell their stories to help keep the next kid from dying. None did.

A conspiracy of silence enveloped Charlotte. Heroin seeped through the city and suburbs in South Carolina with only a few cops, prosecutors, and public health officials battling it.

Jaime, meanwhile, grew philosophical. Opium was a trade good that coursed through civilizations, from Alexander the Great to the Chinese to the Turks and Afghans, snaking out to the Golden Triangle of Burma and Laos. It had been a medicine for three millennia as it changed shape into morphine, welcomed by soldiers, then further morphed into heroin, which street dealers promoted and spread to urban denizens.

Now, in gleaming twenty-first-century Charlotte, the clients were no longer America's outcasts. It wasn't Puerto Ricans in a rainy back alley in Spanish Harlem, or an East L.A. gang member, or some jazz acolyte of Charlie Parker. Many of the users now were the beneficiaries of the wealthiest country the world had known. They were white kids who lived on winding streets, with garages filled with Jet Skis and shiny SUVs, bedrooms with every digital gadget.

Jaime figured that among the Xalisco Boys' greatest innovations was figuring out that a mother lode of heroin demand was now waiting to be mined in these neighborhoods if they'd only offer convenience. The Happy Meal of dope, he called it. Marketed like fast food—to young people.

"'We want what we want when we want it and thus we are entitled to get it,'" he said. "This drug is following the same marketing [strategy] of every other product out there. 'I'll give you good heroin at a great price. You don't have to go to the bad neighborhoods. I'll deliver it for you.'"

In a culture that demanded comfort, he thought, heroin was the final convenience.

A Tidal Wave Forming

Olympia, Washington

Jennifer Sabel felt like she was sinking.

The epidemiologist for the state of Washington stood before a roomful of fourteen prominent doctors at Seattle's Warwick Hotel one cold night in December 2005. Jaymie Mai and Gary Franklin from the state's Labor and Industries had visited her a year before asking if the opiate overdose deaths among disabled workers were also happening in the state's general population.

Sabel and her team pulled together all the death certificates and coroner's reports of people who'd died from opiates. It was a complicated task, identifying potential deaths for each year, then requesting the paperwork on each from coroners around the state. Now she was presenting her findings to a collection of some of Washington's top pain specialists. She kept her eyes on the slides as she spoke.

"We've had dramatic increases in the numbers of opioid-overdose deaths," she said, speaking to the screen.

Twenty-four in 1995. Her pointer followed the graph as it shot up. "In 2004, we found three hundred eighty-six people died of opioid overdoses statewide," she said. A sixteenfold increase.

She went on, detailing some of the cases from each year. Finally, Sabel turned to face her audience. The room was silent. This couldn't be true, said one doctor, finally. There must have been some coding error, another said. Death certificates are notoriously unreliable, said a third. Others spoke skeptically of Sabel's data. The message was clear: Several doctors in the room did not believe her.

Sabel grew queasy, trying to defend the data but aware that she was new to the issue.

"What am I doing here?" she thought. "How did I get into this?"

Gary Franklin jumped in to help.

"This is similar to what we found at L and I and I think there's really something here," he told the specialists.

Sabel sat in silence.

"This group of physicians," she said when we met in 2013. "They've been convinced by the drug companies that it's okay to prescribe these medications for people with chronic pain because here's the studies that show very few of them will become addicted. They don't want to hear that the people they're prescribing these drugs to might die. They're physicians and they're trying to help people."

Sitting near Sabel that night, Jaymie Mai also couldn't believe what the doctors were saying. Four years had passed since Mai first saw those death reports of workers overdosing on the opiate painkillers they were taking for lower back pain and carpal tunnel syndrome. Worker overdose deaths from opiates climbed each year. Mai's backyard rose garden grew ornate as amid expanding death cases she tended it relentlessly to relieve the stress.

Sabel's statewide figures showed a tidal wave forming out in the distance. Overdose deaths, Mai knew, now far outstripped those during the crack rage in the late 1980s and even those when heroin was last popular: the mid-1970s. Overdose deaths advanced in lockstep with the amount of opiates prescribed statewide. These were not pills stolen in pharmacy holdups. The size of the problem could only come from overprescribing.

Mai said, "We couldn't believe the volume, the number of cases. You're looking at the whole state and potentially the whole nation. That [idea] took us a couple days to wrap our arms around. This is a huge problem and it's just going to increase every year unless we do something about it."

L&I came up with a guideline for general practitioners when prescribing these drugs. It went like this: If doctors had patients taking more than 120 mg a day with no reduction in pain, then they should stop and get a pain specialist's opinion before prescribing higher doses.

It was simple and reasonable enough, particularly in light of the new overdose deaths among workers. But it was contrary to an idea central to the pain revolution: that there was no limit on how much opiate painkiller a patient might be prescribed. The guideline Mai and Franklin were proposing would make Washington the first in the country to even suggest some control on how many narcotic pills doctors were prescribing. They could almost hear the criticism if they did this on their own: Government is going overboard, meddling in medicine, taking away rights. So they brought together the state's top pain specialists that night at the Warwick Hotel.

"We asked them," Sabel said. "This is your specialty. At what dose do you say, 'I need to step back and reevaluate this patient because this may not be working?'"

As rough as the Warwick Hotel meeting was for Jennifer Sabel, the pain specialists came around. In later meetings, they themselves suggested that L&I put out guidelines for prescribers suggesting limits, and that not every increase in pain should be met with higher doses of narcotics.

Yet before those guidelines could be issued, Franklin got a letter from two Purdue Pharma executives. They objected to the idea of a ceiling on opiate doses.

"Limiting the access to opioids for people in chronic pain is not the answer," wrote Lally Samuel and Dr. J. David Haddox in the 2007 letter. Haddox is the coauthor of the concept of pseudoaddiction and was now working for the drug manufacturer. One three-year study of 219 patients with arthritis and lower back pain performed by Russell Portenoy and seven other researchers at Beth Israel, they wrote, found patients taking 293 mg of OxyContin a day without a problem.

They were concerned, Samuel and Haddox wrote, that patients needing more opiates "may be undertreated while they are waiting for consultations with pain specialists, as required by the guideline."

Not long after that, a Spokane doctor named Merle Janes sued L&I. Dr. Janes was assisted by five law firms, four of which were from outside Washington State. The guideline, they alleged in a court brief, was an example of "an extreme anti-opioid discriminatory animus or zealotry known as Opiophobia that informs, permeates, and perniciously corrupts the development and management of public health policy" in Washington.

So L&I's prescribing guidelines hung in limbo for two years. Twenty-five workers, each of whom had gone to a workers' comp doc with an injury, died of opiate overdoses in 2008; in 2009, thirty-two more died.

Nevertheless, the state of Washington, L&I, and that Warwick Hotel meeting, however, began a rethinking of the widespread use of prescription painkillers—the first reappraisal since the pain revolution had become conventional wisdom. It was rooted in Mai's investigation into those first worker overdose-death reports in 2001. The paper she wrote with Franklin, and Jennifer Sabel's investigation into overdose deaths for the state, in turn, alerted the Centers for Disease Control in Atlanta. Its epidemiologists began examining the death rates from opiate ODs nationwide. Epidemiologists would follow suit in the state of Ohio, where a few years earlier black tar heroin had collided with aggressive pain pill prescribing, and where the first pill mill emerged.

In May 2011, meanwhile, a judge threw out Dr. Janes's lawsuit. The next year, Washington issued the guidelines on prescribing that Franklin and Mai had come up with—the first state to suggest doctors temper their opiate prescribing. Washington legislators also repealed the intractable pain regulations allowing for unlimited dosing of opiates.

I called Dr. Janes later to ask about his lawsuit and how he could afford the help of so many law firms. A secretary took my message and said they were getting out of prescribing opiates for pain due to "problems that the state was causing for doctors." Dr. Janes didn't return my call.

Pentecostal Piety, Fierce Scratches

Portland, Oregon

In 1906, a delirious Christian revival roared out of Los Angeles. It was an African American movement, but soon was integrated. It took the name of the street where the home church resided. The Azusa Street Revival marked the first explosion of the Pentecostal faith. With it came fervent praying, speaking in tongues, and the belief in a personal rebirth in the Lord. The revival spread east across America to the Midwest and South. Within a decade, the movement arrived in New York City. Among those who embraced it there were numerous Russian immigrant workers.

They returned to Russia to preach their new gospel as communist revolutionaries were toppling the czarist government. These Pentecostal pioneers converted thousands in Russia, the Ukraine, and Belarus. The new Soviet state sent many to gulags. Other believers soldiered on. They held all-day Sunday services in houses where they spoke in tongues, preached baptism by hardship, and became clannish in self-defense. The women wore head scarves. Dancing, jewelry, and makeup were prohibited. They were pacifists and foreswore guns and television. They married young and had lots of children. Higher education was blocked to them, so they became welders and truck drivers.

Their faith was Protestant, but Russian Pentecostals leaned on the severe God of the Old Testament to shepherd them through Soviet oppression. By the time the Soviet experiment ended, seven hundred thousand people, most of them in the Ukraine and Belarus, were fervent Pentecostals. Then, a dream come true. The United States, a land where Protestant faiths were encouraged and even had radio and television stations, opened to them. Tens of thousands emigrated, settling mostly in Sacramento, Seattle, and Portland, Oregon.

Among them was a young couple, Anatoly and Nina Sinyayev, from the city of Baksan. Anatoly was a welder. Nina's father was an evangelist, touring Germany and Israel to preach the gospel. When the Soviet walls tumbled, the Sinyayevs took their two toddler daughters and fled to Portland.

Nina's first baby in America was also their first son, Toviy. From then on, she was always pregnant. The couple had ten more children. Anatoly was always working. They moved eight times, mostly in the Portland suburbs of Gresham and Milwaukie where Russian Pentecostals concentrated. They attended a conservative Russian Pentecostal church, and raised their children in their faith.

But their American dreamland contained hazards they hadn't imagined. Remaining Christian in America, where everything was permitted, was harder than maintaining the faith in the Soviet Union where nothing was allowed. Churches were everywhere. But so were distractions and sin: television, sexualized and permissive pop culture, and wealth.

Leaders turned to the prohibitions that had sustained the faith during the dark decades back home. Girls couldn't dye their hair, pierce their ears, or wear makeup. Young men and women could not talk, or date. If a man wanted to marry, he went to his pastor, who asked the young woman if the suitor interested her. Russian Pentecostals didn't associate much with American society, which they viewed as a threat. Families with televisions were deemed less holy, and they hid the machines from visitors. Pastors called TV the devil with one eye.

The Sinyayevs' daughters were not allowed to wear nail polish or mingle with Americans. But Anatoly kept a television in the basement and turned it on when he thought his children weren't listening. They watched it when he wasn't home. The Sinyayevs' second child, Elina, was their most stubborn. A pretty girl with an aquiline nose, Elina raised her siblings while her mother was pregnant and railed at the church teachings that ruled her home.

"All they preached was that women should wear long skirts, head coverings, no makeup," she said. "They never teach you about love. They didn't want us to know God forgives."

As they moved into adolescence, the Sinyayevs' oldest children hid their lives from their parents. Elina applied makeup on the school bus each morning, and exchanged her long skirts for pants. After school, she donned Pentecostal clothes, removed her makeup, and arrived home looking as plain as she had when she left.

Meanwhile, the U.S. economy frothed. Russian Pentecostals opened auto shops and trucking and welding businesses. After years of Soviet penury, they were suddenly doing quite well, and some grew rich.

Pentecostal kids were steeped in consumerist America at school and old-world Russia at home. They endured church but valued wealth. They eschewed college, worked to buy what they wanted, and quietly rebelled against their parents' old ways.

Then OxyContin appeared. In Portland and other West Coast cities, this seemed to happen in about 2004.

Dr. Gary Oxman watched it arrive from his offices at the Multnomah County Health Department in downtown Portland, and saw overdose deaths again begin to rise. Portland never had many David Procter–style pill mills. Instead, thousands of legitimate doctors began prescribing opiates like OxyContin for chronic pain.

"What we had here is a medical community that's gone along with the idea that pain is the fifth vital sign," Oxman said when we met one day years later at a café in northeast Portland. "It's not this wild abuse. It's that we have a whole medical community prescribing moderately too much."

Gary Oxman had seen this story a decade before, of course. Unstinting supplies of Xalisco black tar heroin lashed Portland addiction and death rates ever higher through the 1990s. Oxman, the group of recovering addicts known as RAP, and others toiled to bring down those numbers, and the numbers did drop. But by 2004, OxyContin was undermining that work. "People are getting recruited into opiate addiction through pills," he said. "Then, because of the cost of the pills, they transfer to heroin."

Oxman plotted the data on a graph, as he had for his heroin overdose study in December 1999. The same steady rise in opiate overdose deaths began again in 2004.

The legless addict Alan Levine had been clean for almost a decade by then. He had emerged as a rambunctious voice for recovering addicts and was named to a local drug-planning committee and the governor's council on drug abuse. But in 2006, pills were everywhere. Levine was treated with Vicodin and then OxyContin for pain related to leg sores brought on by his hepatitis C. He began abusing again and soon fell back onto the street, where I found him, in a downtown motel, a few years later. He had switched to black tar, buying from those who bought from those Mexicans who were still delivering all over town. "I tried to get another number for them," he told me, "but no one wanted to give it up."

Mostly, though, opiates consumed young people in Portland who had never used them, virtually all of them white. As a group, it appears none fell to it harder than the children of Russian Pentecostals who came fleeing persecution and found U.S. pop culture a greater challenge than anything a Soviet apparatchik could invent.

Among them was Vitaliy Mulyar. Born in the Ukraine, Vitaliy grew up in the cocoon of the Russian Pentecostal church in America—first in Sacramento, then Portland. Like his peers, he spoke fluent Russian, and his English carried the hint of an accent from the country he had left when he was two. He, like his peers, found church desiccated and boring.

Vitaliy and his Pentecostal friends grew up in their own world. He found work as a mechanic. Cars became his passion, especially his prized sequoia-green 1999 VW Jetta.

Then a friend at work offered him a Vicodin. Doctors prescribed them, so how bad could they be? With that, he found a new passion. Soon he migrated to OxyContin and his habit rose to four Oxys a day.

To afford it, Vitaliy became one of Portland's first Russian Pentecostal dealers of OxyContin. Many Pentecostal kids had money from jobs they worked. Vitaliy sold into his cloistered network of friends. Many more began selling to support their habit; he supplied them. Pill addiction snuck in among kids whose parents took them to church three times a week and ordered them not to watch television. Vitaliy would look out on the congregation each Sunday as he stood to sing Russian hymns and know that half his peers were high on OxyContin. Some nodded off, their faces in their hands.

By 2006, Vitaliy believed he was the largest OxyContin dealer in Russian Pentecostal Portland. He could easily afford the pills he needed each day. He also put thousands of dollars into his VW. In 2008, however, he was arrested and lost his job. On probation, he could no longer sell pills and thus couldn't afford them either. He switched to cheaper black tar heroin that he bought from the Mexicans who circulated through town. He was in and out of jail, milking his parents for drug money. Russian Pentecostal dealers he owed drove a truck onto his parents' lawn, demanding their money. He lost his Jetta. Soon he was on the street, sleeping on cardboard in downtown Portland.

Hundreds of Russian Pentecostal kids were following this pattern. Their parents were oblivious, or ashamed, and kept their children's addiction as hidden as their televisions.

Elina Sinyayev tried heroin the first time with a friend from work, who told her it would relax her. Her sister started with OxyContin. So did Toviy, her brother. Elina lost her job and, desperate for her dope, began dating a Russian Pentecostal heroin dealer, who also got his tar from the Mexicans delivering it like pizza.

Elina believed she was the only one in her family using heroin. But one night at home she looked at her sister and brother and watched them nod off and knew the truth. Two decades after Anatoly and Nina left the Soviet Union for the freedoms of America, each of their three oldest children was quietly addicted to black tar heroin from Xalisco, Nayarit.

Police arrested Elina's sister for petty theft and Toviy for shoplifting. Anatoly and Nina frantically began checking their children's arms. Elina, meanwhile, shot up in other parts of her body.

One afternoon in March 2011, Toviy told his mother he had the flu. He went out with Elina and they returned hours later. He seemed different but Nina had too many kids to pay close attention. The next morning, she found her eldest boy in bed, unconscious and gasping for breath. Paramedics couldn't revive him. He lasted for three days on life support.

The Portland suburb of Milwaukie in Clackamas County is so small and quiet that its police department has only two detectives. That morning, one of the two, Tom Garrett, was on call. He found balloons of heroin and a syringe in Toviy's bedroom.

Over the next eighteen months, the death of Toviy Sinyayev became a test case for Clackamas County.

Meanwhile, at home, Nina checked the arms of her daughter, Elina, which were always under the long-sleeved blouses of Pentecostal piety. There she found bruises and fierce little scratches.

"We Was Carrying the Epidemic"

Eastern Kentucky

In spring of 2003, a crew of nonunion ironworkers left Greenup County, Kentucky, for Fort Walton Beach, in the Florida Panhandle, to erect the frame of a new Walmart Supercenter.

Greenup County is across the river from Portsmouth, Ohio. It has a long tradition of nonunion ironworker crews, a vestige of the steel industry that once thrived along the Ohio River. Long after steel left, Greenup families were still making their living this way and crews traveled the country for jobs like that Walmart project in Fort Walton Beach.

But by 2003, many of their sons and other young workers were caught up in pill addiction. One addict on that crew was Jarrett Withrow.

Jarrett had already given up a lot for dope. He hoped for a college basketball scholarship. But in high school in Portsmouth, everyone was using pills. Jarrett started in with Vicodin prescribed him by John Lilly, at his clinic downtown. Once addicted, Jarrett stole OxyContin from his father, who was dying of cancer. He remained hooked on OxyContin for eight years. It consumed every plan he had. Before long, he was on a Greenup County iron crew.

That spring of 2003, his crew was on the Fort Walton Beach job for a couple weeks when their pill supply ran short. One afternoon, one of the crew left and came back that night.

"Look what I got," he said, holding up bottles of pills he was prescribed that afternoon.

Turned out, Florida doctors were awfully easygoing when it came to prescribing these pills. Florida had no prescription-monitoring system that checked on each patient to see whether he had visited other clinics, scamming doctors for pills. No one in Florida had seen the business potential. The Greenup crew began going to these doctors, and asking coworkers from Florida to go as well and sell them the pills. Then they sent the pills back to Kentucky and sold them for triple.

"I can remember at first they felt we was crazy doing these

prescription pills," Jarrett said. "We'd have them go to the doctor for us. At first they'd give the pills to us really, really cheap."

They hiked the prices eventually. But "that triggered the idea that this was easy," Jarrett said. "Other people began saying, 'Let's go find doctors.' My friend continued to go down there monthly, like his family doctor was down there [in Florida] or something. He started telling other people. We was carrying the prescription pill epidemic."

As I dug around attempting to understand how the opiate epidemic spread, I found many stories like Withrow's. With pain pills now so easily prescribed, the pills moved among vulnerable populations by a casual contact, a chance meeting—not unlike the way Ebola and AIDS viruses advanced. New opiate addicts spread information on where to find pills the way a cough spread germs.

Some of the most potent early vectors were newly christened junkies from eastern Kentucky, where coal mines were closing and SSI and Medicaid cards sustained life. These addicts, feigning pain and injury, mined local doctors and pharmacists, who quickly got wise. Kentucky, to its credit, was one of the first to put in a system tracking what drugs each patient had been prescribed and by whom. But seven states border Kentucky. Many eastern Kentuckians have relatives who left to find work in other states, and, after decades of out-migration, state lines tend not to matter much to folks from the region. The Kentucky prescription monitoring system, therefore, very quickly had the unintended consequence of pushing the state's new opiate addicts out across state lines in search of pills, tapping first their networks of friends and relatives.

This kind of travel in search of illicit products was also already part of many eastern Kentucky counties, where bootlegging was common. These counties had been dry for years. Generations of bootleggers had grown up illegally selling alcohol they brought in from wet counties, which local cops either winked at or shielded. Among these was Floyd County (pop. 30,000), which finally went wet in 1983.

Before that, though, bootlegging "led us into decades of corruption of the police forces," said Arnold Turner, a former Floyd County prosecutor, and father of the current prosecutor, Brent Turner. "It created a network of criminals and as they lost the ability to deal in alcohol, they had to find another product. Then, with bootlegging, you had a public dulled into low expectations when it came to contraband and illegal activity. People were used to it. No one saw the monster coming. That was the foundation that let this juggernaut [of pills] start coming in."

Many of these bootleggers became almost advance men for the epidemic.

One of them was a man named Timmy Wayne Hall. Hall had grown up on Branham Creek Holler in Floyd County, the son of a factory worker who was also a preacher in the Church of God. Hall's siblings and relatives worked in the nearby coal mines. Floyd County hadn't many jobs outside the coal mines, which were tough places to make a living. Hall had other things in mind and never did work a day in his life.

In 1980, he married into a family of bootleggers. He began driving down to Perry County, buying cases of Schlitz beer, the cheapest available and thus the bootleggers' favorite, and selling them out of the family's house in Floyd for triple. After Floyd County voted to go wet, Hall applied for SSI and, like several families in his holler, began getting the monthly check. He was prescribed Lorcet after a car accident, which he could afford with his Medicaid insurance card. He promptly grew addicted to the pills.

There weren't many drug addicts in Floyd County back then, and most, like Timmy, used 10 mg Lorcets—a pill that combined hydrocodone with acetaminophen. But in 1996 OxyContin came out, and soon people from all over were getting addicted to it. No doctor would prescribe Hall OxyContin at first.

"Nobody was supposed to get them but cancer patients," Hall said. Plus in 1999 the state put in its prescription-monitoring program.

With Kentucky off-limits, Hall found an Oxy connection through a Floyd County friend in Detroit. He also found other connections in Dayton and Toledo. He had read about New York mafioso John Gotti and Colombian drug lord Pablo Escobar years before. OxyContin allowed him, a man without much else in his life, to imagine following in their footsteps. He began driving regularly up to Ohio and Detroit for pills. These connections were reliable enough so that things got bad in Floyd County where OxyContin was concerned.

But in 2004 Floyd County began to get a lot worse. A local trucker named Russ Meade was driving across Louisiana one day. Meade spotted billboards for a clinic called Urgent Care in the town of Slidell that mentioned prescription pain pills.

Being from Floyd, Meade knew pills' value. He stopped in, was prescribed a bunch, brought them home, and sold them. Onto something, he began driving down to Slidell—a seventeen-hour trip—with several Floyd County addicts, paying for their visits, then keeping half the pills they were prescribed. Among them was a man named Larry Goble. Goble was a former miner on disability with black lung, who had briefly been a deputy sheriff. Meade later died, but Goble kept driving down to Urgent Care with addicts, paying for their trips and five-hundred-dollar doctor visits, which he saw amounted to a charade with a physician. In payment, he took half the pills they were prescribed. Goble later testified in federal court that he used some and sold the rest.

Soon dozens of folks from Floyd County were driving the seventeen hours to Slidell. The clinic's owner, Michael Leman, next opened another in Philadelphia, hiring a drug-addicted, alcoholic doctor named Randy Weiss to see patients. Despite the Urgent Care name, Weiss later testified, the clinic had no equipment to treat people with urgent medical needs, such as make casts or stitch wounds. Leman's clinics charged eastern Kentuckians $500 per visit, while locals paid only $250. Then he opened an Urgent Care in Cincinnati. He hired Dr. Stan Naramore, who had been convicted of murder in Kansas, then had that conviction overturned on appeal. Carloads from Floyd County began making pilgrimages to Philadelphia and to Cincinnati each week.

From these Urgent Care clinics, a new flood of pills washed into Floyd County, upsetting a tenuous balance in the hollers. Along these creeks, some families led lives of quiet decency, trying to raise children and hold what jobs they could get in an area where work was hard to find. Other families, though, had been unemployed for generations and on government assistance. Up to then, they had resorted to small-time criminal activities, but remained minor irritants in holler life. When Oxy came along, however, the sorriest families were transformed into dominant and unruly forces.

Timmy Wayne Hall was among the biggest customers of Leman's new Urgent Care clinic in Philadelphia. Hall traveled constantly back and forth, paying others to drive for him because he was heavily addicted.

"I was taking twenty, twenty-five people a month to Philadelphia. The patients would sit in the car. I'd go in there and get their scripts. Then go to the pharmacy in their name; it was only twenty feet away."

With each patient receiving close to five hundred pills, and Hall taking half of that, he was clearing more than four thousand dollars for every person he hauled up to an Urgent Care. He was also scoring pills from Detroit and connections in three other states—though never in Kentucky, as he feared the state's prescription-monitoring program. Back home, he made a killing on the first of the month when the SSI checks arrived in Floyd County.

He began hiring dealers to sell for him. At his peak, he figured he had dealers selling in five counties in eastern Kentucky. When he heard of competitors, he would go to their customers and offer them Oxy 80 mg pills for sixty-five dollars apiece instead of the seventy dollars the competitors were charging. He sold all over, watching as OxyContin seeped into every corner of eastern Kentucky. Men with professional jobs in wealthy Pike County were his pill customers; so were the construction guys who worked on their houses.

Hall, a man who'd never worked, now bought a dozen houses in and near Branham Creek Holler. He often took friends on road trips and paid for everyone's hotel room. A coterie of junkies hung about him, and he paid them to cook, wash his clothes, vacuum his house, cut the grass, and do odd jobs on his properties. He grew intoxicated with the power and the fact that pills allowed him to be, for Kentucky, the magnanimous don. He had a habit of up to twenty OxyContin 80s a day.

Hall was arrested in 2007. During withdrawal, he went into a seizure and was briefly pronounced dead, then spent six months learning to walk again. When he pleaded guilty, Hall confessed to selling two hundred thousand OxyContin and methadone pills, though the real figure was likely far higher.

"I'm sorry for the things I done," Hall said when I spoke to him by phone from the federal prison where he is now serving fifteen years. "I was brought up in the church and didn't want to hurt no one. But I was an out-of-control drug addict who didn't realize who I was hurting."

With money and addiction urging them on, meanwhile, Floyd County addict-entrepreneurs were like bloodhounds sniffing out shady docs in far-flung places.

An oxycodone 30 mg pill cost eight dollars in Florida and could fetch thirty dollars back home. Florida had no prescription monitoring, so any pharmacist would fill a script. The first Floyd County guy to discover Florida was apparently Jim Marsillett II, who ran a stable of addicted women down to Fort Lauderdale in an RV once a week. Marsillett first ventured to Florida after federal investigators closed down the Urgent Care clinics in Philadelphia and Cincinnati, where he had been buying.

With the opening of the Florida territory, a new Appalachian migration began, south this time. Campers voyaged weekly down from the Oxy-wracked regions of Ohio, Kentucky, and West Virginia for doctor visits. The OxyContin Express was the name given to flights from Huntington, West Virginia, to Fort Lauderdale. By 2009, of the top ten oxycodone-prescribing counties in America, nine were in Florida. The other was Scioto County, Ohio, where Portsmouth is located. Broward County had four pain clinics in 2007 and 115 two years later.

Initially, Florida officials didn't seem too concerned as long as the hillbillies left their money and took the pills with them when they left. It wasn't until 2009 that Florida put in a prescription-monitoring system—the last state in the country to do so. By then, customers from as far away as Colorado were heading to Florida.

Yet it was hard-up folks from Ohio and Kentucky who discovered the Sunshine State. Randy Hunter, a Kentucky state police detective from Floyd County, ended up traveling the country, following the Floyd County pill migration. He made cases in New Orleans, Philadelphia, Houston, and cities in Florida against the shady docs and pain-clinic owners who sold to itinerant Floyd County addict entrepreneurs.

"We saw a lot of eastern Kentucky go out of state," said Hunter, now retired, as he took me on a tour of the hollers of Floyd County one day. "They traveled like gypsies, roaming around looking for pills. When they found a honeycomb of pills, they stayed, and not only stayed, but they brought friends and family."

More Cases Than Car Crashes

Southern Ohio

The gaunt addict known as Jeremy Wilder, from the town of Aberdeen, on the Ohio River, left prison and came home in 2007.

He was locked up in 2003 for breaking into pharmacies, his addiction out of control. When he left Aberdeen that year, the town possessed a small group of drug addicts to whom he sold his OxyContins. Now, four years later, his brother and everyone he knew was heading to Florida to buy pills. But things had gone far beyond pills. Many people in Aberdeen were on heroin. They wandered the small town half dead, proud of their needle marks.

"When I was selling Oxys, it was a certain group of people," he told me. "When I come home, it was a certain group of people plus everybody else. Cops' kids. Poor kids, rich kids, smart kids, dumb kids."

The area had spawned a generation of young people who had nothing to look forward to, whose families had been unemployed for years. Many of these kids grew addicted. But kids at the bottom were not who moved the market. It was really the rich kids who did that. Jeremy sold to two brothers whose parents were well-off business owners in town. Another customer was going to inherit several houses.

From his place on the Ohio River in 2007, Jeremy Wilder could see the change. First pills, now heroin. Lots of both. But it was nothing anyone in an official position in Ohio recognized until, as luck would have it, some data passed across the desk of a guy in a state office cubicle up north in Columbus who liked being alone.

ED SOCIE LOVED NUMBERS.

Socie was an epidemiologist with Ohio's department of health. He worked on the eighth floor of the department's building in Columbus, in the Violence and Injury Prevention section. He followed data of deaths from violence and injuries. By mid-2005, he had been at his job for twenty-two years.

An admittedly reclusive fellow, Socie was fascinated with statistics and data and the stories hidden beneath them. He possessed enormous curiosity for the topic.

"I just sat at a computer all day crunching numbers on death data," he said. "I enjoyed crunching the numbers. Out of curiosity, I looked at everything I could."

By 2005, Socie was supervising data for a lot of hot-button topics. Among them were homicides and suicides, which rose and fell with some frequency. One number he counted on to stay put, however, was deaths from accidental poisonings. People just didn't poison themselves to death all that much, nor did the numbers vary much from year to year.

So in 2005 Socie was startled to notice that poisoning deaths in Ohio were climbing.

His data came from the federal Centers for Disease Control. Ohio coroners' death certificates are submitted to the CDC, which codes them according to cause of death and sends the figures back to the state for easier evaluation.

It all began with the figures for unintentional injury deaths. Sitting at his desk one day, Socie saw that deaths coded for unintentional injury were heading up. He dug further and found that most were coded as accidental poisonings. Why would they be rising? Intrigued, he kept digging into the CDC data and codes. The poisoning deaths, it turned out, were actually drug overdoses. This was new. Cocaine and methamphetamine—the popular drugs through the 1980s and 1990s—are damaging drugs, but people don't often fatally overdose on them. Heroin, which people do overdose on, hadn't been a sustained problem since the 1970s. Drug overdoses in Ohio had remained pretty constant for decades.

Socie graphed these new numbers. After remaining stable for decades, the deaths suddenly took off like an airplane, almost tripling in six years.

A good chunk of the deaths—known in CDC coding as X44s—were due to "unspecified drugs." But an equally large segment—the X42s—were from narcotic overdoses. Socie began running his computer through its paces, asking about deaths from specific drugs: oxycodone, hydrocodone, heroin, cocaine, morphine, opium. Opiates were present in virtually all the deaths where the drugs were specified.

The numbers alarmed Socie. He showed them around the

department. At first, his work "fell on deaf ears," he said. "I got no feedback that this was something I should explore much further. I was a little disappointed because I thought it was important."

Socie bided his time, watching as the numbers kept rising over the next eighteen months.

In January 2007, Christy Beeghly took over as the supervisor at the department's violence and injury prevention unit. Beeghly was from a children's hospital, where kids were injured from what was under the sink, not so much from what was in the medicine cabinet. But maybe it helped that she was not an old hand at violence and injury prevention. Socie brought out his data and charts showing the sudden increases in fatal drug overdoses. Ninety five percent of all Ohio poisoning deaths were drug overdoses; the greatest part of these overdoses was due to prescription pills.

Beeghly was astonished. They dissected the numbers further. That's when they realized that right then and there drug overdose deaths were about to surpass fatal auto crashes as Ohio's top cause of injury death.

This was a stunning moment in the history of U.S. public health. Since the rise of the automobile in America, vehicle accidents sat unassailed atop the list of causes of injury death in every state, and in the United States as a whole. Now Ed Socie's numbers showed that would soon no longer be true in Ohio. And by the end of 2007, it wasn't.

"That was a really startling trend," Beeghly said. "It took the pills to get us here. We've exposed a much greater population to these opiates than we had back in the 1970s with the heroin epidemic."

Drug overdoses passed fatal vehicle accidents nationwide for the first time in 2008. But it happened first in Ohio, where two complementary opiate plagues met and gathered strength in the late 1990s: prescription painkillers, especially Purdue's OxyContin, moving east to west; the Xalisco Boys' black tar heroin moving west to east.

The effect showed up a decade later in the death numbers Ed Socie untangled.

Socie and Beeghly also found that quantities of prescription painkillers dispensed annually in Ohio followed the same upward line as overdose deaths. Both rose more than 300 percent between 1999 and 2008. But even that hid the truth. The use of some opiates actually declined: codeine, for example. The real story was in what skyrocketed. Oxycodone. Dispensed grams of oxycodone—the only drug in OxyContin—rose by almost 1,000 percent in Ohio during those years.

They wrote a report revealing once-camouflaged facts.

- The number of Ohioans dead from drug overdoses between 2003 and 2008 was 50 percent higher than the number of U.S. soldiers who died in the entire Iraq War.
- Three times as many people died of prescription pill overdoses between 1999 and 2008 as died in the eight peak years of the crack cocaine epidemic.
- In 2005, Ohio's overdose deaths exceeded those at the height of the state's HIV/AIDS epidemic in the mid-1990s.

DOWN IN PORTSMOUTH, a doctor named Terry Johnson wasn't surprised.

By 2008, Johnson had been Scioto County coroner for six years. He was a family doc and untrained in forensic medicine. But family doctors in small towns often take on the responsibilities of coroner. Johnson was elected to the job in 2002 just as pills were washing across his county in numbers sufficient to create an OxyContin economy. He was still trying to figure out what a small-county coroner did besides assigning cause and manner of death when a deputy called one night.

"We got what looks like a drug overdose, Doc," the deputy said. "Don't know what you want to do. You don't have to come out if you don't want."

Previous coroners hadn't.

"I thought I probably should go out," Johnson said. At the scene, he found a man dead with a needle in his arm.

Fatal overdoses came regularly after that. The office had a small budget and dead junkies would have been easy not to autopsy. But Johnson sent the bodies to medical examiners in larger counties better prepared to do full autopsies and blood tests. These invariably turned up opiates, usually combined with benzodiazepines, the old Dr. Procter cocktail.

Johnson is a trained osteopath, a discipline focusing on a holistic approach to health. He had once convened a summit of Scioto County doctors, pharmacists, and elected officials to address the new and aggressive opiate prescribed for chronic pain. Nothing had come of that.

Now pill mills swept across his city. Fatal drug overdoses increased every year. He saw the lines outside the pill mills, and the junkies wandering down Highway 52 to Walmart. He watched capable young people get themselves declared "simple" to get SSI and the Medicaid card, and thus access to pills. Johnson began tabulating what he termed "drug-related deaths"—a death that probably had to do with the person's addiction but that was officially deemed, say, a heart attack. When he did that, the numbers doubled.

By 2008, Scioto County had twenty-one fatal drug overdoses and twenty-three drug-related deaths—giving it the second-highest death rate in the state. Yet, in Columbus, the legislature had other concerns. The Ohio boards governing the licensing of doctors and pharmacists—believing their hands tied by the state's intractable pain law—kept silent.

"Had [the boards] been the slightest bit creative they could have put a stop to this. They could have put [the pill mills] out of business," Johnson said. "I was trying to bend our prescribing habits down. What I was fighting was a multimillion-dollar ad campaign to liberalize prescribing. Then the epidemiologist showed I was right. But no one was looking at it until the state Department of Health realized our numbers exceeded [fatal] traffic accidents."

NOT LONG AFTER THE report she wrote with Socie, Christy Beeghly called Portsmouth city nurse Lisa Roberts for a meeting with women from around the state to talk about the problem.

Lisa called a friend and public health colleague. This was finally a chance to talk about pills along the Ohio River. They drove to Columbus. It was quickly apparent, however, that the other women in the room would have no conception of what had hit Portsmouth.

"We're setting there and they're telling stories about how wonderful their daughters are. Each one is, like, 'My daughter's in college; my daughter has a Ph.D.,'" Roberts remembered. "I pass a note to my friend: 'What are we going to do?' She passes one back to me: 'I'll tell the truth if you will. These women need a wake-up call.'"

When it was her turn, Roberts told the gathering that her daughter was a pill addict who had stolen from her blind. Lisa had forced her daughter out of the house. "My daughter," her colleague said, "is in jail accused of executing three people for their pills." Half of their coworkers' kids were addicted. They followed with a description of the pill mills, of the OxyContin barter economy, of the constant overdose deaths.

The room was silent.

"I remember coming home and being real mad," Roberts said. "It's not right that our kids are having their futures and freedom taken from them because they've fallen prey to this horrible chemical that steals their soul. Our kids shouldn't be going to the grave. We sent our kids into the military. After she got clean, my daughter had a better chance of surviving a war than she did of surviving the pill epidemic."

Beeghly put together a presentation on overdoses. The PowerPoint showed a red stain of overdoses spreading north out of southern Ohio. Portsmouth held three town hall meetings with Terry Johnson, people from the medical and pharmacy boards, and the DEA. Then-governor Ted Strickland used an emergency executive order to form a state opiate task force to recommend policy changes.

IN ATHENS COUNTY, OHIO, meanwhile, Dr. Joe Gay got hold of the figures that Ed Socie and Christy Beeghly had prepared. A garrulous transplanted Texan, Gay directs a rehabilitation clinic serving four Appalachian counties in Ohio. He also has a passion for statistics.

The Department of Health's graph of overdose deaths looked almost identical to the graph of dispensed prescription painkillers. Gay crunched the numbers to see how exactly they correlated. Then he called a friend and colleague, Orman Hall.

Orman Hall directed a drug rehab clinic in Fairfield County, near Columbus. That afternoon, he was hiking with his son, who was headed to medical school and who, like his father, had a strong interest in statistics. Returning from the hike, Hall checked his phone messages. His eyebrows arched.

"That was Joe Gay," he said, chuckling and shaking his head after he clicked off the phone. "He says he's found a 0.979 correlation between prescription pain pills dispensed and the number of overdose deaths from opiates."

This was preposterous. Never in thirty years of statistical mechanics had Orman Hall heard of a correlation that close to 1.0, which was almost as if the charts were saying that dispensing prescription painkillers was the same thing as people dying.

Gay couldn't believe it either. He ran the DOH numbers again. Each time, 0.979 appeared on his computer screen.

Every statistician knows correlation does not mean causation. But to Gay the correlations did mean that Ohio could all but predict one overdose death for roughly every two months' worth of prescription opiates dispensed.

A Pro Wrestler's Legacy

Seattle, Washington

In 2007, Alex Cahana opened the door to what had been John Bonica's Center for Pain Relief at the University of Washington and found a cobwebbed relic.

The pathbreaking clinic was now in a windowless basement. No signs announced it. Calendars were out of date, piles of papers sat near unread charts and stacks of still-unpacked boxes that sagged like old wedding cakes. As Cahana walked its corridors, the clinic's fifth interim director told him how much he wanted out.

This was what remained of the world's first pain clinic. The concept of pain as a disease, a topic worth study, originated here. So, too, did the idea that chronic pain had many causes and thus needed not just drugs but occupational, physical, and psychological therapy, too; even social workers had a role.

Bonica, the anesthesiologist and former pro wrestler, had founded the clinic. He wrote a classic pain-management textbook from what he learned. He retired in 1977 and died in 1994. Later, his disciple, Dr. John Loeser, expanded Bonica's clinic. Hundreds of clinics followed across the country. But insurance companies gradually stopped paying for the services that made the clinics multidisciplinary. Prescription pills were easier and cheaper, and at least for a while they worked well. In 1998, Loeser resigned as the multidisciplinary clinic was marginalized at the school that had invented the idea.

A decade later, Cahana said, "it was as if [the clinic] didn't exist. It was a metaphor for what happened to multidisciplinary pain management."

The staff called it the Dungeon. Stepping through this wreckage was a bittersweet moment: Alex Cahana had long been inspired by John Loeser. Cahana began his pain specialty in the Israeli army in the late 1980s, with battlefield experience. He attended a conference in Paris in 1993, where he met Loeser, who was then president of the International Association for the Study of Pain.

Cahana remembered Loeser's message: "That pain is the essence of what we do as doctors, that relieving pain is basic medicine. He spoke about Bonica being a military physician who, after witnessing the suffering of his wife during childbirth, decided to create modern pain medicine. And to do that, you had to be multidisciplinary."

That inspired Cahana. Years later, when the University of Washington asked him to resurrect the clinic, Alex Cahana knew its importance in the history of pain management. Succeeding Bonica and Loeser was a dream come true. But he saw why the school went abroad to find someone to take the job.

"It was a completely broken system that no one would touch," he said.

Cahana wrote a forty-three-page contract committing the school to a new aboveground clinic. He wanted windows and the walls made of natural materials and painted with soft colors. He wanted a "bullpen"—an open area where doctors had desks but not offices, so they could better share information. He wanted the best imaging machines to help locate body pain. He wanted a nurse-manager overseeing it all.

The school agreed. On April Fools' Day 2008, Cahana started his new job.

He was immediately shocked at the patients in the UW clinic.

"These were people on tons of opioids for a long time, completely broken and abused. We're talking hundreds of milligrams of morphine-equivalent doses. Doses I'd never seen in my life: four hundred, five hundred, six hundred milligrams a day."

What's more, no one tracked the effects of opiates on a patient's pain, function, depression, sleep. He called colleagues elsewhere and found this to be true across the United States.

"Not one center had measurements-based pain care. This is 2008," he said. "It would all be subjective: They're doing fine or not doing fine. There was a pain rating scale: one to ten. It was insane. A multibillion-dollar industry was based on no measurements whatsoever."

Cahana began resurrecting what Loeser and Bonica had built. He and his staff came up with a computerized questionnaire, and shorter follow-ups, for each time a patient visited. If a patient said his pain was less but things were going poorly, maybe there was another issue.

There Alex Cahana ran into the problem John Loeser faced. An insurance company would reimburse thousands of dollars for a procedure. But Cahana couldn't get them to reimburse seventy-five dollars for a social worker, even if it was likely that some part of a patient's pain was rooted in unemployment or marital strife.

"Nobody thinks those things are of value. Talk therapy is reimbursed at fifteen dollars an hour," Cahana said. "But for me to stick a needle in you I can get eight hundred to five thousand dollars. The system values things that aren't only not helpful but sometimes hurtful to patients. Science has shown things to have worked and the insurance companies won't pay for them."

Great Time to Be a Heroin Dealer

Nashville, Tennessee

When new viruses appear, the discovery is often made by a local physician who stumbles upon a patient with disturbing new symptoms.

Something similar happened when the Xalisco Boys spread east of the Mississippi River, where Purdue's promotional campaign and new opiate-prescribing practices were creating the epidemic's first addicts. Instead of doctors, though, it was usually patrol cops or a local narcotics detective who figured out what was happening. They encountered black tar heroin, saw it delivered like pizza, and wondered, What the *hell*?

So it was in 2005, in the Nashville suburb of Murfreesboro, where a patrol cop came across an off-duty juvenile-court bailiff smoking a black, sticky substance. It tested later as heroin. With the help of the accused bailiff eager to reduce his charges, Murfreesboro police put together a few buys and found it came from Mexicans who delivered the drug; when the bailiff called and ordered more, they came with it. The case expanded and made its way to the desk of Dennis Mabry, an investigator with the Nashville DEA task force, who didn't understand it any better than the Murfreesboro cop. As he and his partner tried to make sense of it, his task force boss, Harry Sommers, dropped by.

Since Tar Pit, Sommers had left his supervising job at DEA headquarters in D.C. He was now in charge of the agency's office in Nashville. But Sommers hadn't forgotten Tar Pit and the Xalisco Boys' system of selling heroin retail. Six years later, he was startled to see they had spread.

"We had not stopped them," he said. "These guys were moving into new territory."

Sommers outlined the Xalisco call-and-deliver system for Mabry. "This is who you're dealing with," he said. "They're all from Nayarit."

Neither Mabry nor his partner had heard the name before. But before long Nayarit was all they thought about. That bailiff's case ballooned to consume fifteen agents for a year. They followed drivers, watched buys go down, and tapped cell phones. The cell of Nayarit heroin delivery boys generated ten thousand cell phone calls a month, more than any wiretap translator could keep up with. The case connected investigators to fifteen cities in eight states. It came to be known as Black Gold Rush.

The Xalisco Boys "got here and took over and made a ton of money," Mabry told me. "They knew how to do it and were professionals. They'd carry the balloons in their mouths. They'd get stopped by police and swallow the balloons."

What Mabry was seeing, it turned out, was a branch of the Xalisco networks that belonged to the Sánchezes, legends in the Nayarit heroin trade. Their story, near as I could piece it together, is typical of how a Xalisco clan spread its heroin operations. The Sánchez clan is rooted in villages near Xalisco—Aquiles Serdán, Emiliano Zapata, and others. Like the Tejedas, the clan is a product of the isolation the Mexican rancho breeds: a bewildering intermarried web of cousins, brothers, sisters, half siblings, in-laws, second cousins, stepfathers, mothers and fathers, aunts and uncles.

The sugarcane-farming Sánchezes were among the first to set up heroin operations in the San Fernando Valley in the early 1980s. From there, they spread to Las Vegas. One trafficker I spoke with said an addict, an Argentine woman they knew as La Sasha, led the first Sánchezes from Las Vegas to Memphis in the early 1990s. Memphis "became one of the biggest markets for a while," he said.

In 2004, a Memphis junkie led the Sánchezes to Myrtle Beach, South Carolina, where he enrolled in the local methadone clinic and gave away their dope to the clients, police said. Police later arrested the junkie on a trafficking charge. But by then the Sánchezes had a foothold from which they expanded to Columbia and Charleston and eventually controlled much of the heroin trade in South Carolina.

Since then, the Sánchez clan has reportedly defended its turf in a very non-Xalisco way, threatening with violence new cell leaders who move into the state.

"You're not allowed to be working in South Carolina without their approval," said one DEA source in Charlotte. "Considering Charlotte is close to South Carolina, we'd expect more overlap of [Charlotte's Xalisco] crews into South Carolina and we don't see much, if any."

In Nashville, Mabry and his partners listened in as the local family boss, Javier "Chito" Sánchez-Torres, spoke often by cell phone with his uncle, Alberto Sánchez-Covarrubias, in Nayarit. Javier had done time in South Carolina for heroin trafficking. He was released in 2003 and somehow ended up in Nashville.

In time, authorities grew to believe that this uncle, Alberto Sánchez—or Uncle Beto, as he was known—was a major source of heroin in the United States. Beto Sánchez was one of the Xalisco pioneers in the heroin business in the San Fernando Valley, informants said, and among the first Sánchezes to sell heroin in parks in Van Nuys, the district in Los Angeles, before the Xalisco crews began using cars and pagers. One informant said Beto Sánchez killed a client in a fight in a park in the early 1980s and returned to Mexico, though Mabry never could find a record of the killing.

Still, Mabry said, "Every time we'd arrest someone, it'd be, 'Beto is my cousin. He's my brother-in-law.' They all knew Alberto Sánchez. They were all related to him somehow."

Uncle Beto frequently instructed his nephew on new markets that might be exploited, on when the next supply was arriving, and, especially, on managing drivers, moving one guy, bringing in another to take his place. "It was like trading cards or players on a sports team," Mabry said. "He'd move guys who didn't get along, or they got along too well and would screw off, spend all night drinking."

Alberto Sánchez's cousin, Gustavo, was his right-hand man and full-time recruiter, trolling Xalisco for potential new drivers. Not only did the family constantly recruit new drivers, but they also never stopped seeking new territory.

Sometime in the early 2000s, according to addicts and police, the Sánchezes sent some workers from Nashville up to start an Indianapolis cell. As time passed, the Sánchezes felt they needed someone to bring more energy to the task.

I had several chats with the trafficker they sent next. This fellow met Javier Sánchez-Torres at a party in Los Angeles. The heroin boss recruited him to come to Nashville to work.

"I began as a driver with balloons in my mouth," the trafficker told me. "After six months, I began to train other drivers. I'm in the house, answering the phones and sending people where they have to go."

By then, he said, the Sánchezes were well aware of OxyContin's role in the business. "It was part of the marketing strategy," he said. "Chiva is the same as OxyContin; just OxyContin is legal. OxyContin users change to chiva. They can get our stuff more easily than going to a doctor for the pills."

As the trafficker earned the Sánchez family's trust, he drove resupply trips from their hub in Nashville to regional cells in Memphis, Charlotte, and Columbia, South Carolina. In 2006, with the family needing new management in Indianapolis, he was given three ounces of heroin and told to go grow the market. He rolled into Indianapolis brimming with the energy and optimism of a newly promoted regional sales manager.

"Let's make good money. Let's get this thing going," he kept saying. He recruited older addicts to spread the cell's number around town, offering them free heroin for every couple hundred dollars in sales they generated. The addicts formed an eager sales force.

"They were looking more for volume than anything, to get it out there," said one Indy addict who worked for him. "You sell the product low enough and it'll create its own demand."

Soon, suburban kids and students from Indiana University in Bloomington were coming in to buy. Xalisco black tar spread out for a hundred miles around Indianapolis.

Occasionally, drivers were replaced; all were from villages near Xalisco, Nayarit. The trafficker I spoke with said he paid drivers fifteen hundred dollars a week, with all expenses covered, including money for beer and prostitutes. When a runner was ready to return to Nayarit, the trafficker would give him three ounces of heroin for free. The runner would sell it, keep the profits, then drive the car back to Nayarit with enough cash to build a two-story house, or buy a business.

"People who are poor and want to progress, you give them a hand," the trafficker said.

Back in Xalisco, by then, more and more young men were turning to chiva for that hand up.

ALL AROUND THE TOWN were the signs of what could be accomplished by selling heroin. Women's clothing stores. Law firms. New markets. Beer dispensaries were six to a neighborhood now—and they were new ones with wooden floors, security cameras, and computerized cash registers. Large houses, owned by young men, were everywhere. No one could build such houses on the wages made working sugarcane.

At the Feria del Elote, cell leaders sponsored basketball teams, importing semipro squads from Monterrey, Mazatlán, Hermosillo. Each team had at least one African American, hired to improve the team's chances. In the town's horse parade, which once featured common farm animals, saddles worth five thousand dollars sat atop horses worth four times that.

The Xalisco system expanded during the 2000s to include families from all over the region. The pioneers from the Tejeda-Sánchez clan had for many years only recruited people they were in some way related to. That changed after Operation Tar Pit sent close to dozens of these workers to jail. The U.S. heroin market was expanding, fueled by Americans' addiction to prescription opiates. Xalisco bosses quickly reconstituted their cells, bringing in workers now from families they were not related to. Over the next few years, as Xalisco cells multiplied, their demand for labor grew voracious and the opportunity to work heroin was now open to many more families. Most of a generation of young men found work in it.

One driver I spoke with, just beginning a prison sentence, told me he began to think of going north when a heroin trafficker he knew in his village built a house with an automatic garage door. Old people stood in amazement and watched it open and close. He saw other drivers, guys he grew up with, return and buy beer for everyone in the plaza. Girls flocked to them. Without land or prospects, he signed up, too.

"It was like a little weed that just keeps growing until it invaded the whole village, and eventually it didn't matter what your last name was," said a former driver I spoke with, who went by the name of Pedro. "Anyone with desire to go up and try his luck could do it."

To most of ranchero Mexico, chiva was a disgusting thing. "But like the song says, 'Dirty money removes hunger, too,'" Pedro said. "When my brother went up north, my mother was saying I don't know how you can sell that garbage. But when she saw the money she was very happy."

Cell leaders had to recruit drivers from new ranchos and, especially, from Nayarit's capital city, Tepic, nearby. The new recruits no longer had family connections to the heroin pioneers. What's more, they had work already; they were painters, construction workers, bakers, butchers. But these were dead-end jobs in Mexico, and humiliating when many other young men had new trucks and houses and money for the banda. So, before long, driving a major U.S. metro area with your mouth crammed with balloons of heroin was a viable economic option—kind of like SSI in eastern Kentucky—for a much larger swath of restless young men in and around Xalisco, Nayarit.

In several Xalisco neighborhoods virtually every able-bodied young man had gone north to sell heroin. The working-class Landareñas and

Tres Puntos neighborhoods, not far from the town's rodeo arena, were among them. The flat neighborhoods, with some still-unpaved streets, were a mix of modest houses of concrete block, mechanics shops, mom-and-pop markets, small beauty salons, and crowing roosters. The neighborhoods became sources of labor supply for the Xalisco heroin stores in the United States. Selling heroin up north became fashionable, almost a rite of passage, for Landareñas and Tres Puntos young men. Most would learn little of America beyond strip mall parking lots in the Xalisco heroin hubs of Columbus, Charlotte, Denver, Portland, and Salt Lake.

Pedro had done many dead-end jobs in Nayarit. His father taught him to hate drugs. Pedro never listened to the ballads—the *narcocorridos*—that recounted how traffickers died in a blaze of glory.

But "I was tired," he said years later, "of work that led nowhere."

A brother-in-law was offered work selling heroin. Soon several of Pedro's brothers went north, too.

"If they need anyone, let me know," Pedro told his brother-in-law.

By then Pedro had watched the business spread across Xalisco. He remembered as a boy seeing a man who'd just returned from the United States. He was sitting atop a fine Thoroughbred horse that no one in town could afford. He was drinking beer, this man, and was the subject of gossip around town. Since then, at least two dozen of Pedro's friends had gone to work as drivers in the Xalisco heroin system as it spread across the United States. Every one of them went with the dream of earning enough to start a car shop, or open a tortilla stand, or buy a taxi. Not one ever did. True, they built houses and bought clothes for their families, those Levi's 501s especially. But they spent the rest on beer, strip clubs, and cocaine, and walked the streets of Xalisco for a week or two the object of other men's envy. When their money dried up, jonesing for that quick cash, they went north as heroin peons again and again. The Xalisco labor pool never dried up. Young men were always eager to return and push heroin, strung out on the high of coming home a king.

When he got a call from a cell boss, Pedro figured he would be different. He wanted to earn enough to open a bakery. The boss sent him and another young man to the border, and paid for them to cross with a group of migrants. The other kid was headed to Minneapolis to sell. Pedro was sent to Columbus, and from there his boss sent him to another city that was deemed virgin territory.

He was given certain rules. No blacks. His boss feared African Americans. Once a customer brought a black customer along. The boss pulled a gun and told them both to get out and never come back. The kids Pedro sold to were all white, always ready to try out their high school Spanish.

"Hola, amigo. Como estas? Me gusta mucho la cerveza."

Pedro and his coworkers found a furnished apartment. Pedro didn't want to stand out, or drive more than he had to. When he wasn't working, he was in the apartment, playing the Xbox. He made a thousand dollars for a few weeks of work. Then he was arrested and convicted of trafficking.

Authorities shipped him to prison. There he studied for his GED, at twenty-five cents an hour, and passed. He also worked as a prison landscaper and cook, making twenty-three dollars a month. It was enough to afford him a television, a radio, and his own food. By the time he was released, he had made nine hundred dollars—almost what he had made selling heroin.

They sent him to El Paso, where an officer took him to the bridge leading to Ciudad Juárez and told him to start walking.

"Don't come back," the officer said.

A month later, back home, Pedro received a letter from the prison. It contained a check for $430, the remainder of what he was owed for working and studying for his GED.

ON THE DAY OF Operation Black Gold Rush, a year after the arrest of the junkie bailiff in Nashville, hundreds of officers fanned out across fifteen U.S. cities gathering up Sánchez clan heroin crews: 138 people in all, drivers, telephone operators, suppliers, as well as numerous local addicts.

That day, federal court looked like a hospital ward. Junkies were throwing up, sweating, and falling off their benches.

"If we didn't arrest them they were going to die," Mabry said.

Marshals rushed doctors to court. Several junkies had arraignment postponed because they weren't fit to understand the judge.

Like Operation Tar Pit six years before, Black Gold Rush showed the vast expanse of the Xalisco system—in this case operated by just one extended family. Nashville was connected to Ohio, to North and South Carolina, to Indiana, Kentucky, and to several states out west.

Indicted in absentia in Tennessee, Alberto Sánchez—Uncle Beto—remains in Mexico, possibly Guadalajara. As happened after Operation Tar Pit, the Sánchez heroin cells quickly reconstituted.

His networks, and those of his family, are believed to encompass most of the state of South Carolina, including Myrtle Beach, where police have six times dismantled the Sánchez heroin cell, only to see it return each time. DEA sources and traffickers themselves tell me Sánchez family cells operate also in Denver, Charlotte, Indianapolis, Salt Lake, Las Vegas, Cincinnati, Columbus, Knoxville, Memphis, Reno, and Portland, Oregon.

Whole new labor pools were becoming available in Nayarit as young men in dead-end jobs signed up for driving stints. Up in America, new, younger, and wealthier customers were emerging everywhere.

It was a good time to be a heroin dealer.

The Criminal Case

Southwest Virginia

L ate at night on October 24, 2006, John Brownlee, the U.S. attorney in western Virginia, received a phone call at home.

On the line was Michael J. Elston. Elston worked in the U.S.
Department of Justice while Alberto Gonzales was attorney general for
President George W. Bush.

Elston said he was calling on behalf of a Purdue Pharma executive.

The investigation Brownlee had approved into Purdue Pharma and
its campaign to market OxyContin was then four years old. The case
was assigned to the tiny Abingdon, Virginia, office, near Kentucky and
West Virginia, a coal-mining region where hundreds of people had
died of OxyContin overdoses. The office issued hundreds of subpoe-
nas, scanned stacks of documents into a database, and interviewed
dozens of people. By 2006, Brownlee's staff believed they had evidence
that the company had knowingly misbranded OxyContin as virtually
nonaddictive.

In Purdue focus groups, doctors worried about OxyContin's addictiveness but yearned for a long-lasting and less-addictive painkiller. The
company that produced a nonaddictive painkiller "would dominate the
pain management market. And that is exactly what Purdue tried to do,"
Brownlee testified later. "[Purdue] marketed and promoted OxyContin
as less addictive, less subject to abuse and diversion, and less likely to
cause tolerance and withdrawal than other pain medications."

Despite its ad claims, Purdue provided no study to the FDA, investigators later noted, that supported those claims. The company taught its
sales force that oxycodone was harder to extract, and thus abuse, than
other drugs—though the company's own studies showed that wasn't
true. In 1995 tests, the company found that 68 percent of the oxycodone could be extracted when the pill was crushed and liquefied and
drawn through cotton into a syringe. In fact, addicts I spoke with said
it was easier to extract the drug from an OxyContin pill than from

other, milder opiate painkillers, such as Vicodin or Lortab, because OxyContin didn't include anything but oxycodone, while the others also contained acetaminophen or Tylenol.

The company's sales staff said in promotional meetings across the United States that OxyContin's twelve-hour timed-release formula meant there were fewer peaks and troughs in euphoria when compared with immediate-release opiates. This was a crucial point. Intense euphoria followed by an intense crash is what produces the cravings leading to addiction to opiates. If OxyContin didn't cause these extreme peaks and troughs, then its salespeople could claim to physicians that the pills carried less risk of addiction than short-acting opiates. I spoke with several doctors who said the graphs showing OxyContin's purportedly mild peaks and troughs of oxycodone in blood plasma were among the most convincing data that Purdue salespeople produced.

But federal investigators later said that these graphs were incorrect and "falsely" exaggerated the difference in euphoric effect between Oxy and its short-acting competitors.

Purdue "phonied up [those] graphs to show a steady level of oxycodone in blood plasmas," said Paul Hanly, a New York City plaintiff's attorney, who brought a class action lawsuit against Purdue. "The true graph shows an incredible spike, then *boom*—you go straight to the bottom."

Purdue supervisors taught salespeople to tell doctors that patients using up to 60 mg of OxyContin could stop abruptly without withdrawal symptoms. However, federal investigators found that company officials knew of a 2001 British study of osteoporosis patients who described suffering withdrawal when they stopped using OxyContin. "Even after receiving this information," federal investigators wrote, "supervisors and employees decided not to write up the findings because of a concern that it might 'add to the current negative press'" surrounding OxyContin.

As I was writing this book, I contacted Purdue's media representatives, requesting an interview with someone at the company about the 2006 criminal case. I inquired about its ad campaign and about how OxyContin was selling lately, among other things. I asked also for interviews with Dr. David Haddox, author of the concept of "pseudoaddiction," and with Dr. Curtis Wright, who had been part of approving Purdue's application while he was at the FDA. A company spokesman sent the following:

For more than 30 years, Purdue Pharma has developed opioid medications to alleviate the debilitating pain experienced by millions of people. As leaders in our field, we are acutely aware of the public health risks that can arise from the misuse and abuse of these medications. We're working with policymakers and health care professionals throughout the country to reduce the risks involving opioids, without compromising the medical care of people suffering from chronic pain.

Purdue is developing innovative technologies to create pain medicines in new forms that include abuse-deterrent properties, making them unattractive to drug abusers. These medicines are designed to provide patients with pain relief when taken as directed, while also deterring abuse by snorting and injection. These new approaches do not prevent abuse, but they are a step in the right direction.

We encourage a transition to abuse-deterrent technologies over time, but it must be accompanied by greater societal efforts to reduce the demand for non-medical use of prescription medications.

In 2005, the federal prosecutors in Abingdon, Virginia, who were preparing the case against Purdue subpoenaed Dr. Hershel Jick up at Boston University. A deputy sheriff delivered the papers. Dr. Jick ignored the subpoena at first. He was too busy to be bothered. Then a federal prosecutor called. They needed him to testify before a grand jury, she said, something to the effect, Dr. Jick later remembered, of a drug company using his 1980 letter to the *New England Journal of Medicine* as proof that their drugs weren't addictive. Hershel Jick was perplexed. He had no idea what she was talking about. What did all this have to do with him?

"I told them I wouldn't go," he told me. "But they threatened to put me in jail, so I schlepped on down there. They had me on the stand asking me irrelevant and obtuse questions for two hours."

Dr. Jick then returned to Boston and with that he exited our story, his tiny letter to the editor in the back pages of the *New England Journal of Medicine* having helped ignite, quite unintentionally, a revolution in American medicine.

In Abingdon, the case against Purdue proceeded. John Brownlee filed criminal charges against the pharmaceutical company. He set October 25 as a deadline for Purdue to accept a plea agreement. In the plea, the company would admit to one felony count of false branding of

OxyContin, or face further charges. In later testimony before the U.S. Senate Judiciary Committee, Brownlee said Michael Elston asked him during his phone call to slow the case, postpone the plea agreement. Elston later said he was calling on behalf of a superior, who in turn received a call from a Purdue defense attorney asking for more time for the company.

Brownlee thought about the request. It was a delicate matter. His political career showed promise. He was being mentioned as a potential candidate for state attorney general, even governor. Still, he saw no reason to postpone the long and complicated case. That afternoon, he had received approval from DOJ higher-ups to proceed with it. He said he told Elston to "go away." Brownlee signed the plea agreement with Purdue the next morning. Eight days later, his name showed up on a list compiled by Elston of federal prosecutors recommended to be fired.

Nine were fired. In the end, John Brownlee was not one of them. But, he testified the next year, he believed his inclusion on the list was retaliation for not delaying the Purdue settlement. The Purdue episode lingered amid the Bush administration controversy in which top attorney general officials were accused of political meddling in the work of their far-flung prosecutors and recommending some be fired for not complying with what were perceived as political orders. Elston later resigned. An attorney for Elston told the *Washington Post* later that there was no connection between the phone call that night and Brownlee's name appearing on the list of prosecutors recommended to be fired.

John Brownlee spent another year as the U.S. attorney from western Virginia. In 2008, he resigned to seek the Republican nomination for state attorney general and lost in the primary. Talk of a future gubernatorial bid wilted. His political career stalled. He is now in private practice.

However, Purdue Pharma pleaded guilty to a felony count of "misbranding" OxyContin. To avoid federal prison sentences for its executives, the company paid a $634.5 million fine, among the largest in the history of the pharmaceutical industry at the time. Three executives—CEO Michael Friedman, General Counsel Howard Udell, and the by-then-departed chief medical officer, Dr. Paul Goldenheim—paid $34.5 million of that. Each pleaded guilty to a single misdemeanor of misbranding the drug. They were also placed on probation for three years and ordered to perform four hundred hours of community service.

In July 2007, the Purdue executives appeared in federal court for sentencing. Lee Nuss, the mother of a Florida man who died of an OxyContin overdose, rose to speak.

"You are," she told them, "nothing more than a large corporate drug cartel."

ABOUT THIS TIME, OVER in southern Ohio, Dr. Phillip Prior had left private family practice to devote himself full-time to his specialty in addiction medicine at the Veterans Administration hospital in the town of Chillicothe. Prior was one of the few addiction specialists in southern Ohio, and this made him something akin to a battlefield medic.

The area around Chillicothe had seen drug problems before, but they'd never involved opiates. Not long after the Purdue campaign hit full swing, however, Chillicothe and the surrounding towns began seeing patients addicted to OxyContin. Many of them used hundreds of milligrams a day as their tolerance grew. Newly liberal prescribing put Oxys everywhere. Pill mills sprouted like fungus. Soon, opiate pills were the party drug for small-town kids who in another era might have been building bonfires and getting drunk.

Then Prior watched in amazement as heroin came to town. Heroin was as foreign to these rural, white communities of southern Ohio as extraterrestrials. Wasn't it an urban drug? For blacks in Baltimore or D.C.? Puerto Ricans in New York? It had never had anything to do with Appalachia.

This heroin, too, was like nothing Prior had ever seen, even in movies. It was sticky and dark brown, like rat crap, yet potent and, above all, cheap. It was called black tar. In Columbus, Mexicans were delivering it by car, like pizza, at prices that were a fourth what Oxy cost, and offering volume discounts. In Chillicothe and towns around Fairfield County, every addict became their salesman, looking for new clients he could parlay into enough orders to make a trip to Columbus worthwhile. From Fairfield County, the news marched south, down through a region where OxyContin had already tenderized a generation of folks to opiate use.

Athens County, ninety miles southeast of Columbus, had seen almost no heroin ever. By 2008, 15 percent of the admissions to a treatment center there were related to heroin, and almost all were injecting it. In 2012, the center was treating more heroin addicts, mostly for black tar, than alcoholics.

And so it went. OxyContin first, introduced by reps from Purdue Pharma over steak and dessert and in air-conditioned doctors' offices. Within a few years, black tar heroin followed in tiny, uninflated balloons held in the mouths of sugarcane farm boys from Xalisco driving old Nissan Sentras to meet-ups in McDonald's parking lots. Others, too, got in on the trade. Black guys from Detroit and Dayton discovered southern Ohio and brought powder heroin.

Phillip Prior was now knee-deep in what was unthinkable a few years before: rural, white heroin junkies.

"I've yet to find one who didn't start with OxyContin," he said. "They wouldn't be selling this quantity of heroin on the street right now if they hadn't made these decisions in the boardroom."

PART III

"Now It's Your Neighbor's Kid"

Nashville, Tennessee

Out on the northwest side of Nashville, Tennessee, Judge Seth Norman has come to expect phone calls to start pouring in around late January every year.

"The legislature comes back in session in January," Norman said.

The calls come from state legislators, each with the same problem: an addicted son, a daughter, a brother-in-law.

"'Um, uh, my nephew down in Camden, you think maybe you might be able to help?' I get those kinds of calls," he told me while we sat in the office adjacent to his courtroom.

Most of the country's twenty-eight hundred drug courts are set up to divert drug abusers away from jail and prison and into treatment somewhere. Seth Norman runs the only drug court in America that is physically attached to a long-term residential treatment center. He takes addicts accused of drug-related nonviolent felonies—theft, burglary, possession of stolen property, drug possession—and puts them in treatment for as long as two years as an alternative to prison. Down the hall from his court are dorms with beds for a hundred people—sixty men and forty women.

I visited Judge Norman's Nashville facility one overcast fall afternoon because this epidemic was not the same as those of the past. For the first time since the years after heroin was invented, the root of the scourge was not some street gang or drug mafia but doctors and drug companies. I went to visit Judge Norman because I wanted to see what changes widespread addiction to a drug, usually associated with the ghetto or barrio might have wrought in America now that virtually all the new addicts were rural and suburban white people.

Seth Norman is eighty and possesses snow-white hair, a genteel Southern manner, and a drawl to go with it. He started the drug court/treatment program in 1996 and built it almost single-handedly by scrounging beds and ovens and lawn mowers from Tennessee state surplus.

Part of his efforts included frequent visits to the state legislature, where his pleadings for more funding fell on deaf ears for a good long time. Norman would go on to the lawmakers about his figures. The drug court and long-term treatment could keep most addicts out of prison—saving the state thirty-two thousand dollars a year over what it costs a prison to house an inmate. The drug court, he would say, boasted a recidivism rate of only 20 percent among those who finished the treatment program; compare that with over 60 percent for those leaving prison, he told them. This was before the pill-and-heroin epidemic swept through. Most legislators took drug treatment for soft-headed do-gooderism and held to the lock-'em-up attitude that voters preferred in a red state like Tennessee.

If Norman's experience is any guide, however, that hard-line attitude has softened recently. "It's taken sixteen years to convince the legislature that it is cheaper to put them [in drug treatment] than to put them in prison," he said.

The cost savings weren't what did the trick, though. Treatment has always been more effective and cheaper than prison for true drug addicts. What's changed, Norman said, is that no longer are most of the accused African American inner-city crack users and dealers. Most of the new Tennessee junkies come from the white middle and upper-middle classes, and from the state's white rural heartland—people who vote for, donate to, live near, do business with, or are related to the majority of Tennessee legislators.

As the opiate epidemic mangled the middle class, these kids doped up and dropped out. Earlier generations of opiate addicts became self-employed construction workers or painters, because that was all they could manage with heroin, and often jail, in their lives. With the new generation, time would tell how they would do, but it wasn't looking good. A large subset of these new young addicts had criminal records now. Many were on probation; a good number went to prison. Either way, their parents were realizing that life with a record was as stunted as life with an opiate addiction. Any dreams these kids' parents once had for them were now improbable. Even qualifying to rent an apartment was hard. With a criminal record, finding a job in the teeth of the great recession was almost impossible.

Some parents were so worn-out that they welcomed a child's departure for prison. But the opiate epidemic also made a lot of criminal-justice reformers out of rock-ribbed white conservatives.

This is what Judge Seth Norman discovered. The experience had, shall we say, modified state legislators' hard-line attitudes toward the proper role of rehabilitation in dealing with addicts accused of drug and property crimes.

"One thing that makes [legislators] more amenable to treatment is that it's hard to find a family now that hasn't been hit by addiction. Started out, fifteen years ago, very few members of the legislature had them. 'Naw, ain't nobody in my family going to touch anything like that.' Not so anymore. Now they have seen it firsthand."

Norman's no dummy. He named several dorms at his treatment facility for friendly legislators—Haynes Hall, Henry Hall, Waters Hall. When I visited he claimed the support of the sitting governor and state directors of corrections, public safety, and substance abuse.

Norman couldn't have imagined this when he was scrounging surplus sofas and coaxing pennies from elected officials in the late 1990s. But as the opiate epidemic ravaged white communities across Tennessee, it had a way of changing the minds of even the hardest hard-liners.

Signs of this were (quietly) appearing nationwide. The opiate epidemic was forcing judges to imagine new kinds of courts—veterans' courts, mental health courts—designed to treat the causes of what landed a suspect in a criminal case.

In Ohio, the opiate epidemic had swollen the prison population beyond capacity. Prison director Gary Mohr, appointed by Governor John Kasich, a Republican, told a newspaper that he favored expanding prison drug treatment—and had done so in four prisons. He also suggested that he would resign if the legislature decided to build more prisons in response to the epidemic.

Republicans across the country, in fact, seemed to be changing their views. In Texas, Georgia, South Carolina, and other states, GOP lawmakers were pushing for what the *Wall Street Journal* termed "a more forgiving and nuanced set of laws."

"You're seeing this huge groundswell for criminal justice reform really being driven by conservative circles," said Chris Deutsch, with the National Association of Drug Court Professionals. "Conservative governors are starting to invest in drug courts. In the last five years, we're really starting to see statewide drug courts in every county."

Texas opened drug courts and was able, therefore, to close prisons.

Kentucky congressman Hal Rogers, a staunchly conservative Republican, has become a strong proponent for drug courts since his district, which included Floyd County, has been hammered by prescription pill abuse. "The epidemic of illegal drugs is by far the most devastating thing I have seen in my more than forty years of public service," Rogers says on the front page of his website, where he also touts the thirty drug courts in his twenty-four-county district.

Kentucky state legislator Katie Stine, a Republican, introduced a bill as I was writing this book that made it easier to charge a heroin dealer with the death of someone who died from an overdose. But key to Stine's bill was increased funding for addiction treatment and education.

"You used to think, 'Oh, the heroin addicted, that would be someone in some back alley, someone I don't know,'" Stine told a local TV station. "Now . . . it is your kid. It's your next-door neighbor's kid."

Georgia governor Nathan Deal heard recovering addicts tell their stories at graduation ceremonies from the drug court where his son is the presiding judge. "They all have their own stories, but a common thread runs through all of them," Governor Deal told the *Journal*, explaining why he had tripled the number of drug courts in three years. "They were given a second chance, and they had been rehabilitated."

Several factors made this politically feasible in states like Georgia. Declining crime rates were certainly one. Stressed budgets during the great recession were another—though treatment has always been proven cheaper than incarceration.

Yes the fact was that, coincidentally or not, this change of heart was happening among conservatives just as opiate addiction was spreading among both rural and middle-class white kids across the country, though perhaps most notably in the deepest red counties and states. Drug enslavement and death, so close at hand, were touching the lives, and softening the hearts, of many Republican lawmakers and constituents. I'll count this as a national moment of Christian forgiveness. But I also know that it was a forgiveness that many of these lawmakers didn't warm to when urban crack users were the defendants. Let's just say that firsthand exposure to opiate addiction can change a person's mind about a lot of things. Many of their constituents were no longer so enamored with that "tough on crime" talk now that it was their kids who were involved. So a new euphemism emerged—"smart on crime"—to allow these politicians to support the kind of rehabilitation programs that many of them had used to attack others not so long ago.

Meanwhile, buoyed by his new purchase with Tennessee's political class, Judge Seth Norman had done some thinking. Four or five drug courts like his could be funded with a one-penny tax on every prescription opiate pill sold in Tennessee. After all, some four hundred million of the pills were prescribed annually to a state of six million people.

By the time I was leaving Nashville and heading again to Portland—where I had heard a Xalisco Boy was just sentenced for the death of Toviy Sinyayev, the Russian Pentecostal kid—no drug company had stepped up to endorse Norman's idea.

Like Cigarette Executives

Portland, Oregon

Because every call means money, Xalisco Boys never ignore their phones during business hours.

Thus Milwaukie police detective Tom Garrett was surprised that after calling the phone of a Xalisco Boy known as Doriro for a half hour, no one answered.

Garrett and his colleagues were now full bore into investigating the heroin-overdose death of Toviy Sinyayev—the son of Russian Pentecostal couple Anatoly and Nina Sinyayev. A dozen harried days had passed since Toviy's mother found him comatose in his bedroom. Under pressure, his sister Elina told police that their dealer was a Russian Pentecostal heroin addict named Aleksey Dzyuba.

They put a wire on Elina. She called Dzyuba. Going through withdrawals and with her brother on life support, Elina met the dealer in a Safeway parking lot, surveilled by a dozen undercover officers. She bought heroin from him, and passed him some marked cash. As he drove from the parking lot, officers descended and arrested him.

With that, a strategy that Portland had adopted to combat the Xalisco Boys was set in motion, named for a college basketball player who died in 1986 after using cocaine a friend had given him.

A so-called Len Bias case is based in federal law. Under that law, a person who supplies drugs that cause a fatal overdose may be charged with a conspiracy that results in death—a charge that carries a twenty-year prison sentence. Cops have to prove the person died from the suspect's drugs; a chain of custody has to be established. But if they can do that, they have a powerful prosecutorial tool and one that was getting a closer look in many parts of the country as the opiate epidemic and fatal drug overdoses spread across the nation. One place that refined the strategy was Portland, Oregon.

The benefit prosecutors see in Len Bias is that it allows investigators to work up a chain of drug distribution. To save himself from a Len Bias prosecution, a dealer needs to flip, and quickly, burning the dealer one link above him in the chain, hoping for leniency at sentencing time. The last man detectives can trace the drugs to faces the twenty years if convicted—a fateful game of musical chairs. Thus, a heart-to-heart takes place in an interrogation room. Investigators can't threaten a suspect, but they do tell him what he faces under federal law. "The tone in the room definitely changes," Garrett said. "You're not joking with them. It's a very powerful conversation."

Speaking through a Russian interpreter, Dzyuba bridled at this idea. People die every day for their addictions, he told his interrogators. He wasn't to blame for their choices. Finally, though, a defense attorney explained the situation. Dzyuba gave up the name of the junkie dealer he bought from. With that, Garrett and his colleagues began working up the chain.

Dzyuba's dealer gave them the name of his supplier, who in turn gave them his dealer. This dealer, three levels up from Toviy, said he bought daily from a Mexican he knew only as Doriro.

This is how, on April 12, 2011, Garrett and his colleagues began calling the number of a man from Nayarit they would later learn went by the name Joaquin Segura-Cordero.

They received no answer. They called through the afternoon. Nothing.

Unbeknownst to them, Segura-Cordero was at that moment being arrested by another department. Portland police had their own Len Bias death case against him. This one originated three hours away, in Bend, Oregon, where a kid named Jedediah Elliott had overdosed and died a couple months before.

Both heroin chains led to Segura-Cordero, who, as it turned out, was a kind of regional sales manager for a Xalisco heroin cell. Normally, as a Xalisco regional manager, Segura-Cordero would have been insulated from the kind of day-to-day heroin sales that would expose him to arrest. But Segura-Cordero had faced a classic small-business problem: a labor shortage. "He had several runners arrested, so he'd run out of runners," said Steve Mygrant, one of the prosecutors in the case. "He was having to expose himself. He was taking calls and making deliveries himself."

Mygrant is a Clackamas County prosecutor deputized to try federal cases. Segura-Cordero was his first Xalisco Boys case. By the time I spoke with him, a couple years after Toviy's death, Mygrant sounded both harried and amazed by the Xalisco system.

"It used to be you go into the ghettos to buy heroin from street corners," he said. "Now these organizations are coming to the neighborhoods, to suburbia. They come to you. That's unique to this organizational model. They're all coming out of Nayarit and all operating off of this dispatch style. Like the fishermen in Alaska; they work seven days a week and go back home and play."

The Segura-Cordero case showed that Xalisco heroin spread for 150 miles around Portland. It went out to the quietest rural counties, where kids, addicted to pills, learned to drive to Portland, buy cheap black tar, and triple their money back home while feeding their own habit. In classic Xalisco style, every junkie became a salesman.

The federal prosecutor who has done more Len Bias cases than any other, who worked out the kinks in the way these prosecutions work, is a woman named Kathleen Bickers. Bickers's first heroin cases in the late 1990s were of Xalisco cells. "We were doing the Nayarit guys but we didn't really realize it," she told me.

But in time she saw the cells' connections to Nayarit and to each other, how they stretched from Portland across the West and out to Columbus and the Carolinas. Now she called the whole thing Corporation Heroin.

"They are the Philip Morris of heroin," she told me in her office in downtown Portland one day. "They think like cigarette company executives. The corporate nature of the model—they depend on that cash flow. They're not going to go away because you incarcerate a few individuals. You have to cut the labor force off at the knees. You have to make the people from Nayarit realize: When you come up here, you may never go back, or it may be fifteen years before you go back."

As she spoke, I thought back to the conversation with that fellow in prison from whom I first heard the name of the town of Xalisco so long ago now. He had lived in Portland, working legally as a mechanic as he watched the Xalisco system expand. "In Portland," he said, "I'd see [the police] grab people with twenty or thirty balloons and they'd let them go. That's why people began to come to Portland, because they weren't afraid. They saw there were no consequences. 'We get caught with this and they let us go.'"

Word spread back in Xalisco that cells did well in Portland, and, furthermore, arrested drivers were only deported. More cells crowded into town, he said.

This reminded me so much of small-town Mexican business culture. I once visited a village in central Mexico—Tzintzuntzan, Michoacán. Tzintzuntzan had at least two-dozen vendors all selling the same kind of pottery on its main street. Once one person did well selling pottery, everyone started doing it. No one thought to vary the offering. The stores stretched for five or six blocks—with each selling identical pots and bowls, eager to undercut the others. Mexican small-business culture, born of crisis and peso devaluations, was risk averse and imitative. That described the Xalisco cells. They came and imitated those who'd come before. In so doing, they dropped prices and raised their potency and the natural result, particularly as OxyContin tenderized the market terrain, was more addiction and overdoses. None of this was on a kingpin's order. It was something far more powerful than that. It was the free market.

Portland's catch-and-deport policy was an important reason why. The policy was designed for the small-time street addict/dealer who city officials didn't want taking jail space from more serious felons. The Xalisco Boys' drivers worked hard to look small-time. In reality, they were the only visible strands of large webs that sold hundreds of kilos of black tar a year across America, by the tenth of a gram. So for many years, when they were caught they were deported and faced little jail time, and no prison time. As farm boys on the make, they drew a very different message from leniency than what these Portland officials intended. To them, catch and release looked more like an invitation.

By the time OxyContin came to Portland in the mid-2000s, the city was famous back in Xalisco, Nayarit. The Boys crowded into the Rose City. What's more, the arrival of OxyContin meant they no longer had to rely on the old street clients like Alan Levine. There were now many hundreds more to help jump-start a heroin cell. The addicts were younger and wealthier. Seizures of a few ounces of heroin were big news a decade ago. Now, Bickers said, cops routinely found pounds of the stuff.

Len Bias became Portland's new strategy to combat the Xalisco Boys. In Portland, and for presumably the first time in the history of heroin in America, police began responding energetically—two or three detectives at a time—to a dead junkie in a gas station bathroom. The deceased's cell phone was mined for contacts that could lead them up the Xalisco ladder. Runners were no longer automatically deported. They were told they faced twenty years in federal prison.

For Len Bias to work, federal, state, and local government agencies had to cooperate completely. The state medical examiner had to be willing to quickly perform an autopsy; the local DA had to give up the case if it appeared the feds had more leverage.

Above all, investigators had to share information. This was because, unlike traditional Mexican drug organizations, Xalisco cells actually shared supplies, even with competitors. Xalisco cases tended to connect like webs. This was forcing investigators to discard turf battles.

"The ego of a narcotics cop is what makes them great," Bickers said. "They're creative, innovative, persistent. They know how to dog a target. But they're very territorial. We constantly have to remind ourselves to break those barriers down, to think organizationally, and not just think that 'it's my case.' You are going to go up a couple levels and you're going to run into somebody else's case. You get down to the dead people, and [the cases] all look like they're separate. But you work them hard and high enough and you keep your mind open, you'll see connections."

Joaquin Segura-Cordero was one example. He was sentenced to fourteen years in prison for selling dope that killed Toviy Sinyayev in a suburb of Portland and Jedediah Elliott out in the Oregon countryside 150 miles away.

Bickers had another case against two brothers from the village of Pantanal, near Xalisco, who were the ninth level up a Len Bias chain. They faced life in prison because of the death of a young woman in Salem from an overdose of black tar that they were accused of importing. As one level led to the next, Bickers watched a web emerge that connected the brothers' alleged Portland cell to suppliers and cells in other parts of Oregon, Las Vegas, and Colorado Springs—and, of course, to Nayarit.

From Bickers's office, I walked a few blocks to the office of a public defender to speak to an attorney who had agreed to talk to me as long as I left his name out of it. He had convinced many Xalisco Boys that their cooperation was the only way to avoid twenty years in prison under Len Bias. The attorney had a standing order to detectives to call him immediately when a Len Bias case began. He supported quick cooperation with investigators—a controversial idea among defense attorneys.

"The value of your information is at its maximum the closer you are to the time of your arrest," he said. "If you're in really quick you can derive great benefit for your client."

Still, he didn't see much effect from prosecutors' new strategy. The pills were so widespread; new kids were getting addicted every day. They were switching to heroin all the time. Against that backdrop, he figured, prosecutors were only temporarily disrupting the market.

"My dental hygienist came to talk to me," he said. "Her son was involved with heroin to the point where he was stealing stuff out of stores. This is a middle-class person you'd think would never be touched by something like this. But it's so prevalent. It's almost like you were trying to stop drinking coffee [with] a Starbucks on every corner."

No Scarface, No Kingpins

Denver, Colorado

That was a daunting thought. I kept it in mind as, not long after that, I stood in an apartment twelve hundred miles away in northeast Denver, watching a thin kid with short-cropped hair tell detectives a story.

Jose Carlos was a classic Xalisco Boy. He was twenty-one and a faint moustache was trying to sprout above his lip. Shackled to a chair, he was shirtless and nervously watched Dennis Chavez and a team of narcotics officers go through every bit of his apartment.

The day before, a narcotics officer named Jes Sandoval had spotted a woman making heroin deliveries at a southeast Denver parking lot. When officers pulled her over, she gave up the apartment and Jose Carlos.

So the narcs busted in. Jose Carlos said he'd been in town for only three months selling heroin. He owned to being from the town of Acaponeta in Nayarit. The cops asked who his boss was. He started tearing up and shutting down at that point. He'd been in Columbus, Ohio, and Charlotte, North Carolina. Working construction, he said. None of the cops in the room were buying that. But as long as he wasn't giving up anybody above him, they didn't care what his story was.

The case, like hundreds before, would go no higher than this scruffy kid. His one-bedroom apartment contained nothing they could use against him. In fact, it contained almost nothing at all: a Walmart card table, four folding chairs, a small flat-screen TV, votive candles to the Virgin of Guadalupe, a pile of clothes, some DVD action flicks, and packets of Pizza Hut hot sauce. No bed, no sofa.

No weapons, no cash, either. On the table were balloons and a plate with only a couple grams of tar heroin. Jose Carlos, it appeared, supplied the Denver drivers with their balloons. There was a slight twist to this operation. This Xalisco cell had its addicts call a Denver number. Those calls were forwarded down to a phone in Nayarit, where an operator answered, then relayed the addict's order to a driver up in Denver. A heroin call center.

This bust was small-time by traditional narcotics standards. Yet, short of arresting the cell owner down in Mexico, the narcotics team, from Denver's District 3, was doing what probably harmed the Xalisco heroin business model most: raising its cost of business.

The Xalisco system succeeded because it reacted to how American cops traditionally worked drugs. Narcotics teams found barren apartments and peons like Jose Carlos; the money and most of the drugs were back in Mexico. This deflated cops and prosecutors. Thus, more so than any traditional drug network in the country, the Xalisco Boys were forcing law enforcement to rethink old strategies, particularly as the opiate epidemic took hold.

The upper- and middle-class junkies scrounging for dope hung around District 3's trendy University of Denver and Washington Park neighborhoods. The Xalisco drivers were there, too. District 3 cops didn't have the manpower or budget to work long undercover cases. Their approach to the Xalisco Boys was simpler, born of necessity, and revolved around Officer Jes Sandoval.

After twenty-two years as a cop and sixteen working drugs, Sandoval had become curiously like the Xalisco runners he tracked. He was as inconspicuous as they were, and about as relentless. In many years as a crime reporter, I have never encountered a narcotics officer as low-tech as Sandoval. He uses only a department-issue flip-up cell phone and a 2007 Honda SUV. He works business hours because the department pays no overtime. He works alone. In his cubicle is a photo of the Lone Ranger, a gift from colleagues. He almost never uses informants, never buys drugs undercover, never works wiretaps.

Instead, Sandoval trolls south Denver strip mall parking lots searching for telltale signs of deals about to happen: Frantic white kids in cars backed into parking spaces, their heads swiveling, surveying all that moves. He watches until the Xalisco runner passes, then follows both cars, calling for backup to arrest them down some side street when the deal goes down.

"I find myself some days traveling all over the district looking," he said.

Doing that, Sandoval made huge numbers of cases. His method is low cost and high volume—the law-enforcement version of the Xalisco heroin system. True, he was arresting the drug world's equivalent of day laborers. They had only small amounts of heroin. They kept quiet, were deported, and were replaced within a couple days. But Sandoval's approach recognized that Xalisco cell owners were small businessmen. They were sensitive to cost, like every small businessman. They weren't *Scarface*-style kingpins, spending wantonly and living for today. Some cell leaders required their drivers to turn in receipts at the end of the day. They had to account for every dollar.

So the way Sandoval saw it, each bust forced a crew chief in Nayarit to buy another car in Denver, find another apartment, and send another driver across the border. Each was a headache for a businessman who already had to make sure that his runners—eighteen- to twenty-five-year-old males most of them—didn't run out of supply, didn't party, didn't get anyone pregnant, didn't use the product they were selling. With each cell phone Sandoval confiscated, the crew chief had to reconstitute his client list, though soon the cells began keeping master lists of clients' phone numbers—on a computer somewhere in Nayarit, Sandoval figured.

"The more drivers we take off, the more desperate they get for drivers," he said as we circled a southeast Denver strip mall.

Amid an epidemic, this was about as good as the cops in District 3 could do. New addicts graduated from OxyContin to heroin every day and dope demand raged across Denver. Drawing from deep labor pools in Mexico, the Xalisco Boys' system appeared impervious. Sandoval's busts were as cost-effective as any other strategy. Denver's District 3 narcs took heart, therefore, from small victories. A couple weeks before I showed up, one Xalisco cell owner, angered that several drivers had been arrested, sent up a guy to act as a consultant, of a sort. The consultant's job was to accompany the drivers on their routes, study how they worked, and suggest ways they might avoid arrest.

Officers arrested him, too.

A Parent's Soul Pain

Ohio

As I tried to chart the spread of the opiate epidemic, one thing dawned on me: Other than addicts and traffickers, most of the people I was speaking to were government workers.

They were the only ones I saw fighting this scourge. We've seen a demonization of government and the exaltation of the free market in America over the previous thirty years. But here was a story where the battle against the free market's worst effects was taken on mostly by anonymous public employees. These were local cops like Dennis Chavez and Jes Sandoval, prosecutors like Kathleen Bickers, federal agents like Jim Kuykendall and Rock Stone, coroners like Terry Johnson, public nurses like Lisa Roberts, scientists at the Centers for Disease Control, judges like Seth Norman, state pharmacists like Jaymie Mai, and epidemiologists like Jennifer Sabel and Ed Socie.

I saw, too, that they were hamstrung. Sandoval and Bickers and Norman were limited in what they could accomplish as long as people remained silent and scary quantities of pills sloshed around America, carrying people to heroin.

So, in time, my focus shifted to the families of those who died, people who were standing up to warn others. Such advocates were few. Most grieving families retreated in shame and never said a public word about how a son died in a halfway house with a needle in his arm. A decade in, with sixteen thousand fatal opiate overdoses a year, only a handful of parent groups had formed to do anything about this public health crisis.

The marketing forces arrayed against these parents made their crusade quixotic. Their lone qualification for the task was a soul pain as relentless as the physical pain that opiates were now commonly prescribed to calm. But no one else was doing the job, and crying days away, arms around a photo album, seemed a waste.

One of them was Jo Anna Krohn, a woman with the soft Southern drawl so common down in Portsmouth, Ohio.

ON MY FIRST GLANCE at Portsmouth, Ohio, I found it hard to see much cause for hope. So many buildings were abandoned. So many folks looked dazed. So many others were on dispiriting disability. The town seemed infected with a pessimism and inertia that I associated with depressed Mexican villages—places that those with aspirations left. I'm glad I kept going back. For in time, beneath that worn-out veneer, Portsmouth revealed another side. The opiate epidemic pushed the town to unimaginable depths. But the town where the pill mill was invented, where an OxyContin/Walmart economy had taken root, a town savaged by economics for thirty years—that led the country into the opiate epidemic and that was flat on its back and forgotten—refused to stay down.

I love a good underdog story. This one seemed exhilaratingly American. As I tracked signs of how the opiate epidemic had changed the country, one place I found myself returning to—a half-dozen times or so—was Portsmouth, Ohio.

And there I met Jo Anna.

Several years before, on April 22, 2008, Jo Anna sat next to the hospital bed that was the end of what seemed to her such a fast road down. In the bed, tubes extruding from his body, lay Wesley, her comatose eighteen-year-old son.

A mother of five and a substitute teacher, Jo Anna prayed with her childhood friend, Karrie, by her side. The two women had grown up on neighboring farms outside Portsmouth.

Snatches of Wes's life appeared before Jo Anna as she cried and prayed some more. Living with his father, Wes began smoking pot at thirteen, and at fourteen dove into the pills that were everywhere in Portsmouth. He was a football player and handsome. He was a linebacker and a ferocious hitter, and thus popular. So a lot of what he did was forgiven and he got used to that. Football players were common among the new rural opiate addicts. Some got addicted to pills prescribed for injuries. Others, like Wes, took them at parties.

By his senior year in 2008, as he starred on the field for Portsmouth High School, Wes had a minor criminal record. He dealt Oxys from his father's house. He bought a gun for protection. One night five weeks before graduation, he was high and partying in his father's basement with younger kids. As a lark, Wes put the gun to his head and pulled the trigger. He lingered on life support for thirty-six hours. Eight hundred people attended his funeral. The family played "Angel," by singer Sarah McLachlan. His death was on the *Daily Times* front page four days running. Five of his organs were donated.

Wes wasn't the first Portsmouth kid to die. McLachlan's song, written about a junkie whose life slips away in a "dark, cold hotel," was becoming a standard at youth funerals, the soundtrack to Portsmouth's swelling opiate epidemic. But ashamed families shrouded their children's passings in a fog of euphemism and palatable lies. One couple Jo Anna knew claimed their son died of a heart attack, when everyone knew his drug use caused the heart attack. Coming on top of everything else that had happened to Portsmouth, this truth was just too painful. As in the early days of the AIDS epidemic, the newspaper was careful not to reveal too much about these deaths.

Wes's death was like that at first. He died of a gunshot. The newspaper never said he was high on OxyContin, had been using off and on for years, sold pills, that his house had been broken into twice, and he bought the gun from a convicted felon for protection from robbers.

That was the full story and the one that Jo Anna Krohn, sitting at her son's side, decided she would tell.

"I was going to be honest," she said when I met her a few years later. "I wasn't going to try to hide what had happened. If I said it enough, maybe another family would never be in my place."

A year after Wes's death, a high school invited her to speak. She told the kids the full story. Another high school invited her. She brought photos of Wes to a town meeting, showed them around, and told what there was to tell.

Kids were dying everywhere in Portsmouth. Soon grieving mothers gathered around her. It was like they were waiting for somebody else to start talking. They put photographs of their dead children on an abandoned building downtown. That finally put faces to the town's unspoken curse. Families of dead kids found the freedom to talk publicly.

It took a decade. But the first voice raised by a parent was that of Jo Anna Krohn as she toured high schools in 2009, telling kids why Wes died. She formed SOLACE, a group for parents mourning the loss of children to opiates. SOLACE became the first parent antidrug organization to grow from the opiate epidemic's ground zero.

When Jo Anna and some mothers appeared at an attorney general's press conference in green SOLACE T-shirts, the media took notice. Jo

Anna began getting phone calls from other counties. She realized then that kids were dying all over Ohio. Nobody had been talking about it. Jo Anna stopped substitute teaching. SOLACE was all she did. Chapters of SOLACE formed in sixteen counties. She spoke in Brown and Knox counties, up in Chillicothe, in Ironton—everywhere except for the high school Wes attended and that now offered a scholarship in his name. Portsmouth High never got around to inviting her.

She grew overwhelmed one day, waiting to give a speech with her friend Karrie. They had grown up doing chores and swimming at the local pond and, as teens, sneaking a beer now and then. They double-dated, imagining how they'd marry and raise kids.

Now in their fifties, each woman had a son dead from dope-related gunshots; Karrie's son, Kent, was murdered in 2000. Each woman also had another son strung out. Jo Anna's oldest lived in a trailer without running water. Karrie's second son had been to prison three times, and she had PTSD from thirteen years of dealing with her two sons' addictions. The women had once found Karrie's son in a KFC bathroom shooting up.

What had become of their girlhood American Dreams? Jo Anna wondered.

"We used to catch snakes in the creek," she told her friend. "Who would've ever thought that we'd be here together?"

I SOUGHT OUT JO Anna Krohn because I couldn't remember any drug scourge so ably abetted by silence.

Cocaine in the early 1980s came with Colombians who shot up Miami strip malls, levitating the murder rate and inflaming the public. My first week as a crime reporter in Stockton, California, in 1989, I walked a street lined by two-dozen crack dealers. When I opened the front gate to a dilapidated house, the crackheads fled like roaches. Bloods and Crips came and warred across Stockton. One of their drive-by shootings paralyzed a toddler. I often wonder what became of her. She would be in her midtwenties by now.

Next came methamphetamine, made in labs that exploded. Meth left users scabbed and twitching.

None of that blight, violence, and outrage accompanied the morphine molecule as it swept the United States. As opiates quietly killed unprecedented numbers of kids, it was as if the morphine molecule narcotized public ire as well. That it began in voiceless parts of the country—in Appalachia and rural America—helped keep it quiet at first. To even see the plague required examining confusing and incomplete data. A generation of coroners had grown up unused to reporting on drug overdoses. The nuances of whether someone died from opiates, and if so, whether that was oxycodone, hydrocodone, methadone, or heroin were sometimes lost.

The signature location of this drug scourge, meanwhile, was not the teeming, public crack houses. It was, instead, kids' private suburban bedrooms and cars—the products of American prosperity. The bedroom was the addict's sanctuary, the shrine to the self-involvement dope provokes. It was their own little dreamland, though quite the opposite of Portsmouth's legendary community pool, where kids grew up in public and under a hundred watchful eyes. Each suburban middle-class kid had a private bedroom and the new addicts retreated to them to dope up and die.

"We lived in our bedroom," said one woman in recovery. "You could have a big, huge house, but you could lock that door, isolated. Everybody I ever got high with, it was always in their bedroom. It was privacy. Don't come knock on my bedroom door."

Most kids also had cars and, when combined with pills or heroin, those vehicles were as destructive as those bedrooms. Their doting parents gave them these cars, which were necessary to navigate pedestrian-proof suburbs. But addicted kids also used them to meet their dealers. Without legions of middle-class kids with cars, the Xalisco Boys' business model didn't work. In cars, kids shot up, gave rides to fellow junkies, hid their dope. When their parents' trust in them finally died, the kids lived in these cars, and the cars became their private bedrooms.

As heroin and OxyContin addiction consumed the children of America's white middle classes, parents hid the truth and fought the scourge alone. They kept quiet. Friends and neighbors who knew shunned them. "When your kid's dying from a brain tumor or leukemia, the whole community shows up," said the mother of two addicts. "They bring casseroles. They pray for you. They send you cards. When your kid's on heroin, you don't hear from anybody, until they die. Then everybody comes and they don't know what to say."

These parents made avoidable mistakes and when a son died or entered rehab for the fourth time they again hid the truth, believing themselves alone, which they were as long as they kept silent. This pervasive lie was easily swallowed. It often lay buried beneath lush lawns, shiny SUVs, and the bedrooms of kids who lacked for nothing.

It was easier to swallow, too, because some of these new addicts were high school athletes—the charismatic golden youth of these towns. Athletes opened the door for other students who figured that if cool jocks were using pills, how bad could it be?

One addict I met was Carter, from one of California's wealthiest communities, the son of a banker.

Carter had been a high school star in football and baseball. With no break from sports during the year, he battled injuries that never healed. A doctor prescribed Vicodin for him, with no warning on what Vicodin contained, or suggestions for how it should be used.

Sports were king in Carter's town. It was a place of gleaming mansions, but he felt no sense that education was of value in providing choices in life, much less for the love of learning. These kids' futures were assured. So sports were what mattered. Dads would brag to friends about their sons' athletic exploits, then berate their boys for poor play, urging greater sacrifice. From the athletic director down to parents and teachers they heard, "You need grades so you can play. That was the vibe we got," Carter told me.

I saw this often. Many new athlete-addicts were not from poor towns where sports might be a ticket out for a lucky few. The places where opiate addiction settled hard were often middle- and upper-middle-class. Parents were surgeons and developers and lawyers and provided their kids with everything. Yet sports were as much a narcotic for these communities as they were to any ghetto. Love of learning seemed absent, while their school weight rooms were palatial things, and in many of them pain pills were quietly commonplace. Just as opiates provided doctors with a solution to chronic-pain patients, Vicodin and Percocet provided coaches with the ultimate tool to get kids playing again.

Carter's coach told him stories of players years before gulping down Vicodin before practices and games. "In my town, the stands were always filled. You wanted to be the hero. So you think, 'I can't look weak. I gotta push myself.' I would get these small injuries. The coaches wouldn't pay any attention. I taught myself to not pay attention to any injuries."

Most athletes on every team Carter played on used pills, for injury or recreation. Soon Carter grew addicted to Vicodin and then to OxyContin. From there, as a student athlete at a Division I university, he began using heroin.

I was coming to see football players as symbols of this American epidemic. Their elevated status on campus left some of them unaffected by consequences. Carter was caught selling pills and was told not to do it again. Above all, though; players were in constant pain and expected to play with it. If opiates were now for chronic pain, well, football players endured more chronic pain than most. Necks, thighs, and ankles ached all season.

Medicating injuries to get athletes playing through pain was nothing new. But as oxycodone and hydrocodone became the go-to treatment for chronic pain, organized sports—and football in particular—opened as a virtual gateway to opiate addiction in many schools. Thus, with the epidemic emerged the figure of the heroin-addicted football player. Though, of course, few wanted to talk too much about that.

By 2008, when Jo Anna Krohn's son died, these kinds of delusions had been accepted for almost a decade in places like Salt Lake, Albuquerque, Charlotte, Minneapolis, and other cities that had for that same decade been the drivers and beneficiaries of the greatest boom in the history of U.S. consumer spending. But it was in beat-down Portsmouth, Ohio, where one mother, and not the wealthiest in town by a long shot, had the gumption to own the truth and say something about it.

ACROSS PORTSMOUTH, AT THE Counseling Center, Ed Hughes thought silence was a huge part of the story.

Opiates had exploded all those plans Hughes had in the mid-1990s to consolidate the Counseling Center's operations and focus on improving its internal workings. The center opened years before in a small house. By 1992 it began residential treatment with 16 beds. When I met Hughes, the Counseling Center had 150 beds, a huge waiting list, a staff of close to 200, and had just moved its outpatient center into an abandoned three-story school—due entirely to the swarms of new opiate addicts.

"We've never seen anything move this fast," Hughes told me.

A decade and a half in, Ed Hughes was still waiting for the arc of addicted clients to plateau and curve downward.

Kids were coming to the center from across Ohio. Many, he said, grew up coddled, bored, and unprepared for life's hazards and difficulties. They'd grown up amid the consumerist boom that began in the mid-1990s. Parenting was changing then, too, Hughes believed. "Spoiled rich kid" syndrome seeped into America's middle classes. Parents shielded their kids from complications and hardships, and praised them for minor accomplishments—all as they had less time for their kids.

"You only develop self-esteem one way, and that's through accomplishment," Hughes said. "You have a lot of kids who have everything and look good, but they don't have any self-esteem. You see twenty-somethings: They have a nice car, money in their pocket, and they got a cell phone . . . a big-screen TV. I ask them, 'Where the hell did all that stuff come from? You're a student.' 'My mom and dad gave it to me.' . . . And you put opiate addiction in the middle of that?"

He winced.

"Then the third leg of the stool is the fifteen-year-old brain."

Hughes saw this all the time, too: adult drug users incapable of making mature choices. This happened because opiates stunted the part of their brain controlling rational action.

"We've got twenty-five- to thirty-year-old, opiate-addicted people who are going on fifteen. Their behavior, the way their brain works, is like an adolescent," he said. "It's like the drug came in there and overwhelmed that brain chemistry and the front of the brain did not develop.

"The front of the brain has to develop through mistakes. But the first reaction of the addicted person is to head back to the family: 'Will you rescue me?' Whatever the person's rescued from, there's no learning. There's no experiences, no frontal brain development. They're doing well and then some idea comes into their head and they're off a cliff. It may not be a decision to use. Most relapse comes not from the craving for the drug. It comes from this whole other level of unmanageability, putting myself in compromising situations, or being dishonest, being lazy—being a fifteen-year-old."

Hughes knew families as addicted to rescuing their children as their kids were addicted to dope. This, too, was an epidemic, Hughes believed.

"I've got forty-year-olds who act like twenty-two-year-olds because their families are so enmeshed in rescuing them. The parents are giving them a place to live, giving them money, taking care of things, worrying about them, and calling me trying to get them into treatment. I try to tell parents it's real important to say no, but say no way back when they're young."

* * *

MOST OF THESE PARENTS were products, as I am, of the 1970s, when heroin was considered the most vile, back-alley drug. How could they now tell their neighbors that the child to whom they had given everything was a prostitute who expired while shooting up in a car outside a Burger King? Shamed and horrified by the stigma, many could not, and did not.

Opiate use in medicine had been destigmatized by crusading doctors. But destigmatizing the new opiate addiction had no prestigious crusaders. That task fell to parents of dead kids and a few individuals with a flair for guerrilla political action, which is how I would describe Brad Belcher.

I visited Belcher because one night he had kicked the shins of the status quo in his hometown of Marion, Ohio.

Like Portsmouth, Marion once thrived. Power shovels built in Marion helped dig the Panama Canal. But those days and those jobs were gone. Inertia had replaced optimism. Decades into the decline, hundreds of Marion kids had grown addicted to pain pills and then switched to heroin. The chamber of commerce desperately devised slogans: "Downtown Marion: Watch Us Grow."

A casual observer could sympathize with Marion's city fathers. Like so many Midwestern towns, Marion was afflicted by forces that were awesome and unseen. A prolonged recession, the steady drip of jobs disappearing, had beaten at Marion. A lot of people with aspirations left. So, too, Belcher felt, did any impulse to look at new ways of attacking problems facing the city.

If you counted all the thefts, the drug dealing, the court cases, the hospitalizations, the pawns, the prison, and the people in jail, the town seemed to Belcher to be running on heroin. Yet the cops never appeared to make heroin arrests. The newspaper never mentioned it.

Belcher, twenty-eight, with cropped hair and way of speaking, is a recovering drug addict. With five years sober, he had the kind of energy common to many in recovery and chafed at Marion's apathy.

One night it occurred to him to go online and order eight hundred large black signs with white letters proclaiming the insurgent message: HEROIN IS MARION'S ECONOMY. They arrived a week later. Late one foggy night, Belcher stuck those signs all over Marion—in cornfields, near the prison, outside churches, by bus stops, schools, and along streets in the better neighborhoods.

"I was generally hoping for some kind of awareness, to get people talking about some kind of solution," he said. "It's in everybody's household."

He was just about to put them up downtown that night when a police officer, a deputy sheriff, and a highway patrolman pulled him over. They roused the city attorney. Marion city government mobilized that night to uproot Belcher's signs. Only ten remained when Marion awoke. But then a drug dealer put snapshots of the signs on Facebook. That created the effect Brad Belcher sought.

The signs became the talk of Marion. Television reporters came. City officials held a town hall meeting. Cops began making heroin arrests and the paper reported them. There was a march to city hall. None of that solved the problem, of course, but it did get people talking, which Belcher took as a start.

Another person I saw cutting through the silence surrounding opiates was Wayne Campbell, a barrel-chested guy with the personality of the football coach he was part-time.

About a year after Jo Anna Krohn in Portsmouth, Ohio, became likely the first parent in the country to raise her voice and organize in response to the opiate epidemic, Wayne Campbell followed suit in the Columbus suburb of Pickerington.

Like Jo Anna's son, Wayne's oldest son, Tyler, had also played football. He was a safety for the Division I University of Akron Zips. In 2009, the school opened a thirty-thousand-seat football stadium, a monument to corporate America in sports. The sixty-one-million-dollar InfoCision Stadium, named for a company that operates call centers, also has a field named for the Summa Health System, a nonprofit hospital; club seating named for FirstMerit Corporation; and a press box named for a local credit union. If ever the Division I school needed a good year from its team, 2009 was it.

Instead, the team disintegrated under the pressure to win and the weight of pills.

The Zip's star quarterback that year, Chris Jacquemain, grew addicted to OxyContin after suffering a separated shoulder. He began stealing and was expelled from the team early in the season, then left school. Jacquemain's life spiraled down. He died of a heroin overdose two years later.

Something like that happened to Wayne's son, Tyler. A walk-on and an eager and aggressive safety, Tyler Campbell was prescribed sixty Percocets after shoulder surgery following the 2008 season. He was given no instructions about the drug and how to use it. Nor was it clear that he needed that many pills to recover from the surgery. Doctors told Wayne it was the usual postsurgical prescription. It seemed to Wayne that doctors wanted to make sure patients didn't return quickly, so they prescribed a lot. That was part of the problem, he figured.

Wayne spoke later with Jeremy Bruce, a wide receiver on the team, who provided a glimpse of the team unraveling that year. The coaches and trainers, Bruce said, felt pressured to field a winning team as the school opened its new stadium. After the games, some of the trainers pulled out a large jar and handed out oxycodone and hydrocodone pills—as many as a dozen to each player. Later in the week, a doctor would write players prescriptions for opiate painkillers, and send student aides to the pharmacy to fill them.

"I was on pain pills that whole season—hydrocodone or oxycodone. I was given narcotics after every single game and it wasn't recorded. It was like they were handing out candy," Bruce told me.

One problem the team faced was a steep drop-off in talent from the first to the second string, Bruce said. As first-stringers got hurt and second-stringers couldn't fill in, he said, "it's a snowball effect because of the pressure and the stress just to get those [first-stringers] back on the field. I think that's where the narcotics came into play and that's why it was handed out so easily—the stress and the pressure to win right now."

J. D. Brookhart, the team's head coach that year, said that he knew nothing of the extent of opiate dependence on the team that Bruce describes. "That wasn't the case, that we knew of," he said. "I don't think it was anything that anybody thought was anything rampant at all. Not from the level I was at.

"It's not like trainers or coaches had any authorization [to prescribe pills]. These pills were ordered by doctors."

Injuries were the team's overriding issue that season, Brookhart told me from his home in Texas, where he has retired from coaching and now works for a Christian nonprofit. Some twenty-four players missed eight or more games apiece due to injuries that year; this included two of Jacquemain's three backups, he said.

By the end of the 2009 season, the Akron Zips football team was a poster squad for America's opiate epidemic. Not only was Jacquemain dismissed for issues related to his addiction, but as the season wore on and the injuries mounted, Bruce said, "I would say fifteen to seventeen kids had a problem. It seems that most who had an addiction problem had an extensive problem with injuries as well."

Toward the end of the season, he said, players had learned to hit up teammates who had just had surgery, knowing they would have bottles full of pills. Meanwhile, a dealer from off campus sold to the players, visiting before practice sometimes, fronting players pills and being paid from the monthly rent and food allowance that came with their scholarship.

The 2009 Zips inaugurated the school's new stadium with only three wins that year. The coaching staff was fired at season's end. But the effect of the season lingered on.

Among the team's weaknesses that year was its size on defense. Overall, its defensive line and linebacking corps were small. So, too, were its cornerbacks; they could cover receivers well, but were unable to provide much help in stopping the offense's running attack.

The team's lack of defensive size was felt acutely at one position: safety, Tyler Campbell's position. Running backs often broke through the defensive line and linebackers. It too often fell to safeties to make tackles. Against a monstrous Wisconsin team, the first game of the 2008 season, with a scholarship now and starting his first collegiate game, Tyler for one week was the nation's leader in tackles, with eighteen—an exploit that coaches attributed to his hard work and perseverance.

His stats, though, highlighted the team's weakness. When a safety is making that many tackles, Bruce said, "there is a serious problem. [Opposing running backs] should never get to the secondary that many times."

As the season went on, Tyler injured his shoulder. His body never fully healed and he had surgery after the season. At the time of the surgery, a snowstorm hit Ohio and his parents couldn't be with him in Akron to ensure he took the pills correctly. Team doctors could give Wayne no records of what Tyler was given after games. But those first sixty post-surgery Percocets following the 2008 season seem to have begun his addiction. By the next season, unbeknownst to those close to him, Tyler had transitioned to OxyContin.

Tyler's 2009 season was spotty. He played eleven games but made only thirty-one tackles, and grew secretive and distant, which teammates and family attributed to his play on the field. In the spring of 2010, his grades dropping and his behavior moody, Tyler was sent home. Over the next year, he was in rehab twice and relapsed. At some point, he switched to heroin.

In June, 2011, his parents put him in an expensive rehab center in Cleveland. Thirty days later, he drove home with his mother, clean, optimistic, and wanting to become a counselor. The next morning she found him dead in his bedroom of an overdose of black tar heroin from Columbus—likely hidden in his room from before he entered rehab, Wayne believes.

With a solid reputation in Pickerington, Tyler's family had kept his addiction a secret. But when he died, Wayne told his wife, "Let's open it up. Come out and be honest."

The Campbells had three hundred wristbands made for the funeral: JUST SAY NO FOR TC. The obituary urged mourners to donate money to a drug prevention group. Fifteen hundred people attended the memorial. As they consoled him, Wayne was struck by how many murmured in his ear, "We've got the same problem at home."

Two weeks later, Wayne met with fathers who wanted to do something in his son's memory. He knew few of them, but learned that several also had addicted kids. That marked a moment of clarity for Wayne Campbell. "When Tyler died, it lifted the lid," he said. "We thought it was our dirty little secret. I thought he was the only one. Then I realized this is bigger than Tyler."

From that grew a nonprofit called Tyler's Light. By the time I met Wayne Campbell, Tyler's Light had become his life's work just as Jo Anna Krohn was now devoted to SOLACE. He spoke regularly to schools about opiates, showing a video of white middle-class addicts, one of whom was a judge's daughter.

Wayne invited others to join him. Among them was Gary Cameron, commander of the Columbus Police Department's narcotics unit. Cameron's team was fighting the Xalisco heroin networks crawling over Columbus; meanwhile, as he told auditoriums full of school kids, his stepson was addicted to their heroin.

Cameron viewed the Xalisco Boys as a new vanguard in narcotics—resembling isolated terrorist cells more than a traditional trafficking organization. Most drivers, he noticed, really didn't know much about the drug they sold. They lived isolated in small apartments. No arrest slowed down these cells. Too many American kids were now hooked on opiates. Neither they nor their parents had much idea of what they were up against. So, in the time of the Xalisco Boys, Gary Cameron viewed education as, fundamentally, police work.

"We were quick to talk about the problems we associated with crack," Cameron said, one day after a Tyler's Light presentation. "We just don't talk about heroin addiction."

About a year after Wayne Campbell formed Tyler's Light, Paul Schoonover called. Could he and his wife, Ellen, help in any way? Schoonover asked. It had been a few months since the Schoonover's son, Matt, had died from a black tar heroin overdose, the day after leaving three weeks of drug treatment.

As I researched this story, the Schoonovers were among the first parents I met on my first trip to Columbus. The death of their son had come well into this epidemic, yet it had blindsided them. Until Matt's death, they knew nothing of it.

So at the funeral Paul stood and told hundreds of mourners the truth of how Matt had died. About the pill use, the OxyContin then the heroin. He told them how through all this, Matt led a normal suburban life; he played tennis and golf. Most of his friends were goal driven and making plans. Matt had goals, but had trouble following through to accomplish them. Still, he was working and part of the family. He never dressed shabbily, and though he ran out of cash quickly, he never stole from his parents. His bedroom door was always open. He never looked like what his parents imagined an addict to be. Yet all the while, it appeared, he led a dual life.

"Was I seeing what I only wanted to see?" said Ellen later. "I might have been."

Shortly after Matt's death, Paul and Ellen Schoonover attended the speech of a motivational speaker with a breakfast group of well-heeled middle-aged couples like themselves. The speaker that day asked them to imagine a second half of their lives about more than just enjoying what they'd accumulated.

"The question was 'How do you take that second half of your life and make something significant from it?'" Paul said when I met the couple in the office of their Columbus insurance agency. "Maybe not a lot of people come to that question. I don't know that I would have. We knew what we were going to do."

Matt's death had led them there. The Schoonovers took it as a calling. They once thought addiction a moral failing, and now understood it as a physical affliction, a disease. They had thought rehabilitation would fix their son. Now they saw relapse was all but inevitable, and that something like two years of treatment and abstinence, followed by a lifetime of 12-step meetings, were needed for recovery.

After kicking opiates, "it takes two years for your dopamine receptors to start working naturally," Paul said. "Nobody told us that. We thought he was fixed because he was coming out of rehab. Kids aren't fixed. It takes years of clean living to the point where they may—they *may*—have a chance. This is a lifelong battle. Had we known, we would never have let Matt alone those first few vulnerable days after rehab. We let him go alone that afternoon to Narcotics Anonymous (NA) his first day out of rehab. He had his new clothes on. He looked good. He was then going to play golf with his friend. Instead of making a right turn to go to the meeting, he made a left turn and he's buying drugs and dying.

"When you start into drugs, your emotional development gets stunted. Matt was twenty-one, but he was at the maturity level of middle-teen years. Drugs take away that ability to act emotionally mature. The drug becomes your god."

The speaker's question that day prompted the Schoonovers to channel their grief. Too many parents were as lost as they'd been. So Paul called Wayne Campbell, hoping to use Matt's story to sound the alarm and prepare parents for what awaited them.

"There was so much evil in all of this," said Ellen Schoonover. "We will turn that into something good. We can embrace it and find meaning from Matt's death."

PART IV

America

Five years after I stood on that Ohio River bank in Huntington, West Virginia, wondering what I was onto, the victims of America's opiate scourge had emerged from the shadow and the silence. They were everywhere now, and known to be so. Heroin had traveled a long way from the back alleys of New York City and William Burroughs's *Junky*. It was even, I discovered as my story wound down, in the upscale pseudo-Spanish subdivisions of terra-cotta tile and palm trees in Southern California not far from where I lived. Especially there.

A half hour from my house, the town of Simi Valley agonized over a spate of opiate overdose deaths—eleven in a year. Simi Valley, conservative and religious, has long been an enclave for cops. Many LAPD officers live in the town. Simi's vice mayor is a Los Angeles police officer. So for years Simi was one of America's safest towns. According to the crime statistics, it still is. But with pills everywhere and heroin sold in high schools, its kids were now also dying of dope. Simi youths clogged the methadone clinic. Nearby Thousand Oaks, Moorpark, and Santa Clarita told similar stories.

Low crime and high fatal overdose rates—this was the new American paradigm. A happy surface over an ominous reality.

"We came to this safe city and we're doing everything society's asked us to do and yet here we are burying our kids," said Susan Klimusko, whose son, Austin, died from a heroin overdose.

Klimusko and others in Simi formed a coalition to fight back, Not One More, supported by the city council and the town's retail core: Starbucks, California Pizza Kitchen, Home Depot, Subway, and others.

Yet these were times when heroin was still invisible, conveniently hidden away, at least to anyone who wasn't a junkie, or a parent of one. Then on Super Bowl Sunday 2014, America awoke to the news that one of its finest actors was dead.

Philip Seymour Hoffman, forty-six, was found that morning in his

Greenwich Village apartment, a syringe in his arm and powder heroin in packets branded with the Ace of Spades near his corpse. Blood tests showed he had heroin in his system, combined with cocaine, amphetamine, and benzodiazepine. The Oscar-winning actor—a father of three—had checked into rehab the previous May for ten days, and then, pronouncing himself sober again, left to resume a hectic film schedule. Just as the death of Rock Hudson thirty years ago forced the country to recognize AIDS, Hoffman's death awoke it to the opiate epidemic.

Within days, media outlets from coast to coast discovered that thousands of people were dying. Heroin abuse, the news reports insisted, was surging. Almost all the new heroin addicts were hooked first on prescription painkillers. This was not new; it had been happening for fifteen years. And there was more to it than drugs. This scourge was, I believed, connected to the conflation of big forces: of economics and marketing, of poverty and prosperity. But this was tough to articulate in four-minute interviews and a lot of it got lost in the media's rush to discover the new plague. Attorney General Eric Holder described an "urgent and growing public health crisis" and called on police and paramedics to carry naloxone, an effective antidote to opiate overdose.

By then, though, a lot about this story had already been changing.

Two decades into the pain revolution, a consensus had emerged that opiates were unhelpful, even risky, for some varieties of chronic pain— back pain, headaches, and fibromyalgia among them. Several clinics and doctors I spoke with had policies against using them for those ailments. One 2007 survey of studies of back pain and opiates found that "use disorders" were common among patients, and "aberrant" use behavior occurred in up to 24 percent of the cases. It was unclear, the authors found, whether opiates had an effect on back pain in the long term.

By the end of the 2000s, it was already common for people to go from abusing OxyContin to a heroin habit. Purdue Pharma recognized this and in 2010 reformulated OxyContin with an abuse deterrent, making the drug harder to deconstruct and inject. The intent was to make Oxy less abusable. It did. Had the company done this in 1996, our story might have been different. But now there was a swollen population of OxyContin addicts nationwide. Without Oxy, they flocked to heroin in even greater numbers.

Fast-food restaurants developed a heroin problem. Across the country, people were using their convenient bathrooms as places to shoot up. There, locked in isolation, many overdosed and died. In Boston, the problem got so bad that the city's public health commission asked fast-food workers to do periodic bathroom checks, and began training workers to notice the signs of overdose: a person's slowed breathing, or lips turning blue.

Alabama now had heroin. Mississippi and southern Louisiana did, too. Rural towns in Indiana and Oregon were bad. Eastern Idaho, North Dakota, and Wyoming were, too. West Virginia saw fatal heroin overdoses triple in five years; Cabell County, where Huntington is located, had the highest number in 2012, with twenty-six people dying from too much heroin. Local media from Upstate New York and Minneapolis ran large and continuing stories about heroin. The *Albuquerque Journal* reported an 80 percent increase in heroin use in New Mexico. The Ohio River valley and Salt Lake City were swimming in it. Heroin was all over New Hampshire and Vermont, and Vermont governor Peter Shumlin dedicated his entire 2014 state of the state speech to the new plague.

Heroin had spread to most corners of the country because the rising sea level of opiates flowed there first. The story resembled the heroin scourge a century before, ushered in on the prescription pads of physicians, the vast majority of whom were sincere in intent. Drug traffickers only arrived later, and took far less profit than did the companies that made the legitimate drugs that started it all. "What started as an OxyContin and prescription drug addiction problem in Vermont has now grown into a full-blown heroin crisis," Governor Shumlin said.

What made New York City the dominant heroin market for so much of the twentieth century—its vast number of addicts, its immigrants, and its proximity to poppy-growing countries—was now true of most of America. Most of the country's heroin was coming from Mexico, and thus through the Southwest, trucked into New York, not arriving on ships from Asia. New York functioned now as more of a regional hub than the nation's central heroin distribution point it once was.

The pharmaceutical industry's sales force arms race ended. Pfizer, Merck, Lilly, and others laid off thousands. One U.S. trade publication suggested that 2014—with sales rep employment down from 110,000 people to 60,000 nationwide—might be the year when the "pharma salesperson really begins his slow walk to extinction." Patents on blockbuster drugs had expired. The image of sales reps walking the halls of hospitals and medical offices, cornering doctors with "the opportunity to 'present, respond and close the deal' is very likely going to be limited," the article lamented.

The arms race left behind massive lawsuits and criminal cases for misbranding and false advertising. Purdue was hardly the only company to have been sued. Its $634.5 million fine was soon dwarfed. Pfizer alone paid more than $3 billion in fines and legal penalties to settle lawsuits alleging, among other things, the misbranding and false advertising of several drugs. That included $2.3 billion to settle a criminal suit in 2009 alleging the company illegally marketed its blockbuster painkiller Bextra. The sum was the largest criminal fine of any kind, though it amounted to less than three weeks of the company's sales, the *New York Times* observed.

Various agencies had tempered their initial enthusiasm where opiate pain treatment was concerned.

The JCAHO was now promoting multidisciplinary approaches to pain, including more healthy behavior, psychological support, and non-opiate medications, along with the education of patients on the addiction risks of opiates. So presumably Vicodin and similar drugs would no longer be prescribed without a word as to what they contained. The FDA was now requiring drug companies to provide patients and doctors with education on addiction risks from timed-release opiate painkillers—a common-sense extension of the patients rights movement, though one that came inexplicably late.

The FDA, meanwhile, reclassified Vicodin from a Schedule III drug to a more restrictive Schedule II. It also denied approval of a generic timed-release form of oxycodone—a no-name OxyContin. But then it approved Zohydro, a timed-release pill similar to OxyContin, containing as much as 50 mg of hydrocodone per pill, though without acetaminophen or anything else to deter abuse. The agency's own advisory committee of pain specialists recommended against Zohydro, and was overruled.

Purdue followed that with an announcement that the company would soon seek FDA approval for its own timed-release hydrocodone pill—though this one would include an abuse deterrent. The FDA approved another Purdue drug, Targiniq ER, which combines timed-release oxycodone with naloxone, the opiate-overdose antidote. OxyContin sales, meanwhile, kept rising. Within a few years of the criminal case brought against the company by John Brownlee's prosecutors in Abingdon, Virginia, *Fortune* reported, Purdue was selling $3.1 billion worth of the drug a year.

At the same time, though, many doctors now seemed to eschew opiate painkillers as energetically as they had embraced them a few years before. Patients who truly needed low-dose opiate treatment for their pain were having difficulty finding anyone to prescribe it.

Primary care docs still didn't have the time, and many hadn't the preparation, to effectively treat chronic-pain patients. That wasn't about to change. In fact, fewer medical students were going into primary care—repelled by long hours, the modest money, and the lack of respect. One study estimated the country would need fifty-two thousand more primary care docs by 2025.

A commentary by four doctors and researchers in the American Journal of Public Health in September 2014 insisted that "It is difficult to believe that the parallel rise in prescriptions and associated harms is mere correlation without causation. [Also] it is difficult to believe that the problem is solely attributable to patients with already existing substance use disorders." They went on, "Appropriate medical use of prescription opioidscan, in some unknown proportion of cases, initiate a progression toward misuse and ultimately addiction . . . Even if an initial exposure is insufficient to cause addiction directly, perhaps it is sufficient to trigger initial misuse that could ultimately lead to addiction."

Pain may well help lessen the euphoria of opiates, as the pain crusaders had contended. Yet the authors noted how little was known about pain and addiction—both enormously complicated topics. Medicine still lacked the tools, they wrote, to identify who was at risk of addiction from properly prescribed opiate painkillers. Nor was there much knowledge of how, in treating pain, to balance that risk with the benefit of relief in patients showing signs of sliding into abuse of these drugs. What little knowledge existed, moreover, had not made it into medical-school training; certainly not to the degree that the pain crusaders, aided by drug companies, had changed medical-school curriculum with "selected evidence" of the benefits of opiate painkillers, the authors wrote.

After more than a decade in which chronic pain was treated with highly addictive medicine, there still was no attempt to bring the studies of pain and addiction together. Specialists in pain and in addiction operated in different worlds. They appeared not to know each other socially. They saw the same patients; a pain patient now might soon be an addict, after all. But there were no conferences where they shared ideas. No journal combined both specialties. Nor could I find any study that attempted to measure this crucial question: How many people grew addicted to pills they were prescribed?

I felt for doctors. Prescribe and they risked a patient growing addicted. Don't prescribe and a patient may have to live with crushing pain. Patient evaluations nipped at their heels. It was a minefield. No wonder so few young doctors were going into primary care.

Multidisciplinary pain clinics were seeing a rebirth, however. Their menu of services had been shown to help many chronic-pain patients over time. Agencies with a financial interest in their patients' long-term improvement were turning to it. Above all, the Veterans Health Administration, once a promoter of opiate therapy for chronic pain, had been turning around. Pain as the fifth vital sign was no longer gospel.

"Opioids are effective pain medication. They do work. But a pill is just not always the answer," said Dr. Gavin West, a top VHA clinician.

After years of watching too many vets with chronic pain become bedeviled by addiction as well, the VHA was opening multidisciplinary pain clinics. The clinics included physical therapy, acupuncture, massage, and swimming-pool therapy, as well as social workers and psychological counselors to help vets suffering chronic pain also find work and housing and resolve marital problems. The VHA has seventy of these clinics around the country, as I write. The numbers of their high-dose opiate patients have fallen dramatically. The goal was to get patients back on their feet, going to work and their kids' soccer games.

"To do those things, you have to approach the patients holistically. We not only have a financial stake, but an ethical stake in this, too," West said. "We're lucky, though. We have the advantage of taking the long view. A lot of [insurance] medical systems don't have that. They'll pay for what helps a person over a couple years. What happens in ten years is probably the next insurance company's problem. If your economic driver is 'I'm going to see a patient for ten minutes and bill them'—that's a bad driver. People who can take a long view are at an advantage to treating a patient holistically."

Insurance companies, notably, have not found the same virtue in multidisciplinary care. But the VHA has figured a more balanced approach to pain will improve patient function while lowering treatment costs in the long run. Their clients, after all, will be with them forever.

I NEVER WAS ABLE to speak with Russell Portenoy. In an e-mail, he politely declined my interview request. However, weeks before that, a remarkably frank interview with him was included in a video released by PROP—Physicians for Responsible Opioid Prescribing.

In the interview, Portenoy acknowledged that as he urged the more liberal use of opiates for chronic pain, he gave many lectures to primary care doctors citing Porter and Jick and several other papers.

None of the papers, he said, "represented real evidence, and yet what I was trying to do was to create a narrative so that the primary care audience would look at this information *in toto* and feel more comfort about opioids in a way they hadn't before. In essence this was education to destigmatize [opioids] and because the primary goal was to destigmatize, we often left evidence behind.

"Clearly, if I had an inkling of what I know now then, I wouldn't have spoken in the way that I spoke. It was clearly the wrong thing to do and to the extent that some of the adverse outcomes now are as bad as they have become in terms of endemic occurrences of addiction and unintentional overdose deaths, it's quite scary to think about how the growth in that prescribing driven by people like me led, in part, to that occurring."

The Treatment Is You

Washington State

Out in Washington State, Jaymie Mai and Gary Franklin continued chronicling the effects of what Franklin called "the worst man-made epidemic in history, made by organized medicine."

Washington addicts in treatment for opiates had skyrocketed through the 2000s from about six hundred to a conservatively estimated eighty-six hundred by 2010. Most were young, suburban, and white. Overdose deaths in the state rose to 512 in 2008.

In 2008, L&I issued its guidelines to doctors aimed to limit opiate prescribing. Overdose deaths had declined since then and by 2012 they stood at 388. The numbers of injured workers dying from overdoses—which had so startled Jaymie Mai years before when she was new to her job—had kept rising, up to thirty-two in 2009; but since the prescribing guidelines came out, the number had been cut in half. So, too, had the numbers of injured workers who ended up as chronic opiate users.

I went up to Seattle, where the Multidisciplinary Pain Center traced its lineage back to John Bonica, the former pro wrestler and pain pioneer. Dr. David Tauben was now its director. Years ago, Tauben was an eager opiate prescriber. He taught the purported message of Porter and Jick. He cheered the introduction of higher-dose OxyContin. Then he watched patients fail to improve. They became disgruntled, demanding ever-higher doses.

During these years, he remembered an applicant to the center's pain fellowship program who was asked why he wanted the post. I want a Bentley, the applicant replied.

"That to me is a metaphor for where pain management is," Tauben told me.

Having changed his mind about opiates, Tauben came to work at the clinic when Alex Cahana took over. Cahana's new approach was to try to get back to the old approach: treat the social and psychological roots of pain, along with the biological. The center staff now included two psychiatrists, three psychologists, a vocational counselor, as well as doctors in family, internal, and rehab medicine.

A generation of doctors had been urged to consider pain the fifth vital sign. "It's just wrong," Tauben said. "I'd say fifteen percent of my patients are probably much better off by being on opiates, but at low or moderate doses."

Tauben took over for Cahana in 2013. Cahana's five years at the center immersed him in America's pain culture wars. The experience had made him something of a philosopher of pain and happiness. Cahana believed that what insurance companies reimbursed for distilled many unfortunate values of the country.

"We overtest, perform surgery, stick needles; these people are worse off," he said. "If we work on their nutrition, diet, sleep habits, smoke habits, helping [them] find work—then they improve. You have to be accountable. If you give a treatment that kills people or makes people worse, you gotta stop. You can't continue making money on stuff that doesn't work."

Cahana saw "stuff" as the problem. Our reverence for technology blinded us to more holistic solutions. "We got to the moon, invented the Internet. We can do anything. It's inconceivable to think there are problems that don't have a technological solution. To go from 'I can do anything' to 'I deserve everything' is very quick.

"All of a sudden, we can't go to college without Adderall; you can't do athletics without testosterone; you can't have intimacy without Viagra. We're all the time focused on the stuff and not on the people. I tell pain patients, 'Forget all that; the treatment is you. Take charge of your life and be healthy and do what you love and love what you do.'"

And he ignored that very advice. Cahana came to Seattle at 260 pounds, and gained forty-five more over the next five years as, stressed and overworked, he battled to rebuild the historic clinic. The clinic won numerous awards, was highlighted as a model. He was on CNN and in *People* magazine, gave a TED talk, and testified before the U.S. Senate on overprescribing in medicine. He grew fatter all the while. He was taking medications for hypertension, cholesterol, and then more for the side effects from the medication—nine pills a day, fifteen hundred dollars a month in co-pays.

"I couldn't walk two flights of stairs without huffing and puffing," he said.

His own doctor was about to prescribe something for elevated blood sugar when Cahana had enough. He seemed to be living like an addict.

He had spent years trying to change public policy, influence academia, and shape legislation on the overprescribing of pills for pain. Now he decided to become the change.

He resigned from the clinic. He is now a consultant to low-income communities on health issues. He went on a regimen of healthy eating and daily training of running, strength conditioning, and yoga. His pills became gradually unnecessary. He lost 110 pounds and runs marathons.

The U.S. medical system is good at fighting disease, Cahana believes, and awful at leading people to wellness.

"They don't know how to do it and the path they offer actually makes people worse."

IN 2013, THE COMMITTEE that John Rockefeller Jr. formed to search for the Holy Grail of a nonaddictive painkiller turned seventy-five.

Its annual conference was at San Diego's Bayfront Hilton under impossibly azure June skies. The seminars took place in darkened conference rooms. Speakers presented data in voices muted by thick carpets.

I attended because I wanted to understand what had become of the search for the Holy Grail. The search for a nonaddictive alternative to opiates had a fairly spotty historical record. It had produced drugs, many of which were once believed, incorrectly, to be nonaddictive: Demerol, nalbuphine, Talwin. But this was the oft-repeated story, as humankind sought heaven without hell. The companies that first manufactured heroin thought it was nonaddictive and marketed it that way. A hundred years later, so did the company that made OxyContin. Maybe this was just nature's way of saying that we can't have it all.

The committee was now known as the College on Problems of Drug Dependence. It had expanded and more CPDD researchers studied addiction treatment. At the conference, I had a beer with Andy Coop, the University of Maryland chemist, who was nice enough to take the time to explain his fascination with the morphine molecule and how it worked.

Drugs that contained variations on the molecule were "damned good at being painkillers," he said. "We are working to find other drugs that are as good, without the undesired effects. My call is it's not going to happen. We have been using morphine clinically for a hundred years and we'll be using it a hundred years from now. I'm not going to say it's never going to happen, but I don't see how it's going to happen."

Then, as if thinking out loud, he added, "If we could only stop the euphoria but not the analgesia, I think we would actually have what I would call the Holy Grail."

Among the conference throngs was Martin Adler, a professor of pharmacology at Temple University. Adler had been a member of the CPDD since the 1960s.

"Virtually all of us, and certainly me, believe the chances of finding the Holy Grail drug are slim to none," Adler told me. "People keep looking and industry keeps looking."

I asked Adler if he thought such a drug was even desirable. Can humans handle having it all? After all, Americans had it all for a brief time and many of the kids who benefited most from the country's embarrassment of riches had turned to drugs used to numb pain.

Perhaps not, Adler allowed. Morphine was, he said, a great metaphor for life. "The bad effects of morphine act to minimize the use of the drug, which is a good thing. There are people born without pain receptors. [Living without pain] is a horrible thing. They die young because pain is the greatest signaling mechanism we have."

Adler believed the lesson of the last fifteen years was that the conception of pain needed to change.

"I don't think you're going to find one treatment for pain," he said. "You don't use one drug to treat all cancers; if you do it's because you don't know how to treat [each cancer] specifically. I think where we're headed is to find the most effective treatments for different kinds of pain. Chronic back pain, neuropathic pain—we just don't know enough about them. That may be because pain isn't a single disease.

"The body is incredible," he went on. "The most amazing thing we can imagine. What you do learn is that there is nothing that's so isolated from everything else that you can just attack that. Everything is tied to everything else. When you're dealing with the brain, they all intersect."

I called Nathaniel Katz, the pain specialist in Boston. In the years since his patient Peter's death and his encounter with Peter's sister, Katz had come to see the foibles of human nature at work in all this.

"My instructors told me that when you take opioids for pain you can't become addicted because pain absorbs the euphoria. That was at Harvard Medical School. It was all rubbish, we all know now. Why do we listen to those messages? Because we wanted them to be true."

I told him I had spoken with people who pointed to Foley and Portenoy's 1986 paper in the journal *Pain*, and then to Portenoy's funding from pharmaceutical companies, including Purdue Pharma, as he traveled the country urging doctors to adopt a new view and use of opiate painkillers. These critics saw the potential for a conflict of interest.

One of them was Andrew Kolodny, a physician who watched the epidemic unfold from his addiction specialty in Brooklyn. Kolodny later cofounded Physicians for Responsible Opioid Prescribing, an organization of doctors critical of the new opiate prescribing.

Portenoy "starts lecturing around the country as a religious-like figure," Kolodny said. "The megaphone for Portenoy is Purdue, which flies in people to resorts to hear him speak. It was a compelling message: 'Docs have been letting patients suffer; nobody really gets addicted; it's been studied.'

"[Purdue] created organizations that were meant to look grassroots. They gave loads of money to front organizations, which approached state medical boards about liberalizing regulations for prescribing. Every effort to control the problem, if it ended in less prescribing, you had all these groups saying what you're going to do is bad for pain patients.

"You now have an industry of pain specialists and this is their business model: They have a practice of patients who'll never miss an appointment and who pay in cash. The whole thing is really outrageous."

Katz, however, saw another story at work. Katz admired Portenoy, who, he said, had spent a career searching for better ways to relieve his patients' real and considerable pain. Portenoy had helped make pain a topic of research. Moreover, Portenoy was always clear that pain treatment needed balance and time; doctors needed to be selective in the patients who received this treatment.

But "people want simple solutions," Katz said. "People didn't want to hear that and the commercial interests didn't want to emphasize that."

Meanwhile, Katz said, physicians everywhere faced insistent patients who felt entitled to relief. "You're standing there with keys to the opioid cabinet. Suffering is certainly real," he said. "For years, the doctor has had to say, 'I wish I could give them to you, but they're addictive; you can overdose. I want to but I can't.' The keys to the kingdom were there but the doctor as gatekeeper could not in good conscience open them."

In this context, Portenoy and Foley's 1986 paper became influential because, Katz said. "[It] was telling doctors what they already wanted to hear: 'Your patients are suffering. Aren't we so much smarter than scientists of many years ago? Now we know that if you take [opioids] for chronic pain, you can't get addicted.'

"You had a new priesthood that emerged, a priesthood of prescribing opioids for chronic pain and a small number of pharmaceutical companies collaborating with these doctors. These companies had these tools—these new drugs. Doctors were being told by the mechanics—the pain specialists—that the tools worked. I think it's more useful to look at people as fundamentally reasonable—looking at why they did the things they did. You had a whole bunch of reasonable people doing what they thought reasonable and it didn't work well."

As Katz spoke, I thought back on all I'd heard and seen and thought it remarkable that all this could be part of the story behind why a town in Nayarit, Mexico, was now selling gobs of heroin in some of the wealthiest and safest places in America. I told him that I thought it just as bizarre that all that reasoning he referred to could, in some measure, hinge on the misinterpretation of a one-paragraph letter to the editor of the *New England Journal of Medicine* in January 1980 written by Dr. Hershel Jick, who intended nothing of the sort.

"Porter and Jick is amazing for the absence of information in it," Katz said. "[But] that paragraph gives you relief from your inner conflict. It's like drinking from the breast. All of a sudden the comfort washes over you."

The Internet of Dope

Central Valley of California

I might be down in Mexico next time you come through," the Man said to me one morning as I sat again in his living room in California's Central Valley.

He slouched in his easy chair, skullcap over gray hair, smiling hazily through the anemia, a once-handsome face now pale and without the bronze gleam it once possessed. He stared out the screen door of the home his family bought for twenty-two thousand dollars years ago, and onto the street of cracked asphalt, prim lawns, and working-class stucco houses.

We'd spoken for hours on my visits over many months since his release from the years in prison that he served for his part in Operation Tar Pit. He had a gripping story of how heroin dealers from one small Mexican town spread black tar to new markets across the United States. I spent hours in his presence, listening to his faint voice speak slowly of the past.

Much of what he said I knew to be true or found ways of confirming. His knowledge of Xalisco was detailed; so, too, his knowledge of methadone clinics in cities of America. The rest sounded entirely plausible. But in the underworld, as many people want to exaggerate what they've done as want to hide it. So I didn't know what to believe until I tracked down a DEA agent who'd worked Operation Tar Pit from the beginning. He confirmed the Man's role, which he knew from listening to endless hours of wiretaps.

"He expanded the organization's network into other cities, especially into cities where there wasn't any competition," the agent said. "He would target methadone clinics where they'd find a client base and build upon it."

Now, fifteen years later, the crews the Man had set up were still dealing misery. Countless young men from Xalisco, Nayarit, were doing long federal prison terms.

Xalisco avoided the notice of Mexico's drug cartels for a long time. After all, what did cartel traffickers care about crews that sold a kilo of heroin at a time? In 2010, however, the Zetas and the Sinaloa Cartel went to war in southern Sinaloa. The violence spread south and engulfed tiny Xalisco, Nayarit. The results were predictable. Dead bodies appeared here and there. In one shootout, eleven people were killed, including Jose Luis Estrada, known as El Pepino, the Cucumber, a reputed local drug boss. Xalisco officials spoke of canceling the Feria del Elote and the State Department warned Americans against traveling to Tepic. Cell leaders, who'd already been moving to Guadalajara, moved there even faster; they kept a low profile and couldn't live in the houses they'd spent so much heroin money building.

This went on for more than a year until it appears the Zetas triumphed. Cell leaders began paying protection to the cartel and things calmed down.

The flow of Xalisco black tar into the cities of America never slowed, however. East of the Mississippi, Xalisco drivers tormented Nashville, Memphis, Indianapolis, several cities in South Carolina, Cincinnati, Charlotte, and, of course, Columbus, and the suburbs for miles around each city.

In Florence, Kentucky, narcotics officers arrested a cell of Sánchez family operators, including one local woman who'd been a go-between for the family in Nashville during Operation Black Gold Rush in 2006. The cell had been using only local white drivers to deliver heroin, providing them with cars and cell phones—presumably because it could no longer find laborers back home to do the job.

Apparently a rumor spread around Xalisco that the commonwealth states (Kentucky, Pennsylvania, Virginia, and Massachusetts) had more lenient drug laws. Several Xalisco drivers had been arrested in Weymouth, Massachusetts, a suburb of Boston.

The Boys remained decentralized, resilient, and adaptable. They embodied America's opiate epidemic: they were quiet, nonviolent. They focused on new opiate markets where the only customers they wanted were the white people. They were, it seemed to me, the Internet of dope, a drug delivery system for the twenty-first century, working in as many as twenty-five states, and all of this coming out of one small town in Mexico. These drivers had their own addiction nipping at their heels. It was the ranchero's dream to return home a king, to pay the banda, to dance with the girls, to see other men's envy, and to feel the embrace of their families as they opened boxes containing precious Levi's 501s and designer jeans. Meanwhile, the local government noted in a report that Xalisco was the 111th wealthiest of Mexico's 2,445 counties (municipios).

The Xalisco crews owed a good part of their success to the prescription pill addiction that was now in every corner of the United States. Whether any of them knew this is an interesting question. I knew drivers who'd never heard the name OxyContin. This made sense to me; they spoke no English and socialized only with other drivers. I also spoke, though, with Harry Sommers, the DEA honcho who'd coordinated the Tar Pit investigations years before. Maybe the Xalisco peons knew nothing, Sommers said. But, he told me, "we know from information provided by members of these Nayarit networks and other intelligence that some of them were well aware of painkiller abuse and targeted areas where they believed it was rampant and knowing those areas would be fertile ground for their product."

Whatever the Xalisco Boys knew, the way they flogged black tar heroin early on combined with the aggresive marketing of pain pills in virgin territories then forming into the OxyContin Belt to create catastrophic synergy, and presaged the transition from pills to heroin that would happen in the rest of the country years later. Kids who started on pills ended up alone and dead in their cars, slaves to a molecule. The forces set up to insist people consume it were as relentless as the molecule itself. Pills had been prescribed with wanton carelessness. Then black tar heroin from the Nayarit mountains was sold to them like pizza. More and more parents continued on without their children. They suffered pain as chronic and life mangling as any those doctors and Purdue Pharma decided should be treated with opiate pills.

A lot was changing for the Xalisco Boys. By 2014, heroin trafficking was expanding dramatically across America, with new dealers, many of them addicts, getting in on the action every day. None had the Xalisco Boys' franchised heroin delivery system; nevertheless, they gnawed at markets the Boys had been cultivating for years, and they found new ones full of pill addicts ready to switch. The potency of brown powder heroin, from other regions of Mexico and sold by black gangs out of Detroit and the East Coast, was getting stronger. The Sinaloa Cartel seemed to have massively upped its heroin exports to Chicago and New York City and elsewhere. Heroin seizures at the U.S.-Mexico border had risen sixfold since 2007.

Back in Xalisco, meanwhile, an incipient avocado industry was overtaking sugarcane and coffee, and providing work for many. The industry dates to about 2009 when growers from the state of Michoacán,

Mexico's avocado center, brought money and partnered with local farmers to plant avocado orchards. By 2014, those orchards were bearing fruit. The coffee warehouse where David Tejeda was gunned down was now an avocado warehouse. Many of the young men who applied for jobs were those who'd been arrested and served prison terms in the United States for selling heroin. Now with a criminal record, they faced lengthy prison terms if they were caught again up north. So they were turning to work in the avocado industry.

Still the town continued to live from tar heroin revenue in one way or another. Hundreds, perhaps even thousands, of men from Xalisco County had gone north to sell heroin. Cars with U.S. license plates were common around town. Mostly they bore plates from California, Ohio, North Carolina, Utah, Colorado, and Oregon, and many of the vehicles had been used to hide and move large amounts of cash back home. Yet few men from Xalisco seemed substantially better off. Cell owners did well. But heroin-cell workers remained tied to a cycle of boom or bust, spending money with ostentation, then having to return to the U.S. to work some more. In the Landarenas and Tres Puntos neighborhoods, the money's effect was hard to see, other than in the men who hung out on street corners drinking and using cocaine. Several streets there were still unpaved.

Little of the drug trade lucre trickled back to the Man anymore. "I don't ask them for nothing," he told me. "I hope they make a lot of money. As long as they acknowledge me when I'm over there. I just want respect. That's all. I don't tell them 'You owe me,' or 'If it wasn't for me you wouldn't have this.' They earned what they got."

He had used the cartel peace in Xalisco to return for Christmas. He saw many of the older guys. Some were still going hard. Others were barely getting by. The onetime black tar wholesaler, Oscar Hernandez-Garcia—Mosca—was back in Xalisco with his wife. He and his brothers were rumored to own the local rodeo arena at the entrance to town. The Man had seen the Nayarit, his friend from the Nevada prison and partner in his first heroin cells. During the cartel conflicts, masked gunmen broke into the Nayarit's home while he and his family were out and took the television, jewelry, and a lot more. They brought a trailer to the robbery and made off with prized horses that he often rode in the parade through town.

The Man came back to California. Here in the Central Valley, he was frail and anonymous. None of his neighbors knew the story of the heroin cells of Xalisco, Nayarit. So he spoke often of going home for good—to Xalisco, his adopted town, the big rancho, where families knew all he had done for them.

That looked unlikely. Life as a drug merchant, from the pills in Tijuana in the 1960s to the countless kilos of black tar, had left him slouched, gray, and weak with liver problems. As we talked that morning, his body seemed to slowly deflate into the chair. A wide television and a lamp on a stand stood nearby. His speech grew faint and slurred. His eyelids fell to half-mast.

"You never apologize for what you are. I don't. I did what I did," he said, grazing a palm down his face. "I never intentionally set out to hurt anybody. Payback's a sonofabitch, but, what the hell, you live with it."

ONE FRIDAY MORNING MONTHS later, I sit in a Columbus, Ohio, courtroom.

The room is so crowded that it looks at first like it could be traffic court, except that almost everyone is young and white. Guys in backward baseball hats and splotchy whiskers. Girls with fading dye jobs, designer jeans, and rhinestone-studded sweatshirts.

This is heroin court.

Fifteen years ago, the Man brought black tar heroin to Columbus. The city became the jumping-off point for the expansion of the Xalisco Boys' system through large parts of the eastern half of the United States just as prescription pills were accepted in medicine as "virtually nonaddictive" when used to treat pain.

Now, in a city that once never had heroin, almost every seat in heroin court is filled.

All are junkies, most started on pills, and three quarters of them use black tar heroin.

Judge Scott VanDerKarr annually handles about four hundred heroin addicts convicted of nonviolent felonies dropped to misdemeanors, which the clients are trying expunge. A few months back, this court was standing room only. VanDerKarr finally divided the court and extended the hours to accommodate the demand. The early two-hour session is for people whose last names begin with *A* through *L*. *M* through *Z* come later in the morning.

Franklin County has several specialized courts—one for veterans, and one for people with mental health problems. There's even a drug court—for offenders with drug- and alcohol-related crimes. But heroin users overwhelm them all. This weekly court was formed in 2010. But even it couldn't contain the demand. In another court, for prostitutes, almost half the women are also heroin addicts.

VanDerKarr wears a black robe and sits high on the bench, and a very large gavel is mounted on the wall behind him. But the atmosphere is relaxed, resembling a group meeting more than court. A table to one side offers stacks of brochures about treatment centers and drug and mental health resources for veterans. VanDerKarr calls several clients before him, applauds their days clean, and asks about their job searches and whether they have 12-step sponsors. Each must seek counseling, submit to random drug tests, and attend ninety NA meetings in ninety days. After that, they attend his session every week for up to two years. Almost half finish the program. But many relapse; some die.

VanDerKarr is a former prosecutor with almost twenty years on the bench. He counts himself one of Franklin County's more understanding magistrates. But years in heroin court have also taught him that addicts, like children, need clear limits and consequences.

"What it's taught me is that jail is actually a good thing" for those who relapse, he tells me after court adjourns. "I mean, give them a consequence of a couple weeks or thirty days. A lot of time it takes maybe two of those" to motivate them.

THE FEAR OF INCARCERATION pushed Robert Berardinelli after his arrest in Operation Tar Pit in Santa Fe.

After more than a year in which he put Xalisco Boys cars and apartments in his name, Berardinelli was given probation by a judge who threatened him with a long prison sentence if he didn't get clean. With that, he finally kicked. He spent a couple years as a counselor in a treatment center. He spoke weekly at a jail and kept on though many people weren't listening. Years later, Berardinelli was a leader in NA and a delegate to the group's 2014 international convention in Southern California, where we met.

"There's no logical reason why I should be sitting right here and not in some federal penitentiary. I'm so blessed that I got out of it and never did time," he said as we sat near a fountain outside a hotel in the San Fernando Valley, only a few miles from where the Xalisco Boys got their start. "I believe in the power of the twelve steps. It's why I'm here right now. It's tailor-made for people like me."

Neither Santa Fe nor New Mexico had escaped the opiate plague. Crews of Nayarit black tar vendors had rotated through Santa Fe and northern New Mexico. In the Española Valley, pills had combined with heroin. In 2012, the local newspaper reported, the area set an overdose-death record. "We remain firmly at the top of the national list for drug overdose deaths per capita," an editorial stated.

The number of kids involved had alarmed Berardinelli and changed the makeup of NA in his region. Now the discussion within the organization was how to reach these youngsters. This had been happening in 12-step groups across America, from Portsmouth to Portland. Grizzled, veteran recovering addicts in their fifties and sixties were seeing their sparsely populated NA meetings overwhelmed with kids in their twenties, enough so that special meetings were created for the new opiate addicts.

I asked if he ever wondered what became of the boss called Enrique and the drivers who gave him all his dope. Not really, he said. It seemed so long ago. But he felt no rancor. They were nice guys, clean-cut, not killers, just working-class boys trying to get ahead and were probably living back in Mexico somewhere. He marveled that they were the only dealers he'd encountered in forty years doing heroin who didn't use their product. He was still startled at how organized they were. After Tar Pit, he remembered, there was no dope on Santa Fe streets for exactly one day. *That's* how organized they were.

He vividly remembered the moment early that morning fourteen years before when DEA agent Jim Kuykendall and his team rolled up to arrest him. Their indictment held a dozen Mexican names and his. They had phone bills and car titles in his name. Berardinelli was gaunt, pocked, scabbed, and worn-out. He could lie no more.

Kuykendall led him to a patrol car in handcuffs.

"This is the first day of the rest of your life," the agent said as he put him in the car.

It took a while, but Robert Berardinelli came to see that as the truth. He was now a grandfather and felt lucky to have survived decades of enslavement. At his request, I passed a message from him to Kuykendall.

"Jim Kuykendall saved my life," Berardinelli said. "For years now, I've wanted to just say, 'Hey, man, thank you.'"

OUT IN PORTLAND, FOLLOWING the death of her brother, Toviy, Elina Sinyayev assured her parents she had cleaned up. She was actually using more than ever. She was rarely at home, escaping Toviy's memory and her own responsibility in his death.

One night, her father came to her room, knowing something was wrong. They had never understood each other. As he sat down, he took her purse from the chair and heard metal clinking. Inside, he found two heroin spoons.

She expected rage. Instead, his eyes grew teary. For the first time in her life, he pleaded with her.

"Elina, you need help," he said.

Elina broke down and cried, too. That night, rushing to heroin, she texted a friend and asked for money. The friend texted back, "No, but I know a church. It's different."

A Russian Pentecostal junkie named John Tkach had started a rehabilitation clinic in the Portland suburb of Boring. Tkach saw the Russian Pentecostal churches trying to hide the sight of hundreds of addicted kids. Parents who asked a pastor's help with their addicted child were shamed as running a sinful house. Tkach sold his trucking business, took out a second mortgage on his house, and opened a rehabilitation center. A church formed around it, the first to make the rampant opiate addiction of Russian Pentecostal kids the focus of its ministry. God Will Provide, as the new church was called, rested on Jesus's message of love, forgiveness, and transformation. Traditional Russian pastors called it blasphemy and sinful. Russian Pentecostal kids called it the Rehab Church. But soon God Will Provide had spread its church/rehab center model to Sacramento, Seattle, and elsewhere.

There, Elina met Vitaliy Mulyar. Vitaliy had crashed since those heady days when he was one of the first Russians to sell OxyContin in Portland. In 2010, Vitaliy faced a two-year prison term if he failed another probation drug test. Terrified, he turned to God Will Provide, where he felt warmth in church for the first time. He kicked heroin, became a Bible teacher, and, with a judge's permission, went on a mission to the Ukraine and Austria as the church, fired by the new energy of its recovering-addict congregants, opened a school for missionaries.

A year into his recovery, Vitaliy encountered Elina at the center. He told her his story. She mistrusted her own capacity to change. But it struck her, the way he had risen from the street. A chaste romance followed, in keeping with Russian Pentecostal tradition, though with a modern American twist. They grew acquainted via hundreds of texts while he was on mission. Vitaliy came home and asked Elina to marry him before they ever kissed.

Two years later, their daughter was born. They named her Grace.

Nobody Can Do It Alone

Southern Ohio

On March 26, 2013, Dr. Phillip Prior died of liver cancer in a hospice in Lancaster, Ohio. He was fifty-nine.

As a kid, Prior had wanted to be a paleontologist, a herpetologist, an archaeologist, and a biologist—all before he was ten. He raised snakes. In open rebellion to his father who was insisting he cut his hair, he went to the barbershop and got his head shaved. When his family's church urged blacks in its congregation to find their own church, Prior walked through the corridors yelling that he would never step foot in it again.

His parents prized education above all else. Prior alarmed them by spending the first seven years after high school getting a degree in auto mechanics and learning bicycle repair, and opening a bike shop in Cincinnati.

He finally entered college at twenty-four, got a medical degree from Ohio State, and worked for many years as a family doctor in Chillicothe. Later, as a recovering alcoholic, Prior turned to a specialty in addiction medicine.

He lived on a farm in Stoutsville, Ohio. He built rockets and for several years he and three others held a world record in amateur rocketry—sending a homemade rocket twenty-three miles up in the air above White Sands, Nevada. He loved to hunt. A mountain lion he killed in Wyoming was mounted on his living room wall. His garage was a meeting place for men with a zeal for auto mechanics.

Real family doctors touch lots of people. Two hundred of Prior's friends gathered to remember him a few days after his death. His kids chose to play the Beatles' "Let It Be" and Jimi Hendrix's "The Wind Cries Mary" as mourners comforted the family. At his farm, friends fired up a bronze Chevy van with mag wheels he was working on before he got sick. They met again months later for a hog roast at which his ashes were scattered on the farm. Some of the ashes were shot up into the sky in a homemade rocket, along with messages from friends.

Prior's life had been marbled by addiction, elevated by exploration, and studded by acts of defiance. He drove a simple Toyota Camry and owned a couple suits he rarely wore. But he had been a lonely voice at America's opiate ground zero for his final half-dozen years sounding the alarm about the excessive prescribing of OxyContin as a gateway to heroin. He was one of the first in the region to urge the use of medication in the treatment of addiction—the judicious use of Suboxone, particularly—feeling that abstinence too often led recovering addicts to relapse, and, with low tolerance, to die when they did.

I spoke with Prior on the phone, but never in person. I intended to, but he grew ill. By the time I made it to Ohio, he was in a hospice.

"There'll only be a handful of us who'll ever remember who Dr. Prior is, but in southern Ohio he is the crucial doc," said Orman Hall when we met for lunch, coincidentally a few hours before Prior died. Hall now directed the state's substance abuse program.

Opiate addiction was everywhere in Ohio. I asked Hall how long he thought the country might be living with this generation of opiate addicts. Some Vietnam-era addicts were still using, hanging on forty years later.

"Let's hope we can keep people alive," Hall said. "Our experience is that people go from zero to sixty pretty quickly."

An Ohio State physics honor student Hall had met started out using 10 mg of Percocet recreationally every other day. Eleven months later, he was mainlining a large amount of heroin daily.

Phillip Prior "was the guy who articulated the treatment approach we need to take to deal successfully with this population of opiate addicts," Hall said. "He was the guy who painted the bigger picture of the complicity of Purdue Pharma in starting this epidemic. He was the guy who did it for me.

"The profound irony in all of this is that opiates are providing him with some level of quality of life as he expires."

Indeed, after years fighting prescription opiate abuse and the heroin addiction that followed, Phil Prior, in the weeks before his death, was administered, and grew dependent on, the opiate painkillers that he received from hospice nurses to relieve his considerable pain. He even called a doctor to intervene when hospice nurses wouldn't up his dose.

"He's ending his life opiate dependent," Hall said. "There's an appropriate role for opiates in our health care system and how they're being used for Dr. Prior is a prime example of how they need to be used."

*   *   *

MILES NORTH, IN THE town of Marion, Brad Belcher's guerrilla tactics had ignited a discussion. One person taken up in it was Jennifer Miller, Marion County's chief probation officer. By 2013, almost 80 percent of Miller's caseload was opiate addicts.

Miller had begun her career in the mid-1990s as a gung-ho officer who saw her job as locking up as many folks as she could. She wrote presentencing reports that urged prison for pot smokers. But now a mother, and watching opiates take hold of her county, Miller noted how little success the old ways were having. Addicts went to prison, got out, and started using right away.

"I've come a long way in opening my mind," she said when I spoke with her in 2014.

A doctor at one seminar she attended described how opiates overwhelm the brain receptors. Miller began studying addiction and brain research online. She had never imagined this stuff would be necessary to do her job as a probation officer. But the opiate epidemic turned her into a social worker as much as a cop.

In 2013, Governor John Kasich, a Republican, went around the Republican-dominated legislature and expanded Medicaid health insurance to every Ohioan, which in turn gave thousands of families a way to pay for long periods of outpatient drug treatment. The next year, Miller applied for a state grant to use the opiate-blocking drug, Vivitrol, on addicts. Four months in, Miller had a waiting list for Vivitrol, and some of the county's worst junkies were clean. But each shot cost twelve hundred dollars and an addict needed it once a month.

"The million-dollar question," Miller said, is how long addicts will need to be on Vivitrol. So far, no drug company had stepped forward to help defray the cost. However, in Marion County, opiates, and the Vivitrol experiment, got police, jailers, court officials, and probation officers all working together in ways that hadn't been necessary or common before. Brad Belcher had inherited an old school building that once held a rest home. He offered it, three years rent-free, for a sober-living house with a dozen beds. So it seemed that the damaged county was rediscovering community.

"Some of the myths are being debunked," Belcher said. "People are understanding that this is a chronic illness. People are complaining when people are shooting up in parking lots. But it ain't over."

DOWN IN COLUMBUS, AS the second anniversary of Matt Schoonover's death approached, Paul and Ellen felt the shock lifting.

They tried to piece together their shattered lives by speaking publicly about how Matt had died. That felt like therapy. Doing nothing, they thought, would have crushed them. They had known little about addiction when Matt was alive. So they learned about drugs and the brain, about *mu* receptors and endorphins, and that helped.

Sharing grief publicly required taking care not to go too far in using it to push public awareness of the plague. Grief could become an occupation. But so many parents around the country were facing the loss of a child to this now. Strangers told them about addiction in their own lives. Ellen, in fact, felt she had suddenly been let in on a national secret. Addiction was everywhere. "People try to keep this happy façade," she said. "You realize there are a lot of people who suffer in silence."

It soothed her to write occasional letters to Matt and speak to parents with addicted kids on the topic "What I Wish I'd Known." A main point: that after three weeks of rehab, no addicted child is "fixed."

In Ohio, opiate prescribing had declined 40 percent. The legislature had a roster of bills aimed at regulating prescription opiates and expanding treatment options. One of them was modeled on the Counseling Center, the treatment clinic run by Ed Hughes in Portsmouth. The bill required counties to provide addicts with a full range of services—from housing and psychological counseling to help finding work. Still the state's problem raged. The Department of Health released numbers for fatal drug overdoses in 2012: a record 1,272 Ohioans had died that year, and of those 680 were due to heroin. In one three-month period, fully 11 percent of all Ohioans were prescribed opiates. Officials expected the number of heroin overdose deaths to more than double in the next couple years.

One way to view all that had happened was as some enormous social experiment to see how many Americans had the propensity for addiction. I ran this idea by an addiction specialist named Dr. Richard Whitney in the wealthy Columbus suburb of Dublin.

"That's an interesting way to put it: Let's feed this to everybody in the society and see what pops up," he said. "Let's, as a society, watch all of our potential alcoholics become opiate addicts instead. Had these opiates not appeared, I think we'd have seen a similar number of alcoholics, but later in life. My field used to be middle-aged alcoholics. It usually took twenty years of drinking to get people in enough trouble to need treatment. But with the potency of these drugs, the average age has dropped fifteen years and people get into trouble very quickly with oxycodone, hydrocodone, and heroin."

Nationwide opiate addiction had achieved a few things—albeit at frightening cost. There was the remarkable change of heart regarding prison and treatment that was under way, especially in red states, and led by Republican politicians.

Parents seemed to be losing their fear. A PR consultant named Barbara Theodosiou near Fort Lauderdale had two sons addicted amid the height of the Florida pill mill boom. Figuring there must be others like her, she started a website—addictsmom.com—and a Facebook page with the motto "Sharing without shame." By 2014, the page had grown to fourteen thousand mothers, who consoled and prayed for each other as they wrote in the rawest terms about collect calls from jail, forty-thousand-dollar rehabs, syringes found in sofas, funerals planned, and their kids reaching three hundred days clean of the morphine molecule. Theodosiou added a page for grandparents raising their addicted kids' children. At times the comments reached the pitch of a primal scream of maternal agony, a kind of mass group therapy for a drug epidemic in the virtual age.

"For 6 long years I've begged, pleaded, screamed, yelled, cried, grounded, took things away, called the police, kicked him out & not to mention the countless hrs feeling guilty & terrified for him," one woman wrote about her heroin-addicted son who'd just been thrown out of rehab again for a dirty drug test. "And the thousands of dollars spent on rehab, hospital bills & therapist as well as bailing him out of jail. I have prayed prayed prayed & prayed . . . "

A deeper understanding was emerging of how addiction was created in the brain. Functional MRI scans had revealed a lot since the 1990s about the brain's pathways of reward.

"It verified a lot of what we did intuitively," Whitney said. "Once people get addicted they really lose the power of choice. It takes thirty to ninety days for the brain to heal enough to make decisions. Otherwise, it's like putting a cast on a broken bone and expecting someone to run five miles."

Nationwide, attitudes toward addicts and addiction seemed to be shifting, though slowly. Addicts were not moral failures, deviants, and criminals—the image that stuck in the popular mind following the Harrison Act. Instead, they were coming to be seen as afflicted with a disease that happened to manifest itself in stealing and conning in the relentless search for dope to calm the beast.

As I followed this story, I took as given that kicking opiate addiction required a dozen attempts at rehabilitation. The figure I kept hearing was one in ten—the number of people who succeeded in each rehab. That was true, Whitney said, only because so few people get the full treatment they need. Too often they go in for three weeks or six weeks. Brain chemistry needs far more time to recover from the blast it takes from opiates.

"We have as good or better treatment results as they do for asthma or congestive heart failure—if we have the tools to work with," he said. "But people do not get enough treatment to get well. It's as if we said you only get half the chemotherapy you need to treat your cancer. People wouldn't stand for that. Insurance companies don't want to [fund] addiction treatment with enough duration and intensity because we as a society do not demand it."

CENTRAL OHIO WAS GROUND ZERO in the opiate scourge and that had given folks a lot to think about.

For Paul Schoonover, the best hour of the month was the time he spent sharing his son's story with kids at the rehab center that Matt left the day before he died.

Paul was also working with the nascent college recovery movement at Ohio State. The movement began years ago in response to alcohol and pot abuse on college campuses. Rutgers, Brown, and Texas Tech pioneered the movement's hallmarks: dorms free of drugs and alcohol, 12-step meetings, counseling, drug-free social events, full scholarships for recovering addicts, majors in addiction therapy. But the movement gained huge momentum and spread to many more schools with the opiate scourge, and Ohio State was part of it.

"It's been white middle- and upper-class kids," a young woman at Ohio State named Sarah Nerad told me. "Their parents are the ones who are going to the schools saying, 'What are you doing for my kid?' It really gets the attention of parents and schools when you have kids heavily addicted to opiates and heroin."

Nerad, a recovering heroin addict from the Houston suburbs, was getting a master's degree at Ohio State University and had a grant to help start the movement on campus.

The roster of universities with new recovery movements sounded like the top college football rankings, and reflected how dope addiction had swept red states: the Crimson Tide of Alabama and the Bulldogs of Georgia, Ole Miss and Southern Mississippi, Baylor, Texas, Vanderbilt,

Tennessee, Virginia—as well as Oregon, Michigan, Michigan State, Penn State, and several smaller schools—all had campus recovery movements in response, largely, to pill and heroin abuse. Ohio State had opened a twenty-eight-room recovery dorm.

Meanwhile, apart from expanding Medicaid, Governor Kasich had begun a program called Start Talking! that was intended to bring the opiate epidemic into the public conversation. Attorney General Mike DeWine had a heroin initiative, a main goal of which was to connect disparate groups in Ohio towns and get them working together.

These measures recognized a recurring theme: the most selfish drug fed on atomized communities. Isolation was now as endemic to wealthy suburbs as to the Rust Belt, and had been building for years. It was true about much of a country where the streets were barren on summer evenings and kids no longer played Kick the Can as parents watched from porches. That dreamland had been lost and replaced, all too often, finally, by empty streets of bigger, nicer houses hiding addiction that each family kept secret.

Chronic pain was probably best treated not by one pill but holistically. In the same way, the antidote to heroin wasn't so much naloxone; it was community. Paul Schoonover felt that.

So when he wasn't speaking to kids at the rehab center, Paul spent his time connecting groups of parents, nonprofits, and schools—and talking about Matt.

"Nobody can do it on their own," he said. "But no drug dealer, nor cartel, can stand against families, schools, churches, and communities united together."

PART V

Up from the Rubble

Portsmouth, Ohio

In 2012, a lanky, hollow-eyed white man arrived in Portsmouth, Ohio, his arms purple and scraped with needle marks, a third of his teeth gone, and half his life wasted. He carried with him ten bucks, a couple Percocets, and a few sheets of scrawled poetry.

The addict Jeremy Wilder was escaping rural America. He was thirty-five. His entire adult life had coincided with the opiate epidemic and the decline of small towns like his own. Years before, OxyContin spilled over his town of Aberdeen downriver in Brown County. He spent the best years of his youth in quacks' clinics and selling more pills than he could count. He bought heroin in Cincinnati from those Mexicans and their delivery business. He had two kids, but didn't know what it was like to raise a child sober. He'd gone to prison and returned to Aberdeen.

Aberdeen looked to be the salt of America's earth. Lots of farmland. Barns. Families growing corn and kids. The kind of place where the country songs say boys liked to drink a beer and raise a little hell on Saturday night, but made sure to give thanks to the Man upstairs on Sunday. But it had been quite a while since Jeremy had seen that kind of town. The Aberdeen he knew was a sewer of pills and needles, which was why little old Brown County had the highest rate of drug over-doses in Ohio. Jeremy could name a dozen towns like it along the mighty Ohio River, once a vital vein in the country's industrial arm, now contaminated with heroin.

He called a childhood friend living in Portsmouth. The friend was also an addict, but Wilder didn't know what else to do. Portsmouth was far from Brown County. The guy said he didn't have much, just a couch in a small apartment, but Wilder was welcome to it. Jeremy left his cell phone in Aberdeen—every contact in it was an addict or a dealer. His father drove him to Portsmouth and gave him a little cash and those Percocets to tide him over.

"Good luck," his father said, and drove off.

Jeremy watched him go. He was alone and hoping to get clean in the pill mecca of America.

His poetry was among the few accomplishments in which Jeremy took pride. He never liked to write as a kid. But in 2003, locked up and bored in Brown County jail, he began scrawling. Mostly he wrote verses about the addict life and poems for guys in prison to send to their girlfriends. A lot of it was bad. But some of it, he felt, had value. Through a couple prison stints, he began to write every day in his cell. When you wrote, inmates avoided you and conflicts went by you like water around a rock.

> *Will I wake up from this nod or will this be the end?*
> *Will it be just like the day when I buried my best friend?*
> *Would I be truly missed by my family and my wife?*
> *Sometimes I really wish I'd lived a different life . . .*
>
> *I walked up to the casket so I can truly see.*
> *I take a moment to stare inside, but I was staring down at me.*

He never wrote when he was using. He thought only of his next hit when he was using. Heroin numbed not just the body but also the emotions. Writing was the opposite of dope. So he turned to it when he was sober, as a way of staying so. He was surprised that it helped.

It surprised Jeremy just as much that he had turned to Portsmouth for the redemption he figured he didn't deserve. He knew the town once had jobs, now had none, and instead teemed with dope fiends. The docs who prescribed his pills learned the trade in Portsmouth. But with no other hope, he hugged Portsmouth like a life raft.

As it happened, the curious fact was that as the addict Jeremy Wilder sought rebirth in this beat-down town, he was not alone.

IF PORTSMOUTH HAD A survivor from its industrial glory days, it was a shoelace company called Mitchellace.

Mitchellace was founded in 1902 to supply the many shoe factories in Portsmouth. Charles Mitchell invented a shoestring braiding machine—bobbins pivoting and weaving like the Harlem Globetrotters—and once had twelve hundred of them running full-time as the company's five thousand employees made 120,000 pairs of shoestrings a day. Back then, Mitchellace was the country's largest shoelace manufacturer.

Making, packaging, and exporting shoelaces to the United States was apparently something few foreign companies could do profitably. Effervescent management under Kerry Keating, the husband of the great-granddaughter of the man who took over the company from Mitchell, kept the company expanding even as Portsmouth's shoe companies died. The company moved into a hulking eight-story building that had once housed the Williams Shoes factory.

Keating retired and his three sons took over. Around town, the Keating boys were known as "third-generation." In Portsmouth, and probably in most of America's Rust Belt, that was shorthand: the first generation built their companies; the second, with business degrees, managed and expanded them; but the third generation was raised with an appetite for leisure and their companies often declined. A lot of folks around Portsmouth had seen far too much third generation.

The Keating boys made the decisions but they weren't often on the premises. Kerry Keating had opened a shoelace plant in Honduras to satisfy demands from Kiwi, a shoe-products firm, for lower prices. The Keating sons began moving production for other companies there as well—companies that hadn't been so adamant about cost reductions.

Bryan Davis had started as a kid at Mitchellace, working the lowest jobs and rising through the years to become vice president of sales.

"We could still do it twice as fast here, with half the people, as they could abroad," he said. "But they shut down the braiding and weaving operation here that had been in their family since 1902. They shut it down and were doing it overseas."

Portsmouth workers trained to make shoelaces were let go. By 2009, the company employed eighty people. The Keatings bought a California shoe-supply company. Paying that debt, Mitchellace couldn't pay for the yarn and wax needed to make what it sold.

"We had orders coming out our ears," Davis said. "We just didn't have the money to fill them."

Customers abandoned the company. Finally, a bank called in its note on Mitchellace. The company's employees were furloughed. The company that had invented the shoelace industry, and survived foreign competition, now faced bankruptcy.

Most around town accepted the company's fate. Years of defeat convinced folks of the ideas propounded by business schools and Wall Street: Outsourcing was inevitable; growth came from sexy acquisitions and not from expanding a business's abilities to win new customers. This dogma judged towns like Portsmouth as unredeemable as a street junkie. The town itself, as enslaved to this way of thinking as the heroin addict is to the drug that destroys him, seemed to believe that it wasn't worth saving.

"You can only be knocked down so many times," Davis said, "until you start buying into the idea 'Oh, well, it's over. We lost.'"

And so it was that in 2009, with a pill plague consuming its children, and the news that its last shoe-industry factory was about to close, Portsmouth, Ohio, found itself at rock bottom.

But any addict knows that rock bottom is where recovery begins. That's what happened with Mitchellace. Then it happened in Portsmouth, too.

Nelson Smith was at a bank a few days later when he heard about the company's bankruptcy. Smith owns a construction company in Portsmouth, and knows nothing about shoelaces. But Bryan Davis did, so Smith called him.

"This isn't going to happen," Smith said. "We're going to save these jobs. We're going to save this industry in Portsmouth. Are you on board?"

"Well," Davis said, "I don't have a whole lot else going on."

Smith assembled a group of local businessmen who put up their own money to keep the plant afloat: a lawyer, an insurance agent, a financial planner, Davis, and Ryan Bouts, Mitchellace's vice president of manufacturing. The team wrote a forty-page business plan called Project Goliath, and named their proposed company Sole Choice. Also in the bidding for the remains of Mitchellace were the Kiwi shoe company and an equity firm the Keatings now partnered with.

Two weeks later, the parties went to court to decide the future of shoelace manufacturing in Ohio. All the creditors were there. The judge began calling the former owners "the Keating Four," then awarded the company to Smith, Davis, and their Sole Choice investors.

I met Bryan Davis a couple years later. We walked the hulking plant and talked over the roar of the bobbins that spun out long streams of laces to be used for boots, medical supplies, tennis shoes, lanyards, and Oxfords.

"It took individuals to say, 'No more,'" Davis said. "'We're not going to lose any more jobs and we're not going to lose another industry in this town.' We were the last bastion of what was a great shoe industry: shoelace manufacture. And we were going to let it go."

Three floors of the plant were empty. Davis took that to mean there was room to grow. By the time I visited, Davis said, Sole Choice had three hundred customers—up from twenty-four. Forty people had their jobs back and more were coming on. The company exported shoelaces to thirty countries, including China and Taiwan.

"The outsourcing mentality has cost us millions and millions of jobs. We have now done that for thirty-some years and we have literally destroyed our manufacturing base in this country. It's all been about money, the mighty dollar. The true entrepreneurial spirit of the U.S. has to be about more than that. It has to be about people, relationships, about building communities. Money—that comes. You'll get that eventually, but happiness comes from these other things."

I never spent long reporting this story about pills and heroin without people getting around to happiness and how to achieve it.

"It wasn't about the laces; it was about the people," said Davis, who is also a Republican Party leader in Scioto County. "America bought into Charles Dickens's Scrooge; they couldn't get past making the money. But it *is* about taking care of the family of Bob Cratchit. It *is* taking care of Tiny Tim that matters, that actually brings joy into your life. We forgot that. We were quite content to have our workers throw a piece of coal on the fire to stay warm. America did that. Charles Dickens gave us the warning, told us, 'Don't go down this road.' Think of the chains on Scrooge's business partner who died lonely, miserable; then you see him as a ghost with chains all around him. That kind of reminds you of what Portsmouth's been forever—a ghost town with chains all over it."

BY THE TIME MITCHELLACE was becoming Sole Choice, Scioto County coroner Terry Johnson had spent most of a decade raising hell about the mounting corpses from pill overdoses in and around Portsmouth—to little avail.

Johnson had watched a generation walk Highway 52 like zombies and get themselves declared simple to go on SSI and get the Medicaid card. He'd seen family members grow addicted and he had rethought every stereotype he had about addicts. Doctors had failed people, he felt.

"We visited incredible harm on the people of America as a profession," he said. "Pharmacists did also. Every single pill that was killing people in my county was legitimately prescribed, legitimately filled, legitimately paid for."

Ohio had at the time that intractable pain law that exempted doctors from prosecution for responsibly prescribing opiates. But nothing in state law regulated pain clinics.

"So I decided I have to go to Columbus and write and pass a bill before anybody catches on to what I'm doing," Johnson told me one afternoon in Portsmouth.

In 2010, Johnson was elected to Ohio's House of Representatives, the first Republican to hold the Portsmouth seat that had once belonged, seemingly in perpetuity, to Vern Riffe Jr.

Johnson took office in 2011. He and fellow representative Dave Burke, a pharmacist, wrote House Bill 93. This was a rare event. Term limits in Ohio mean that legislators come and go and acquire little knowledge of the issues on which they pass laws by the time they're termed out. Legislation is often written by lobbyists who are the power that accumulates in Columbus as lawmakers rotate through.

"Instead, we came out of left field," Johnson said, "and wrote our own legislation."

For a month he and Burke worked in the shadows like French resistance fighters. They forged a bill that defined and regulated pain clinics. Their House Bill 93 made it illegal, among other things, for a convicted felon to run one. Doctors could no longer dispense pharmaceuticals from their clinics—a widespread pill mill practice up to that point. Jo Anna Krohn and members of SOLACE showed up to support the bill, and Governor Kasich promised to sign it.

In the country's quintessential battleground state, House Bill 93 passed unanimously in May 2011. Together, Ohio Republicans and Democrats repealed the state's intractable pain law.

Down in Portsmouth, meanwhile, churches formed an alliance against the pill mills—the central banks of the town's OxyContin economy. Tom Rayburn, a member of the First Apostolic Church, was tasked to come up with a plan. "The Lord said, 'Have seven marches,'" Rayburn told me. "Seven is God's number."

Marches went by two notorious housing projects, and around the jail, and through downtown. One march circled a pill mill seven times. Marchers stopped at the clinic door. A nurse came out. They were blocking traffic, she yelled. The marchers started singing "Amazing Grace." A local pastor pulled out a shofar—a ram's horn like the one Joshua used at Jericho—and blew.

The seventh march was scheduled to go through East Portsmouth. The East End is wedged between the railroad tracks and the Ohio River. Portsmouth's decline had crushed the area. It was now a ghetto of white families on unemployment and SSI, and pills had settled on the East End like a biblical plague.

But the week had been a good one. House Bill 93 had just passed. The largest drug raid in county history took place as agents swarmed in and shut down a half-dozen pain clinics. Their closure ended the era of pill mills in Portsmouth. None has reopened.

Still, the afternoon of that seventh march felt ominous. The skies stayed dark all day and delivered a cold rain on the hundred marchers as they snaked through the East End. But as the march ended, the torrents ceased. Marchers stood there shivering and drying off. As they did, a rainbow arced over the massive Mitchellace factory. The skies cleared. The sun came and a strange light, cleansing rain fell. As it did, another rainbow appeared, crossing the first in the sky. People stopped and gazed up at the double rainbow embracing Portsmouth from the East End to the west.

"People were coming out of their doors," said Lisa Roberts. "I looked around at everybody. It got real bright. We had been a town in constant mourning. Every week there was another death. Now the flood was over, this flood of pills. It was like receiving visions of the Virgin Mary or something. It was as if this devil, this evil was lifted."

PORTSMOUTH DID NOT AVOID the new heroin scourge. Quite the contrary. Many in the town's enormous population of opiate addicts switched to heroin. Crime went up. Detroit dealers of powder heroin began flowing down through Portsmouth. Addicts began going to Columbus for the cheap black tar that the Mexicans were selling like pizza. Before long, you could get either powder or tar heroin in the town where Dreamland once stood.

The Scioto County pill mills illustrated how generalized opiate prescribing had become in America. In their last year of operation, 9.7 million pills were legally prescribed in the county of eighty thousand. But even two years after the pill mills were done, 7 million pills were still prescribed there.

Nevertheless, closing the cynical clinics was a necessary beginning. Like the rescue of Mitchellace, it was an action townspeople took to determine their own future, instead of letting it happen to them.

That became a theme of sorts. Portsmouth also returned to a city-manager form of government. The council hired a man who had actually managed other towns before he came to Portsmouth. No longer would supermarket clerks try to run the town's affairs. Residents might finally know the trash pickup schedule.

Scott Douthat, the sociology professor at Shawnee State, had a class study the town's problems and propose solutions that required no extra budget. Douthat and colleagues had earlier surveyed residents. What bothered them most "wasn't crime, it wasn't drugs, it wasn't the economy," Douthat said. "It was the way the city looked."

City officials first ignored the survey. "We don't need no egghead academics coming in here and telling us how to do our jobs," said one.

But since then, there'd been turnover at city hall. So when Douthat's students shaped proposals, they were heard. The students urged the city to apply for a federal Community Oriented Policing Grant, which it won. Now there were more officers on the streets. Buy a floodlight for a beleaguered downtown park, the students suggested. Prostitutes magically moved elsewhere. Students proposed a fifty-dollar annual fee on each rental property to pay for code inspectors, and volunteered to input the rental-property data. The town hired code inspectors, whose presence motivated landlords. The students suggested including litter pickup as part of each probationer's sentence and volunteered to help a judge organize the program because the city didn't have money for staff. Probationers picked up ninety tons of litter in the first three months.

This was all Municipal Governance 101, but it seemed radically refreshing to a town emerging from a thirty-year narco-economic fog. Residents, meanwhile, realized that the city had almost no budget. Churches, Boy Scouts, and other groups began regular civic cleanups at parks and along the river.

For the first time since the 1960s, someone named Vern Riffe would not be in political office in Portsmouth. Riffe Jr. retired from his powerful post as speaker of Ohio's House of Representatives in 1995 and died two years later. In 2014, his son, Vern Riffe III, retired after a quarter century as a commissioner of Scioto County. Nine people came out to run for his job.

Meanwhile, gyms began opening in Portsmouth. One of them, Iron Body, moved into an old car dealership downtown and had four hundred members in six months. "People got so tired of seeing addiction and fat people," said Bill Dever, a local defense attorney who belongs to the club. "So there's this big turn toward health and fitness. It's palpable."

Several buildings downtown were under renovation. A Cincinnati clothing store owner named Terry Ockerman moved back to Scioto County where he grew up. Ockerman bought and renovated an empty four-story furniture store in downtown Portsmouth into gleaming, modern lofts, and had a waiting list to rent them. Next door, he was putting in a café with outdoor tables, a place where people could actually meet and converse.

"Loft living and cafés—what's hipper than that?" he said. "What we're selling is a lifestyle." The town seemed to be welcoming the new, scuttling the old.

In that regard, as I was finishing this book, I received an e-mail from David Procter. He recalled my interview request, which he'd turned down while incarcerated. He was out of prison and had been deported to Canada, he wrote. Thus he was now willing to talk.

I was very interested in speaking with him, and outlined a few topics we might discuss. In response, he wrote that he had a lot to offer on topics that included pill mills and pharmaceutical company promotional campaigns and their effect on his prescribing. But then he added, "Any consultation be it medical or legal always carries a price . . . If you feel that it is worth pursuing then make me an offer when you call me." He provided an e-mail address and a Toronto-area phone number.

I responded that I do not pay for interviews. "Your participation in the Pill Mill industry indeed makes your perspectives and history very interesting," I wrote. "I would hope that, given your past, you'd want people to know all that happened, you'd want to help illuminate . . . You might again truly help people in pain, which I can assure you is real. You can help atone for some of that by helping shed light on this nationwide problem."

I haven't heard back from him. Too bad, he probably had something interesting to say. But what was happening in Portsmouth with an eye to the future as the town battled back engrossed me far more than a disgraced doctor trying to harvest the last few bucks from his criminal past.

Far more vital, for example, was the kind of stuff a young guy named Clint Askew was creating. As I was writing this book and spending time in Portsmouth, Askew had assembled a clan of nine or ten friends obsessed with rap music. Late at night, at his job as a market clerk, he began working out raps and choruses, and beats to go with them. His friends added lyrics of their own. Raw Word Revival was born.

Askew had grown up in Portsmouth and took the town as his raw material, shaping rhymes, like a journalist, from what was around him. He had never used pills, but watched the best of his generation die or walk the streets in tatters looking for a fix. One friend, addicted to pills, used a heated clothes hanger to burn dots on his arm in the shape of a

W—for "whore." Each dot was a girl he had slept with. This kid was once so straitlaced that he never cursed.

"I always felt I was supposed to do something with my life," Askew said.

One night at the market where he worked, a hook occurred to him. What did people really know about this forgotten place? He fastened on its area code, 740, and came up with a chorus:

> *What the hell you know about the 7-4-0?*
> *If you ain't lived here, worked here, sold here*
> *If you ain't caught a case here.*
> *What the hell you know about this place here?*

Others in RWR added raps, telling what they knew of growing up here. The song was a cry from out of the Walmart world of rural heartland America, white Appalachian rap about American decline and rebirth.

> *Used to be known as the 6-1-4*
> *Now it's just known for the devil at your door*
> *Pain clinics, pill mills*
> *Factories, drug deals . . .*

> *Yes I'm aware an' I care*
> *An' I'm ready to revive our greatness*
> *But be patient*
> *'Cause a big black cloud's hang'n over our town*
> *Flash flood a lotta people going my route wound*
> *Up gettin' drowned . . .*

They filmed a video on an iPhone at locations around town. Thousands of people watched it on Facebook. The track boomed from cars, people sang it in Walmart. People who hated rap loved the song. Portsmouth suddenly had some rousing, truth-telling art to rally around.

It didn't take long for folks to see the 740 elsewhere. The 740 was in Floyd County, Kentucky, and in Marion, Ohio. It was in Chimayo, New Mexico, and in the meatpacking towns in southwest Kansas. It was in those long, dreary lines outside the offices of David Procter, down any Walmart aisle, and in that parking lot where Dreamland once stood.

"7-4-0 reminds me of my hometown, Elkhart, Indiana (574)," one woman commented after reading several blog posts I wrote on the song.

BY MY LAST VISIT, it was clear that Portsmouth was starting over, throwing off old dogmas and a dependence culture. The town seemed now to hold itself a bit more accountable, looking to recover shredded community and take control of its future.

The most remarkable sign of this by far was that slowly, but without a doubt, hundreds of addicts were turning away from dope and tending to their own recovery. Close to 10 percent of the town was in recovery. The town that led the country into the opiate epidemic, ground zero in the pill explosion, was now poised to lead out of it as well.

With the quacks and the clinics gone, townspeople found that their children, now clean, began wandering home. They'd been gone a long time, and many never returned.

Hard-held attitudes in conservative Scioto County softened. Recovering addicts now had an easier time finding work. Everyone had friends or family on dope. Some employers believed in second chances. Others saw little choice. Those who were in recovery were at least going to pass a drug test. A job wasn't a panacea and many people relapsed even after finding work. But it was a start.

Getting clean awoke a creativity and imagination in those who made it back. At times it felt as if a new workforce had moved in. Addicts in recovery were injecting Portsmouth with what other American cities relied on Mexican immigrants to provide: energy, optimism, gratitude for an opportunity.

Portsmouth's resurrection, like that RWR video, was sprouting from the rubble of the town's decline. The town was positioned to be a national center for addiction research and treatment. It had thousands of addicts—both active and recovering—and lots of vacant buildings to expand into. Not since the Narcotic Farm closed in Lexington, Kentucky, in the 1970s did the country have an opportunity for the study of so many addicts in so small a place.

"The steel mill towns got ate up," Lisa Roberts told me one day at lunch. "To replace our industrial base we got prisons and nuclear plants. Then heroin became the new industry. This was allowed to percolate in Appalachia for at least a decade. What happened then is it moved out like a cancer across the country. Now we're being looked at as leaders because we have the experience and we know how this works."

Indeed, Scioto County was ahead of the country in a lot. As fatal overdoses set records in the state and the nation, they fell in Scioto County. The county had a needle exchange program that took in a hundred thousand syringes a year; new hepatitis C cases dropped by half. Addicts saved twenty-three people overdosing by injecting naloxone they were given through a state-funded pilot project in Scioto County.

China, having lost two Opium Wars waged on it by the British Empire, cured itself of its opium addiction by relying on former addicts to mentor their dope-sick brothers and sisters. Portsmouth was doing the same. Twelve-step meetings were all over town, sometimes several a day. Addicts saw examples all around them of people getting clean and happy. A newly recovering addict now had mentors to call at three A.M. who knew how hard things could get. Many recovering addicts had applied to Shawnee State, hoping to become social workers or drug counselors. The school was adding professors and a bachelor's of social work, and a psychology master's degree, all with a focus on addiction.

Above all, the Counseling Center had doubled in size during the epidemic. It now occupied some of Portsmouth's many abandoned buildings, and provided jobs to two hundred people, most of whom were in recovery and had criminal records.

The Counseling Center employed Jarrett Withrow, who'd been part of that ironworking crew that went to Florida and found a pill haven. Kathy Newman, who'd gone to David Procter for help with pain from her car accident, was now clean and working at the Counseling Center, too. Addicts intent on recovery could now have fun without drinking or using dope. The Counseling Center opened the Clubhouse, the largest drug-free hangout of its kind in Ohio. It held dances and card games and 12-step meetings.

Managing the Clubhouse, of all people, was Mary Ann Henson. Mary Ann, facing felonies, had finally gotten clean in 2010. Her husband, Keith Henson, had stopped using, too. Their son, Luke, was eight, and with two sober parents he was a chipper kid, a redhead with a big mouth of pearly teeth. Now in her forties, Mary Ann was a soccer mom, squiring Luke around, and mothering the newly recovering folks who hung out at the Clubhouse.

Angie Thuma, the veteran Walmart shoplifter, was hoping one day for a job at the Counseling Center. She was twenty months clean and working as a cashier for minimum wage, earning $230 a week, with which she supported her two sons while living with her parents. Shoplifting charges got her banned from Walmart, so shopping now was a chore. And she wasn't going to apply for the assistant manager's job where she worked, fearing a background check would reveal her past.

Yet, she told me the last time we spoke, "when I think about all the things I went through and I'm still alive, it gives you courage to keep bettering yourself."

That seemed to be Portsmouth's attitude. The town still looked as scarred and beaten as an addict's arm. Wild-eyed hookers strolled the East End railroad tracks, and too many jobs paid minimum wage and led nowhere. Portsmouth still had hundreds of drug addicts and dealers. But it also now had a confident, muscular culture of recovery that competed with the culture of getting high—a community slowly patching itself.

Proof of that was that addicts from all over Ohio were now migrating south to get *clean* in Portsmouth. No place in Ohio had the town's recovery infrastructure.

On my last trip to Portsmouth, I met a young woman from Johnstown, a rural town northeast of Columbus that from her description sounded a lot like the 740 that RWR rapped about. She had been buying heroin from the Xalisco Boys in Columbus for a couple years. When she tried to quit, a driver who spoke English called her for a week straight.

"But, señorita, we have really good stuff. It just came in."

Finally, she threw away her phone. There wasn't much on it but dope contacts anyway. She was twenty-three, alone with a ten-month-old son, and—seeking to get clean with nowhere else to turn—she found refuge in Portsmouth.

"I love it here. I'm really afraid to go back," she told me in the lilting drawl of rural Ohio, when we met at a party for a woman celebrating her first year clean.

So the battered old town had hung on. It was, somehow, a beacon embracing shivering and hollow-eyed junkies, letting them know that all was not lost. That at the bottom of the rubble was a place just like them, kicked and buried but surviving. A place that had, like them, shredded and lost so much that was precious but was nurturing it again. Though they were adrift, they, too, could begin to find their way back.

Back to that place called Dreamland.

AFTERWORD

In 2011, black-tar heroin overdoses ravaged Upland High School. Upland, "the City of Gracious Living," is a middle-class suburb forty miles east of Los Angeles. Kids at the school had grown addicted to pills, then to heroin. Now they were buying heroin from a few dealers on campus, who were in turn getting their supply from some Mexican traffickers in the area, including one in particular whom everyone called Chato.

The agents who told me this story said they'd already been hearing of Chato's crew from informants. They tried once or twice to penetrate it, but the Upland High outbreak gave the investigation new urgency.

As wiretaps and informants made clear, Chato was from Nayarit, possibly Xalisco, and resided in Riverside, twenty-five miles east of Upland. He ran a crew of heroin-delivery drivers around the area, and had another working in Las Vegas. He had four cellphones: one each for customers in the city of Ontario, near Upland, and Las Vegas, a third phone to contact his drivers, and a fourth, which the agents never had a number for, to talk to Mexico.

The investigation into Chato's crews would last three years, and connect his operation with other crews, and with Nayarit wholesale suppliers, in fourteen U.S. states. Piecing through these networks, agents seized a thousand pounds of heroin, and believed that was only a moderate fraction of what those crews were bringing in, most of it a couple kilos at a time.

What's more, Chato appeared not to be one guy. It was a name used by whoever happened to rotate in to run these crews, which had been operating quietly for a decade. The crews' owner, the agents assumed, lived in Mexico.

In the months following the release of *Dreamland*, people often asked me whether the Xalisco Boys continue to operate. My answer is yes, and I point to cases like the one that blew up out of Riverside, Ontario and Las Vegas. The Xalisco boys continue to sell dope across America. That has not changed.

But the Xalisco Boys' heroin world has shifted dramatically. Above all, America's heroin market ballooned, as ever-more pill addicts were transitioning to the drug. The CDC found fatal heroin overdoses had tripled from 2010 and 2013. Announcing a new study of the extent of heroin use, the agency, along with the FDA and DEA, issued a press release that began: "Heroin use has increased across the United States among men and women, most age groups, and all income levels. The greatest increases have occurred in groups with historically lower rates of heroin use, including women and people with private insurance and higher incomes."

The Xalisco Boys were the first to recognize and systematically exploit the new market for heroin that the overprescribing of narcotic pills was creating. But now the word was out. Everyone in the underworld knew that heroin was the thing to sell. The numbers of dealers seemed to expand ferociously, crowding the markets that the Xalisco Boys once had largely to themselves in many states. Street dealers who sold meth or cocaine were reported to have switched to selling heroin. In Cincinnati, I was told, large numbers of black guys, who seemed younger than ever, stood on corners selling dope to white addicts driving in from suburban and rural areas in the tri-state area. To announce their intentions, the dealers woofed like dogs—"dog food" being a moniker for heroin in the age of black tar.

Mexican cartels were also now fully aware of the new heroin market. They appeared to be taking over the Colombians' dominion in the eastern United States, much as they had wrested the cocaine business from them two decades before. "Colombians have almost totally removed themselves from the distribution [of heroin] directly in the U.S.," one New York law enforcement source told me. "What happened to cocaine in the late 1980s . . . is now happening to heroin as well."

Not long before our conversation, New York cops had seized one hundred fifty pounds of heroin imported from Sinaloa, Mexico, but which had originated in Colombia. Colombians figured they'd take less profit for less risk, and were now content to sell their dope to Mexican cartels that were avid to exploit the burgeoning U.S. market.

Moreover, every new addict was a dealer-in-waiting because selling dope is the way many support their habits—full-time work being at odds with the demands of the morphine molecule.

At the same time, though, a critical mass seemed to form. Shortly after *Dreamland* appeared, families who had just lost children began mentioning their kids' struggles with addiction in their obituaries for all to read. While noting their son's "comical and charismatic personality," parents of 24-year-old Daniel Wolanski, from Avon Lake, in northern Ohio, wrote that "unfortunately his five-year battle with addiction took over," and eventually beat him, though he spoke often before he died of the many friends he'd lost to overdoses.

"They say it takes a community to raise a child," his parents wrote. "It takes a community to battle addiction."

Feeling this, more anti-heroin groups began to form on Facebook. Unlike when I began my research, it was no longer difficult to find parents willing to tell their stories. Opiate addiction was shedding the stigma and taboo that had stifled these voices just a few months before. It all reminded me of the AIDS epidemic, during which families of the deceased at first made up euphemisms for how loved ones died. That had changed. Families, parents, were feeling emboldened, losing their shame, and going public.

Fourteen years after running a story that called the Porter and Jick letter a "landmark study," *Time* put the issue of widespread opiate addiction on its cover. *Sports Illustrated* ran a long piece on athletes' addiction to these drugs. Newspapers across the country ran major stories on heroin in their communities, often with photos of a needle in an addict's arm.

One result was that doctors ratcheted back on their prescribing in some areas of the country. But again, this too often seemed to be done without much nuance or consideration of who might actually need the drugs—just as they had once been prescribed to almost anyone. So folks who really needed the pills for chronic pain reported trouble getting them.

I spoke twice at the White House Office of National Drug Control Policy—office of the so-called Drug Czar—where I was assured the opiate abuse epidemic was the top priority. The new drug czar, Michael Botticelli, came from a background in public health; he was the first czar not to come from law enforcement or the military. He was also a recovering alcoholic with twenty-five years sober. The office put together a Heroin Task Force, which as I write is shaping recommendations for what to do.

An advisor to Hillary Clinton's presidential campaign called. Mrs. Clinton, she said, had been hearing a lot of from parents with addicted children as she campaigned in Iowa and New Hampshire. We spent an hour on the phone, talking about pain pills, pill mills, Mexican heroin trafficking, and about the quiet surrounding this epidemic that had allowed it to spread. A month later, Mrs. Clinton was reported to be coming up with policy proposals to address the problem.

As the 2016 presidential campaign gets underway, I hope this topic will be discussed frequently and that parents of addicts, in particular, will raise their voices and tell their stories.

Indeed, widespread addiction of white kids in rural and suburban America was having the effect nationwide that Judge Seth Norman had already noticed in Nashville. Ideas that I suspect many people had thought settled were now up for reexamination. What was the proper role of drug treatment versus imprisonment? Parents were pushing politicians to find alternatives to incarceration and felony records for their addicted kids. Most remarkably, through the fall of 2015, Republican candidates vied to appear the most compassionate when it came to drug treatment. Chris Christie, Carly Fiorina, and Jeb Bush told stories of the addicts they had known, loved ones and friends, in ways that might well have lost them any chance of winning a Republican primary a decade earlier. It was as if years of "tough on crime" talk had closeted many Republicans, intimidating them into silence on the issue of addiction. Now they were feeling liberated, free to talk about it, free to question old shibboleths.

It occurred to me that heroin, so fearsome and scary, was emerging as a ferocious agent of change in America.

The opiate scourge was making once-unthinkable strategies politically palatable. When Scott County in rural Indiana exploded with HIV infections due to needle sharing, the state's Republican governor ordered up a syringe exchange. The director of Ohio's prison system, serving a Republican governor, began signing up inmates for Medicaid so they could get rehab treatment paid for on the outside. "Our investment is in communities, not prison," he told a reporter. "I'm not going to build another damn prison." Leonard Campanello, Gloucester, Mass, police chief, announced he would not arrest, but look to find treatment for, those who came into the department with their drugs or drug paraphernalia. In an act of inspired guerrilla theater, he also posted the names and contact information of the CEOs of the five largest pharmaceutical companies, together with their salaries and perks of the job.

I visited conservative, libertarian northern Kentucky for *The New Yorker* magazine and found counties were transforming wings of their jails into full-fledged rehabilitation clinics. In northern Kentucky, Democrats had a tough time getting elected. But so did Republicans who hadn't signed on to the idea that addiction was a disease best dealt with not by incarceration and felony records, but by treatment. In Kenton and Pulaski counties, jails had actually hired recovering addicts to run their rehab programs and mentor others. Jail, it seemed, was slowly evolving into a place where an addict could get help, taking advantage of the time he spent away from easy access to dope and the drug life.

The opiate epidemic had swamped available rehab infrastructure on the outside. Few but the wealthiest families could afford the kind of inpatient treatment that opiate addiction seemed to require: nine months to a year, minimum, addiction specialists told me. So the question of what form jail took had become enormously important to families that had never had to consider the question. Years into the opiate scourge, the prospect was weirdly real in some areas that if you wanted treatment help, you would have to go to jail.

This marked a new way of thinking about jail—as an investment rather than a cost. Jail had been a cost, a drain on county budgets, for decades. Inmates spent months vegetating, conniving, planning their criminal escapades. Now some counties were taking a new view of jail as a place where they could create new drug-treatment capacity very quickly and relatively cheaply, and make use of addicts' time that once was spent vegetating, and thus help some out of the drug life.

Jail as an investment, not a cost. Heroin, again, as an agent of change.

Within this, though, were also huge challenges. There was a reason, after all, that prison was our answer to addiction. In the face of addicts relapsing again and again, prison seemed a safe option. At least there addicts were isolated; they couldn't break into houses, steal money from parents, shoplift, and get into more serious crime. Now state and county governments seemed to be assuming the task, in the public's mind at least, of somehow "curing" addiction—changing behavior, rewiring brain pathways, in essence. That was a lot to ask when it came to the morphine molecule. We'll see how it goes. Addicts would relapse. Indeed, relapse is assumed to be part of recovery. Some folks I spoke with, in fact, were redefining recovery as a series of periods of sobriety, growing in duration, but interrupted by relapse. "It's kind of a cliché, that we can't arrest our way out of this problem," one prosecutor told me. "Well, we can't treat our way out of this problem, either. We're never going to solve the heroin epidemic on the back end—incarceration or treatment."

A sobering thought, and probably correct.

I returned to Portsmouth in the fall of 2015 and found the town continuing to improve. Lisa Roberts told me of a plan to put blue silhouettes of angels in the houses in East Portsmouth where the residents had supplies of naloxone, the heroin overdose antidote.

A couple new restaurants had gone in downtown. A couple more abandoned buildings were being gutted for remodeling. Hipsters were starting the kind of businesses that hipsters start, and a monthly public event downtown—Final Friday. "Most people will just call them the Blue Hairs. They're definitely adding some progression to the town," Lisa said.

The Counseling Center had expanded to five hundred clients, and there was talk of it beginning a service of finding permanent housing for those who'd finished all its programs. Some people would object to this idea, but the more I learned, the more I became convinced that a new crew of recovering addicts could give the town the jolt of energy and gratitude that it needed after so many years of debilitating fatalism.

Jo Anna Krohn, meanwhile, had turned SOLACE into a Suboxone clinic, handling a hundred patients a month, with a doctor on staff and a very expensive urine analysis machine to test the folks who came in every month. Her oldest son, who when I met Jo Anna had been living in a camper without electricity or water, was now clean and working at the clinic alongside her.

Most of SOLACE's clients were on Medicaid. This was made possible by Gov. John Kasich, a Republican who had gone around his party and the legislature it controlled to expand Medicaid for all Ohioans, specifically to cover drug treatment.

It seemed more likely than ever that this once-great American town had continued to shrug off the old dogmas of dependency that kept it low, and was indeed returning to some self-reliance and perhaps a measure of the Dreamland it had once been.

When I wrote this book, I decided not to include a scene of any addict shooting up. I'd seen too many newspaper stories with photos of such things, and thought it over done. But I also believed that those scenes were a distraction, for this book is only on one level about dope. It occurred to me, as I researched *Dreamland*, that talking about heroin—opiates in general—was really a way of talking about America.

Where we stand as a country has a lot to do with the nature of drugs containing the morphine molecule.

By the time I began research for this book in 2012, we had, I believe, spent decades destroying community in America, mocking and clawing at the girdings of government that provide the public assets and infrastructure that we took for granted and that make communal public life possible. Meanwhile, we exalted the private sector. We beat Communism and thus came to believe the free market was some infallible God. Accepting this economic dogma, we allowed, encouraged even, jobs to go overseas. We lavishly rewarded our priests of finance for pushing those jobs offshore. We demanded perfection from government and forgave the private sector its trespasses.

Part of the private sector developed a sense of welfare entitlement. Certainly, in this opiate scourge, it is the private sector that has taken the profits; the costs of dealing with the vast collateral damage have fallen to the public sector. A couple months after this book's publication, *Forbes* counted the Sackler family, and Raymond Sackler, the last remaining of the brothers, as the richest newcomer to the magazine's list of "America's Richest Families"—with an estimated net worth of $14 billion. All of that was due to sales of OxyContin, which the magazine estimated at $35 billion since the drug's release in 1996.

We seemed to fear the public sphere. Parents hovered over kids. Alarmed at some menace out in public, they accompanied their kids everywhere they went. In one case, a couple was actually charged with allowing their nine-year-old daughter and her sister to go to the park alone. The term "free-range parenting" was coined to describe the daring parents who let their kids out of their sight. No wonder so many kids—boys mostly—were diagnosed with ADHD and prescribed Adderall and other drugs. (I wish someone would study the incidence of opiate addiction as teens and young adults of people who as kids were diagnosed with ADHD and prescribed drugs like Adderall.) They spent their lives indoors, cooped up, bouncing off the walls. I can say this because I was one: Boys are like dogs; they need to run and run and run. When I was a boy in suburban Southern California, we spent our entire free time outside playing—football, basketball, riding bikes, or just running around. We probably ran three or four miles a day every day. My knees were in an almost permanent stated of being skinned, with scabs growing and being torn off by my roughhousing. My mother had a bell from her family's farm in Iowa that she used to ring us home at dinnertime—because we were always running around of the house. I've been back to the street when I grew up eight times in the last few years and have yet to see a human being outside. The park where I used to play is always empty.

Keeping kids cooped up seems to me connected to the idea that we can avoid pain, avoid danger. It doesn't surprise me to hear that in universities, students, raised indoors on screens, apparently lived in some crystalline terror of any kind of emotional anguish. A 2015 story in the *Atlantic* called "The Coddling of the American Mind" reported on the phenomenon of college students—kids who grew up in the era of hyper-protection from physical pain—demanding to be protected as well from painful ideas. They were demanding professors provide "trigger warnings" in advance of ideas that might provoke a strong emotional content—for example, a novel that describes racial violence. This new campus ethos, the authors wrote, "presumes an extraordinary fragility of the collegiate psyche, and therefore elevates the goal of protecting students from psychological harm. The ultimate aim, it seems, is to turn campuses into 'safe spaces' where young adults are shielded from words and ideas that make some uncomfortable."

Psychology Today ran a story on "Declining Student Resilience" that noticed increased "neediness" in college students, that students had called campus police after seeing a mouse, blaming teachers for poor grades, and "increasingly seeking help for, and apparently having emotional crises over, problems of everyday life." Professors, the author continued, "described an increased tendency to see a poor grade as reason to complain rather than as reason to study more, or more effectively. Much of the discussions had to do with the amount of handholding faculty should do versus the degree to which the response should be something like, 'Buck up, this is college.'"

All of this seems the predictable result of the idea that we should be protected from pain at all cost.

As a country, meanwhile, we acted as if consumption and the accumulation of stuff was the path to happiness. We leave family Thanksgivings to go stand in line to buy products—Xboxes, tablets, and the like—that keep us isolated and that poison our kids, and we go do it as if we have no choice in the matter. We have built isolation into our suburbs and called it prosperity. Added to that mix is the expansion of technology that connects us to the world but separates us from our next-door neighbor.

We wound up dangerously separate from each other—whether in poverty or in affluence.

Kids no longer play in the street. Parks are underused. Dreamland lies buried beneath a strip mall.

Why then do we wonder that heroin is everywhere?

In our isolation, heroin thrives; that's its natural habitat. And our very search for painlessness led us to it.

Heroin is, I believe, the final expression of values we have fostered for thirty-five years. It turns every addict into narcissistic, self-absorbed, solitary hyper-consumers. A life that finds opiates turns away from family and community and devotes itself entirely to self-gratification by buying and consuming one product—the drug that makes being alone not just all right, but preferable.

I believe more strongly than ever that the antidote to heroin is community. If you want to keep kids off heroin, make sure people in your neighborhood do things together, in public, often. Form your own Dreamland and break down those barriers that keep people isolated. Don't have play dates; just go out and play. Bring people out of their private rooms, whatever forms those rooms take. We might consider living more simply. Pursuit of stuff doesn't equal happiness, as any heroin addict will tell you. People in some places I've been may emerge from this plague more compassionate, more grounded, willing to give children experience rather than things, and show them that pain is part of life and often endurable. The antidote to heroin may well be making your kids ride bikes outside, with their friends, and let them skin their knees.

I found the rough beginnings of that in the town of Portsmouth, Ohio—much to my surprise and delight. The encouraging signs in Portsmouth I also recently found in the suburbs of northern Kentucky, where pills and heroin have hit hard.

That's the good news: We don't just sit around and take the beating. We act. Like Americans always have. Heroin is fearsome enough to force us to action. What it does to users, their families, and their neighborhoods is so harrowing that heroin reminds those who live through it of the ties that bind them to others—producing in some places the opposite of the isolation that that produces in users.

So there are even times when I think I'm right—that perhaps heroin is the most important force for positive change in our country today.

Anyway, after years of writing about it, that's what I'd like to hope. And if it is, and for all it has taught us and forced us to recognize about ourselves and how we live, as one woman told me, "we may thank heroin some day."

ACKNOWLEDGMENTS

As this book tells a story that spreads nationwide, I encountered and relied on people across America for help in telling it.

I met parents transformed by this epidemic, and the loss of children, into activists of one sort or another: Carol Wagner, Margie Fleitman, Barbara Theodosiou, Susan Klimusko, Jodi Barber, Krissy McAfee, Tracy Morrison and her daughter Jenna. Wayne Campbell spent many hours with me and allowed me to attend his Tyler's Light presentation. Jo Anna Krohn sat with me several times sharing the story of her son Wes, and the creation of SOLACE. Paul and Ellen Schoonover, and their son Myles, were kind enough to share the story of how Matt had died. I believe they understand that this problem has spread because people have remained silent. I am grateful to them for sharing their story.

In Denver, Dennis Chavez was, of course, a fountain of information about the Xalisco Boys, a term for them that he coined and I borrowed for this book. I also spent time with other police officers who helped me understand how the Xalisco Boys were working in Denver today: Jimmy Edinger, Jes Sandoval, Nicole Shacklee, Dale Wallis, and Teresa Driscoll-Rael. I spoke also with several junkies who shared their thoughts. My wonderful aunt and uncle, Cal and Dick Van Pelt, provided me with welcome lodging in the Denver area.

Several people in Charlotte were kind enough to spend time with me to talk about the Xalisco Boys in that city. I spent a lot of time with Detective Brent Foushee, who also shared with me his master's thesis on the topic. Grateful appreciation also to Detective Don Queen, attorney Rob Heroy, deputy county prosecutor Sheena Gatehouse, Bob Martin from the Carolina Medical Center. Charlotte police officer Chris Long, a narcotics investigator, was the first law enforcement officer in the country to confirm to me that all these crews of heroin traffickers were in fact from the same town, and that that town was Xalisco, Nayarit. In South Carolina, I thank Dean Bishop, Max Dorsey, Marvin

Brown, and Walter Beck. I spoke with, and thank, other assorted folks as well, police officers and the opposite of police officers, whose names I can't include here.

In Columbus and Marion, Ohio, I'm grateful to many people who helped me understand the black tar heroin problem, but also the gravity of the state's opiate plague: Columbus police captain Gary Cameron, Orman Hall, Judge Scott VanDerKarr, Andrea Boxcil, Ed Socie, Ronnie Pogue, Christy Beeghly, Jennifer Biddinger and the folks at the Ohio attorney general's office, Sarah Nerad, Brad Belcher, Jennifer Miller, Dr. Richard Whitney, and the family of Dr. Phillip Prior. Dr. Joe Gay in Athens County, Ohio, was an early source, full of facts, perspective, and enthusiasm for the story.

In the state of Washington, I received essential help from Jaymie Mai, Jennifer Sabel, Caleb Banta-Green, Drs. Alex Cahana, John Loeser, David Tauben, Gary Franklin, Michael Schatman, and Michael Von Korff. I thank them for taking the time to help educate a reporter with a lot to learn.

One of the great pleasures of writing this story was visiting Portsmouth, Ohio, where people welcomed me and spoke forthrightly about their town. I am enormously grateful to Bryan Davis, Randy Schlegel, Joe Hale, Andrew Feight, Scott Douthat, Mary Ann and Keith Henson and their son, Luke, Terry Johnson, Danny Colley, Angie Thuma, Nate Payton, Kathy Newman, Melissa Fisher, Terry Ockerman, Chris Smith, John Lorentz, Jarrett Withrow, and Abbi Andre. As always, several others who helped me enormously probably prefer not to be named.

In Portsmouth, Ed Hughes spent many hours educating me on the multidisciplinary approach to drug rehabilitation and the history of the Counseling Center. Finally, Lisa Roberts was a huge fount of information about the town, its pill mill history, and the addiction that followed. I thank her also for the numerous contacts she provided me.

In Portland, Vitaliy and Elina Mulyar were nice enough to share their story with me, and help me understand the history of Russian Pentecostalism and the denomination's battle with opiate addiction among its youth in America. Dr. Gary Oxman told me the story of his investigation that attempted to understand the spate of heroin overdoses in Portland in the 1990s. Federal prosecutor Kathleen Bickers was a wonderful and encouraging source of information on the Xalisco Boy phenomenon. Early on, Portland police lieutenant Mike Krantz helped me see the extent to which Xalisco heroin had invaded that town. I thank, too, Steve Mygrant, Wayne Baldassare, Tom Garrett, Sean Macomber, and John Deits.

The story of RAP was told to me by Ed Blackburn, Alan Levine, and others who I also thank but probably can't name. I thank also Dr. Rachel Solotaroff at Central City Concern.

My dear friends Amy Kent and Steve Daggett, and their son, Colin, provided conversation and lodging that was a welcome respite from motel rooms while I was in Portland on several visits.

Folks in law enforcement from around the country were hugely helpful in adding their pieces to this nationwide puzzle. I thank Jim Kuykendall, Harry Sommers, Rob Smith and the Charlotte DEA, Adam Hardin and the South Carolina DEA, Chuvalo Truesdell, Dennis Mabry, Hal McDonough, Judge Seth Norman, Jeri Holladay Thomas, Chris Valdez, Rock Stone, Frank Harrell, Leo Arreguin, Lisa Feldman, and William Mickle, and some others whose names I cannot print here.

In Boise, Idaho, Ed Ruplinger very generously shared with me his recollections of the case he made against the Xalisco Boys, one of the first in the country. I also thank Steve Robinson and Joe Wright for their help.

Early on, as I attempted to track the Xalisco Boys to towns around America, I spoke with narcotics officers of various kinds, too many to mention, who helped by confirming, or not, the presence of the Nayarit traffickers in their areas.

From the small town of Xalisco, Nayarit, a major center of heroin supply to the United States, I spoke with numerous traffickers, drivers, telephone operators, and suppliers. Most would speak only of what they did, and would not discuss the activities of others. This was especially true of the man known as Enrique. I was happy to listen under any conditions they imposed. Most were or are in U.S. prisons, which I find are wonderfully contemplative places to sit and talk with people. Now, if only federal prison wardens would understand that in their custody are people who can tell the entire story of Mexican trafficking to the United States, that this is an important story for the public to hear, and that making it easier on a reporter trying to tell it wouldn't kill them. To those prison officials who did help in that regard, I say thank you. I also spoke with people from Xalisco: professionals, business owners, and some others. Most I tried to know only by first names, for their protection and my own. But even these I'll keep private, though I thank them nonetheless.

Early on, Professor Marcia Meldrum at UCLA instructed me on the historical background and context to the current opiate epidemic.

Dr. Nathaniel Katz and Dr. Marsha Stanton provided me with wide and deep perspectives on the history of pain, and on the pain revolution. Drs. Andrew Kolodny, Jane Ballantyne, Art Van Zee, and Mike McNeer, now firmly opposed to the liberal prescribing of opiate painkillers, shared with me the evolution of their thinking. Finally, I thank Dr. Hershel Jick, who told me the essential story of his 1980 letter to the editor.

Professors Andrew Coop, Martin Adler, and Herbert Kleber helped greatly with understanding addiction and the brain, methadone, and the College for the Problems of Drug Dependence.

Though some of them didn't appear in this book's final draft, several recovering addicts helped me understand the heroin street scene, past and present. Among them are Robert Berardinelli in Santa Fe, Dean Williams in Indiana, Bobby Melrose in Columbus, Pickles, Bob Wickham, the ex-RAPsters in Portland, several guys in rehab at the Counseling Center in Portsmouth, the three kids in Denver, and that waitress I met at a speech at the University of New Mexico in Albuquerque who drove for the Xalisco Boys for nine months.

While I was at the *Los Angeles Times*, I came upon the story of the Xalisco Boys and from that this book grew. My editors, Davan Maharaj, Marc Duvoisin, and Geoff Mohan, encouraged my research and shepherded the story along, and I'm grateful to them.

At Bloomsbury Press, editor George Gibson provided very welcome, energetic, and cheerful support for this project throughout. I'm indebted to Pete Beatty for buying my book proposal for the Press, and then editing the manuscript with calm and professionalism. My agent, Stephany Evans, at FinePrint Literary, saw the value of this project when other agents did not, and this was long before the storm of opiates and heroin was being widely covered in the media, as it is now. Stephany helped me hone my book proposal and then went into battle for it. For that, too, I'm very grateful to her.

I'm indebted to several editors who have corrected my prose throughout my career. Sam Enriquez, probably the best editor I've had, who hired me at the *Los Angeles Times* and is now at the *Wall Street Journal*, was kind enough to read and correct sections of this book.

I thank my father, Ricardo, and his wife, Roberta Johnson, for their support and interest in this book. When I was three and we were moving to California, my father, a now-retired literature professor from Claremont McKenna College, recounted to me the stories of Odysseus that were every bit as consuming as a television serial. My own love of storytelling was born from that, and from the care that he and my mother, who died in 1979, placed on the values of education and experience. I thank my brothers, Ben and Josh, and their families, and remember, again, our brother, Nate, and our mother. I thank also my in-laws, the Tullys, the Lotkas, and the Pennys, for their generosity and good-natured tolerance of my endless stories of opiate addiction and heroin trafficking in America.

More than anyone, though, my wife, Sheila, and my daughter, Caroline, lived with this book and helped give it life, tolerating my reporting trips and collecting me at airports with hugs and kisses that I badly needed. I could not have done this without them and I love them so.

SOURCE NOTES

This book was written based primarily on interviews I did over a five-year period, but especially in 2009 as a reporter for a story for the *Los Angeles Times*, and from 2012 to 2014.

I interviewed parents of addicts in several states, and many addicts themselves, public health nurses and epidemiologists, defense attorneys, doctors, local cops, drug rehabilitation counselors and administrators, pain specialists, chemists, a pain historian, state and federal prosecutors, DEA and FBI agents, as well as more than a dozen Xalisco Boys, most of whom were in prison at the time. The fellow I call the Man I interviewed eight or ten times, in person and over the telephone.

I traveled widely to get those interviews. Several times I visited Columbus and Portsmouth, Ohio, and went to Marion twice, and Cincinnati once. As the research proceeded I found myself three times in both Portland, Oregon, and Denver. I went to Indianapolis and Nashville; to northern and eastern Kentucky; to Charlotte, North Carolina; Boise, Idaho; Phoenix, Arizona; Huntington, West Virginia; and Albuquerque and Chimayo, New Mexico.

Part of my research involved a trip to Xalisco for four days during the Feria del Elote while I was employed at the *Los Angeles Times*, and from which I wrote a three-part series on the town and its pizza-delivery model for retailing heroin. That trip remains the only time in my career when I've lied when asked what I did for a living. I told people who asked that a photographer colleague and I were tourists, Spanish teachers in California. At this point in Mexico, beheadings and mass slaughter were the order of the day. Bodies were hung from overpasses and left in piles on street corners. Many reporters were murdered. Against that context, I hope the journalism gods will forgive my trespass in Xalisco. We left the town when, in an encounter that seemed far too coincidental, I was introduced to a man I was told was the Nayarit state police supervisor of the antikidnapping squad, who watched me far too closely while I watched a basketball game during the fair.

A trial transcript is a great friend to a crime reporter. But because Xalisco Boys almost always plead guilty to their cases, I had very few trial transcripts available in piecing together their story. One important and early one, though, was a large case against Luis Padilla-Peña in Omaha, Nebraska. That case came just as the Boys were beginning their expansion out of the San Fernando Valley. I'm indebted to prosecutor William Mickle for his help in procuring that very long transcript.

Indictments against the Xalisco Boys, on the other hand, are plentiful, and helpful for two reasons, mainly. Though they were not intimately detailed, the indictments did tell the same story over and over. They resembled each other so much that reading indictments from Charlotte to Portland to Phoenix and points in between gave me confidence early on in my research that this system was being faithfully duplicated across America. Also, indictments gave me names—of prosecutors and sometimes investigators with whom I later spoke, and of Xalisco defendants, by then in prison, to whom I wrote requesting interviews.

Another invaluable transcript, by the way, was from the trial against Michael Leman, owner of the Urgent Care clinics in Slidell, Louisiana, Philadelphia, and Cincinnati. Along with interviews, they provided a fascinating view of how the pill problem exploded in one eastern Kentucky county—Floyd. I added to that with interviews with local prosecutor Brent Turner, and his father, Arnold Turner, a former prosecutor, and with Randy Hunter, a recently retired state police detective, and with a prison interview with Timmy Wayne Hall, one of the biggest pill dealers in Floyd County.

Most of my research into Portsmouth, Ohio, came from interviews with residents on visits I made to the town, as well as a Facebook page devoted to the town's diaspora and how Portsmouth used to be. Much of my information about Dreamland came from people on that page. There were occasional news and historical journal articles as well that filled in parts of the story of the town's decline and the history of that fabulous pool.

Information on David Procter and his physician progeny I obtained from, first, interviews with people in Portsmouth. I also relied on reports from Kentucky's Board of Medical Licensure for Procter as well as several of the doctors who had worked for him. Newspaper articles about those doctors and other pill mill owners who came later were also invaluable.

Several books informed my sections on opium, morphine, heroin, the Harrison Act, and the Narcotic Farm. Martin Booth's *Opium: A History* is the classic history of the poppy and the goo it produces that has been so much a part of human history. Other books that I turned to were:

The American Disease: Origins of Narcotic Control, David F. Musto (Oxford University Press, 3rd edition, 1999)

One Hundred Years of Heroin, ed. David F. Musto (Praeger, 2002)

Creating the American Junkie: Addiction Research in the Classic Era of Narcotic Control, Caroline Jean Acker (Johns Hopkins University Press, 2005)

Dark Paradise: A History of Opiate Addiction in America, David Courtwright (Harvard University Press; enlarged edition, 2001)

Smack: Heroin and the American City, Eric C. Schneider (University of Pennsylvania Press, 2008)

The Narcotic Farm: The Rise and Fall of America's First Prison for Drug Addicts, Nancy Campbell, J. P. Olsen, and Luke Walden (Abrams, 2008)

Junky: The Definitive Text of "Junk" (50th Anniversary edition), William S. Burroughs (Grove Press, 2003)

Wellcome Witnesses to Twentieth Century Medicine, Volume 21: Innovation in Pain Management, ed. L. A. Reynolds and E. M. Tansey (QMUL History C20 Medicine, 2004)

Opioids and Pain Relief: A Historical Perspective, ed. Marcia L. Meldrum (IASP Press, 2003)

For the sections on the revolution in pain treatment, I relied on recollections from doctors who were practicing or in residency in the late 1980s and early 1990s. *Innovation in Pain Management* provided essential details on the early approaches to pain management, into Cicely Saunders and Robert Twycross at St. Christopher's in England, and into Jan Stjernsward's development of the WHO Ladder. I also relied on oral histories that Professor Marcia Meldrum did with Kathleen Foley and Russell Portenoy, which are available at the John C. Liebeskind History of Pain Collection at UCLA.

To chronicle the spread of the abuse of opiates I relied on studies by several government agencies, primarily SAMHSA and the Centers for Disease Control. The GAO, now renamed the U.S. Government Accountability Office, produced two important reports. One was a report analyzing the state of methadone clinics in America. The other was a 2003 analysis of Purdue Pharma's promotion campaign for the first half-dozen years after releasing OxyContin.

To describe Purdue's campaign, I also used interviews with doctors, including the late Phillip Prior, news articles, advertisements from medical journals, parts of Barry Meier's book *Pain Killer*, and an interview with former U.S. attorney John Brownlee.

Through this odyssey, I relied also on my experience over twenty-seven years as a journalist. I learned reporting covering crime for four years in the great town of Stockton, California. In my decade living in and traveling across Mexico, I had a chance to tell much longer stories. I reveled in the sagas of *ranchos, valientes, corridos, pistoleros,* and in the novel that each immigrant life comprises. You can read more about that in my two previous books: *True Tales from Another Mexico: The Lynch Mob, the Popsicle Kings, Chalino, and the Bronx* and *Antonio's Gun and Delfino's Dream: True Tales of Mexican Migration.*

Finally, I invite you to visit my website, www.samquinones.com. There I've listed, and linked to, many more resources—including recorded audio and video interviews and several relevant music videos on YouTube—that I used to tell this true tale.

INDEX

Aberdeen, Ohio, 247, 333
Accreditation Council for Continuing
    Medical Education, 135–36
addiction
    of Civil War soldiers, 54
    as disease vs. moral failing, 299, 327
    emotional development stunted by, 300
    as human nature, 326–27
    to Lorcet, 243
    to OxyContin, 6, 8, 137, 138, 147,
        154, 159, 165–66, 191, 213, 214,
        333–34
    pain caused by, 327
    personality of patient taking opiates and,
        92–93
    political solutions, 275–76, 325, 329,
        338
    pseudoaddiction, 109
    research on, 78–79, 98–99, 325, 327
    of school athletes, 287, 291–92,
        295–98
    selling heroin as an addiction, 104–5,
        261, 316–17
    theory that pain reduces risk of
        addiction, 94, 96–98, 106–8, 137,
        188
    See also heroin addiction; revolution in
        pain treatment
"Addiction Rate in Patients Treated with
    Narcotics" (Porter and Jick), 15–16,
    92, 106–7, 109, 188–89, 203, 314
Addiction Research Center (ARC), 78–79
addicts. See heroin addicts
addictsmom.com, 327
Adler, Martin, 312

advertising. See pharmaceutical company
    advertising campaigns
advocates for staying clean
    ex-addicts as, 116–17, 294–95, 320
    parents as, 207, 286–89, 298–300,
        303, 325–26
African Americans. See blacks
Alinsky, Saul, 116
America. See United States
American Pain Foundation (APF), 137
American Pain Society (APS), 94–95
anesthesiology, 84–85, 94
Appalachia, 26
Arlington, Virginia, 178
Arreguin, Leo, 57
Askew, Clint, 341–43
Athens County, Ohio, 252, 268

Baker, Connie, 96
Baldassare, Wayne, 68–70
Ball, Alice Huffman, 198
Baltimore, Maryland, 191
Barela clan, Chimayo, New Mexico,
    151–52, 170, 171
Barela, Felix, 171
Baxter, 94–95, 96
Beeghly, Christy, 249–50, 251–52
Belcher, Brad, 294–95, 325
benzodiazepines, 25–26, 304
Berardinelli, Robert, 173, 175–77,
    320–21
Bias, Len, 278–79
Bias, Tracy, 198
Bickers, Kathleen, 280, 282
Billiter, Gary "Rocky," 160, 198

Blackburn, Ed, 116, 117
blacks, 45, 128, 144, 163, 259, 261, 323
black tar heroin
    about, 7, 17–18, 41, 59
    attracting young addicts, 116, 165–66,
        194–95
    injecting, 55, 166
    managing sales efforts, 100
    Mexican ounce measure, 58
    price of, 58, 70, 162, 228, 239, 268
    purity of, 120–21, 150, 175–76, 268
    See also heroin addiction; Xalisco Boys;
        Xalisco, Nayarit
Blevins, Tony, 200
Blood and Crip gangs, 115
Boise, Idaho, 100–102, 104–6, 172, 179
Bonica, John, 86, 253
Booth, Martin, 52, 355
bootlegging, 242–43
Boston, Massachusetts, 15–16, 187–89
Brompton cocktail, 80
Brookhart, J. D., 296
Brownlee, John, 220–21, 264, 266–67
Bruce, Jeremy, 296
Buenos Aires, Argentina, 82
buprenorphine, 36
Burke, Dave, 338
Burton, Jack and Jackie, 200, 201
busts. See Xalisco Boys busts and jail time

Cahana, Alex, 253–55, 309, 310–11
Caldwell, Idaho, 105
California, 37
Camarena, Enrique "Kiki," 90, 148
Cameron, Gary, 298
Campbell, James, 94–95
Campbell, Nancy, 79
Campbell, Tyler, 295, 297–98
Campbell, Wayne, 295, 297–98
Canoga Park, California, 47–, 47–49
Carlos, Jose, 283–84
Carnegie, Pennsylvania, 166
Carter (high school athlete), 291–92
Center for Pain Relief, University of
    Washington, 86–88, 108–9, 253–55,
    309–11
Centers for Disease Control, 234–35, 248,
    355
Central City Concern, Portland, Oregon,
    116

Charles, Karen and Jerry, 145–46
Charlotte, North Carolina, 168, 226–31
Chattanooga, Tennessee, 167
Chavez, Dennis, 40–46, 283
Chicago, Illinois, 57, 58
children, 96, 291–92, 293, 295–98. See
    also middle class junkies
Chillicothe, Ohio, 198, 268–69
Chimayo, New Mexico, 149–52, 169–71,
    175
China and morphine, 52–53
Christmas Carol, A (Dickens), 337
chronic pain treatment
    cordotomies as, 82
    holistic methods, 329
    opiates for, 92–94, 95–97, 99, 189,
        203–5
    and OxyContin, 132–33, 137–38
    pain clinics, 86–88
    for school athletes, 292, 295–98
    and time-release pain medications, 99
Cincinnati, Ohio, 65, 157, 244
class action lawsuits, 201
CME (continuing medical education)
    seminars, 31, 135–36
cocaine, 45, 60–61, 100, 191, 289
Cohn, Frederick, 159
College on Problems of Drug Dependence
    (CPDD), 311–12
college recovery movement, 328–29
Colley, Danny, 155–56
Columbus, Ohio, 20–21, 22, 144,
    161–65, 193, 194–96, 295–300,
    319–20
Committee on Problems of Drug
    Dependence (CPDD), 77–78
Community Oriented Policing Grant,
    340
conflicts of interest, 134–36, 312–13
conspiracy cases, DEA, 149, 169–71
Coop, Andy, 36–37, 38–39, 311–12
Corn Fair, Xalisco, 56, 113–14, 141, 183,
    259, 353–54
coroners, 250–51, 290, 337–38
Corporation Heroin, 280. See also Xalisco
    Boys
Counseling Center, Portsmouth, Ohio,
    145, 146–47, 292–93, 326, 344
Courtwright, David, 55
crack cocaine, 45, 60–61, 100, 191, 289

Creedmoor mental hospital, New York, 28
criminal justice reform, 275

Dark Paradise (Courtwright), 55
Davis, Bryan, 335, 336–37
Dayton, Ohio, 143–44
Deal, Nathan, 276
Denver, Colorado, 40–46, 283–85
Detroit Steel, Portsmouth, Ohio, 24
DeWine, Mike, 329
Dickens, Charles, 337
diet pills and stimulants, 26
disability, 154, 210
doctors
    belief that opiates were not addictive,
        232–34
    CME seminars, 31, 135–36
    failure of, 337
    lack of training for treating pain
        patients, 137–38, 187–88, 189, 211,
        306–7
    lawsuit against L&I for pain pill
        guidelines, 234, 235
    locum tenens lists of unemployed
        doctors, 198
    patient load, 97–99
    and pharmaceutical companies,
        134–35
    post-surgery overprescribing of opiates,
        295
    See also pill mills; revolution in pain
        treatment
Dole, Vincent, 63
Doriro (Joaquin Segura-Cordero), 278,
    279–80, 282
Douthat, Scott, 207, 339–40
Dreamland swimming pool, Portsmouth,
    Ohio, 1–3, 4, 206, 207
drug courts, 273–75, 275–77, 278–79,
    319–20, 354
drug enforcement. *See* police
Drug Enforcement Administration (DEA)
    Black Gold Rush operation, 256–57,
        262–63
    in Columbus, 20–21
    connecting Nayarit to black tar heroin,
        178–80
    and Herreras crime family, 57–58
    Kuykendall family of agents, 148–51
    on OxyContin, 135

in Phoenix, 172
physician registration numbers, 155
in Portland, 121
and Procter, 160
Tar Pit operation, 178, 179–80,
    181–84, 193, 256, 315
drug-related deaths. *See* overdose deaths
drug traffickers
    about, 317
    Herreras crime family, 57–58
    in New York City, 22, 28–31, 54–55,
        305
    Sinaloans, 60–61, 62, 90, 223, 317
    Tierra Caliente, 223
    See also Xalisco Boys
Dzyuba, Aleksey, 278

El Gato (dealer), 71, 73
Ellis, Kim, 117–18
Elston, Michael J., 264, 267
Enrique
    busted, 182
    in Canoga Park, 47–50, 73–74
    flying to Phoenix, 13
    and the Man, 321
    in Phoenix, 111–12, 113
    in Santa Fe, 174, 175, 176–77
    in Tijuana, 47
    in Xalisco, 14, 32–35, 51, 72, 74–75,
        111, 112–14, 173, 174–75

FACES scale, 96
FamilyPractice.com, 137
fast food restaurants, 304–5
FDA (Food and Drug Administration),
    126, 136, 264, 306
Federal Medical Center (Narcotic Farm),
    Lexington, Kentucky, 76–77, 78–79
Feldman, Lisa, 181
Fishman, Scott, 108
Florence, Kentucky, 316
Florida, 167, 245, 246
Floyd County, Kentucky, 210–11, 242–46
Foley, Kathleen, 82, 92–93, 125–26
Fonseca, Ernesto "Don Neto," 90
Fordyce, Bill, 86–87
Fort Walton Beach, Florida, 241–42
Foushee, Brent, 226–28
Franklin, Gary, 203–5, 232, 309
Friedman, Michael, 267–68

From One Pain Patient to Another (Purdue
   Pharma video), 126, 136, 355

Gallegos, Josefa, 151–52, 171
Garcia-Langarica, Cesar "Polla," 179
Garrett, Tom, 278–79
Garrison, Kentucky, 156
Gatehouse, Sheena, 228–29, 231
Gay, Joe, 252
Georgia and drug courts, 276
Gergely, William, 127
Gerson, Win, 30, 125
Goble, Larry, 243–44
God Will Provide church/rehab center, 322
Goldenheim, Paul, 267–68
Government Accountability Office (GAO),
   126, 136, 355
government workers fighting the epidemic
   coroners, 250–51, 290, 337–38
   drug courts, 273–75, 275–77, 278–79,
      319–20, 354
   in Ohio, 325, 329
   See also Drug Enforcement
      Administration; police
Greenup County, Kentucky, 241

Haddox, J. David, 109, 234
Hale, Joe, 199–201
Hall, Orman, 252, 324
Hall, Timmy Wayne, 243, 244–45
Harrison Narcotics Tax Act (1914),
   53–54, 76
Hawaii, 61, 66, 179
Health and Human Services Department,
   134
Henson, Keith, 212, 214, 344
Henson, Mary Ann, 208–9, 212–13, 218,
   344
Herb & Thelma's Tavern, Covington,
   Kentucky, 8–9
Hernandez-Garcia, Oscar, 164, 178, 179,
   181–82, 318
heroin
   about, 7–8, 53–55, 77
   appeal of, 195
   breaking into the spotlight, 303–7
   business models for selling, 55, 61,
      120–21 (*See also* Xalisco Boys: retail
      sales)
   consumption in United States, 82

injecting, 55
New York City as heroin center, 54–55
physicians arrested for prescribing to
   addicts, 54
as replacement for morphine, 54
research, 78–79
social stigma against, 82, 84, 93, 94,
   260, 294
See also black tar heroin; drug traffickers;
   Xalisco Boys
heroin addiction
   about, 37
   in Chimayo, 150–52
   in colleges, 328–29
   educating children about, 298
   examples of, 5–7, 8
   of school athletes, 292
   transition to heroin from OxyContin,
      157, 165–66, 191–92, 238, 239,
      268–69, 291–92, 295, 297, 304,
      317
   withdrawal symptoms, 26, 38–39
heroin addicts
   about, 170, 177
   addicts helping other addicts, 344
   age of, 116
   attempts to quit thwarted by Xalisco
      Boys, 167–68, 224, 345
   attitudes toward, 327–28
   dream of making money off heroin, 176
   ex-addicts helping other addicts,
      116–17, 294–95, 320
   functional, 121
   funeral home owner, 173
   in Heroin Court, 319–20
   Hoffman as ground zero for waking up
      America, 303–4
   junkie guides for Xalisco Boys, 62–63,
      65–66, 168
   junkie salesmen, 280
   junkie shoplifters, 103, 213, 214–18,
      344–45
   Levine, Alan, Portland, 68, 70–71
   the Man, 90–91
   relapses, 6–7, 77, 238, 293, 297, 320,
      324
   relationships with Xalisco Boys, 70–71,
      105, 118, 167–68, 224, 229
   teenagers as, 187, 194–96, 291–92,
      295–98

in wealthy neighborhoods, 17–18, 194, 229–30, 291–92
and Xalisco Boys arrests, 262
as Xalisco Boys sales force, 259
See also middle class junkies; parents of addicted children
heroin overdose deaths
about, 7–8, 220
autopsies of victims, 17, 250
as barometer of heroin problem, 122
in Chimayo, 150, 151, 169–70, 175
college athlete, 295
in Columbus, 163
in fast food restaurants, 304–5
in Huntington, 17–18
from injecting, 53
Ohio department of health investigation, 247–50, 252
OxyContin as precursor, 8
in Portland, 116–17, 119–20, 121–23, 278
post-rehab, 6–7, 297
statistics on, 119–20, 238
Herrera-Nevarez, Don Jaime, 58
Hoffman, Philip Seymour, 303–4
Holder, Eric, 304
horse dancing, 56
hospice care, 80
Huff, Kevin, 198
Huffman, Denise, 198
Hughes, Ed, 145, 146–47, 292–93
Hunter, Randy, 246
Huntington, West Virginia, 17–19, 245
hydrocodone, 190, 191–92, 208, 291, 292, 306

I Got My Life Back (Purdue Pharma video), 136
India, 82
Indianapolis, Indiana, 143, 259
Innovation in Pain Management (Reynolds and Tansey, eds.), 355
insurance companies
and heroin addiction in children, 196
and managed care movement, 97
methadone covered by, 190
refusal to pay for multidisciplinary approach to pain management, 87–88, 108–9, 124, 254–55, 307, 310

International Association for the Study of Pain, 82
Italian gangsters and heroin, 55

Jacquemain, Chris, 295
jail. See Xalisco Boys busts and jail time
Jaime (Charlotte undercover police officer), 230
Jalisco, Mexico, 43
Janes, Merle, 234, 235
jazz bands at the Narcotic Farm, 77
Jefferson, Tracy, 65–66
Jick, Hershel, 15–16, 92, 106–7, 109–10, 188–89, 203, 266–67, 314
Johnson, Adam, 17
Johnson, Teddy, 17
Johnson, Terry, 250–51, 337–38
Joint Commission for Accreditation of Healthcare Organizations (JCAHO), 95, 96, 98
junkies. See heroin addicts

Kallir, John, 29, 31
Kasich, John, 325, 329
Katz, Nathaniel, 187–89, 312–14
Keating, Kerry, and sons, 334–36
Kelley, Sharron, 115–16, 117
Kentucky, 241–46, 242, 244, 275–76
Kentucky Board of Medical Licensure, 153
Klimusko, Susan, 303
Kolodny, Andrew, 313
Krohn, Jo Anna, 287–89
Kuykendall, Jaime, 148
Kuykendall, Jim, 148–52, 169–72, 178, 321

law enforcement. See Drug Enforcement Administration; police
Leman, Michael, 244, 354
Len Bias cases, 278–79, 281–82
Levi 501s, 103–4, 112–13
Levine, Alan, 68, 70–71, 116–17, 238
Lewis, John, 36
Lexington, Kentucky, 76–79
Lilly, John, 156, 208, 212
L&I (Labor and Industries workers' compensation system), Washington state, 202–5, 233–35, 309
Lockhart, Jerry, 213–14
Loeser, John, 86–88, 108–9, 253–54

Lopez, Marina, 178, 181, 182
Lorcet, 243
Lorentz, Chuck, 3
Lorentz, John, 3
Lortab, 191–92, 208
Los Angeles, California, 89–91, 164
Los Angeles County, California, 60–61
Lucasville Bottoms, Ohio, 199–201
Lucasville, Ohio, 199

Mabry, Dennis, 256–58, 262
Mai, Jaymie, 202–5, 233, 234, 309
the Man
    about, 315
    arrest and jail time, 128–29, 183
    in California, 318–19
    in Columbus, 144, 161–65, 222–23
    in Los Angeles, 89–90
    in Nevada, 130–31, 141–42
    scouting towns for dealing
        opportunities, 143–44, 165–67, 168
    and shipments from San Fernando
        Valley, 178
    in Wheeling, 165–66
    in Xalisco, 90–91, 140–41, 142–43,
        183, 318
managed care movement, 97
maps, ix–x
marijuana (pot), 37
Mario (in Columbus, Ohio), 222
Marion, Ohio, 294–95, 325
Marshall, Donnie R., 182
Marsilette, Jim, II, 245
Martinez clan, Chimayo, New Mexico,
    151–52, 170–71
Meade, Russ, 243–44
measurements-based pain care, 254
Medicaid, 209–10, 211, 242, 243, 325
Medical Tribune, 31
Meier, Barry, 126, 127
Memphis, Tennessee, 257
mentor system for recovering addicts, 117
methadone, 63, 64, 78, 190–91
methadone clinics, 63–66, 143, 144, 164,
    168
methamphetamine, 289
metopon, 79
Mexican immigrants to the United States,
    21–22, 43–46, 61–62, 182–83
Mexican Mud heroin, 57, 58

Mexico, 13, 33–34, 35, 37–38, 280–81,
    316, 353–54. See also ranchos and
    rancheros
middle class junkies
    about, 276, 303–7
    and college recovery movement,
        328–29
    in Columbus, 6–7, 298–99
    in Denver, 284–85
    heroin addicts in wealthy
        neighborhoods, 17–18, 194, 229–30,
        291–92
    in Ohio, 290, 291–93
    in Portland, 282
    in privacy of their bedrooms and cars,
        290
    in Tennessee, 274
    and treatment centers, 274–77
    as Xalisco Boys' target, 22, 45, 63
middle class pill addicts, 208–10, 218
Miller, Jennifer, 325
miners, 210–11, 243
Mitchellace, Portsmouth, Ohio, 334–36
Mormons and prescription painkillers, 93
morphine molecule
    about, 36–37, 38–39, 311–12
    heroin as replacement for on streets,
        54
    research, 78–79
    as silent killer, 289–91
    time-release pills, 81, 84, 99, 124
    wars and, 52–53
    and WHO Ladder, 81–82
    See also opiates
MS Contin, 84, 99, 124–25
Multidisciplinary Pain Center, Seattle,
    Washington, 309–11. See also Center
    for Pain Relief
Mulyar, Elina, 322. See also Sinyayev, Elina
Mulyar, Vitaliy, 238, 322
mu-opioid receptors, 38
Mygrant, Steve, 65, 279–80
Myrtle Beach, South Carolina, 257

naloxone antidote to opiate overdose, 304,
    344
Napp Pharmaceuticals, 81
Naramore, Stan, 244
Narcotic Farm, Lexington, Kentucky,
    76–77, 78–79

Narcotic Farm, The (Campbell, Olsen, and
   Walden), 79
Nashville, Tennessee, 166, 256–57,
   262–63, 273–75
National Institutes of Health, 107
National Pharmaceutical Council, 97
Nationwide Children's Hospital,
   Columbus, Ohio, 193–96
Nayarit, Mexico, 43–46, 140, 172. *See also*
   Xalisco, Nayarit
Nayarits. *See* Xalisco Boys
New England Journal of Medicine
   (NEJM), 16, 92, 99, 106–7, 266
Newman, Kathy, 154, 156, 344
New Mexico, 320–21
New York City, New York, 22, 28–31,
   54–55, 305
Nixon, Richard, 63
Norman, Seth, 273–75, 276–77
Northern California, 223
Northern Nevada Correctional Center,
   Carson City, Nevada, 128–29
Not One More coalition, 303
Novocain, 78
Nuss, Lee, 268

obesity epidemic, 37
Ockerman, Terry, 340–41
Ohio, 138–39, 247–50, 252, 275, 325,
   326, 329, 338
Ohio State University, 328–29
Olsen, J. P., 79
opiates, 53, 80–85, 92–94, 93, 109, 190,
   260, 294, 324. *See also* heroin;
   hydrocodone; morphine molecule;
   prescription painkillers; revolution in
   pain treatment
opiate class system, 213–14
opiate epidemic
   America's awareness of, 303–7
   in Columbus, 194–96
   speed of spread, 292–93
   spread of, 61–63, 65–66, 74, 90–91,
      100, 105, 143–44, 165–68, 193,
      241–46, 305
opium, 38, 52–53, 194–96
Opium: A History (Booth), 52, 355
opium poppies, 38, 52–55
Opium Wars, 52–53
outsourcing mentality, 335, 337

overdose deaths
   about, 251
   from methadone, 191
   Ohio department of health investigation
      of, 247–50, 252
   one decade into epidemic, 16,000/year,
      286
   from opiate pain pills, 188–89, 190,
      199, 203, 205, 232–34, 238,
      248–52
   from OxyContin, 139, 200, 208–9,
      249–50, 264
   See also heroin overdose deaths
Oxman, Gary, 115–16, 117, 119–20,
   122–23, 238
oxycodone, 124, 190. *See also* OxyContin
OxyContin
   about, 124–25, 281
   abuse deterrent added to, 304
   abuse of, 138, 145, 155, 157, 165–66,
      191–92, 209
   addiction of children, 207, 291, 297
   addiction to, 6, 8, 137, 138, 147, 154,
      159, 165–66, 191, 213, 214, 333–34
   addicts and dealers obtaining
      prescriptions of others, 208–9,
      212–13, 218, 238, 241–46
   advertising campaign, 125, 126–27,
      132–38, 211–12, 220–21, 264–65
   as business model, 155–56
   death from teenage prank, 287–88
   doctors overprescribing, 26–27,
      145–46, 155–56, 238, 241–42
   as economic currency, 212–13
   and heroin addiction, 91
   injecting, 126, 138, 159, 165, 191–92,
      200
   opiate class system, 213–14
   overdose deaths, 139, 200, 208–9,
      249–50
   pills into cash technique, 208–10, 211
   Purdue Pharma guilty of misbranding,
      267–68, 269
   sales per year, 306
   as street drug, 138, 139, 145, 147,
      165, 190, 211
   tolerance to, 165, 192, 204, 264, 268
   transition to heroin from, 157, 165–66,
      191–92, 238, 239, 268–69, 291–92,
      295, 297, 304, 317

withdrawal from, 265
Xalisco Boys' awareness of, 193, 224,
    258, 260, 317
See also middle class junkies; pill mills

Padilla-Peña, Luis, 65–66, 354
Pain (journal), 92, 93, 109
pain clinics. See pain management with
    multidisciplinary approach; pill mills;
    revolution in pain treatment
pain, conception of, 312
pain conferences, 96
Pain Killer (Meier), 126, 127
pain management, 93, 94, 136, 304–7.
    See also revolution in pain treatment
pain management with multidisciplinary
    approach
    Center for Pain Relief, UW, 86–88,
        108–9, 253–55, 309–11
    with injections, 84
    insurance companies' refusal to pay for,
        87, 108–9, 124, 254–55, 307, 310
    measurements-based pain care, 254
    medical school failure to teach about,
        138, 187–88, 306–7
    and theory that pain patients would not
        become addicts, 92–93, 108–9
    by VHA, 307
Pain Medicine and Palliative Care
    department, Beth Israel Medical
    Center, New York City, 95–96
Pain Physician (journal), 190
pain pills. See OxyContin; prescription
    painkillers
pain receptors, lack of, 312
Paintsville, Kentucky, 159
palliative care, 80–84
parents of addicted children
    as advocates, 8–9, 207, 286–89,
        298–300, 303, 325–26, 327
    in Chimayo, 170
    denial of, 230–31
    rescue as addiction, 293
    silence about the problem, 239,
        251–52, 290–91, 292, 322, 329
    supporting heroin habit, 218–19
Parker, Charlie, 77
Partners Against Pain, 137
patients, 96, 97–99, 98, 153, 158
Pedro (driver), 260–62

Pentecostal revival, 236–37
Percocet, 297, 324
Pfizer, 29–30, 133
pharmaceutical companies, 96, 137,
    305–6. See also Purdue Pharma
pharmaceutical company advertising
    campaigns
    about, 133, 135–36
    HHS guidelines, 134
    for OxyContin, 125, 126–27, 132–38,
        211–12, 220–21, 264–65
    for Terramycin, 29–30
    for Valium, 30
Pharmaceutical Research and
    Manufacturers of America, 134
Philadelphia, Pennsylvania, 167, 244
Phoenix, Arizona, 111–12, 113, 172, 179
Physicians for Responsible Opioid
    Prescribing (PROP), 308, 313
pill dealers, 157
pill mills
    about, 156–59, 158–60, 165, 197,
        198–99
    alliance against, 338–39
    and fatal drug overdoses, 250–51
    Ohio regulations for, 338
    and OxyContin, 155
    Portsmouth as nation's capital of,
        197–99
    in Portsmouth, Ohio, 25–27, 156,
        197–99, 207, 208–10, 212–13
    prosecution against doctors, 220
    in South Shore, 25–26, 145–47,
        153–56
    standards and patient demands, 197
    Urgent Care brand, 243–44
police
    in Boise, 100, 101–2, 104–6, 172, 179
    in Chicago, 58
    Community Oriented Policing Grant,
        340
    in Denver, 40–46, 283–85
    education as work of, 298
    in Floyd County, 246
    in Huntington, 18, 19–20
    living in Simi Valley, 303
    in Marion, 294–95
    in Portland area, 68–70, 120–22,
        278–82
    rethinking strategies, 120, 229, 284–85

teamwork, 281–82
in Xalisco, 67
and Xalisco Boys, 61, 62, 120, 256,
   281–82
and Xalisco Boys' cell phones, 171–72,
   229, 257
See also Drug Enforcement
   Administration
police informants, 42–45
political help for addicts, 275–76, 325,
   329, 338
Polla (Cesar Garcia-Langarica), 100,
   101–2, 105–6, 179
Portenoy, Russell, 83–84, 85, 92–93,
   95–96, 99, 108, 136, 307–8,
   312–14
Porter, Jane, 16, 92, 106–7, 109, 314
Portland, Oregon, 68–70, 115–22, 179,
   182, 236–40, 278–82
Portsmouth Daily Times, 146
Portsmouth, Ohio
   about, 3–4, 23, 24–25, 218–19
   alliance against pill mills, 338–39
   cleanup of, 339–41, 343–44, 345
   Dreamland swimming pool, 1–3, 4,
      206, 207
   hope for, 287–89
   industry in, 334–37
   OxyContin economy, 206–8
   pill mills in, 25–27, 156, 197–99, 207,
      208–10, 212–13
   and Procter's pill mill, 25–26, 145–47,
      153–56
prescription-monitoring systems, 242,
   244, 246
prescription painkillers
   about, 84–85, 132, 138
   addiction to, 15–16, 341–42
   addicts and dealers obtaining
      prescriptions, 208–9, 212–13, 218,
      241–46
   age of abusers, 190
   doctors overprescribing, 25–27, 53–54,
      95–99, 109, 155–56
   and doctors' time constraints, 97–98
   doctors underprescribing, 94, 95, 108
   L&I guidelines for, 233–35
   Lorcet, 243
   methadone as, 190–91
   and Mormons, 93

MS Contin, 84, 99, 124–25
   and opiate epidemic, 241–42
   overdose deaths, 188–89, 190, 199,
      203, 205, 232–34, 238, 248–52
   overdose deaths investigation, 232–33,
      247–50, 252
   Percocet, 297, 324
   for school athletes, 287, 291–92,
      295–98
   search for nonaddictive forms of,
      311–12
   transition to heroin from, 191–92, 324
   Vicodin, 191–92, 208, 291, 306
   See also OxyContin
Press Ganey surveys, 96, 98
Prior, Phillip, 132–33, 138, 268–69,
   323–24
Procter, David, 23–24, 25, 145–46,
   153–59, 197, 341, 354
pseudoaddiction, 109, 234
Purdue Frederick, 30, 31, 84, 98–99
Purdue Pharma
   about, 266, 355–56
   abuse deterrent for OxyContin, 304
   false claims, 264–65
   and FDA, 136, 264
   guilty of misbranding OxyContin,
      267–68, 269
   lawsuits against, 201, 220–21, 266–68
   MS Contin, 84, 99, 124–25
   and pain revolution, 98–99
   and Portenoy, 313
   salespeople of, 132–34, 138–39, 221,
      265, 305
   threatening Counseling Center,
      Portsmouth, 146
   See also OxyContin

Quinones, Sam, 19, 353–56

Raices, Toño, 66–67
ranchos and rancheros, 20–22, 45–46,
   49–50, 51, 57, 72, 91, 103–4,
   112–13. See also Xalisco, Nayarit
Raw Word Revival, 341–43
Rayburn, Tom, 338
recovery, 294–95, 343–45. See also
   rehabilitation/recovery programs
Recovery Association Project (RAP),
   116–17

rehabilitation/recovery programs
continuum of care, 146–47
court facility in Nashville, 273–75
limitations of, 299–300, 326, 328
overdose shortly after, 6–7, 297
and OxyContin addicts, 138–39
for Russian Pentecostal kids, 322
12-step groups, 299, 320, 321, 328,
344
relapses, 6–7, 77, 238, 293, 297, 320,
324
Reno, Nevada, 65–66, 130
Republican Party and opiate epidemic,
275–76, 327
research
on addiction to heroin and morphine,
78–79, 325, 327
on opiates for pain leading to addiction,
98–99
on pain management, 81, 83, 93–94
on surgical anesthesia, 84–85
on workers' comp claim deaths from
opioids, 203, 204
on Xalisco Boys, 58–59
revolution in pain treatment
about, 313–14
and black tar heroin, 165
doctors taking advantage of (See pill
mills)
and FDA, 126
general practitioners as prescribers,
137–38, 187–88, 189, 211, 306–7
and OxyContin, 124
pain clinics as result of, 197–99
and Porter/Jick, 15–16, 92, 106–7,
109, 188–89, 203, 314
push back against stats proving
addiction issues, 232–35
recognition of danger of opiates, 304
and spread of Xalisco Boys, 193, 224,
258, 260, 317
theory that pain reduces risk of
addiction, 94, 96–98, 106–8, 137,
188
See also opiates; pharmaceutical company
advertising campaigns
Reynolds, L. A., 355
Richardson, Bruce, 151
Riddle, Billy, 23
Riffe, Vern, Jr., 206–7, 340

Roberts, Lisa, 25, 155, 207, 251–52,
343
Robinson, Jody, 197
Rodriguez-Zepeda, Aurelio, 171–72
Rogers, Hal, 275–76
Rogers, Peter, 193–96
Roybal, George, 170
Ruplinger, Ed, 100, 101–2, 104–6, 172,
179
Russia, Pentecostal revival in, 236–37

Sabel, Jennnifer, 205, 232–35, 234
Sackler, Arthur Mitchell, 28–31, 125, 133
Sadler, Nancy, 198
Salazar, Lynette, 170
Salt Lake City, Utah, 93–94, 105, 130–31
Samuel, Lally, 234
Sánchez clan, 168, 257–58, 262–63, 316
Sánchez-Covarrubias, Alberto "Beto,"
258, 262
Sánchez-Torres, Javier "Chito," 257
Sandoval, Jes, 283–85
San Fernando Valley, California, 48–49,
60–61, 73–74, 178, 180
Santa Claus bust, 101–2
Santa Fe, New Mexico, 171–72, 320–21
Santos, Rodolfo, 159, 160
Santuario de Chimayo, New Mexico, 150
Saunders, Cicely, 80
Schoonover, Ellen, 6–7, 9, 298–99
Schoonover, Matt, 5–7, 298–99
Schoonover, Myles, 5–6
Schoonover, Paul, 6–7, 9, 298–99,
325–26, 328
Seattle, Washington, 86–88, 253–55
Segura-Cordero, Joaquin "Doriro," 278,
279–80, 282
Sertürner, Friedrich, 52
"7-4-0" (rap song), 342–43
Shawnee State, Portsmouth, Ohio,
339–40, 344
shoe manufacturing, 24
shoplifters, 103, 214–18, 344–45
Shumlin, Peter, 305
Simi Valley, California, 303–7
Sinaloa, Mexico, 60
Sinaloans, 60–61, 62, 90, 223, 316, 317
Sinyayev, Anatoly and Nina, 236–37, 322
Sinyayev, Elina, 237, 239–40, 278,
321–22

Sinyayev, Toviy, 237, 240, 278–79, 282, 321
Slidell, Louisiana, 243–44
Sloan Kettering Cancer Center, New York City, 83
Smith, Dennis, 170
Snyder, Steven, 159
Social Security Disability Income (SSDI), 210–11
Socie, Ed, 247–50
SOLACE, 288–89
Sole Choice, 336–37
Sommers, Harry, 178–79, 256, 317
source notes, author's, 353–56
South Carolina, 257
Southern Hills Hospital, Portsmouth, Ohio, 25
South Shore, Kentucky, 23–24, 145–46, 153–54
Stanton, Marsha, 93–94, 99, 107, 108
Start Talking! program, 329
state laws protecting doctors who prescribe opiates, 95
St. Christopher's Hospice, London, 80
Stine, Katie, 276
Stjernsward, Jan, 81
Stone, Paul "Rock," 120–22, 178, 180, 182, 183–84
Substance Abuse and Mental Health Services Administration (SAMHSA), 190, 191, 355
sugarcane farms in Mexico, 59–60, 74–75, 111
Sullivan, Carl "Rolly," 138–39
Supplemental Security Income (SSI), 209–11, 242, 243, 244–45
Swing Is Alive (OxyContin ad campaign CD), 134

Tansey, E. M., 355
Targiniq ER, 306
Tauben, David, 309
Tejeda-Cienfuegos, Enrique, 71
Tejeda, David, 56, 60, 61, 66–67, 91
Tejeda-Sánchez clan, Nayarit, 183–84
terminology guideline, xi
Terramycin advertising campaign, 29–30
Theodosiou, Barbara, 327
Thuma, Angie, 217, 344–45
Tierra Caliente traffickers, 223

Tijuana, Mexico, 47
time line, xi–xiii
Time magazine, 107
Tkach, John, 322
tornado, 143
Tri-State Health Care and Pain Management, Portsmouth, Ohio, 198–99
Turner, Brent, 210–11
12-step program, 299, 320, 321, 328, 344
Twycross, Robert, 80–81
Tyler's Light nonprofit, 298–300
Tzintzuntzan, Michoacán, 280–81

Udell, Howard, 267–68
unemployment, 25, 154, 210–11, 243, 244–45, 247, 338
United States, 37, 95, 125, 137, 189, 190, 234, 303–7, 337
University of Akron football team, 295–98
Urgent Care pill mills, 243–44
urine black market, 213

Valdez, Chris, 150–51, 169
Valium, 30–31
VanDerKarr, Scott, 319–20
Vaqueros Musical, 66, 67
vehicular accident deaths, 249
Ventafridda, Vittorio, 80
Veterans Administration Hospital, Chillicothe, Ohio, 268 69
Veterans Health Administration (VHA), 95, 96–97, 307
Vicodin, 191–92, 208, 291, 306
Virginia, 166
Vivanco-Contrerases clan, Phoenix, Arizona, 179
Vivitrol, 325
Volkman, Paul, 198–99

Wagner, Carol, 8–9
Wald, Alan, 28
Walden, Luke, 79
Wallis, Robert, 41
Wall Street Journal, 275
Walmart, 214–18
wars and morphine, 52–53
Washington, 202–5, 233–35
Webster, Lynn, 84, 93, 94

Weissman, David, 109
Weiss, Randy, 244
Wesley, 287–88
West Virginia, 18
Wheeling, West Virginia, 165–66
Whitney, Richard, 326–27, 328
Wilder, Jeremy, 156–57, 247, 333–34
William Douglas McAdams, 29–31, 125
Williams, Fortune, 156, 159, 160, 212
Williams, Jaime, 1
withdrawal symptoms, 26, 38–39, 69,
    78–79, 194, 216, 245, 265, 278
Withrow, Jarrett, 241–42, 344
Wong–Baker FACES scale, 96
Wong, Donna, 96
Wood, Alexander, 53
Woodling, Gary, 172
workers' compensation system,
    Washington state, 202–5, 233–35
World Health Organization (WHO),
    81–82
Wright, Alder, 53
Wright, Curits, 126

Xalisco Boys
    about, 59–61, 174
    avoiding traditional heroin towns, 223
    blending in and following rules, 162–63
    brand of, 223–24
    customer service, 70–71, 105, 118,
        167–68, 224, 229
    dispatcher position, 43, 44, 222–23
    driver position, 22, 43, 44–45, 61
    expanding their market, 61–63, 65–66,
        74, 90–91, 100, 105, 143–44,
        165–68, 193
    Heroin Cells in the U.S., map, ix
    junkie guides, 62–63, 65–66
    living quarters in the U.S., 49, 104,
        112, 283
    persistence and resilience of, 193, 228,
        316–17, 321
    phone code system for deliveries, 121
    research on, 58–59
    retail sales strategy for Denver, 283–84
    retail sales strategy for United States

cities, 43–46, 49, 70–71, 91, 101–2,
    130–31, 164, 279–80
    returning home with money from
        dealing, 21–22, 33–34, 45–46, 111,
        112–14, 259, 261
    robbery of, 112
    selling heroin as an addiction, 104–5,
        261, 316–17
    sending money home, 45, 112, 163,
        166, 176, 183
Xalisco Boys busts and jail time
    in Boise, 101–2
    in Columbus, 22
    DEA operations, 178, 179–80, 181–84,
        193, 256–57, 262–63, 315
    earning a GED and money in jail, 262
    Enrique, 182
    Herrera clan, 58
    in Nevada, 128–29
    police realize ineffectiveness of, 120,
        228–29
    returning home after jail time, 262, 318
Xalisco, Nayarit
    about, 91, 129, 140, 259–61
    avocado industry, 317–18
    clans in, 59
    construction boom, 103
    Corn Fair, 56, 113–14, 141, 183, 259,
        353–54
    drug cartel violence in, 316
    drug culture permeating the area,
        259–61
    map, x
    middle class farmers, 102–3
    satellite dish as status symbol, 74–75
    selling heroin as way of life, 72–73
    sugarcane farms, 13, 59–60, 74–75,
        111
    treatment of farmers vs. people with
        money, 113, 114
    See also ranchos and rancheros

Yuma, Arizona, 13–14

Zohydro, 306